WTO AND INDIAN ECONOMIC REFORMS

Edited by
Talwar Sabanna

SERIALS PUBLICATIONS
NEW DELHI

First Published - 2008

ISBN: 978-81-8387-149-5

Published by

SERIALS PUBLICATIONS
4830/24, Prahlad Street, Ansari Road
Darya Ganj, New Delhi-110002 (India)
Phone : 23245225 Fax : 91-11-23272135
E-mail: serials@satyam.net.in

CONTENTS

Part-II
Indian Economic Reforms

PREFACE

The recent process of globalisation has changed not only the territorialisation aspects of human endeavors but also the focus on competitive compression and efficiency in many sectors, its growth being beset with varying phases of transformation depending on the pace of gloablisation as measured by openness in trade finance and commodity and service markets. Further, the WTO is a vehicle to take us on the path of development in the 21st century. To get on this vehicle is not all that easy, nor is it simple to stay on it without losing balance because of the WTO's unique power of "cross retaliation". Thus, implementing the WTO agreements will mean an upheaval in our attitudes to work hard, meet agreed schedules and deliver quality products in far concerns of the earth or perish.

Further, globalisation process in the world economy in the form of free flow of goods and services across nations, international movements of finance, capital and labour migration has been strengthened, particularly after the revolution of information technology and concerned global actions to initiate the process of policy reforms based on the trade liberalization, technological collaboration and participation of foreign equity and portfolio investment in different parts of the world. The emergence of WTO at the conclusion of the Uruguay round of trade negotiations of the GATT has marked the beginning of the multilateral surveillance of the trading arrangement that are evolving under the new global order. The book focuses its attention on the matters like WTO and its impact on various fields, need and success of Economic reforms and sustainable development.

The collection of papers was a great task but the generous help and assistance given by the numerous eminent scholars spread all over India mad it easy to collect the papers. All the paper writers, with their broad vision and clear outlook, have made possible in taking up this book. I record my sincere thanks to all contributors.

Talwar Sabanna

OUR CONTRIBUTORS

Francis Gnansekar, Reader in Commerce, St.Joseph's College (Autonomous), Tiruchirapalli.

R. Krishnaraj, Research Scholar, P.G. & Research Department of Commerce, St.Joseph's College, Tiruchirappalli.

Chandra Prakash Azad, Centre for Regional Studies, T.M. Bhagalpur University, Bhagalpur.

A.K.Jha, Head, P.G. Department of Economiocs, B.N.Mandal University(WC), P.G.Centre, Saharsa.

Revansiddappa Veershetty, Guest Lecturer in Economics, Government First Grade College, Bidar-1, Karnataka.

Devendrappa M.Madari, Lecturer, Department of Economics, Gulbarga University, Gulbarga-6, Karnataka.

Prakash Basanna, Guest Lecturer in Management, Gulbarga University, Gulbarga-6, Karnataka.

Shoukath Azim, Reader, Department of Sociology, Karnatak University, Dharwad-3, Karnataka.

Prem Chand Tiwari, Reader, Department of Economics, Handia P.G.College, Handia, Allahabad.

Bipasha Chowdhary, Research Scholar, Department of Economics, Allahabad University, Allahabad.

Mahesh Kumar Tiwardi, Research Scholar, Department of Economics, Handia P.G. College, Handia, Allahabad.

S.Vasanthi, Senior Lecturer in Commercer, Providence College for Women, Coonoor-643104.

Vasudev Sedam H., Reader, Department of Economics, Gulbarga University, Gulbarga-585106, Karnataka.

Mohammed Younus K., Research Scholar, Department of Economics, Gulbarga University, Gulbarga-585106, Karnataka.

Rameshwari Pandya, Senior Lecturer, Department of Home Science Extension and Communication, Faculty of Home Science, M.S. University of Baroda,Vadodar, Gujrat.

K.Alamar, Reader and Head, Department of Economics, Centre for Research, Arul Anandar College(Autonomous), Karumathur, Madurai.

N. Murali, Faculty Member, Department of Economics, Centre for Research, Arul Anandar College(Autonomous), Karumathur, Madurai.

Prakash S.Kamble, Venutai Chavan College, Karad, District-Satara, Maharashtra.

Zainab M.Khurram, Lecturer in Economics, Zakir Hussain College (Evening), University of Delhi, J.N.Marg, New Delhi-2.

Rekha Mehta, Associate Professor, Department of Economics, J.N.V. University, Jodhpur.

Pallavi, Research Fellow, Department of Economics, J.N.V.University, Jodhpur.

W.N. Salve, Shri Venktesh College, Ichalkaranji, Kholapur district, Maharashtra.

Shamkutty George, Reader in Commerce, Henry Baker College, Melukavu, Kottayam District, Kerala.

L.T.Nayak, Senior Scale Lecturer, Department of Geography, Karnatak Science College, Dharwad, Karnataka.

B.Hymavathi Reddy, Reader (Retd), Department of Studies in Geography, Karnatak University, Dharwad, Karnataka.

Suryakant N.Waghamare, Guest Lecturer, P.G.Department of Geography, Karnatak University, Dharwad, Karnataka.

S.I.Biradar, Reader in Geography, Karnatak University, Dharwad, Karnataka.

Benson Kunjukunju, P.G. & Research Department of Commerce, St.Thomas College, Kohencherry-689641, Kerala.

Mohan P.Philip, P.G. & Research Department of Commerce, St.Thomas College, Kohencherry-689641, Kerala.

D.R.Albal, Reader in Sociology, Karnatak University Kittur Rani Chennamma P.G. Centre, Belgaum-591156, Karnataka.

Z.A.Pathan, Research Scholar in Sociology,, Karnatak University Kittur Rani Chennamma P.G. Centre, Belgaum-591156, Karnataka.

A.V.Melvanki, Research Scholar in Sociology,, Karnatak University Kittur Rani Chennamma P.G. Centre, Belgaum-591156, Karnataka.

M.B.Chalwadi, Guest Faculty in Geography,, Karnatak University Kittur Rani Chennamma P.G. Centre, Belgaum-591156, Karnataka.

Debnarayan Sarker, Professor, Centre for Economic Studies, Presidency College, Kolkata.

Megha Sidhpur, Research Scholar, Department of Home Science Extension and Communication, Faculty of Home Science, M.S. University of Baroda,Vadodar, Gujrat.

Bibekananda Mishra, Lecturer in Economics, Konark Bhagabati Mahabidyalaya, Konar, Puri-752111, Orissa.

Dilip Kumar Ghosh, Senior Research Officer, State Institute of Panchayats and Rural Development, Kalyani, Nadia.

A.Y. Kamble, Research Scholar in Sociology,, Karnatak University Kittur Rani Chennamma P.G. Centre, Belgaum-591156, Karnataka.

Jayashree Dam P. Choudhury, Sr. Lecturer, Department of Economics, K.C.Das Commerce College, Guwahati.

Vijaya B. Korishetti, Senior Scale Lecturer, Department of Studies in Sociology, Karnataka State Women University, Bijapur.

Akash S.B., Lecturer, Department of Commercer, Karnatak University, P.G.Centre, Karwar, Karnataka.

S.Sagayadoss, Lecturer, Department of Economics, Sacred Heart College, Tirupattur.

S.M. Jawed Akthar, Senior Lecturer, Department of Economics, Aligarh Muslim University, Aligarh-202002, UP.

Ashwini Kant Jha, Professor and Head, P.G. Department of Economics, BNM University (W.C.), P.G.Centre, Saharsa, Bihar.

Bhavna Jha, Lecturer in IRPM, MAM College, Nangachia, T.M.Bhagalpur University, Bhagalpur, Bihar.

Hemant Kumar, Research Scholar, DNM University, Madhepura.

G.N.Joshi, Professor, Department of Economics, Veer Narmad South Gujarat University.

V.Aditya Srinivas, Faculty, Department of Economics, Veer Narmad South Gujarat University.

Part I

WORLD TRADE ORGANISATION

1

WTO AND CONSUMER PROTECTION IN PHARMACEUTICAL INDUSTRIY

I. Francis Gnanasekar and R. Krishnaraj***

INTRODUCTION

In 1947, Indian Pharmaceutical industry was estimated as Rs.10 crore and it was dominated by German and UK based Multinational Companies (MNCs). After independence, government established Public Sector Enterprises such as Hindustan Antibiotic Limited (HAL) and Indian Drugs and Pharmaceuticals Limited (IDPL) to ensure the availability of essential medicines at an economical cost and to face the competition posed by the Multinational Companies. Public sector enterprises contributed remarkably for the growth of pharmaceutical industry in both formulations and basic drugs.

INDIAN PATENT ACT (IPA) 1970, DPCO

Indian Patent Act 1970, (process patent) and DPCO brought tremendous improvement in the private-sector companies. Increase in the import duty of pharmaceutical goods reduced the market share of MNC's.

NEW INDUSTRIAL POLICY AND WTO AGREEMENT

New industrial policy supported by the IMF and World Bank was introduced. Imports were largely freed. India entered the

* Reader in Commerce, St. Joseph's College (Autonomous), Tiruchirapalli.

** Research Scholar PG & Research Department of Commerce, St. Joseph's College.

International Product Patent Regime in the place of IPA 1970 by 1st January, 2005.

TRADE RELATED ASPECTS OF INTELLECTUAL PROPERTY RIGHTS (TRIPS)

Trade-Related Aspects of Intellectual Property rights agreement of WTO came into force from 1st January, 2005. It is mandatory to include both product and process patents in the patent laws of member states. The TRIPS agreement requires all member countries to adhere to minimum stands of intellectual property protection.

PROSPECTS OF INDIAN PHARMACEUTICAL SECTOR

The global pharmaceutical industry is estimated as US $ 550 billion and is likely to grow at 7% per annum, while Indian Pharmaceutical industry is estimated at US $ 6 billion, which has a current growth of 10% per annum. In the global scenario, Indian Pharmaceutical industry occupies the 4th rank in terms of volume and 13th rank in terms of value. (CII, 2005).

Indian Pharmaceutical industry has been providing employment for millions. India is not only self-sufficient but also self reliant in the production of both bulk drugs and finished formulations. India has the technology to produce chemical intermediaries and raw materials for their needs. It also exports them at various competitive prices. Indeed, the drug prices in India are one of the lowest in the world.

The United Nations Industrial Development Organisation (UNIDO) has classified, India into second category, countries with innovative capabilities. In this category only 5 countries have been selected from developing countries. At present, India has the highest number of United States Food and Drug Administration (US-FDA) plants outside of US and largest bulk drug filling facilities with lesser cost.

In the context of TRIPS agreement, Indian Pharmaceutical Industry mainly focuses on research and development to make and sell self-patented products. India has the advantage of scientific talent with highly skilled manpower, advances in biotechnology and latest information technology facilities with lesser cost.

The United States Pharmacopoeia (USP), the independent regulatory authority, plans to set up a research-based center in India. This will help all the Indian Pharmaceutical companies who are exporting drugs to US and other regulated markets to get regulatory approvals at a much faster pace. USP wants to work in close coordination with those scientists in a more harmonious way in establishing drugs standards and reference standards, monographs, quality aspects of products etc.

PROBLEMS AND PROSPECTS OF PHARMACEUTICAL CONSUMERS

Research and Development (new product discovery) has always taken the back seat amongst Indian pharmaceutical companies. Most of the drugs available in the global markets are based on the research of Multi National Companies'. MNC's concentrate mainly on highly profitable segments instead of essential drugs and less profitable service segments. This trend causes *"favour for the rich and challenges for the poor"*.

Due to the flow of recently designed high profit drugs into the drug market, essential drugs are produced inadequately, which leads to a hike in the prices of such drugs. Most of the patented drugs are very expensive. In India, on the average, more than two fifths of the populations have low income; they cannot afford to buy patented drugs for huge price and more over they cannot pay high premium to insurance companies to cover their expenditure. Per capita, consumption of drugs around the world is estimated to be around 87 US $ whereas in India it is 3 US $. (Sathya sundaram, 2005)

Drug Price Control Order (DPCO) ensures that essential and life-saving drugs do not fall out of price control. Over the period of time, as a result of sustained lobbying of the pharmaceutical industry, the number of drugs listed in DPCO was reduced from 347 in 1979 to 76 in 1995. The National Pharmaceutical Pricing Authority (NPPA) set up in 1997, is supposed to monitor the prices of the drugs. Despite this authority and monitoring practice, drug prices are going up and posing a threat to the consumers.

It states that the lowering tariff protection and New-MRP based excise duty regime threatens the existence of many small scale pharma units, that were involved in contract manufacturing for larger players.

According to Indian Drug Manufacturers Association (IDMA), big manufacturing firms would now prefer in-house production to contracted work, leading to a closure of several units that provide employment. Industry many be forced to hike prices to meet out excise duty advance reserve. Closure of small and medium pharma companies would pave the way for monopolies situation and result in increased cost of medicines and shortages. Various research studies reveal that high-cost profitable products will flow into the drug market and essential drugs will be at short supply, which can lead to a hike in the prices of such drugs.

International generics majors are setting up their own manufacturing and research outfits in India. This will result in fixing up of higher prices for their products. It will affect consumers, as they have to pay higher prices even for generic products.

In Pharmaceutical industry promotional strategies include personal selling, market survey, action plan, core doctor strategy, monitoring competitors action, communication theme, promotional inputs, sample distribution plan, gifts, free goods offer, customer relation management, market information system, providing continued medical education tools to doctor, distributing journals, latest references, conducting conferences and sponsoring doctors for international meetings.

Personal selling is essential for the survival of growth of pharmaceutical organization. This is done by sales force (Medical Representative). The main objective of salesman is providing customer's satisfaction and thereby achieving company's objective. Normally Multi National Company follows better marketing promotional strategies than Indian companies. They utilise their latest information technology, market survey system, market research tools, and research organisation's data to formulate better marketing strategies to win over the competition. Indian companies have been facing lot of problems in marketing their own cheap products in the market place. So, it results in better sales of MNC's high cost products than cheaper Indian products.

Doctors are the ultimate deciding authority, in prescribing products for the consumers. By better marketing strategy and sponsorship, MNC's used to exhibit better talents and win over doctor's confidence thereby making their sales. In this context, consumers are not getting an opportunity to buy cheaper Indian products, if doctors do not prescribe them.

Table 1
Productivity of Sales Force in Indian Pharmaceutical Market

Name of the Company	*Total number of Medical Representatives*	*Sales in Rupees Crore*	*Productivity*
Glaxo group (MNC)	2000	1514.8	7.5
Ranbaxy Cipla	1650	1012	6.1
Pfizer (MNC)	1750	1351.7	7.7
Dr.Reddy's	1200	659.7	5.5
	1000	453	4.5

Source: HDFC Securities, 2005.

Indian companies adopt a strategy of tie-up partnerships with other Multinational companies. Indian companies are concentrating on Novel Drug Delivery Systems (NNDS) to create slightly differentiated products and patent them. For example, Ranbaxy's copy of Bayer's Ciprofloxacin was a significant improvement in terms of dosage; Bayer's Cipro needs to be taken twice a day to be effective, whereas Ranbaxy's is a once-a-day formulation. (Sridharan, 2005).

Indian companies are entering into technologically tougher sector to reduce higher competition. Indian companies are challenging the innovators' patents in court, ahead of its expiry. Generics manufacturer has to file such an application called Abbreviated New Drug Application, or (ANDA) with USFDA and successfully challenge the relevant patent of the innovator to get a 180-day marketing exclusivity and better price. Though it is a good beginning for the Indian companies in overseas market, but their concentration should not be confined to overseas high profit market alone; they should also provide their services to the Indian domestic consumers in a better way.

Table 2
Top Selling drugs in Indian Pharmaceutical Market

Rank	*Products*	*Sales in Rupees (Crore)*
1	Corex	89.7
2	Human mixtard	84
3	Voveran	83.2
4	Becosules	77.7
5	Taxim	74.3
6	Liv-52	67.6
7	Asthalin	66.8
8	Sprodex	63.5
9	Digene	63.4

Source: Forbes, IMS Health Data, 2003.

The spurious drug industry is growing beyond control in India. According to the World Health Organisation (WHO) 2001 Statistics, 35 per cent of the world's spurious drugs are produced in India. Spurious drugs are life threatening, and not life-saving drugs.

Thus, spurious drugs claim a market share of 20 per cent of the total drug market in India. (Sathya sundaram, 2005).

CONCLUSION

Globalisation, regulations, TRIPS, stiff competition, increasing costs, non-availability of essential drugs, lesser per capita income, lack of R&D efficiency, spurious drugs and drying product pipelines are those factors posing challenges to Consumer's of India. Major discovery of many more drugs by Indian companies will solve these challenges. If drugs are available locally, it will suit our people price. Indian companies can utilise our available source of cheap labour, scientist, doctors and technicians. The Indian Pharmaceutical Industry also needs to take advantage of the recent advances in biotechnology and information technology. Experts say that India can be a super power in pharma R&D. Top global companies now look at India as the partner of choice. Indian companies should improve their R&D efficiency and thereby should provide more services to the consumer's welfare.

REFERENCES

CII (2005), "Indian pharmaceutical industry can reach US $ 48 billion by 2007".

Chemical Weekly, Vol. L, No. 42, June 7, p. 128.

Sathya sundaram (2005), "New opportunities in pharmaceuticals". Facts for you, Vol. 25, No. 11, August, p. 15.

Sridharan (2005), "Indian Pharma's Mid-life Crisis". Business Today, Vol. 14, No. 4,

February 27, p. 53.

2

IMPLICATIONS OF WTO ON SMALL SCALE ENTERPRISES: OPPORTUNITIES AND CHALLENGES

Chandra Prakash Azad & A. K. Jha***

World trade organization fulfils the need for an organization to regulate world trade and ensure production of trade and related property rights. The Uruguay Round of the GATT, in 1994 has gone down in history by establishing the World Trade Organisation at Geneva in 1995. The eight round of Multilateral Trade Negotiation of the GATT participants, commonly referred to as the Uruguay Round was launched in Uruguay. This negotiation concluded on the 15th December, 1993 at Geneva. The Treaty of the Uruguay became effective in April 1995.

WTO has been established for implementation of the various provisions of Dunkel Treaty. To expedite the negotiations in 1991, Sir Arther Dunkal, Director General of GATT and the official chairman of the Trade Negotiations Committee, tabled a scheme of proposal (known as the Dunkal Draft) for the consideration of the participating countries. The Dunkel Text covered seven areas for negotiations, *viz.*: (i) Market Access (ii) Agriculture (iii) Textile & Clothing (iv) GATT Rules (v) Trade Related Intellectual Property Rights (vi) Trade in Services and (vii) Institutional Matters.

In the 21st century of today it has been clearly embarked in the era of global society. In the economic sphere, the combined

* Centre for Regional Studies, T.M. Bhagalpur University
** Head, P.G. Dept. of Eco., B.N. Mandal Univ. (WC), P.G. Centre, Saharsa

effects of technological progress, rationalization of management methods, optimization of productivity, institution of World Trade Organization and working of major corporations have increasingly globalized the world. The economic world is inextricably woven in gorgeous net works making the world inevitably global with each passing year.

In the financial sphere, with deregulation, the simplification or end of exchange controls, financial innovation and advances in telecommunications, the financial world has become effectively globalized.

In the information sphere, news and data can be transmitted worldwide and video conferencing at the two ends of the world arranged at the drop of a hat. The world is truly a global village and the world market, a global market.

Most countries in the world are now forced to increase their integration within and dependence on the international market economy in one way or another. In numerous cases, the impact of the market on the whole of social life leads to dramatic consequences, reflected by the policy of structural adjustment, which has seen the state withdrawing from its main economic and social responsibilities. In the minds of a growing number of decision-makers throughout the world, it has become increasingly self-evident than the market should no longer be viewed as an institution, which must be regulated by external social forces, but, on the contrary, that it should be used to regulate societies as a whole.[2] Gerald Berthoud points out:

...... our time is characterized by a deep belief in the power of the market to solve the world's development problems.

Development now means integration into the national and international capitalist market, with a condition that this integration alone is the minimal condition for a region or country to be considered 'developed'. However, the initial process of globalization has confirmed for a growing number of Third World Countries or the countries of the South, that they are no longer or they were at no time in a position to engage in utilitarian exchanges with the rich countries. Development through the market is essentially a selective process; it caters to those who have economic resources; those without purchasing power are thrown on the fringes and excluded from the market to be captured by the resourceful. Market is a heartless institution.[4] Third World, whose majority population is struggling to obtain the strict necessities of life, consumption remains far beyond their means, and as such, they are out of the global market even before they could integrate with it properly.

This paper proposes to discuss the process of globalization, which is actually an attempt to integrate the markets of the world and create a market economy on a global scale and assess the future of the people in the developing countries where large populations survive on the functioning of their small and medium industries or local art and craft industries. No attempt has been made to define the terms, as it is assumed that the readers are well acquainted with these words and concepts which have been used in their general connotative sense and meaning.

Development, for the Third World Countries, from colonial times to the present day, is fundamentally an imposition, in one form or another, of a new institutional framework with its concomitant values as the prerequisites for the dynamism of the market. For the greater part of the World's population, development has proved to be the destruction of their ethnic identities, loss of their ecology, ruination of their culture and emaciation of their social solidarity networks and loss of their traditional handiwork of art and craft. More often, development has resulted in a social divide in which a small minority has made large profits at the expense of the majority. The forced development has thrown up three categories of people.[5]

I A small class of ultra rich businessmen, corporate managers, politicians, bureaucrats. They are able to collect much wealth while spending lavishly.

II A varying number of people in an intermediary position – doctors, teachers, office-workers, etc. who represent the middle classes. They actually balance production and consumption.

III Lastly, there are the poor, excluded from any share in the nations' wealth and preoccupied by problems of mere survival.

Though profits are exploding: the poor are losing out. Globalization and market (read privatization) has both winners and losers. Its market is an extremely ambivalent phenomenon, facing both ways like a head of Janu. The Human Development Report 1999 produced by the UNDP contains plentiful evidence of "Globalization without a human face". There are images of a "global apartheid", of life chances derived from the huge social disparities between the richest and poorest fifths of world population. According to the UNDP, the gap in income between the countries of North and South more than doubled in the four decades between 1960 and 2000.[6]

Globalization, development and market have released, what the sociologist Ulrich Beck, often describes the forces of "global social Darwinism",[7] increasing the wealth of the few while pauperizing the many. The mass of the world population who are excluded from globalization is depicted in Fred Scholz's following horror scenario:

It can act as a dumping ground for all kinds of used goods and cheap products, and may sometimes be the recipient of alms and disaster aid and the target of military peacekeeping exercises. But this marginalized left – over world, the New South, will generally be doubly out of touch and left largely to its own devices. It would fret out its own internal contractions and fragment through its own morbidity, and it will suffer from violence, poverty and backwardness.[8]

This description would not seem an exaggeration if we look into the reports from impoverished regions of Africa and South Asia, and from the slums of Bombay, Manila, Cairo, Rio or Harlem, though the mass of world population does not live in such dreadful conditions. Globalization has already been marked by greatly increased disparities, within countries and between countries. The gap in per capita income between developed and developing countries has more than tripled between 1960 and 1990. Between 1960 and 1991, the income, share of the richest 20 per cent of world's population rose from 70 per cent to 85 per cent, while the income share of the poorest 20 per cent of the population fell from 2.3 per cent to 1.4 per cent. The ratio of income shares of the richest to the poorest groups doubled from 30:1 to 60:1. Latest data indicates a marked worsening of such disparities. It has reached 74:1 in 1999, and it is projected to reach 100:1 in 2015.[9] The bulk of the people across the world find themselves in more fragile and vulnerable economic circumstances because many of the earlier welfare state provisions have been reduced or removed, public services have been privatized or made expensive and hence less accessible, and employment conditions have become much more insecure and volatile.

The disaster of *neo-liberalism* with its antecedent companions – globalization, privatization, market economy and multinational corporations – has brought the Third World countries to the brink of social revolt. Thanks to the economic system imposed on one countries by the World Bank, International Monetary Fund (IMF), International Development Agency (IDA), World Trade Organization (WTO), the poor are much poorer and are becoming progressively worse off, and the wealthy are wealthier and becoming increasingly better off. P. Xavier Gorostiaga, S.J. has collected data on the distribution and utilization of the wealth of the world according to percentages. This data divides the world's population into five groups of twenty per cent each. The twenty percent who are the most affluent have 82 per cent of the world's wealth. 11 per cent of the world's riches belong to the next group, 2.3 per cent of the riches is held by the third group, 1.9 percent belongs to the fourth group, and merely 1.4 per cent to the fifth group. A graph depicting this discrepancy is designed in the form of a champagne glass. It is wide at the top, but the rest is very thin. Things always break at their weakest point.

And the point in question here is the portion of the population excluded from the world's wealth, a population figure of 60 per cent.[10] With such an unequal distribution of wealth and riches where individual incomes exceed the total income of many developing countries combined together, the world would be in danger of completely losing its social stability.

The world is already in the "Globalization Trap". The way it is working it must almost automatically lead to an 80/20 society, in which 80 per cent will be losers and only 20 per cent winners.[11] Though democracy, market economy and human rights are considered to be the three equal sides of the globalization triangle, but social and human rights are undermined by deterioration in living and working conditions, women's rights by greater exploitation in, "world market factories" and the growing intercontinental trade in women, and children's rights by the expansion of child labour and child prostitution Globalization and its economic pressure pose a systematic threat to human rights itself, including right of self-determination of states. The opened up markets for capital, goods and services, and competition between locations, have weakened the ability of the states to impose minimum social standards and have strengthened the negotiating power of multinational corporations. Their transnational structure further weakens the power of national trade unions to counter their excesses and organize against them. Globalization has not only meant economic interconnectedness. Thus there are five distinct types of globalization visible today:

1. Economic globalization
2. Social globalization
3. Ecological globalization
4. Political globalization and
5. Cultural globalization.

All five are closely interwoven and have proved harmful for the developing countries. It was too deeply preoccupied with assessing the damages of economic globalization that it has paid little heed to other segments. This has been mainly due to the fact that the recent phase of globalization has been marked by forces of the strongest and most sweeping waves of concentration of economic activity that we have known historically. In terms of multinational corporations' activities, the possibility of vertical disintegration of production, which has allowed parts of the production process to be relocated and geographically separated, has been associated with greater vertical integration of the control and ownership of production internationally.[12] In addition, the last decade has, in particular, witnessed a wave of cross-border mergers and acquisitions across not only major manufacturing industries but even in the service sector and in utility provisions such as education, telecom, media and entertainment. More alarming, however, is the domination of financial flow in cross border transactions, as well as the greater role played by speculative elements and the separation of finance capital over productive capital. They are too well known to require elaborate mention.

It is worth mentioning here that globalization is also a struggle to control newer forms of economic territory besides keeping natural resources, markets and labour under control. Indeed, control over natural resources – particularly oil and energy resources – remains central concern of the globalization leaders.[13] It is amply demonstrated by a number of events like interventions in Afghanistan, Venezuela, Iraq and US military geo-politicking in Middle East, South Asia and Africa besides in Latin America.

Indeed, the current trend is towards a blatant capitalist/ imperialist/ neo-imperialist/ hyper-imperialist subjugation of the globe in the garb of globalization and the call for neo-liberalism. So far as the developing countries are concerned, the issue is still not state versus market, but changing the character of the state in order that a "vital power shift can take place from the bourgeoisies-feudalism-bureaucracy combine to a genuine people's democracy."[14] The market-friendly and marginalized state has already begun to pave way for capitalist world development, whereas the developing countries, which have not even been able to consolidate and build upon the gains of their five six decade old independence have been compelled to abandon their socialist welfare policies and follow an altogether culturally alien development model. These countries need a different model of development that will assure general welfare of the masses leading to an equalitarian social life free from exploitation and deprivation. The World Bank, IMF sponsored state-minimalism and market-friendly approach to the problems of developing countries pose serious hindrances in their development efforts where the governments have to mobilize social efforts to struggle against poverty, ill-health, malnutrition and the forces of inequity and injustice in a feudal-capitalist social regime. By granting the forces of marauding capitalism a free play in the name of overarching and determinate power of global economy, there is a covert attempt to put a stop to any serious consideration of alternative notions of collective action to reshape socio-economic destiny. Despite various instances of having been duped and cheated in the past, the developing world has not learnt its lessons properly.

While leading the national movement, Gandhi wrote in Young India of 1931, spelling out the meaning of Swaraj in these words:

Swaraj would have no meaning which was not the Swaraj for workers and peasants...... I am working for winning Swaraj not only for you, but for those toiling and unemployed millions who do not get even a square meal a day.[15]

Gandhi, deeply rooted to the Indian political culture, realized the basic facts of life of the Indian masses and knew the social, economic, political and spiritual responses to it. Gandhi said in 1924 and the situation has hardly changed despite nearly six decades of independence, various plans and projects and heroic assertions of development decades and manifestoes voicing conquest of unemployment and regeneration of rural earth into blooming gardens:

There is on the face of the earth no other country that has the problem that India has of chronic starvation and slow death-a process of dehumanization. The solution must, therefore, be original. In trying to find it, we must discover the causes of the tremendous tragedy.[16]

Instead of these warnings, we have decided to sell our souls to the Moloch of globalization that brings to us the message of "eat drink and be merry". We are caught in the web of 'Coca-Colanization' and "MC Donaldization" and do not have the vision of Gandhi to understand the problems of the common masses. The western materialists are today leading a people who rejected their own Charvakas[17]. Gandhi had realized the ruse and deception of the western imperialists and that is why he had opposed even western political institutions. He was of the opinion that they "have systems suited to their own genius.

We must have ours suited to ours."[18] Spelling out the economic constitution of India, Gandhi wrote way back in 1928:

The economic constitution of India, and for the matter of that of the world should be such that no one under it should suffer from want of food and clothing. In other words, it should be able to make the two ends meet. And, this ideal can be universally realized only if the means of production of elementary necessaries of life remain under the control of the masses.... They should not be made a vehicle of traffic for the exploitation of others. Their monopolization by any country, nation or group of persons should be unjust.[19]

Gandhi had warned, in his own inimitable way that a "non-violent system of government is clearly an impossibility so long as the wide gulf between the rich and the hungry millions persists."[20]

The globalized world is not paying heed to needs of the marginalized is visible in the fact that more than a quarter of the 4.5 billion people in the developing world still do not have some life's basic necessities. Nearly 1.3 billion people do not have access to clean water. About 480 million are malnourished. In India, as per the India Development Report 1999 to 2000, out of every three persons one is poor earning less than a dollar a day. If we add to this the undernourished or malnourished, the proportion becomes two out of three. The share in global income of the richest fifth of the world's people is 74 times that of the poorest fifth. The world GDP increased from 30 billion to 3 trillion in the past 50 years, but the share of the poor countries fell from 20 per cent to 10 per cent.[21]

The advocates of globalization promised to usher in an era of unprecedented economic growth, technological progress, rising living standards, and material prosperity. In fact, the world economy has slowed towards stagnation in the new era. The average annual growth rate of world GDP declined from 4.9 per cent between 1950 and 1973, to 3.0 per cent between 1973 and 1992, and to 2.7 per cent between 1990 and 2001. Between 1980 and 1998, half of all the developing countries suffered from falling real per capita GDP.[22] It follows a decline in the real earnings of workers all over the world including the

United States, the leader of globalization. In US the real weekly earnings of production and non-supervisory workers (in 1992 dollars) fell from $ 315 in 1973 to $ 264 in 1989. After a decade of economic expansion, it reached $ 271 in 1999, which remained lower than the average real wage in 1962. In Latin America about 200 million people or 46 percent of the population live in poverty. Between 1980 and early 1990s (1991-1994), real wages fell by 14 per cent in Argentina, 21 per cent in Uruguay, 53 per cent in Venezuela, 68 per cent in Ecuador, and 73 per cent in Bolivia.[23]

Globalization has meant in many ways the globalization of stagnation tendencies and financial crisis, which has resulted in steep fall of the purchasing power of the great majority of the world population. The global market has proved non-friendly to the majority of the people.

Globalization threatens the masses with scarcity and pauperization. The poor and the weak are most vulnerable to the risks of globalization. Recent studies in India point to the adverse effect of the economic reforms on the poor. Liberal policies have led to increase in prices, reduction in the consumption of nutritious items like cereals, downsizing of the work force, increase in unemployment, reduction in social services, reduction and elimination of subsidies on essential items. The existing rural industries are becoming unviable. Disruption of traditional crafts and small-scale industries seem imminent because of competition from large industries and MNCs. The onset of joint ventures with multinational participation has accentuated the erosion of small-scale production because of capital-intensive export-oriented enterprises. Unemployment is growing as traditional labour intensive cottage, small-scale and medium industries are displaced by new technologies. Liberalization of imports has brought to the doorsteps of the people even basic goods required for their daily needs. Even in remote areas, processed foods and bottled drinks are making inroads. Essentially local products like picles, *vadis, papads,* incense sticks, sweets, jams, jellies, herbal medicines etc. have also attracted the attention of the corporate houses. Cheap electronic toys have replaced the clay and wooden toys from the local market. Khadi industry in India survives on subsidy from the government, both central and state. Silk industry is facing crisis due to cheap and better Chinese silk products and yarns. Ready-made garment industries require highly skilled workforce. Gem and precious stone market too has tough competition from global competitors. In all, the future of small-scale industries, which can absorb large work force, is quite bleak.

It would like to substantiate this point by the example of handloom industry, which is an ancient cottage industry in India. It is a highly decentralized set up, spread throughout the country. The industry provides employment to over 150 lakh people, besides providing indirect employment to several lakhs of persons who are engaged in pre-loom, post-loom and marketing activities. The handloom weavers constitute the largest work force, next only to agriculture in India.[24]

Nearly four million handlooms are engaged in weaving nearly 23 different varieties of cotton fabrics. The industry meets around 30 per cent of the total clothing requirement of the country. Tamil Nadu accounts for nearly 30 per cent of total handloom. Textile production and constitutes 50 per cent of India's textile exports. The state has over 6 lakh of handloom units and 1400 cooperative societies. In many of the districts like Salem, Namakkal, Bharampuri, Cuddalore etc. the number of handlooms have dropped sharply. The crisis in this industry is attributed to sharp rise in prices of cotton yarns, chemical dyes, and indiscriminate import of yarn of various counts.[25] Competition from mill and imported clothes is very sharp. Likewise, readymade garment industry has ruined livelihood prospects of the tailoring business where wages are little and competition very high. The same is the fate of brassware industries, which are now being captured by large industries with huge capital.

IMPACT

Small, Scale Enterprises in India has been functioning amidst protected environment, i.e.; reservation for products to be manufactured by these units, quantitative restrictions of imports, wall of high import tariffs, preference in sanction of loans, concession from the Government and purchase of product by government department/ public sector undertaken, etc. After implementation of WTO, the protected environment for SSI sector is gradually vanishing. SSI, now, are facing increased competition from the multinational companies and survival of the fittest has become the buzz-wood in the Indian industrial sector today.

Not only that, the entry of multinational in ordinary consumers goods like ice-cream, agarbatti manufacturing, food processing, minerals water etc. is also adversely affecting the SSI sector since these were the traditional areas of this sector. The MNCs (Multi National Companies) are not interested in high tech product. Rather they prefer low technology, quick profit yielding volume products with regular demand throughout the year. In the name of consumer interest, MNCs continue to swallow SSEs and eliminate them from the market.

Small, tiny, artisan-based industries are on their way out in this era of globalization. To end the examples with Bihar, of the 130 thousand small, tiny artisan based industries[26] hundreds are getting closed everyday. This may not always be due to globalization, but market economy, the global economy, definitely has its impact.

The hope of economic globalization providing the developing countries a free access to the global market has remained a dream. They are already in the vortex of negative impact of global economy. No doubt, since 1980 there has been a dramatic growth in some 15 countries, bringing rapidly rising income to many of their 15 billion people. But over the same period of time, economic stagnation or decline has affected 100 countries. In 70 of these countries average incomes are less than they were in 1980, and in 43 countries less than they were in 1970. The international economic scene is quite grim. The WTO is the latest instrument by which they are creating new bonds to bind the developing countries. Modern, sophisticated technology is used for exploiting the poor, instead of helping them out of their ill-fed, malnourished existence and survival.

The latest World Bank report (2005) has stated:

When direct poverty reduction is given priority, the key will be to understand how political climate improvements impact the poorest members of society in their various capacities; as employees, as entrepreneurs, as consumers, as users of public services and as recipients of tax funds services or transfers.[27]

The masses in the developing countries are neither employees, nor entrepreneurs and also do not have access to public services worth the name. They live in utter squal our and wretched conditions which possibly the World Bank planners and experts coming from Europe and America cannot even conceive. The only way to improve the living conditions is to develop their skills and improve their traditional art and craft.

CONCLUSIONS

The world market, once projected as a weapon against despotism and economic of a few countries, has itself turned into a powerful dictator following selective destruction of the weak and dominance of the economically powerful. The categorical imperative of world market competition is a challenge to any attempt to organize individual societies and economies creatively and differently. Small scale industries are bound to yield to the pressure of multinationals and go into extinction unless people come to the fore to save them and their cultural heritage.

NOTES AND REFERENCES

Boutros Boutros-Ghali, "Global Prospects for United Nations", *Aussen Politik,* Vol. 46, No. 2, 1995, p. 108.

World Bank Development Report 1996: From Plan to Market, Oxford: Oxford University Press.

Gerald Berthoud, "Market", in Wolfgang Sachs (ed.), *The Development Dictionary : A Guide to Knowledge as Power,* London and New Jersey: Zed Books, 1992, p. 70.

J.M. Buchanan, *Liberty, Market and State: Political Economy in the 1980s,* Brighton: Wheatsdheaf Books, 1986, and A.H. Shand, *Free Market Morality: The Political Economy of the Austrian School,* London:

Routledge, 1990 and R. Heilbronner, *Behind the Veil of Economics*, Cambridge: Cambridge University Press, 1988.

n. 3, P. 81.

Human Development Report, New Delhi: Oxford University Press, 1999.

Franz Nuscheler, "Globalization: Is the South Losing Touch?", *Adult Education and Development*, 58, 2002, p. 124.

Ibid, pp.

See n. 6. Data collected from different pages. For 2000 and projected figures see United Nations, *Human Development Report*, Oxford, Oxford University Press, 2000 and 2002. See also James Petras and Henry Veltmeyer, Globalization Unmasked, London and New Yrok: 2ed books, 2001.

Fernando Cardenal, "The Validity of Utopias", *Adult Education and Development*, 44, 1995, p. 175.

n. /, p. 125.

Jayati Ghosh, "Imperialism, Fundamentalism and the Uses of 'Terror'," 18th A.K. Gopalan Memorial Lecture, organized by Jana Sanskriti on July 18, 2003 at Vithalbhai Patel House, New Delhi. Text also published in *Janata* in two parts August 31, 2003.

Ibid. p.

Mohit Bhattacharya, "Rolling Back the State : Public Administration in the Age of Market Supremacy", *The Indian Journal of Public Administration*, Special Number on Liberalisation Policy and Social Concerns, Vol. 42, No. 3, 1996, p. 251.

M.K. Gandhi, *Socialism of My Conception*, Edited by Anand T. Hingorani, Bombay: Bhartiya Vidya Bhavan, 1957, p. 243.

Ibid, p. 97.

The Charvaka materialism is characterized by direct orientation against idealist and religious doctrines propagated in Indian Philosophy. The Charvakas said: "While life is yours, live joyously: None can escape death's searching eye; when once this frame of ours they bun how shall it ever again return?" See for details S. Radhakrishnan, *Indian Philosophy*, London: George Allen & Unwin Ltd., 1977, Vol. 1, p. 281.

N. 15, P. 115

Ibid. P. 272

Ibid. P 276

N. 6; P. 25

Mingi Li, "After Neoliberalism: Empire Social Democracy and Socialism?, *Analytical Monthly Review*, January 2004, p. 22.

Ibid.

E. Mubarak Ali, "Handloom Industry in Tamil Nadu", *Kisan World*, June 2004, p. 45.

Ibid.

Institute of Human Development, *Bihar Development Report (Draft)*, New Delhi, 2003, p. 17.

Dhurjati Mukherjee, "Challenges of Poverty Eradication: Can the MGDS be Achieved" *Young Indian*, December 25-31, 2004, p.3.

3

WTO AND INDIAN AGRO-BASED INDUSTRIES

Revanasiddappa Veershetty Devendrappa M Madari***
*Prakash Basanna****

INTRODUCTION

Agro-based industries are based on the processing of agricultural produce, or they cater to the input needs of the agriculturists. Agro-based industries may be organised on i) Cottage scale, ii) Small scale and iii) Large scale . Large scale agro - based industries are generally set up in large cities, or in semi-urban areas. Rural agro-based industries are generally organised either on a cottage or small-scale basis and possess most of their characteristics[1].

The World Trade Organisation (WTO) is the principle international body concerned with solving trade problems between countries and with negotiating trade-liberalising agreements [2]. The WTO takes the place of the former General Agreement on Tariffs & Trade (GATT) and is the embodiment of the results of the 1986-1994 Uruguay Round of trade negotiations concluded under GATT. The WTO was established on 1st January 1995 and it encompasses previous GATT legal instruments, as they existed when the Uruguay Round was completed. However, the WTO extends new disciplines to economic and trade sectors not covered in the past. While the GATT was limited to trade in goods, the WTO

---

* Guest Lecturer in Economics, Govt. First Grade College, Bidar-01
** Lecturer Dept. of Economics, Gulbarga University, Gulbarga-06
*** Guest Lecturer in Management, Gulbarga University, Gulbarga-06

covers trade in services, including such sectors as banking, insurance, transport, tourism and telecommunications sectors as well as the provision of labour. In addition, the WTO covers all aspects of trade related intellectual property rights. The WTO joins the International Monetary Fund (IMF) and the World Bank as the third pillar of the global economic management system. The WTO and the agreements under it are treaties concluded by member states and therefore forms part of international economic law as opposed to international trade law.

WTO is a strong rule-based system, more powerful when it handles disputes. The most important benefit of WTO agreement is strengthening of the rules-based multilateral trading system. This is of particular importance to economically weak nations. If commercial relations of a country were based on economic and political strength, developing countries, like India, would be virtually helpless and increasingly dependent on richer and more powerful countries. Their situation would be nearly as bad if multilateralism were rejected in favour of an exclusive focus on regionalism. Had the Uruguay Round not been held - worse, if it had failed - economic and political power would have come to dominate commercial relations. In that sense, rules-based multilateralism is a declaration of economic and political independence for less powerful countries.

Opportunities and Benefits for Agro-Based Industries Under WTO Regime

OPPORTUNITY OF GETTING JUSTICE AND LEVEL PLAYING FIELD

The Uruguay Round significantly strengthened the dispute settlement procedures. Individual countries, no matter how big, can no longer block the process. Now the lower-income developing countries are in a better position to defend their rights and to insist other members to fulfill their legal obligations as laid down in the WTO's rules [3].

OPPORTUNITY FOR GLOBAL MARKET ACCESS

The increase in market access provides opportunities to increase and diversify exports.

OPPORTUNITIES

The above said opportunities can be availed of only by following certain guidelines laid by WTO are:

1. Introducing fundamental reforms in agricultural policies that affect trade,
2. Removal of subsidies from agriculture and allied sector
3. Phasing-out of quotas on developing countries' exports,
4. Reductions in industrial tariffs and an increase in tariff bindings by a broad cross-section of actual and potential trading partners,
5. The decision to phase-out so-called quantitative restrictions
6. Harmonization of quality systems around the world

ENSURING STABLE DOMESTIC POLICY ENVIRONMENT

Indian agriculture and agro-based industries suffered more because of various shortsighted domestic policies than any other factor. The Uruguay Round Agreements are a "single undertaking", requiring all WTO members to accept essentially the same rights and obligations. This was not the case under the former GATT where many lower-income members undertook fewer obligations than developed countries did. Those obligations, including additional disciplines, can be very helpful to reform oriented governments.

Policy discretion is a two-edged sword. Indian agriculture policies are classical case of this. No doubt, it gives governments freedom, but it also allows them to change their policies frequently, sometimes in response to the demands of politically powerful special interest groups, not necessarily acting in the country's overall interests. The recent large-scale inflow of edible oils in India, higher MSP to already surplus Rice and

Wheat and low MSP to scarce pulses are certain examples. The credibility of economic reforms can then be undermined, discouraging both domestic and foreign investors and making domestic and foreign investors hesitant to commit funds to projects other than those who promise a very quick pay-off. Therefore, the "burden" of accepting additional multilateral disciplines on one's own trade-related policies, can often be a blessing in disguise for a government interested in promoting economic growth and development. That is why this is an opportunity for hard working and quality conscious agriculture and agro-based organizations in India.

MORE OPPORTUNITIES IN FUTURE

The Uruguay Round will boost global GDP and stimulate global demand for the exports of lower-income developing countries. Estimates of the increase in global GDP from the market access part of the Uruguay Round range from $40 billion to $315 billion, a part of which will be spent on goods and services exported by the lower-income developing countries. This is an opportunity for Indian farmers and farmers' organizations, provided we work hard to meet the international quality requirements and requirements of product presentation.

WHO WILL BE THE LOSERS?

Those organisations and people who are not willing to change and upgrade quality and productivity and the government and management systems those who are not willing to change with time will be the losers. In fact, India is in a position to gain a lot provided we take this change as a challenge and start working to adopt ourselves to the new global economic order.

Indian organisations in agriculture and agro-based industry are likely to gain, perhaps more than any other sector, from a strengthened multilateral trading system, from the phase-out of quantitative restriction on products, and from the opportunities to use new WTO obligations to promote badly needed domestic economic reforms especially in agriculture sectors.

As export subsidies and domestic support are reduced in the major developed exporting countries, the artificially low world market prices which prevailed as a result of dumping surplus production through the extensive use of agricultural export subsidies, will phase out with time. This will take some time, till than we should utilize out time and resources on the up gradation of domestic agriculture marketing and production systems as well as quality.

The progressive implementation of the results of the Uruguay Round as a whole will generate increasing opportunities for trade expansion and economic growth to the benefit of all countries. The possible negative effects visible in imports are only of a short-term nature, at the same time the dumping from subsidized exports must be controlled because this is not a fair competition. This is not because we were not prepared to accept the competition and want to live in protected environment because we don't want to destroy our delicate agricultural base for short-term gains. The ray of hope is that every one has accepted that WTO is a reality and we have to work hard. The islands of excellence are emerging within India and we are proud of them.

OPPORTUNITIES TO INVEST AND EXPAND:

Moreover, it is generally accepted that artificially low world market prices have undermined agricultural production and investment in many developing countries like India and have inhibited essential domestic agricultural re-structuring, productivity and quality improvements.

More realistic and stable world market prices for agricultural products will help to reverse these trends and enhance agricultural production and trade prospects in developing countries like India. This will be possible provided we provide appropriate trade and domestic agricultural policies environment to farmers and agro-based industries [4].

HOW CAN THE INDIAN AGRICULTURE AND AGRO-BASED INDUSTRIES EXPLOIT THE IMPROVED MARKET ACCESS ?

Challenge is to face the reality that WTO is here to stay and not try to ignore it. This is a genuine challenge. The answer lies in a combination of measures:

- By improving policy-making and macroeconomic management,
- By boosting training and investment to upgrade quality,
- Upgrade business management practices and
- Enhancing knowledge base about the global markets.

The thrust of Centre for Indian Trade Association (CITA) will be to work on these lines.

It is now widely accepted that the major obstacle to increased exports and growth in the developing countries like India is the inadequate response of domestic producers ("supply constraints") to market access opportunities abroad[5]. Removing, or at least significantly reducing, domestic supply constraints and quality problems in these countries must be a priority.

The economies of the countries like India have been hampered by a number of structural factors. They are:

- Macroeconomic imbalance (fiscal, monetary and exchange rate policies),
- Biased government policies in favour of non-agricultural sector supported by strong lobbies; (now failed to deliver under competition)
- Lack of appropriate human and physical capital at large
- Poorly developed infrastructure especially in rural areas
- Inadequate and outdated regulatory regimes (including state-run or state-tolerated or government supported private monopolies) many times supported by vested private sector lobbies, and
- Poorly functioning institutions, including Universities and R&D institutions, for enforcing the rules necessary for a functioning market system.

The strengthening and professionalization of public administrations and institutions, and improvement in physical transportation and communications infrastructures, is an immediate need and necessary.

Indian Agriculture and Agro-based industries need institutional back up: A key contribution of the domestic as well international institutions should be to provide technical assistance for building the institutional infrastructure to support trade and trade policy.

These efforts include technical assistance to help the private sector become more outward looking i.e. to develop global view. The focus should be on product and market development, (with a priority on diversifying exports means more products and more markets), trade finance, export quality management, export packaging, and training in international purchasing and supply management.

Strengthening business information networks are also important. In all this, the needs of small and medium size farmers and agro-based enterprise warrant special attention. Domestic and International lending institutions have to play an important role in removing these bottlenecks.

Domestic economic reforms that improve the domestic supply response along with, if necessary, revised foreign direct investment regulations are likely to help the developing countries like India in improve their disappointing record in attracting private investment from, within India or abroad, in agriculture and agro-based sector. The additional capital, together with the technological know-how (including organizational, managerial and marketing skills) that often accompany private investment, can play an important role in further strengthening India's ability to expand and diversify their exports by taking advantage of market access opportunities abroad.

Within the broader area of economic reform, there is also a role for trade liberalization especially in the field of agriculture trade within in India. In India, trade liberalization is now being combined with exchange liberalization, liberalization of investment conditions but the deregulation of the internal market for agriculture is still long overdue to form a complete market opening package. Agriculture trade liberalization is vital and in the interest of all the stakeholders (farmers, consumers and government) to create stable economic conditions for investment and trade[5].

An important element in this area is the adoption of trade legislation and rules that are consistent with WTO disciplines and to make India competitive. This makes for a more predictable, secure and transparent trade environment.

CONCLUSION

In competitive world our strategy should be to produce the best quality at the lowest cost. This can be encouraged and supported by proper policy reforms and public investments in strengthening agriculture infrastructure and research. At the same time it is important to read between the lines, why few countries are so much interested in India and pushing WTO provisions to enter the Indian markets. India is located in ideal location with all possible natural advantages for most of the crops and animal products. There is every possibility to become an agricultural superpower in the world in the days to come.

Government and private sector joint efforts in policy reforms should be to achieve the dream to make Indian agriculture strong enough to face the competition. The political stability and economic prosperity of India depends upon how well we do in our agriculture and agro-based industries because this is the only sector which can feed and provide jobs to majority of over one billion human as well as another one billion animal population and that too with self-respect and dignity. Profitability in Indian Agriculture will decide the future of India and the social and political stability of India. Economically viable agriculture is the only insurance for stability of Indian social, political and economic system.

REFERENCES

Ishwar C. Dingra (1995), "The Indian Economy", Sultan Chand and Sons, New Delhi, p. 165.

Mishra and Puri (2005), "Indian Economy", Himalaya Publishing House, New Delhi, p. 132.

Keayla BK (2002), " WTO and India", Swadesh Jagran Prakashan, New Delhi, p. 14.

Sinha PN , "Scope for Agro-Based Industries", Commerce, Vol. 127, Nov. 17, 1973, p.28.

Gulati, Ashok et. al. " From Marakkesh to SEATTLE – Indian Agriculture in Globalisaing World",Economic EPW, Vol. XXXIV, Oct., 1999, p. 12.

4

TRADE IN HIGHER EDUCATION: A STUDY OF WTO, GATS AND THEIR PROS-CROS IN INDIA

*Shaukath Azim**

End of the 20th century witnessed an excited debate in the country about the impact of opening up banking, insurance and telecom services. Every country has vital social and economic compulsions in these services. But, with the commencement of 21st century, the intense dispute on these services almost passed away. These days we never come across any hue and cry about the impact of LPG on the services stated in the beginning. In the present century, the most important aspect engrossed is the GATS and its consequences on higher education in the entire world. Owing to the outcome of GATS, January 1, 2005 onwards, India is obliged under the WTO to open its higher education sector to foreign nations. Therefore, it has both positive and negative consequences on the quality and availability at higher education in India.

In the backdrop of WTO and GATS, an attempt has been made in this paper to examine the impact of WTO and GATS on the prospect of higher education in India. The present paper has been divided into 4 parts. In the first part a succinct note is specified on WTO and GATS and the manner of trade in higher education. This part also furnishes the information about the key elements, rules of GATS. In the second part an effort has been made to study the blow of GATS on higher education in

---

* Reader, Department of Sociology, Karnatak University, Dharwad-03. e-mail: shabbuazim@yahoo.co.in.

India. In the third component a depiction of poor status of higher education in India and in the last part few proposals have been given to face the challenges of GATS.

WTO AND GATS

An attempt in this segment made to know about WTO and GATS and the policies of GATS on higher education. An effort has also been made here to the response of India to GATS. The GATS is the first ever set of multilateral rules covering international trade in services. Previous international trade agreements covered trade in products, but never services. The GATS was negotiated in the Uruguay round and came into effect in 1995. It is administered by World Trade Organization (WTO), which is made up of 144-member country. The WTO is the only global international organization dealing with the rules of trade between nations. At its heart are the WTO agreements, negotiated and signed by the majority of the worlds trading nations and ratified in their parliaments. The GATS is one of these key agreements and is a legally enforceable set of rules.

The GATS has three parts. The first part is the frame work that contains the general principles and rules. The second part consists of the national schedules that list a country's specific commitments on access to their domestic market by foreign providers. The third part consists of annexes which detail specific limitations for each sector can be attached to the schedule of commitments. Therefore, it is essential to understand what kind of education services will be covered by GATS and what is meant by higher education services.

MODES OF TRADE IN SERVICES

The GATS defines four ways in which a service can be traded, known as 'modes of supply'. These four modes of trade apply to all services sectors in GATS. Table-1 provides a generic definition for each mode, applies them to the education sector and comments on the relative size of the market supply and demand. It is important to note that the current use of the term "borderless education" covers all four modes of supply.

Table 1
Mode of Supply

Sl. No.	*Mode of supply According to GATS*	*Explanation*	*Examples in Higher Education*	*Size/ Potential of Market*
1.	Cross Border Supply	The provision of services where the service crosses the border (does not require the physical movement of the consumer)	# Distance learning # e-learning # virtual universities	# Currently a relatively small market # Seen to have great potential through the use of new ICTs and especially the internet
2.	Consumption Abroad	Provision of the service involving the movement of the consumer to the country of the supplier.	# Students who go to another country to study	# Currently represents the largest share of the global market for education services
3.	Commercial Presence	The service provider establishes or has presence of commercial facilities in another country in order to render service	# local branch or satellite campuses # Franchising arrangements with local institutions	# growing interest and strong potential for future growth # Most controversial as it appears to set international rules on foreign investment
4.	Presence of Natural Persons	Persons traveling to another country on a temporary basis to Provide service	# Professors, Teachers, Researchers working abroad	# potentially a strong market given the emphasis on mobility of professionals

Source: Jane Knight, 2002

CATEGORIES OF EDUCATION SERVICES

Trade in education is organized into five categories or sub-sectors service. These categories are based on the United Nations Provisional Central Product Classification (CPC) and are described in Table-2. The three categories that are most relevant to this report are 'higher', 'adult', and 'other'. The four modes of services described above apply to each of the categories.

Critics of this classification system believe that it does not reflect the reality of today where non-traditional and private providers exist and alternate forms of delivery using new technologies are being used. However, countries are able to add their own qualifications or supplements to the UN CPC classification scheme and therefore, in principle, should not be limited by the scheme.

KEY ELEMENTS AND RULES OF THE GATS

The overall framework contains a number of general obligations applicable to all trade in services regardless of whether a country has made a specific commitment to sectors or not. These are called unconditional obligations. Fundamental to this discussion is the Most Favored Nation (MFN) rule.

Each WTO member lists in its national schedules those services for which it wishes to provide access to foreign providers. In addition to choosing which service sectors will be committed, each country determines the extent of commitment by specifying the level of market access and the degree of national treatment they are prepared to guarantee. Table-3 lists the key elements of the GATS and provides brief explanatory notes.

GATS AND INDIA

Under the compulsion of GATS, our country has to take out, what the WTO labeled, obstacles or barriers in free trade in higher education. India has to unlock the door to foreign universities to function in India. By removing all the existing obstacles, most of the developed countries, especially the United States, want to further liberalise the world economy

Table 2
Classification System for Education Services

Sl. No.	*Category of Education service*	*Education activities included in each category*	*Notes*
1.	Primary Education (CPC 921)	# Pre-school and primary education services # Does not cover child-care services	
2.	Secondary Education (CPC 922)	# General higher secondary # Technical and vocational secondary # Also covers technical and vocational services for the disabled	
3.	Higher Education (CPC 923)	# Post secondary technical and vocational education services # Other higher education services leading to University degree or equivalent	# Types of education (i.e. business, liberal arts, science) are not specified # assumes that all post secondary training and education programs are covered.
4.	Adult Education (CPC 924)	# Covers education for adults outside the regular education system	# Further delineation is needed
5.	Other Education (CPC 929)	# Covers all other education services not elsewhere classified # Excludes education services related to recreation matters	# Needs clarification recoverage and differentiation from other categories # For example – are education and language testing services, student recruitment services, quality assessment covered

Source: Jane Knight, 2002.

Table 3
Key Elements and Rules

Sl. No.	*GATS Element of Rule*	*Explanation*	*Application*	*Issues*
1.	Coverage	All Internationally traded services are covered in the 12 different service sectors (e.g. education, transportation, financial tourism, health, construction)	Applies to all services – with two exceptions : 1. Services provided in the exercise of governmental authority 2. Air traffic rights	Major debate on what the term "Exercise of governmental authority" means.
2.	Measures	All laws, regularities and practices from national, regional or local government that may affect trade.	A generic term that applies to all sectors.	
3.	General or Unconditional obligations	Four unconditional obligations exist in GATS. -Most favored nation (MFN) transparency -dispute settlement -monopolies	They apply to all Service sectors regardless of whether it is a scheduled commitment or not.	Attention needs to be given to "most favored nation"
4.	Most favored nation (MFN) treatment	Requires equal and consistent treatment of all foreign trading partners	May apply even if the country has made no specific commitment to	MFN has implications for those countries who already are

Contd....

Sl. No.	*GATS Element of Rule*	*Explanation*	*Application*	*Issues*
		MFN means treating one's trading partners equally. Under GATS, if a country allows foreign competition in a sector, equal opportunities in a sector, equal opportunities in that sector should be given to service providers from all WTO members. This also applies to mutual exclusion treatment For instance, if a foreign provider establishes branch campus in Country A, then Country A must permit all WTO members the same opportunity/ treatment, Or if Country A chooses to exclude Country B from providing a specific service, then all WTO members are excluded.	provide foreign access to their markets. Exemptions, for a period of 10 years are permissible.	engaged in trade in educational services and/or who provide access to foreign education providers MFN is not the same as national treatment.
5.	Conditional obligations	There are a number of conditional obligations attached to national schedules: -Market access -National treatment	Only applies to commitments listed in national schedules Degree and extent of obligation is determined by country	GATS supporters believe that a country's national educational objectives are protected by these two obligations.

Contd....

Sl. No.	*GATS Element of Rule*	*Explanation*	*Application*	*Issues*
6.	National Treatment	Requires equal treatment for foreign and domestic providers Once a foreign supplier has been allowed to supply a service in one's country there should be no discrimination in treatment between the foreign and domestic providers.	Only applies where a country has made a specific commitment. Exemptions are allowed.	GATS critics believe that this can put education as a "public good" at risk.
7.	Market Access	Means that degree to which market access is granted to Foreign providers in specific sectors. Market access may be subject to one or more of six types of limitations defined by GATS agreement.	Each country determines limitations on market access for each committed sector.	
8.	Progressive Liberalization	GATS has a built in agenda which means that with each round of negotiations there is further liberalizations of trade	Applies to all sectors and therefore includes education	

Contd....

Sl. No.	*GATS Element of Rule*	*Explanation*	*Application*	*Issues*
		in service. This means more sectors are covered and more trade limitations are removed.		
9.	Bottom-up and Top-down approach	Bottom-up approach refers to the fact that each country determines the type and extent of its commitments for each sector. Top down approach refers to the main rules and obligations as well as the progressive liberalization agenda there will be increasing pressure to remove trade barriers.	Sceptics maintain that the top down approach will have increasing importance and impact thereby increasing pressure to liberalise.	

Source: Jane Knight, 2002

and then control, manage and provide higher education in the global market. In this process, only developed countries can make huge profits. They attract not only in higher education, but also in every field of socio-economic life. Naturally this may happen to higher education field as well. In India already some foreign universities tried to market their higher education programmes. Representatives of several countries visited India to market certain percentage of their medical and engineering seats. Some foreign universities have also engaged Indian agencies and firms to recruit students to study in their universities. Others have started franchisee or commercial presence in India by allowing students to be enrolled in India and carry out studies for a part of the period in India and completing the other part of the degree in the institutions abroad (Sharma, 2002).

Thus the export of higher education to India by Universities of several countries has been through modes of consumption abroad, cross border supply, franchisee, and virtual universities. In 2005, about 75,000 students went abroad for education mostly to USA, Australia, UK, Canada and France. However, on an average only 2000 students per year came to India. But, most of them were from Gulf and South Asian countries.

A recent estimates given by Global Alliance for transnational Education Indicate that about $27 billion worth of higher education is exported to Asia and Pacific by three countries namely USA, UK and Australia. A business of $37 billion trade in tertiary education services in Asia and Pacific region is projected in future. Largest number of universities advertising in India is from UK followed by Australia, Canada and Austria.

As far as India is concerned, the foreign education providers are interested in higher education with the use of all the four modes of trade. They are targeting at economically well to do group in society in order to maximize profits. The force of GATS so much that, the non-organized private education providers, in India, are the first one to take its advantages. The public education providers would be marginalized in the race due to unequal rules of the game.

There is bound to be an unfavorable balance in the trade of education services. (Sharma, 2002).

GATS AND POOR STATUS OF INDIA HIGHER EDUCATION

It is significant to note that India has a bulk contingent of higher education institutions, students and teachers. Now every one has an opportunity to pursue higher education in India. Before the Independence higher education in India was in the hands of few classes and castes and was accessible mostly in city centres. Most of them who got higher education, served loyally to colonial masters. Today, however, there has been a shift from class to mass. Since more and more children completing their primary and secondary education and many wish to continue to gain a degree. There has been a tremendous growth in higher education centres and learners and gained prominence. 'Today global wealth is concentrated less and less in factories, land, tools and machinery. The knowledge, skills and resourcefulness of people are increasingly critical to the world economy. Human capital has gained more prominence than physical capital. Most of the developed countries responded quickly to the changing global phenomenon and started investing heavily on the generation of human capital. They are providing advanced skills that command premium in today's work places.

And what about the developing country like India? Will she be able to participate in the knowledge economy? Is she facing a future of increasing exclusion, unable to develop the skills required for the Twenty-first country? It is disheartening to note that Higher education in India is becoming more and more old-fashioned. But "The world is moving from industrial revolution to knowledge revolution. Industrial economy to knowledge economy, Industrial society to knowledge society. The world's Silicon Valleys are pushing the technological envelope. Advances in information technology have made knowledge as more important and made more accessible, effective and powerful. Therefore participation in the knowledge economy requires a new set of human skills. People need to have higher qualifications and to be capable of intellectual independence. Without improved human capital India will inevitably fall behind and experience intellectual and economic marginalization and isolation.

Due to GATS, India has to maintain international standard in her higher education system. Students have to be trained and prepared to face global market. LPG has opened the vistas to every young men and women. For that reason, our men and women have to be trained on par with international level. Hence, our higher education institutions clearly need well-designed academic programmes and a clear mission. Most important to their success, however, are high quality faculty, committed and well-prepared students and sufficient resources. But most of the higher educational systems in India suffer severe drought in each of these areas. Some of them are:

1. To keep the tune of GATS Agreement in higher education, we need a well-qualified and highly motivated faculty. Otherwise the level of knowledge imparted to students will be limited and restricts the students' ability to access existing knowledge and generate new ideas. In India, the teaching methods of most of the teachers are often outmoded. Most of them have become *"dictators"* in the classroom because they simply *"dictate"* notes to students. Teachers simply give them marks without assessing the quality of answer scripts. Therefore, they have become *"Marxists"* (Marksists). Since every student is getting first class and above, there is no *"class struggle"* among the students. Teachers have made *"classless society"*.
2. In many institutions, students face difficult conditions for study. Severely over crowded classes, inadequate library and laboratory facilities hamper the learning process. Many students start their studies academically unprepared for higher education. Most of them join to colleges due to the lack of choices other than higher education. Poor basic and secondary education also affects the performance of students at higher education.
3. International agreement of services means, students in India need to learn any one of the international

languages, in particular, English. Since most of the Universities allowed the students write their exam in their regional languages, the ability of students to write and speak in English is further deteriorated. Corporate companies value those who have got the ability to communicate freely in English. Unless learning English be made compulsory, Indian students may fail miserably in grabbing the opportunity offered by GATS.

4. No doubt GATS agreement has some advantages like regularly updated curricula, more practicability, learner centric and more importantly it develops marketable skills. But in India most of the higher education institutions depend on government for its expenditure. But GATS stressed on drastic cut in public expenditure on education. In the support of GATS, Ambani-Birla committee in its report recommended "there should be a freeze on recruitment of staff in all the universities at all levels. In addition, an ad-hoc cut of 10% in the total staff strength should be imposed in all these institutions. Following these footsteps the UGC issued a directive that only 80% of the teaching vacancies be filled up and that too on temporary basis. Due to impact of this committee report most of departments of universities facing acute shortage of teachers. In some departments of the universities only guest lecturers teach all the papers. Conventional universities started losing their original quality and strength. These universities are lagging behind in the race of global competition.
5. Imbalances in the enrollment ratio in higher education are also a cause of concern in India. Most of the institutions of higher learning are in metros and city centres. There has emerged "higher educational divide" between rural and urban students. Most of institutions of higher learning in urban areas possess adequate infrastructural facilities, which can be compared to international standards. Metro students

are better equipped to face the onslaught of internationalization of higher education. But now-a-days majority of students who are studying in conventional universities are drawn from rural areas. Most of them fail miserably in IQ tests and communication skills. Therefore GATS policy on higher education to a great extent affects rural students than urban, poor students than rich.

6. The expansion and differentiation of higher education is occurring at the same time as the pace of knowledge creation is dramatically accelerating specialized and a revolution has occurred in peoples' ability to access knowledge quickly. These changes are fundamentally altering what economies produce as well as where and how they produce it. Organizations are changing. India's higher education system is not fully developed to those skills that are needed to run the changing organizations.

HOW TO FACE GATS IMPLEMENTATIONS ON HIGHER EDUCATION?

Therefore in the 21st century, Indian, higher education must keep a number of considerations. Some of them are:

1. Students in India must learn not only what is known how, but also how to keep their knowledge, up to date. New technology based tools for gathering knowledge must become central elements of their education and curricula should be designed so that students learn how to learn.
2. Today is the age of specialization. Therefore specialization gained more prominence in modern society. Institutions of higher education will need to provide opportunities for in-depth study of particular fields. Indian students must be offered general education that can serve them as a solid foundation for life long learning and later specialization.
3. Comprehensive policy of implementing different and new type of premier institutions in rural areas so that

specialization will be created among rural students also. Because new institutions can best serve the interests of modern day students.

4. We all know that knowledge is being produced throughout the world. Therefore we should actively involve the scholars from other countries. This is crucial for developing and maintaining a largely intellectual community. "Much new knowledge has how become an international public good. Its benefits should extend well beyond the borders of the country in which it is created". Therefore we should import new information from the developed countries. Countries that allow information to flow freely will benefit more.
5. The advances in communication and information technology are important in knowledge revolution. They should be available more and more to those students who are deprived of these advances.

X-FIVE-YEAR PLAN PROPOSAL TOWARDS GATS

In order to face the GATS implications X five-year plan made following observations. They are:

- "Although India has approved to complete liberalization on trade in educational services, it may not be able to withstand the international pressures unless she prepares well for the second round of WTO negotiations. The matter is urgent and the government should therefore appoint committee/task force to advice on (a) negotiation on higher education issues in WTO, and (b) issues relating to erecting the safeguards for the post-negotiations market access regime".
- "Serious thinking is required to extend the benefits of higher education to the less privileged section of society. For this an Educational Development Bank should be created."
- "Private relevant institutions of higher education should be encouraged provided they adhere to equity

parameters determined by appropriate regulatory mechanism."

- "Optimum utilization of public infrastructure and manpower in the higher education sector should be ensured".
- "Universities should also consider setting up a cell for taking care of internationalization of higher education, both for import and export. Universities may devise ways and means to mobilize their own resources through various means".

Explaining its approach for internationalization of higher education Tenth Five Year Plan proposal suggests special incentives to universities: Universities which are willing to rise say 25-30 percent of their recurring expenditure from the fees of foreign students should be permitted to retain 10 percent of collection towards a designated fund for updating equipment and facilities. The university should be within its rights to admit as many foreign students as necessary to raise the target amount. For five year government should also consider making a matching grant towards their designated fund. This would progressively reduce the dependence of such a university on the government. (Sharma, *ibid*)

For the universities that accept the above scheme, recommends the proposal, the NAAC (National Assessment and Accreditation Council) should set up a special and professional method for evaluation so that the foreign students who receive training in India are accepted as "World class" on their return to home. The evaluation should aim at ensuring not only high academic standards but also decent living conditions for the foreign students.

The proposal further states, Deemed universities, which are rapidly growing in number and receive no support from the government, should be encourage to admit higher percentage of foreign students. It emphasizes that if private enterprise is "willing to set up world class educational facilities in emerging areas such as IT or biotechnology, where the full cost will be recovered from the fees of foreign students they should be given encouragement.

The UGC has allowed deemed universities to set up their campuses in other countries. In view of this, the proposal wants this facility to be extended to all universities who wish to export education. It is also proposed that as an incentive for the universities, "their earnings from abroad should not be deducted from the annual government grants for say, 5-10 years", and they should have "access to soft loans" for the purpose.

CONCLUSION

In conclusion we can say that in the era of LPG, knowledge has become a springboard for social and economic growth and development. It promotes the cultures that support its creation and dissemination a vital task. Universities must take a leading role in shaping young men and women according to the changing global scenario. In this context the president of Tanzania remarked that 'our universities must produce men and women willing to fight an international battle for self confidence and self assertion as equal players in the emerging globalized world.

REFRENCES

A fair globalization: Creating opportunities for all (2006), World commission on the Social Dimension of globalization, Academic foundation, New Delhi.

Gills, Malcom (1999), Quoted in *Higher Education in Developing countries: Peril and Promise*, 2000 pp. 15.

Higher Education in Developing Countries: Peril and Promise, (2000), The task force on Higher education and society, World Bank.

Knight, Jane (2002), *Trade in Higher Education Services: The implications of GATTS*, The observatory on borderless higher Education, London.

Krishnaraj, P.M. (2005) Gats and its implications for Higher Education in India or *http://execcindia.indiainfo.com.*

Peer Mohammed (1994), *Higher Education and Employment*, Rawat Jaipur.

Shama, Vijendra (2002), "WTO, GATS and the Future of higher Education in India" in *Peoples Democracy*. Vol. 26, No. 6 Feb. 10.

5

W.T.O. AND INDIAN AGRICULTURE: ISSUES AND IMPACT

Prem Chand Tiwari, Bipasha Chowdhary** & Mahesh Kumar Tiwari****

After the great depression in 1930s, there was a decline in the level of international trade. To prevent another global recession it was decided in a meeting of Brettonwoods that there should be some international institution regarding trade. This has paved a way towards the establishment of GATT in 1947. The General Agreement on Tariff and Trade (GATT) was an international organisation, which was created in 1947. The basic objective of GATT was free trade through multilateral trade negotiations. There were three basic objectives of GATT –

- Non discrimination (i.e. non-discrimination between countries for the source of good)
- Elimination of non-tariff barriers.
- Solving the trade disputes by consultation among the nation.

The present world trading system had evoloved from the former GATT, envisaged in 1947 in the aftermath of second world-war. The evaluation of WTO from GATT was the Uruguay round (1986-1994) which have Paved the way for the establishment of WTO. The main subject of discussion for

* Reader, Department of Economics, Handia P.G. College Handia, Allahabad.
** Research Scholar, Department of Economics, Allahabad University, Allahabad.
*** Research Scholar, Department of Economics, Handia P.G. College, Handia, Allahabad.

Uruguay round were – tariffs, non-tariff barriers, textiles and clothing, agricul.ures, trade in services, trade related aspect of intellectual property rights, trade related investment measure anti-dumping and countervailing measurer subsidies etc.

WORLD TRADE ORGANISATION

World Trade Organisation was established on 1st January, 1995 formally signed by 115 countries. India is one of the founder member of WTO. WTO is established for free, fair and undistorted trade in commodities, services and related aspects. The emergence of WTO ushered a new are of consensus on several issues, which were not in the jurisdiction of GATT. There basically four types of agreements. First kind is related to commodities and known as GATT (1994). It includes Agreement on Agriculture (AOA), textiles, subsidies, sanitary and phyosanitory measures, automobiles etc. The second agreement is related to trade of services. 254 kind of services have been listed. The third kind of agreement is related to intellectual property which include patent. Copyright, geographical indication etc. The fourth kind of agreement are called plurilateral agreements i.e. countries have to sign independently to become member of these agreements. They include agreement on Civil defence, Civil airways, milk etc.

The World Trade Organisation is headed by a ministerial conference of all member that meet at least once in every two years. After ten years of the establishment of WTO six ministerial conference had taken place so far. Singapore (1996), Geneva (1998), Seattle (1999), Doha (2001), Concun (2003), Hong-Kong (Dec. 2005).

One of the significant feature of WTO agreement was that it contained a subject of special concern to developing countries i.e. agriculture. Agriculture is an area of great concern for all developing countries including India. Agriculture Contribute substantially to national income and gives employment to a large number of people in these countries. Agriculture was most debatable issue at the ministerial conferences.

Agriculture plays on important role in Indian economy. Agriculture contributes in three ways in the economy factor contribution, market contribution and foreign exchange contribution 60% of people are employed in agriculture sector in India, around 21% of national income comes from this sector. The percentage share of agriculture exports in total merchandise exports is around 12%.

AGREEMENT ON AGRICULTURE (AOA)

The Agreement on agriculture had basically three elements–

1. Market Access
2. Export Subsidy
3. Domestic Support

1. **Market Access–** Market access commitments basically regarding the tariffication of all non-tariff braises. All member countrier were required to go through the process of tariffication by removing quantitative restriction. At the same time they have to reduce their tariff rates. Tariff duties had to be reduced by 36% by developed countries over a period of six year with a minimum rate of reduction of 15% for each tariff item. On the other hand developing countries had to reduce the tariff rate by 24% over a period of ten years with a minimum reduction of 10% on individual product. The base year for the calculation was 1986-1990.
2. **Export Subsidy–** Member countries are directed to reduce export subsidy. In the case of developed countries reduction is required by 36% in terms of value and by 21% in terms of volume in 6 years and in case of developing countries, direct export subsidy was to be reduced by 24% and the quantity of subsidized exports by 14% over a period of 10 years. The base period for calculation was 1986-90. It should be mentioned here that India had not used any form of export subsidy during 1986-88. The member may continue to use their existing export subsidies, but may not introduce new one within the limits agreed.
3. **Domestic Support–** Aggregate Measure of Support (AMS) is the mechanism to quantity the domestic support. The AOA limits AMS within a maximum limit

10% in case of developing countries. The domestic support to agriculture produces by developed countries is to be reduced by 20% within a time period of six years and for developing countries it has to be cut by 13% over a period of 10 years. Domestic support has been classified under three categories–

Amber Box– It comprises all form of domestic support which are trade distorting, therefore they have to be reduced.

Green Box– It includes government services such as research, disease control, infrastructure and food security. They also include payments made directly to formers that do not stimulate production, such as certain form of direct income support; assistance to help formers to re-structure agriculture and direct payments under environmental and regional assistance programmes.

Blue Box– It include certain direct payments to formers where the farmers are required to limit production.

Impact of AOA on Indian Economy– Agriculture for India is not only a matter of trade but a matter of sustenance because a large number of people depend on it for their livelihood. In Indian Agriculture sector gives employment to around 60% people where as in the developed countries only 2 or 3% people depend on agriculture.

India's stand on the issue of agriculture in WTO is that it is ready for talk on tariff reduction (market access) only if the developed nations are prepared to relent on heavy domestic and export subsidies from the view point of providing domestic support and export subsidy. India is in a better position than the other countries. India, has no obligation as it is not providing export subsidies on agriculture. As regard to domestic subsidy. Aggregate Measure of Support (AMS) of Indian agriculture is well below the deminimis of 10% in term of AOA stipulation.

Indian enjoys the advantages of low wages in agriculture in comparison to the most of the developed countries. The prices of most of agriculture commodities are lower than the world prices. Therefore after the removal of trade barriers these countries will export larger amount of agriculture products and this will lead to the equalisation of Prices of agriculture produces world wide and the countries like India will loose their comparative advantages on these products. On contrary there are few items like oil-seeds, sugar in which the Indian prices are higher than the international prices. Due to liberalisation India will import a large amount of these commodities in near future. Liberal import of agriculture commodities may create difficulties for supply demand balance for essential commodities specially for foodgrain in India.

WTO has provided both the challenges and opportunities to countries whether developed or developing. The world market would gradually be distortion free and those countries pursuing international competitiveness be able to take advantage of free and fair trade. Although there are some threat like food in security instability in prices yet India should try to cash the opportunities which WTO has provided. Indian agriculture sector has great potential, to increase its market share it agriculture trade it has to adopt some strategies. For example Process of liberalisation in the domestic market should be accelerated, improvement of agro processing units etc.

REFERENCES

Gulati Ashok, Kelly Tein (1999), *Trade Liberalisation and Indian Agriculture* Oxford University Press, New Delhi.

Mishra and Puri *Indian Economy.*

Sengupta A.K. and Wadhava R.K. (1994), *Impact of Uruguay Pound on Agro. Exports.* Trade in Agriculture : Uruguay Round and After. Ed. By Bhattacharya, B. and Sengupta, A. K. (IIFT, New Delhi).

Rao M. B. (2001), *WTO and International Trade* Vikas Publishing House, New Delhi.

Understanding the WTO Published by WTO, Geneva.

Economic Survey of Indian 2004-05 and 2005-06.

6

IMPACT OF WTO & GATS ON SERVICE SECTOR: WITH SPECIAL REFERENCE TO "PROBLEMS AND PROSPECTS OF LIFE INSURANCE CORPORATION OF INDIA"

S. Vasanthi *

INTRODUCTION

The Marginal role of developing countries in the World Trade Organization is now well known. India is a founding member of the GATT (1947) it actively participated in Uruguay Round Negotiations. The General Agreement on Trade in services (GATS) is an offshoot and came into force on January 1, 19995, with the establishment of WTO. GATS cover 12 areas which are divided into 161 sub-sectors.

ROLE OF LIC

Life Insurance made its debut in India 100 years ago. The Life Insurance sector was nationalized and consolidated in LIC in 1956 jointly with the General Insurance sector. LIC adopted the motto of "Yogakshemam Vahamyham" which means "your welfare is my responsibility". LIC has been contributing substantially towards infrastructure development in the country, like drinking water, electricity, housing etc. for upgrading the quality of life. The Total Investments of the Corporation as at 31st March 2005 stood at Rs. 4,14,557.22 cr (provisional), excluding house property loan. LIC is the largest Financial Institutional Investor-both in equity and term loans.

---

* Senior Lecturer in Commerce, Providence College for Women, Coonoor.

LIC is the largest Insurance Company in India with the 16.82 crore policyholders.

STATEMENT OF THE PROBLEM

Entry of foreign players has not only increased consumer awareness and reach, but also has forced government firms to become more efficient and aggressive. LIC could take effective steps to improve its total quality management to capture excellent/good market share to face the global competiton. LIC can plan for better portfolio allocation for its effective survivial. By facing its present challenges thus LIC has had a longstanding and evidenced by Indian population through many years, while private players have no past records.

REVIEW OF LITERATURE

1. S. Krishnamurthy, S.V. Money, Nani Jhaveri, Sandeep Bakhsi, Ramesh Bhat, M.R, Dixit and Sunil Maheswar, 2005. had discussed about the Insurance Industry in India, structure, Performance and the future challenges, (Vikalpa Vol-30, No.3 July-Sept 2005.)
2. Yogakshema- LIC House Magazine Vol- 49, No.10,Oct 2005.
3. Papers published in a Two days International Training programme on"Life Insurance Insights"organized by the Southern Zonal Training Centre (SZTC) of the Life Insurance Corporation Of India, Chennai, on 22/12/05 and 23/12/05 were as follows:
   (a) Glimpses of world insurance with refernce to the Indian context, and III as a provider professional education – Shri S.J. Gidwani, Secretary General Insurance Institute of India.
   (b) A Journey through Life Insurance contracts – Shri. V.N.S.Pillai, Faculty member, LIC, SZTC .
   (c) Mortality, Interest & Expenses-Underwriting for risk cover and corporate profit-An Actuary's assessment and practical problems- Shri. R. Ramakrishnan, Consulting Actuary, formerly Chief Actuary LIC.

(d) Stay Healthy– D. Thirupathi, Faculty member SZTC.

(e) Lif Insurance- New Dimensions in marketing- Shri Basavaraju, Principal, LIC, SZTC.

(f) Ancillary Insurance Services – Smt. Niranchana Rangarajan, Faculty member LIC, SZTC.

(g) Claims Shri- R. Masilamani, Faculty member LIC, SZTC.

(h) Policyholders' Rights and Duties– Shri. K. Sukumar, Faculty member, LIC, SZTC.

4. Dr. P. Stanley Joseph. 2005, had highlighted his views on LIC on the topic "Change Scenario of Insurance Companies in India after Liberalisation" presented a paper in the UGC sponsored Two days National Seminar on "World Services Trade" organised by the Dept of Economics St. Joseph's College, Tiruchirapalli on 4th, 5th, Dec 2005. On the same day Mrs. K. Rajeswari, had expressed her views on WTO and Insurances Services followed by Dr. S. Sudalaimuthu, highlighted his views on "Globalisation –Its Impact on Insurance Industry"

6. Problems and Prospects of Services Sector in India in the context of WTO's Gats Proposal, an UGC sponsored National Level Seminar organised by the Dept of Commerce, Jamal Mohammed College, Tiruchirapalli on 8th 9th and 10th Novmber 2005 highlighted many papers on Insurance sectors.

LIC TODAY

LIC is one of the largest life insurers of the world and during the year 2004-05, 2.39 crore policies were issued by LIC, bringing First Premium of Rs. 12174.11 crore in the conventional business. In Pension and group schemes, LIC secured 81.42 lacs lives and new premium of Rs 3680 crore. The total business in force with LIC is 16.59 crore policies for Rs 12,89885 crore sum assured, under individual assurances and 3.19 crore lives for sum assured for Rs 1,37,837 crore under group business. Over the years the LIC has grown into a financial conglomerate of international significance. It has, through its subsidiaries and associate companies, namely the LIC Housıng Finance Limited and the LIC Mutual Fund, contributed substantially to the housing stock and the capital market of the country. Its international ventures, the LIC (Interantional) B.S.C.(C), LIC (Nepal) Ltd, and LIC (Lanka), along with the LIC branch offices in London, Mauritius and Fiji have successfully tapped the vast potential for life insurance in the respetive countries. LIC rededicates itself for the well being, extending financial security to its people-INSURING LIVES & LIVES ENSURING SMILES ALL THE WAY. LIC has emerged as number one in the world, in settlement of claims settling over 42,112 claims every working day i.e. 1.90 claims per second. During the year 2004-05, LIC settled over 115.04 lakh claims for Rs 23658.75 cr.

The total income of LIC during the year 2004-05 was Rs 1,12,346 crore including total premium income of Rs.75083 cr and income from investment portfolio of Rs. 33718 crore. Today LIC has grown into a 100 bn dollar Corporation with the Asset Value Rs. 4,38,079 cr and the Total Life Fund as on 31st March 2005 being Rs.3,85,639 cr.

CITIZENS' CHARTER

Citizens' Charter was presented to the Nation in November, 1997. In the Charter the bench marks were prescribed for 30 servicing areas. These bench marks are revised every year. The revision of Citizens' Charter is under process.

Insurance Regulatory and Development Authority Regulations, 2002:

The IRDA (Protection of Policyholders' Interests) Regulations, 2002 has been implemented in all our offices with effect from 30th April, 2002.

CLAIMS SETTLED DURING THE LAST THREE YEARS

Year	*Number (in Lakh)*	*Amount (in Crore)*
2000-01	75.86	11,637.98
2001-02	87.67	14,519.25
2002-03	95.34	16,952.34
2003-04	103.46	19,596.11

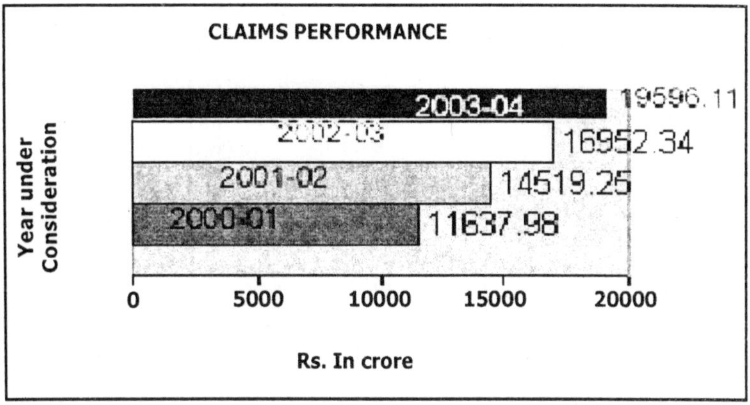

Claim settlement performance (2004-2005)

- Total Claims settled-over 114.91 lakh for Rs. 23560.66 cr
- LIC settles over 42112 claims every working day i.e. 1.90 claims per second
- 95.65 % of Maturity claims are settled on or before the date of maturity
- 9.86% of Non-early Death Caims are settled within 20 days of intimation.

Highlights of the Corporation as on 31.3.2005 (Provisional)

• Total Income	:	Rs. 1,07,969 Crore
• Total Premium Income	:	Rs, 70,857.98 Crore
• Income from Investment	:	Rs.33,652.00 Crore
• Total Life Fund	:	Rs.3,85,000 Crore
• Total Assets	:	Rs. 4,40.043 Crore
• Total No. of Claims paid	:	Rs.115 Lakhs

More than 40 different places catering to the changing needs of different segments of the society. The efficient services of LIC with further improvement in quality and improved bench marks have been formed as a policy service. LIC has introduced social responsibility/security Group Schemes like Janashree Bima Yojana, Swamajayanthi Gram Swarojgar Yojana and

Lic's Investments - Some Highlights

Type Of Investment	*Investments Up To* 31.3.1977	31.3.1987	*(Rs. In Crores)* 31.3.1997	31.3.1998	31.3.1999	31.3.00	31.3.01	31.3.02	31.3.03	31.3.04
Central Govt. Securities	981	4675	37330	45876	56185	70533	85181	109938	137276	166939
State Govt & Others	715	1683	8906	10471	12928	14156	17877	21463	28988	37402
Electricity (Sebs)	733	2603	8214	9153	10591	11931	12402	13447	14508	14805
Housing	618	1872	10967	12242	14207	15885	17998	19054	19944	20694
Water Supply& Sewerage	203	718	2028	2264	2508	2997	3657	4000	4420	7111
State Road Transport Corp	-	180	540	551	671	736	784	893	1358	1373
Loans To Industrial Estates	9	37	45	45	45	45	45	45	45	45
Loans To Sugar Co-ops	22	37	37	37	37	37	37	37	37	37
Development Authority	-	1	1	1	1	1	1	1	1	1
Roadways, Port, Railways	-	-	-	25	25	85	325	681	781	1272
Power Generation (Pvt Sector)	-	-	-	276	801	1478	1615	3797	6105	6412
Municipalities	-	-	-	4	4	4	4	4	14	14
Total	3281	11806	68068	80945	98003	117888	139926	173370	213477	213477

Note: (1) Item 1 & 2 Are Shown As At Book Value As On 31.3.04.
(2) Items 3 To12 Are Gross Investment Made So far.

Jeevan Shiksha Sathayog Yojana. LIC has donated Rs. Five Crore in response to the Prime minister Shri. Manmohan Singh's appeal to donate generously to the Prime Minister's National Relief Fund to help fund the relief and rehabilitation measures taken up in the Tsunami hit areas.

CHALLENGES FACED BY LIC

1. Privatization of Insurance business.
2. Entry of banking sector into the field of insurance business.
3. Entry of private sector into insurance business (both from local and foreign).
4. Moving away from a state controlled system to market orientation in interest rates as well as price determination.
5. Reducing the proportion of funds to be invested in government securities.
6. Encouraging technological up gradation of existing business.
7. Encouraging domestic private sector insurance companies.
8. Enhancing human resources and skills in areas like investment analysis and portfolio management.
9. Constitution of a regulatory authority for insurance business.
10. Attempt to divest the controlling interest of government in existing insurance business.

PROBLEMS OF LIC

1. As a regulatory norm, IRDA had placed the condition that only insurers with the minimum capital of Rs. 1 billion could apply for registration, but in life insurance, despite such minimum capital requirements, and despite govt. re-insurance guarantee guarantees, the company stood out way beyond private entrants, is "LIC" the only public life insurer.
2. A contentious issue for LIC has been directed by IRDA to keep a solvency margin of 150%. But LIC argued

that in terms of market values, its hidden reserves-estimated to at above 500 billion- could be considered as the same. With the current solvency margin of 110%, LIC would approximately require an additional whopping Rs 80 billion to fulfill the 150% norm.

3. The premium growth of LIC showed in 2003-04 of only 6.34% over the previous years, especially after a decline in 2002-2003. It is also a fact that during the same period of 2003-2004, private sector premium grew by a tremendous 152.74%. Mr. S. Krishnamurthy, MD and CEO of SBI Life states, "Private insurers have done well by capturing a significant chunk of the market share". But LIC monopolizing a mind-boggling 87% of Indian life insurers.
4. Only due to private entry the whole market pie of LIC is growing and has responded to the competition admirably.
5. LIC has initiated only now to expand its product line and to me more innovative like the private players, to concentrate more on up gradation of new technology by updating new changes in technology, infrastructure etc. to face the present global competition.

PROSPECTS OF LIC

1. LIC settles 1.90 claims per second.
2. LIC has very well past records.
3. LIC had reached its 50th year as No.1 Life insurer in the world with 16.82 cr policy holders.
4. LIC had taken initiative steps to expand its product line (i.e.) more than 40 different plans catering to the changing needs of different segments of the society, implement various I.T enabled initiatives, modification in bench marks reducing time lags, customer education and display of all possible information on website and effective grievance redressal machinery at all levels.
5. LIC has taken enough steps to do service efficiently with further improvement in quality and improved bench marks.

6. With the entry of private insurers, LIC today had spread life insurance widely and in particular to the rural area and to the socially and economically backward classes with a view to reaching all insurable persons of the country and providing them adequate financial cover against death at reasonable cost.

CONCLUSIONS

LIC should recognize the importance of training and education in insurance, and initiate greater industry-academic collaboration. The areas of education and training can still seriously be extended to academic interaction, investment expertise, information technology, research etc. An analysis of the commitments made in financial services indicates that very limited liberalization has been realized under GATS. Therefore, for India the GATS commitments fail to expand market access for India's exports of labour intensive services. Given our requirement of additional equity for the financial services sector as well the potential for providing for labour intensive services, it is perhaps to be more ambitious and improve under GATS, including financial services. Of course, we need to have a good regulatory system in place.

Finally to conclude, it is imperative that this industry becomes pioneer if the following steps are taken to meet the global challenges today. Insurance education and training, academic interaction, information technology, professionalism in insurance marketing, Research, Industry-Academic Partnership, management education, Financial Support are the important factors are to considered as very important needful criteria for a sustained and continuous growth of the industry in India.

REFERENCES

S. Krishnamurthy, S.V. Money, Nani Jhaveri, Sandeep Bakhsi, Ramesh Bhat, M.R, Dixit and Sunil Maheswar, 2005, "The Insurance Industry in India, structure, Performance and the future challenges", (Vikalpa Vol-30, No. 3 July-Sept 2005).

Yogakshema- LIC House Magazine Vol- 49, No.10,Oct 2005.

"Life Insurance Insights"organized by the Southern Zonal Training Centre (SZTC) of the Life Insurance Corporation Of India, Chennai, on 22/12/05 and 23/12/05 were as follows: (a) Glimpses of world insurance with refernce to the Indian context, and III as a provider professional education – Shri S.J. Gidwani, Secretary General Insurance Institute of India. (b) A Journey through Life Insurance contracts – Shri. V.N.S.Pillai, Faculty member, LIC, SZTC. (c) Mortality, Interest & Expenses-Underwriting for risk cover and corporate profit-An Actuary's assessment and practical problems- Shri. R. Ramakrishnan, Consulting Actuary, formerly Chief Actuary LIC. (d) Stay Healthy– D. Thirupathi, Faculty member SZTC. (e) Life Insurance- New Dimensions in marketing- Shri Basavaraju, Principal, LIC, SZTC. (f) Ancillary Insurance Services – Smt. Niranchana Rangarajan, Faculty member LIC, SZTC. (g) Claims Shri- R. Masilamani, Faculty member LIC, SZTC. (h) Policyholders' Rights and Duties – Shri. K. Sukumar, Faculty member, LIC, SZTC.

Dr. P. Stanley Joseph. 2005, "Change Scenario of Insurance Companies in India after Liberalisation" - UGC sponsored Two days National Seminar on "World Services Trade" organised by the Dept of Economics St. Joseph's College, Tiruchirapalli on 4th, 5th, Dec 2005.

Mrs. K. Rajeswari, "WTO and Insurances Services"& Dr. S. Sudalaimuthu, "Globalisation –Its Impact on Insurance Industry"

Other paper refernces from" Problems and Prospects of Services Sector in India in the context of WTO's Gats Proposal", an UGC sponsored National Level Seminar organised by the Dept of Commerce, Jamal Mohammed College, Tiruchirapalli on 8th 9th and 10th Novmber 2005 highlighted many papers on Insurance sectors.

7

AGRICULTURAL DEVELOPMENT AND OPPORTUNITIES: AN ANALYSIS IN THE CONTEXT OF W.T.O REGIME

Ashwini Kant Jha, Bhavna Jha**, and Hemant Kumar****

INTRODUCTION

The Uruguay Round in 1986, launched by the Punta del Este Declaration, was the most ambitious multilateral trade negotiation to demolish all types of trade hurdles to open world trading system and usher-in international economic renaissance as the main objective of this round. If fact, Uruguay Round led to several agreements of understanding among the global partners of trade, like (i) Market Access Agreements (ii) Rules and discipline of multisafeguards etc. and (iii) New areas of agreements (TRIPS, TRIMS and Patent). The later meetings added fresh issues to these agreements like labour-standard, environment, competition policy, electronic commerce and so on.

India is more concerned about agricultural, textiles, garments, small industry products, and the new areas of trade policy like TRIPS, TRIMS, Sanitary and Phyto-sanitary issues, Micro organism, Plant seeds of various plant varieties, chemical fertilizers, quantitative restrictions and tariffs. Indian

* Professor and Head, P.G. Department of Economics, BNM University (W.C.), P.G.Centre, Saharsa, Bihar.

** Lecturer in IRPM, MAM College, Nangachia, T.M.Bhagalpur University, Bhagalpur, Bihar.

*** Research Scholar, DNM University, Madhepura.

agricultural costs are quite competitive except in a few areas. The yield rate is by far below the international average. Liberalization shall imply better price for producers leading to a better gain to them. This shall push-up technological change as well as quality change in out-put. Some imports in agro-products are bound to come to compete with domestic out put but the overall consumers preference for domestic products due to tastes, the rush for imports is not expected.

The World is changing into a global village. There is a visible change in multiple forms and from multiple directions. Starting from reforms with emphasis on liberalization, privatization and globalization, the world has witnessed emergence of World Trade Organization (WTO) and its conditionalities which have altered the basic principles of trade, regional groupings, barrier free movements, mergers and acquisitions, foreign direct investments, bilateral and multi lateral agreements, etc., and which have become the order of the day. The World is in the grip of technological changes and revolution in the field of information technology.

The global economy has arrived as a consequence. Global markets in a global economy are characterized-and driven-by competition: competition by firms and competition between countries. A dramatically increasing number of firms are going international, and a growing percentage of their overall sales is coming from overseas markets. There are new opportunities-and pressure-to utilized them. At the same time advance in information, communication and transportation technologies, as well as in managerial and organizational methods, facilitate the transnationalisation of many firms, including Small and Medium Enterprises.

The service sector has emerged as the most powerful segment of national income in most of the economies including India. Labour standard and environmental situation in our country affect the cost of production and competitiveness of products in other countries. Marketing strategy has changed. There has been a major change in consumers' attitudes and preferences. Their pressure for better quality and hygienic products has transformed sellers marked into buyers market.

This situation has forced the organization become market centered and customer focused.

Amid so many changes around us, the Indian Small and Medium enterprise Sector has been playing a very important role in terms of its contribution to wards employment, output and exports has remained relatively oblivious to these changes. So far, it has survived amid somewhat protected environment which exist in the form of product reservation, market reservation, price preference, priority sector lending fiscal exemptions/concessions etc. With the emergence of WTO along with its conditionalities, protection may be considered as discriminatory or barrier to trade. Many of the existing support systems in place for protection and promotion of SEM sector will have to compete on their own and to find a place for themselves in domestic as well as international market.

The world today is more closely knit, using different means of organization, communication and production, and is more subject to rapid change then ever before. Patterns of international trade, capital and competition have been changing dramatically in recent time, with serious consequence for suitable business strategy.

It is a against this back drop, the paper examines the implications of WTO regime, both in terms of threats and opportunities and discusses response of SMEs in meeting WTO environment challenges.

The International trade was not so smooth during 1940s, when there were many restrictions imposed by different countries with a view to protecting their domestic industry. After the end of the Second World War, some countries realized that restrictions on international trade were affecting their growth. It was therefore, felt that the artificial restrictions imposed on international trade be removed and fore this purpose, a "World Trade Organization" (WTO) could be set up. This did not materialize due to opposition from the USA. Thus, GATT was born, as an alternative to WTO.

GATT: In 1948, 23 countries, including India, formed General Agreement on Tariffs and Trade (GATT) as an international body headquartered in Geneva, Switzerland to pursuer the objective of free trade in order to encourage group and development of all member countries. The principal purpose of GATT was to ensure competition in commodity trade through the removal or reduction of trade barriers. GATT was an international trade and rules formed under it were binding on all its member countries, two-thirds of which were developing nations. In addition to being a forum for trade negotiation, GATT was a kin to an international court, which resolved the trade disputes of its member countries.

It was after the formation of GATT that the average import tariffs in the world were reduced to substantially lower levels, which enable remarkable growth in world trade. Since the setting up of GATT, eight rounds of negotiations on trade matters have been held. The first seven rounds of negotiations conducted under GATT were aimed at stimulating international trade through reduction in non-tariff restrictions on imports imposed by member countries. GAAT did provide a useful forum for discussion and negotiation on international trade issues. The first round was held at Havana in 1947, the second at Annecy in France in 1949, the third at Torquay in Britain in 1950-51, the fourth, fifth and sixth rounds in Geneva in 1955-56, 1960-62 and 1964-67 and the seventh in Tokyo from 1973 to 1979. The 8th round of Multi-lateral Trade Negotiations, Popularly known as Uruguary Round covered 7 years (1986-93) and took place at Punta del Este in Uruguay. World Trade had undergone a structural change during the four decades since the establishment of GATT in 1948. The share of agriculture in worked merchandise trade which was 46 per cent in 1950 had declined to 13 per cent in 1987. Simultaneously, the structure of employment and contribution of various sectors to GDP of developed countries was rapidly increasing. It ranged between 50-70 per cent of the GDP by 1986. The share of employment in the service sector was also increasing. For instance, in USA, services represented two thirds of GDP and employed over 70 per cent of work force,. In 1980, US exports of services amounted to 35 billion. In the commodity sector, the comparative cost advantage had moved in favour of Japan and several other newly industrialized nations. These factors impelled developed countries, under the leadership of USA to take the initiative of bringing service sector into trade negotiations. Thus, the Uruguay Round (UR) contained the mandate to have negotiations in 15 areas. In part I, negotiations on Trade in Goods were to be conducted in 15 areas and Part II negotiations on Trade in services to be carried out.

Part I (Trade in Goods) declaration in UR contained the (1) tariffs, (2) Non-tariff measures, (3) Tropical, products, (4) Natural Resource-based products, (5) Textiles and clothing, (6) Agriculture, (7) GATT articles, (8) Safe guards, (9) MTN (Multilateral Trade Negotiations) agreements and arrangements, (10) subsidies and countervailing measures, (11) Dispute settlement, (12) trade Related Aspect of Intellectual Property Rights (TRIPS), (13) Trade Related Investment Measures (PRIMS), (14) Functioning of the GATT systems (FOGS). Thus, besides the traditional GATT subjects such as tariff and non-tariff barriers and improvements in GATT rules and disciplines on subsidies and countervailing measures Property Right (TRIPS), Trade Related Investment Measures (TRIMS) and Trade in Services were included for the first time for negotiations.

These negotiations were expected to be concluded in four years, but on account of differences in participating countries on certain on certain critical areas, such as agriculture, textiles, TRIPS and anti-dumping measures, agreement could not be reached. To break this deadlock, Arthur Dunkel, Director General of GATT compiled a very detailed document, popularly known as Dunkel proposals and presented it before the member countries as a compromise document. It was here that the Dunkel Draft came into being and a need for the setting up of WTO was emphasized once again.

There was no multilateral or international organization that dealt with trade issues between countries before second word war. The international trading system had functioned without such an organization for almost fifty years under the ageis of the General Agreement on Tariffs and Trade (GATT). But it vdid not have the standing of international organization like International Monetary Fund (IMF) or the World Bamk.

However, the scenerio changed in 1994, when the Uruguay Round of trade negotiations under the GATT ended with an agreement to establish the World Trade Organization (WTO), along with considerable progress in strengthening the international trading system. The WTO came into existence on 1 January 1995.

GATT AND THE WTO'S PRINCIPLES

The main principle of GATT was to establish an open and now-discriminatory trade, thus giving rise to term "open multilateral system". It enjoins each signatory to commit it self to tread all other signatories according to the most favoured national (MFN) standard. *Most Favoured Nation (MFN)* treatment requires that tariffs and other regulations should be applied to imported or exported goods without discrimination among countries. *National Treatment* rule prohibits countries from discriminating between imported products and equivalent domestically produced goods. However, member countries did not commit to free trade with zero tariffs. Under GATT all member countries agreed to undertake a series of negotiating round in which 'tariff concession' would be exchanged. The contracting parties would negotiate with their key trading partners for reduction of tariffs on items they export in return for 'concessions' on items of interest to their trading partners. Once tariff concessions were agreed, there extended to all contracting parties (the MFE or non discrimination, clause). The tariff rates were subsequently 'bound' so that tariffs could not be raised unless the 'escape clause' was invoked.

The WTO is also to administer the provisions of Dispute settlement Understanding (DSU) and also Trade Policy Review Mechanism (TPRM).It would also work in coherence with IMF and world Bank for achieving greater coherence in global economic policy making. As per underlying principle, there shall be Ministerial Conference composed of representatives of all ;the Members, which shall meet at least once every two years, The Ministerial conference shall carry out the functions of the WTO and take actions necessary to this effect. There shall be General council composed of representatives of all the

Members, which shall meet das appropriate. In the intervals between meetings of the Ministerial Conference, its functions shall be conducted the General Council.

THE AGREEMENT ON AGRICULTURE (AO A) UNDER WTO

The Agreement on Agriculture (AoA) under WTO is committed to achieving specific binding commitments in each of the following areas – market access, domestic support, export competition , Trade Related Intellectual Property Rights (TRIPs) and to reach an agreement on sanitary and Phyto –Sanitary issues.

The Government can intervene by three ways of subsiding farmers. The Government can have a set of domestic and external policies which are basically intended to fetch higher prices for their output than would have been possible, were trade to become globally free. This can be done by various measures like tariffs, quotas, export enhancement programmes, price stabilization measures, import licencing, canalization other domestic price support policies. It is very much possible that is through direct cash payments to cultivator. The third method of subsidization can be through the supply of inputs below their cost of production. For example, subsidies in electricity, credit, fertilizers, transport and irrigation, farm fuel tax exemptions, livestock feed and crop insurance.

Thus we see that the measures, which distort agricultural po9licies, can be both domestic policies and border measures. In order to know the level of support by the Government, it needs to be quantified and aggregated in some sense. It is this need which has given birth to the notion of Aggregate. Measure of Support (AMS).

The following were the main proposals made by Arthur Dunkel, then Director General of GATT in relation to agriculture.

All Domestic Support in favour of agricultural producers with the exception of certain measures which have been exempted (in view of their non distortive effect) shall be reduced within a period o six years (i.e.from 1995 to 2001) by 20 percent. Export subsidies, which are in the nature of direct subsidies, shall be subject to commitments for reduction of budgetary outlay and quantities by 36 percent and 24 percent respectively within a period of six years, beginning 01january 1995.

There shall be comprehensive tariffication. Ordinary customs duty, including those resulting from tariffication shall be reduced within a period of six years on a simple average basis of 36 percent with a minimum rate of reduction of 15 percent for each tariffline.

As envisaged in the Dunkel proposals, calculation of AMS has to be made by each Government and to be reduced over a period of six years. The AMS is to be calculated separately for subsidies, which are product specific, and subsidies which are non product specific. As mentioned above, in the case of developing countries, a limit of l0 percent has been stipulated separately for product specific and non product specific AMS bellow which there is no obligation to make any reduction.

The benchamark for product specific support is 5 percent of the total value of production of the agricultural products. In simple words, if product specific support is greater than 5 percent of the total value of the production of the agricultural product then it has to be brought down by 20 percent over a period of six years, beginning in 1995 and if it is less than 5 percent, then there is no reduction commitment. Similarly for non-product specific support the specific support is less than 5 percent, there are non-reduction commitments. However for developing countries like India, there is special clause which stipulates 10 percent as the benchmark figure for reduction commitments. It means, for developing countries, a limit of 10 percent has been stipulated separately for product specific and non product specific AMS below which there is no obligation to make any reduction.

There are three components of Border Measure

(a) Reduction in tariffs
(b) Other market access commitments and
(c) Requirement on export subsidies.

(a) Reduction in tariffs: First of all, there is a requirement of tariffication. What it amounts to saying is that all non-tariff measures like Quantitative. What it amounts to saying is that all no tariff measures like Quantitative import restrictions, minimum import prices, discretionary import licencing, variable import levies, non – tariff measures maintained through state trade enterprises, voluntary exports restrains and other such measures must be replaced by tariffs. Once this tariffication requirement is complete, developed countries have the binding to reduce the tariffs by an average of 36 percent over a period of six years Similarly developing countries have the commitment to reduce the tariffs by an average of 24 percent over a period of ten years. For each line, the minimum tariff reduction has to be 15 percent apart from the average reduction. In case of developing countries, minimum tariff reduction for each line is 10 percent. The tariff reduction does not apply to least developed countries.

(b) **Other market access commitments:** The market access commitments require that the countries which maintain Quantitative restrictions on agricultural imports must provide for minimal imports at low customs duties. This minimal limit is defined as 3 percent of domestic consumption rising to 5 percent of domestic consumption rising to 5 percent of domestic consumption at the end of six years.

A lot of myth prevails regarding this commitment. It is generally perceived that, India must import 3-5 percent of domestic consumption requirement but this is not true for two strong reasons. First, market access commitments apply only to those countries that maintain Quantitative restrictions that are inconsistent with GATT. Under article XVIII B as long as any country has Balance of payment (BOP) problem, they are exempted from the above commitments. Since India has BOP problems, India's Quantitative restrictions are not GATT inconsistent. Further, assuming that India no longer has BOP Problem, the minimum market access clause will be really relevant. But even then there is no compulsion that 3-5 percent consumption needs must be imported. But even then there is no compulsion that 3-5 percent of consumption cannot be on the negative list, but will have to be on the open General Licence (OGL) list, subject to whatever tariff exists. In India, the tariff on agricultural products is very high. It is up to 100 percent on primary products, up to 150 percent on processed products and up to 300 percent on edible oils.

There are certain safeguard provisions if the market access leads to an import surge or if imports take place at an extremely low price. There are disciplines on export prohibitions and restriction but these do not apply to developing countries.

(c) Requirement on Export Subsidies– There are certain expert subsidies which are subject to reduction commitments. The Dunkel proposals stipulate that Budgetary Outlay on such export subsidies must be brought down by 36 percent over a period of six years. The volume of agricultural exports that receive subsidies must be brought down 21 percent, also over a period of six years. However, these commitments are for developed countries. There is a differential and special treatment again for developing countries. That is, the timeframe for reduction is ten years and not six years. However these commitments are for developed countries. There is a differential and special treatment again for developing countries. That is the timeframe for reduction is ten years and not six years. For developing countries, budgetary outlays on export subsidies must be brought down by 24 percent and the volume of exports that receive subsidies must be brought down by 14 percent. In case of least developed countries, there are no reduction commitments on export subsidies. The benchmark year for all these reductions is 1968-90. In such cases, where subsidized exports may have increased in importance, the base used will be 1991-92.

Table 1
A summary of commitments under AOA of WTO by Member Countries are given below

Particulars	*For Developed Countries*	*For Developing Countries*
Period of commitment	*6 years 1955-2000*	*10 years 1995-2004*
TariffsAverage cut for all agricultural products Minimum cut per product	-36%-15%	-24%-10%
Domestic SupportTotal AMS cuts for Agriculture Sector (Base period : 1986-88)	-20%	-13.3%
ExportsValue of subsidiesSubsidised Quantities	-36%-21%	-24%-14%

CERTAIN IMPLICATIONS

1. Since the Aggregate Measure of Supply (AMS) calculated by various experts for India turned out to be negative, there is no ground to reduce the domestic support for India. Hence the product specific and non-product specific subsidies shall largely be untouched for the time being.
2. As opposed to the prevalent myth that the PDS will have to be scrapped, there is no reason to worry on this account. The PDS will very be there in place. However, greater disciplines on the PDS is on the cards which do not conflict with the Indian objective of better targeting and revamping of the PDS. It must be more transparent and directed a urban and rural poor on the basis of clearly defined nutritional criteria. Moreover, food purchases by the Government for the PDS will have to be made at current market prices. The Export subsidies listed for reduction in the Dunkel package, does not include export incentives, Therefore, while industrialized countries would have to reduce export subsidies, there is no requirement for India t reduce these incentives, There is also a view that elimination of subsidies by the industrialized counties

will create market opportunities for the Indian products.

As per the general safeguards and exception there is no obligation to convert non-tariff measures into custom duty equivalent, for those countries, which are having BOP problems. Since India maintained QRs (Quantitative Restrictions) for BOP reasons, the removal of QRs was done in phases. It was done gradually only on a few commodities to begin with. But with WTO panel's ruling that India should remove QRs before March 2001, from January 1997, India made a series of commitments to remove QRs with the removal of Qrs, foreign trade is going to pick up in the coming years.

TRADE PERFORMANCE OF AGRICULTURE AND ALLIED ACTIVITIES

The agricultural sector has undergone enormous changes over a period of time. The share of Gross Domestic Product (GDP) in agriculture to total GDP has come down from 58.9 percent in 1951 to about 24 percent in 2002. However, the employment in agriculture has come down from 72 percent of total labour force in 1991 to 65.5 percent in 2000.

Agricultural exports are the major components of the international trade in India. It hovered around $ 3.2 billion in 1990-91 to 1992-93. It jumped to $4 billion in 1993-94 and witnessed further jump to 6.1 billion in 1995-96. This tempo of growth continued till 1996-97, which took agricultural export close to $7 b7 billion. The spectacular increase in agricultural exports during 1992-93 to 1996-97 raised export surplus of this sector from a modest $1.4 billion to $4.5 billion. Agricultural imports including fertilizer showed a mixed trend during this period. Agricultural exports tool a down turn after 1996-97 and plummeted to $5.6 billion during 1999-2000. In contrast to this, agricultural imports witnessed 80 percent increase in dollar terms after 1996-97. Due to this, net foreign exchange earnings of agriculture declined. However, the declining trend of agri exports has reversed since 2000-01 and it has again gone up to $ 7.4 billion in 2003-04.

Table 2
India's Agricultural Trade In Pre And The Post Wto Period

	Year	*Exports $ Million*	*Imports V Million*	*Net Exports V Million*
Pre WTO Period	1991-92	3338	1256	2028
	1992-93	3028	1618	1410
	1993-94	4023	1317	2706
	1994-95	4227	2544	1683
Post WTO period	1995-96	6120	3001	3119
	1996-97	6868	2303	4565
	1997-98	6634	2893	3741
	1998-99	6033	4012	2021
	1999-00	5615	4402	1213
	2001-01	6256	2738	2275
	2001-02	6146	3350	2796
	2002-03	6734	2804	3930
	2003-04	7425	NA	-

Source: Economic Survey, Ministry of Finance, GOI, various issues.
* Foreign Trade BOP, CMIE, August 2004.

TREND IN AGRICULTURE EXPORT

During early 1990s marine products topped the list of agriculture export followed closely by export of oil meal. Other import items of export are tea, cashew nut, basmati rice, spices, tabacco etc. Liberalization of non basmati rice in mid 1990s provided big boost to its exports, As a result of this, rice export figured at the top during 1995-96 and during 1998-99. Out of two grades of rice, basmati rice showed a steady trend in its export but non basmati rice showed violent year to year fluctuations.

Export of marine products has been consistent around $ 1.1 billion. Export of traditional items like tea, cashew and spices did not show adverse impact in post WTO regime but coffee exports has been hit badly. Castor oil and guargum meal are emerging as important items of exports. However oil meal is the worst affected export item. After witnessing 90 percent growth between 1992-93 and 1996-97, oil meal exports dwindled to less than 40 percent of level attained in 1996-97 by end of 1990s. Export of cotton have declined from $ 444 million in 1996-97 to meager $ 19 million in 1999-2000. Almost similar has been the case with export of sugar.

TRENDS IN AGRICULTURAL IMPORTS

India no more depends upon rice imports and import of cereal preparations has reduced to very low level. As far as import of food grains is concerned, India occasionally imports wheat. This, some researches say, is because of export of wheat in previous year, besides production fluctuation. Import of pulses was increased till 1997-98 and declined thereafter. Like wheat, India some times goes for huge import of sugar & raw cotton. Import of vegetable oil has increased drastically after 1993-94. As a result, vegetable oil import now constitutes about 2/3rd of import of all agricultural items including fertilizer. Vegetable oil import during late 1990s, has reached staggering level of more than $1.8 billion. It is reported that India is now biggest edible oil importer in the world except China and 40 percent of total requirement of edible oil is met through import. Among agricultural inputs, India has imported fertilizers to the tune of $1.28 billion during 1999-2000. However, this has dropped to almost half during 2000-01 ($0.66 billion) and 2001-02 ($ 0.62billion). Issues for Agriculture and Agro based Industries in the wake of WTO Agreements.

INDIAN-EXPORTS AND ITS QUALITATIVE CHANGE

With WTO agreement and consequent Sanitary and Phyto Sanitary (SPS) measures, Indian agro-processing sector may face non-tariff barriers for its products. Several past instances are there to prove this. Interestingly, many countries are setting their health standards at a level higher than the international prescribed ones. For example, in case of tobacco exports, the internationally prescribed level of Dischloro-Dimethyle-Trichlorethane(DDT) residue is 4 parts per million (ppm), while Japan and the USA had set their permissible level at less than 1 ppm. The idea is to block tobacco exports,the internationally prescribed level of Dichloro-Dimethyle-Trichlorethane (DDT) residue is 4 parts per million (ppm), while japan and the USA had set their permissible level at less than 1 ppm. The idea is to block tobacco exports originated from countries like India. Another instance is shrimps' exports from India. The USA had placed restrictions on the ground that these are not caught with turtle excluding devices. This may well be aploy for blocking shrimps' exports knowing well India's fisherman lacks adequate resources to catch shrimps with turtle excluding devices.

There should be a proper mechanism to monitor the entire commodity chain to maintain quality and hygiene standards. There is a serious need to link up farmers with processing and exporting agencies and firms so that quality can be ensured right from the raw material processing and exporting agencies and firms so that quality can be ensured right from the raw material production stage. This can be achieved through appropriately designed arrangements like contract farming or the procurement cooperative alignment with processing and marketing companies.

There has to be an all round realization at every level that quality production of international standards is the watchword for survival now. The processors, small or big, have to take steps to improve quality right from the selection of the raw material and that of the ingredients. Steps have also to be taken to upgrade the hygienic and sanitary conditions of the workers, plant and machinery so as to ensure quality of the finished products. There has to be much greater emphasis to invest in research and development and in product innovation.

Raising production and Export Base of Agro- Agro-Processed commodities has to be enlarged. Based on the past trends of exports, natural advantages, quality and productivity parameters, India has a comparative advantage and is the world leader in producing certain good quality agro- products, like fruits and vegetables and certain other cash crops. These products are usually low volume and high value, not essential food and India's Production capacity is higher than the competitors. The productivity of certain crops has to be improved for greater value addition, export and to cut the unit cost.

PREVENTION OF POST HARVEST LOSSES.

Post Harvest Management practices is important for prevention of post harvest losses, value addition, maintenance and improvement of quality, enhancing the shelf life of food and ensuring remunerative price for farmers. With production of about 600 MTs of food , India is the 2nd largest producer after China in the world. However, p9ost harvest management of food products in India has not kept pace with the progress achieved in the production. The need for high degree of efficiency in the post harvest management is as essential at about RS. 50.000 crore per year. The cold chain may be provided to help in retaining quality, freshness and to freshness and to reduce post-harvest losses. These developments would result in the greater availability of quality raw materials to the industry, thus, resulting in better capacity utilization and producing a wider range of products and of international quality. The multinationals now entering the food industry have an international marketing network and have their brand loyalties all over the world. This will enable the Indian products reaching all over the world in the form and packing required.

UTILIZATION AND MANAGEMENT OF LIVESTOCK

There is a regional imbalance in creation and utilization of processing facilities for milk in the country. Moreover, only a few processing plants are meeting the ISO standards. In order to maintain the quality of milk, bulk milk coolers have to be installed by the milk union/ daireis . Further, Indian dairy products have to compete with the international players, like EU,USA and Oceania countries like Australia and New Zealand. In the absence of import restrictions, domestic dairy products have to compete with cheaper imported products in domestic market. If this happens, it will totally topsy turvey the pattern of dairy development in the country, affecting income distribution.

As for the poultry sector, with quantitative restriction (QRs) being lifted, producers will be exposed to the threat of uneven competition from developed countries. No subsidies exist for this sector in India, although the governments of developed countries give their industry heavy subsidies $394.7 per ton (approximately Rs.18 per kg.) the poultry meat is subsidized to the extent of $295.2 per ton in EU (Rs. 13.50 per kg.) It is reported that in Orissa, West Bengal, the farms are small , with about 500 birds per farm. The poultry gives employment to about 1.6 million people. Many ancillary industries support the poultry industry. Agriculture that provides many ingredients essential for poultry feed, will be hard hit along with the poultry industry if the foreign players are allowed tobring in cheap chicken.

SUGGESTIVE MEASURES FOR COMPETITIVENESS OF .INDIAN AGRICULTURE

While India has some surplus for export of agricultural products, our international competitiveness is adversely affected because of the existence of heavy subsidies in developed countries land the non tariff barriers faced by Indian exports of agricultural products. India should maintain sufficient level of border protection for our farmer who are largely subsistence and marginal producers At the same time we want substantial reduction in the domestic support, lowering tariffs and export subsidies by developed countries with a view to eliminating export subsidies within a reasonable period of time.

There is need for finding greater market access for Indian agricultural products especially in the markets of developed countries.

Food security of four people, protection interest of domestic farmers and their livelihood as also to boost our exports should be given due importance. There is need to raise productivity, providing better irrigation facilities ,developing rural infrastructure including cold chains, increasing expenditure on agricultural research and strengthening the market net work and effectively managing the supply chains. Public investment in agriculture should be accelerated by adopting the cost reducing.

Technologies and by removing restrictions on agricultural trade, marketing and processing in the country. This can be achieved through appropriate policy frame work and institutional arrangement. Institutional reforms for augmenting and managing infrastructure and other services through Self

Help Groups ,Watershed Development Committees, etc. needs to be strengthened.

Indian agricultural sector needs to be diversified. Farmers should grow and export cereals, fruits, dairy products, vegetables and flowers in a big way. The increased revenue from exports could then be used for new investment in agriculture. Through the multiplied effect, this new investment can double or triple agriculture output for further exports.

A shift of sizeable proportion of the work force to the non-agricultural sectors such as industrial and services sector is also needed. This is because of the fact share of agriculture in India's GDP has fallen to about 24 percent, while 65 percent of the work force is still employed in this sector.

CONCLUSION

With the advent of WTO regime, there is a need prepare an agriculture and allied activities for the global competition with cost effective production and efficient management. It is obvious that benefits to developing countries like India, in terms of increasing their exports will occur only after the elimination export subsidies and substantial adoption in domestic support in the developed countries has been effected. The opening up of agricultural trade should be looked at as a major opportunity for raising the overall economic growth rate by exploiting India's competitive as well as comparative advantage in agriculture, for improving the efficiency of resource use in agriculture and for technologically upgrading the rural sector we need to devise a multi pronged strategy to face the emerging challenges under the WTO regime and make Indian agriculture a sustainable and internationally competitive.

REFERENCE

Bhattacharya, B (1995), world Trade Organisation, Yojana, February 28, Vol.39, No.3.

Centre for Monitoring Indian Economy (2002), Foreign Trade and Balance of Payments, October, CMIE publication, Mumbai.

Centre for Monitoring Indian Economy (2003), Foreign trade and Balance of payments, September, CMIE.

FISM, A Brief Guide to the WTO for small Business May 1999.

Planning Commission: Draft Tenth Five Year Plan (2002-2007), New Delhi 2002.

Vibha Mathur (2002), Indian Economy and the WTO-New Challenges and Strategies, New Delhi New Century Publication, Delhi.

Uruguay Round – Final Act Marrakesh (15th April 1994).

8

NEW AGRICULTURAL STRATEGY AND GREEN REVOLUTION– ISSUES, CONCERNS AND THE WAY AHEAD

*S. M. Jawed Akhtar**

INTRODUCTION

The new agricultural strategy was introduced in India during the Third Five Year Plan i.e. during sixties. This period was of great significance to Indian agriculture. It was marked by a near disaster on the one hand and much achievements were made on the other. Agriculture was stagnated, foodgrains production and the production of other crops was not picking up even in the face of rising population. However, in order to tackle this problem, the Government of India invited a team of experts sponsored by the Ford Foundation in the latter half of the Second Five Year Plan. The team submitted its report entitled 'India's Food Crisis and Steps to Meet It' in April, 1959. This report suggested intensive efforts for increasing agricultural production and productivity in selected regions of the country with stress on modern inputs, especially fertilizers, pesticides, irrigation, credit etc. Initially, the new technology was tried in 1960-61 as a pilot project in seven districts and was called Intensive Area Development Programme (IADP). In October 1965, the net was widened to 114 districts and the programme was called as Intensive Agricultural Areas Programme (IAAP). Later, the high-yielding varieties (HYV) programme was also added and the strategy was extended to cover the entire country.

* Senior Lecturer, Department of Economics, Aligarh Muslim University, Aligarh.

This strategy has been called as 'Green Revolution'. The Green Revolution is composed of dwarf high yielding varieties (HYV), fertilizers, pesticides and new efficient water management techniques etc.

The term 'Green Revolution' refers to marked improvement in a short period, and a higher level of agricultural production over a fairly long period of time. In a broad sense Green Revolution means a transformation of agriculture, reduction in food shortage and undernourishment and elimination of the traditional agricultural sector as a bottleneck to progress. In a narrow sense, it means an increase in production due to plant improvement to solve the food problem. However, the advocates of the new strategy considered the intensive approach as the only means of making a breakthrough in Indian agriculture in the shortest possible time. As a result of new agricultural technology, India has achieved relative self-sufficiency in foodgrains and its imports became negligible. India is also able to accumulate larger buffer stocks of rice and wheat so that she could face any eventuality resulting from drought in a particular year.

Under the new agricultural strategy, special emphasis has been placed on the development and widespread adoption of high-yielding varieties of seeds. Though the government had been paying attention to induce qualitative improvements in seeds in ever since the initiation of planning process in the country, yet the real impetus to these efforts was given by the adoption of the new agricultural strategy in the khariff season of 1966. In Mexico, Prof. Norman Borlaug and his associates developed new varieties of wheat which were early maturing, highly productive and disease resistant and these varieties were imported and planted in selected regions of India having adequate irrigation facilities. Within a year of their introduction it was conclusively demonstrated that the yields from the new varieties exceeded 25 to 100 per cent compared to the yields from traditional varieties (Misra, Puri – 2004)

GREEN REVOLUTION AND AGRICULTURAL PRODUCTION

As a result of new agriculture strategy, foodgrains production increased substantially from 82 million tonnes during 1960-61 to 212.0 million tonnes during 2001-02. Table-1 gives the foodgrains production in India during last four decades. Table-1 reveals that the production of rice increased from 34.6 million tonnes during 1960-61 to 93.3 million tonnes during 2001-02 (but declined to 72.7 million tonnes during 2002-03). The production of wheat stood at 11 million tonnes during 1960-61 which rose to 72.8 million tonnes during 2001-02 (but declined to 65.1 million tonnes during 2002-03). Table-2 gives the yield per hectare of major crops. It shows that there is tremendous increase in the yield of wheat, which rose from 851 per hectare during 1960-61 to 2778 per hectare during 1999-2000 (but declined to 2618 during 2002-03). Likewise, the yield of rice increased from 1013 per hectare during 1960-61 to 1986 per hectare during 1999-2000 (but declined to 1804 per hectare during 2002-03. On the other hand, yield of pulses shows marginal improvement during the same period. The production of coarse cereals- jowar, bajra and maize – continues to remain static or has moved very slowly upwards. The production of these crops is subject to wide yearly fluctuations. It is interesting to observe that the ratio of wheat to rice has steadily increased from one-third during 1960-61 to more than three-fourth during 2002-03. The green revolution did not cover pulses. The output of pulses fluctuated from year to year between 13 to 15 million tonnes. Thus, the Green Revolution was confined only to high yielding varieties (HYV) cereals.

As a result of the Green Revolution, the crop pattern in India has undergone two significant changes. Firstly, the output of cereals has risen at the rate of 3 to 4 per cent per annum, but the output of pulses has remained stagnant or even declined. This has resulted in a decline in the relative importance of pulses in foodgrains output over the period of time. The stagnant production of pulses and the consequent rise in the price of pulses has an adverse effect on the economic condition of the poor. Secondly, among cereals, the proportion of rice in total cereals output has come down marginally, while that of wheat has increased. The rising output of wheat indicates a substitution of coarse grains with wheat, both on the side of production and consumption.

Table-1
Production of Major Crops in India

(million tonnes)

Crop	*1960-61*	*1970-71*	*1980-81*	*1990-91*	*1995-96*	*1996-97*	*1997-98*	*1998-99*	*1999-00*	*2000-01*	*2001-02*	*2002-03**
1. Rice	34.6	42.2	53.6	74.3	77.0	81.7	82.5	86.1	89.7	85.0	93.3	72.7
2. Wheat	11.0	23.8	36.3	55.1	62.1	69.4	66.3	71.3	76.4	69.7	72.8	65.1
3. Cereals	69.3	96.6	119.0	162.1	168.1	185.2	179.3	188.7	196.4	185.7	198.5	163.0
4. Pulses	12.7	11.8	10.6	14.3	12.3	14.2	13.0	14.9	13.4	11.0	13.4	11.1
5. Percentage of Wheat to Rice	31	56	67	74	80	84	80	82	85	82	78	89
6. Total Foodgrains	82.0	108.4	129.6	176.4	180.4	199.4	192.3	203.6	209.8	196.8	211.9	174.2

* Provisional
Source: Economic Survey– 2003-04

Table-2
Yield Per Hectare of Major Crops

(Kg. per hectare)

Crop	*1960-61*	*1970-71*	*1980-81*	*1990-91*	*1995-96*	*1996-97*	*1997-98*	*1998-99*	*1999-00*	*2000-01*	*2001-02*	*2002-03**
1. Rice	1013	1123	1336	1740	1797	1882	1900	1921	1986	1901	2077	1804
2. Wheat	851	1307	1630	2281	2483	2679	2485	2590	2778	2708	2761	2618
3. Cereals	753	949	1142	1571	1703	1831	1775	1856	1926	1844	1974	1783
4. Pulses	539	524	473	578	552	635	567	634	635	544	615	556
5. Total Foodgrains	710	872	1023	1380	1491	1614	1552	1627	1704	1626	1739	1562

**Provisional*
Source: Economic Survey– 2003-04

GREEN REVOLUTION AND AGRICULTURAL INPUTS

Increase in agricultural production and productivity to a large extent depends on the availability of agricultural inputs. The main elements of the new agricultural strategy are:

(i) expansion of irrigation coverage;
(ii) increased provision and utilization of key inputs such as HYVs of crops, fertilizers and plant protection chemicals;
(iii) expansion and improvement of institutional support services such as research and extension; and
(iv) price policies favourable to producers of major food grains (Abrol, I.P., 2004).

Irrigation development has been the cornerstone of the new strategy. Alt the time of independence the net irrigated area was 20.9 million hectares, while gross irrigated area was 22.6 million hectares. Recognizing large-scale development of irrigation facilities as critical to rapid agricultural growth, the country has spent about Rs. 45,000 crores on irrigation development in the first four decades after independence. As a result, the net irrigated area increased from 31.1 million hectares in 1970-71 to 57.2 million hectares in 1999-2000. Table 3 gives the details of gross and net irrigated area in India.

Table 3
Gross and Net Irrigated Area in India

(million hectares)

Year	*Net Irrigated Area*	*Gross Irrigated Area*	*Net Irrigated Area as Percent Net Sown Area*	*Gross Irrigated Area as percent of Gross Cropped Area*
1950-51	21.0	23.0	—	17.0
1970-71	31.1	38.1	22.1	23.0
1980-81	38.7	49.7	27.6	28.8
1990-91	48.0	63.2	33.6	34.0
1995-96	53.4	71.3	37.5	38.2
1996-97	55.1	73.2	38.6	38.6
1997-98	54.9	73.0	38.7	38.3
1998-99	57.0	75.9	40.0	39.4
1999-2000	57.2	76.3	40.5	40.2

Sources: CMIE, Statistics on Agriculture, Feb. 2004

As a consequence of development of irrigation facilities, gross irrigated area as a per cent of cropped area increased from 17 million hectares during 1950-51 to 40.2 million hectares during 1999-00 (Table-3). Further, there has been a gradual improvement in area irrigated more than once. In 1950-51, area irrigated more than once was 1.7 million hectares or 8.1 per cent of net irrigated area, in 1998-99 this had increased to 18.6 million hectares or 33 per cent of the net irrigated area (Datt, Sundharam-2004). As far as sources of irrigation are concerned, the importance of wells and tube wells has increased over the period of time. Table-4 gives the details of sources of irrigation in India. It shows that well irrigated area has increased from 6 million hectares to 336 million hectares during 1951-2000. Wells irrigation in 1999 –2000 accounted for 58.7 per cent of the total irrigated area as compared to only 29 per cent in 1950-51. On the other hand, canal irrigated area has increased from 8.3 million hectares in 1950-51 to 17.9 million hectares in 1999-2000. Even then, its relative importance has come down from 40 per cent to 31.4 per cent during the same period. The growth of wells irrigation has been at the expense of irrigation from tanks and other sources. During this period, it is wells irrigation, particularly tube wells irrigation which has made the most spectacular progress. In 1960-61, only 0.1 million hectare was irrigated by tube wells, but in 1992-93, over 14 million hectares were served by tube wells irrigation. Tube wells account for 30 per cent of total irrigated area.

Table-4
Area Irrigated by Sources in India

Sources of irrigation	*1950-51*		*1980-81*		*1995-96*		*1999-2000*	
	Area (m.ha.)	*Perce-ntage*	*Area (m.ha.)*	*Perce-ntage*	*Area (m.ha.)*	*Perce-ntage*	*Area (m.ha.)*	*Perce-ntage*
1. Canals	8.3	40	15.2	39.4	17.1	32.0	17.9	31.4
2. Wells and Tube wells	6.0	29	17.6	45.7	29.6	55.6	33.6	58.7
3. Tanks	3.6	17	3.1	8.2	3.1	5.8	2.7	4.7
4. Other Sources	3.0	14	2.5	6.5	3.5	6.4	2.9	5.0
Total	20.9	100	40.5	100	53.0	100	57.2	100

Source: CMIE, Statistics on Agriculture, Feb. 2004

However, the irrigation potential created over the years (in major and medium works) has not been fully utilized. Over the years, the gap between the potential created and the actual utilization has been widening. For instance, during 1989-90, the irrigation potential created and the actual irrigation utilized were 77 million hectares and 69 million hectares respectively – the gap was 8 million hectares. By 1999-2000 this gap between potential and actual irrigation has widened still further – against irrigation potential of 95 million hectares created, the actual utilization was only 85 million hectares, the gap was 10 million hectares. The non-utilization of the created irrigation potential occurs mainly due to delay in the construction of field channels and drains and in land leveling/ shaping. Lack of involvement of farmers is also an important constraint in achieving full utilization of created potential. With a view to narrowing this gap, the Government has started the Command Area Development (CAD) Programme. The basic objective of CAD Programme is to maximize productivity in the irrigation of command areas through an integrated approach – covering farm development works including construction of filed channels and field drains, land shaping whenever necessary and the introduction of rotational supply of water to ensure equitable and assured distribution to individual farm holdings.

Moreover, the emphasis in the recent years is on minor irrigation works using ground water resources. Minor irrigation works are relatively less capital intensive and do not take long time to be constructed. Expansion of minor irrigation works, however, depends on private initiative and naturally it depends upon the farmers' perception of profitability, easy and cheap availability of such facilities as electric power, supply of diesel, construction material, credit etc. Expansion of rural electrification works helps to optimize returns from minor irrigation works. Minorirrigation works are of special importance in raising pulses and oilseeds as these crops require only limited irrigation facilities. There is almost no time lag between the creation of irrigation potential and its utilization in the case of minor works.

Fertilizers have constituted yet another key input in addition to expanded irrigation in achieving goals of high production and productivity. India's soil though varied and rich, is deficient in nitrogen and phosphorous. With population rising at a fast rate, the use of larger doses of chemical fertilizers is the only way to augment our foodgrains production. Table-5 gives the details of production, consumption and imports of fertilizers in India. It shows that since the adoption of new agricultural strategy in the sixties, the consumption of chemical fertilizers has been growing rapidly. From a mere 70 thousands tonnes in 1950-51, consumption of fertilizers rose to 292 thousands tonnes in 1960-61 and further to 17474 thousands tonnes in 2003-04. At the same time, there is a tremendous increase in the consumption of fertilizers per hectare area from 0.5 Kg in 1950-51 to 90.1 Kg in 2001-02 (but declined to 84.8 Kg. in 2002-03). As internal production of fertilizers has been short of continuous demand, the govt. had to depend upon imports. From 52 thousands tonnes in 1950-51, total imports has risen to 2018 thousands tonnes in 2003-04. The Government has been promoting the consumption of fertilizers through heavy subsidies. In the recent years, special measures were taken to streamline distribution of available supplies. However, large imports of fertilizers through the use of scarce foreign exchange and heavy subsidies was the result of the absence of a clear-cut and vigorous policy of setting up fertilizer units within the country. Inspite of rapid increase in the consumption of fertilizers in the country in recent years, India's position is much behind other progressive countries. Consumption of fertilizers in India per hectare during 2001-02 was 90 kgs., while in South Korea (400 Kgs.), Japan (340 Kgs.) Netherlands (275 Kgs.), Belgium (225 Kgs.), etc.

Another basic and crucial input for attaining sustained growth in agricultural production is the seed. It is the carrier of new technology to crop production, propagation and multiplication. In the past, Indian farmers generally used seeds of very indifferent quality either because the special good quality seeds kept for sowing were consumed away during the off-season or because good seeds deteriorated through bad

Table-5
Production, Imports and Consumption of Chemical Fertilizers in India

Year	*Production (000 tonnes)*	*Imports (000 tonnes)*	*Consumption (000 tonnes)*	*Consumption per hectare of cropped area (Kgs.)*
1951-52	39	52	70	0.5
1960-61	150	419	292	1.9
1970-71	1059	629	2177	13.1
1980-81	3005	2759	5516	31.8
1990-91	9045	2758	12546	76.8
2001-02	14628	2399	17360	90.1
2002-03	14465	1757	16094	84.8
2003-04 (P)	14200	2018	17474	—

Source: - Economic Survey - 2003-04

storage. However, over the period of time Agricultural Department and the Indian Council of Agricultural Research (ICAR) have done much to evolve and popularize improved and disease-resisting varieties of seeds suitable for different local conditions. In fact, it is the success of this policy initiative, which is the main reason of India's current self- sufficiency in foodgrains. The Government set up the National Seeds Corporation (NSC) in 1963 and the State Farms Corporation of India (SFCI) in 1969, to produce and supply quality seeds. In India, the organized seed sector particularly for food crops and cereals is dominated by the public sector. The Government is giving considerable attention to:

(i) research in evolving better seeds suitable to Indian conditions,
(ii) larger production and better distribution of quality seeds,
(iii) provision of adequate credit facilities to enable even the poorest farmers to purchase and use quality seeds, and
(iv) expansion of irrigation, fertilizers and pesticides which are necessary for the efficient use of quality seeds.

The Government of India announced the New Policy on Seed Development in September, 1988. The thrust of this policy is to secure for the Indian farmer high quality seed available any where in the world with a view to maximize his yields and increase productivity and farm income. After the introduction of the new seed policy, the private sector has began to play a significant role in the production and distribution of seeds. The new seed policy permits the import of the best seeds under open general license, and enables the Indian farmers to make use of the best seeds of oilseeds, pulses and coarse grains after multilocational trials by the ICAR. The Government of India has also set up a Seeds Bank in 1999-2000 to make available seeds for meeting any contingent requirement and also develop infrastructure for production and distribution of seeds. The Seeds Bank is being implemented through National Seeds Corporation, State Farms Corporation of India and State Seeds Corporation of various states.

ISSUES RELATED TO GREEN REVOLUTION

An important consequence of the strategies adopted since sixties has been to boost production chiefly of two crops rice and wheat. Their share in total foodgrains production went up from 56 per cent in 1970-71 to 74 per cent in 1990-91 and further to 78 per cent in 2001-02 (Table 1). However, production of foodgrains other than rice and wheat did not increase significantly (Table 6) and in the eastern region even the yield of rice did not increase.

Table 6

All India Compound Growth Rates of Production of Major Crops – Green Revolution Period (Base T.E. 1981-82 = 100)

(Percent per annum)

Crop	1967-68 to 1980-81	1980-81 to 1989-90	1990-91 to 1999-00	2000-01 to 2002-03
1. Rice	2.22	3.62	1.90	-5.6
2. Wheat	5.65	3.57	3.81	-0.28
3. Pulses	-0.40	1.52	0.61	0.91
4.Total Foodgrains	2.15	2.85	1.94	-3.73
5. All Crops	2.19	3.19	2.28	-3.13

Source: GOI, Ministry of Agriculture, Agricultural Statistics at a Glance, Various Issues.

Table-6 reveals that a growth rate of 2.85 per cent was recorded in foodgrains production during eighties. This decade was the turning point in India's foodgrains economy leading to self-sufficiency through significant productivity increase first in wheat and later in rice. An annual increase of 2.85 per cent in foodgrains in eighties was the hallmark of Green Revolution that enabled India to become self-sufficient and even a marginal exporter. The pace of growth slowed in nineties considerably and even slower than the population growth rate. Further, during 2000-03 the compound growth rates of all crops became negative and there is large decline in the production of rice equal to 5.6 per cent. This is a matter of concern. Likewise, for the country as a whole, while per capita availability of cereals has increased substantially that of pulses has declined significantly (Table 7). The net availability of cereals increased from 394.9 grams per day during 1951 to 492.2 grams during 2002, but that of pulses declined from 60.7 grams to 35.0 grams during the same period.

Table 7
Net Availability of Cereals and Pulses

(Per capita per day) (Grams)

Year	*Cereals*	*Pulses*	*Total*
1951	334.2	60.7	394.9
1961	399.7	69.0	468.7
1971	417.6	51.2	468.8
1981	417.3	37.5	454.8
1991	468.5	41.6	510.8
1996	442.5	32.7	475.2
1997	466.0	37.1	503.8
1998	414.0	32.8	447.0
1999	429.2	36.5	465.7
2000	422.0	31.8	454.7
2001	386.2	30.1	416.2
2002	457.3	35.0	492.2
2003 (P)	409.9	28.2	438.2

Source: Economic survey, 2003-04

An important impact of the strategies pursued in the Green Revolution period has been intensification of regional disparities and imbalances in agricultural development (Table 8). Agricultural production and income rose substantially in the north-western states of Punjab, Haryana,

Western U.P., parts of Rajasthan, Tamil Nadu and Andhra Pradesh. By contrast productivity and output growth have been modest in eastern and central India and in Deccan plateu. Progress was particularly slow in rainfed areas, which account for over 60 per cent of the cropped area where a great majority of rural poor are concentrated. Technological changes have contributed to widening the disparities in income between the small and large farms and between landowners on the one hand and landless labourers and tenants on the other. In absolute terms, however, the grains from technological change have been shared by all sections. This is indicated by the rise in real wages and employment and incomes of small farmer, in regions experiencing technological change (Rao, Hanumantha-1975). It is now well-known that the so-called Green Revolution which helped the country to raise its output of foodgrains has also been accompanied by a widening of the range of inequality in rural incomes, the loss of their status as tenants by a number of small farmers and the emergence of social and economic tensions in the countryside. The challenges that Indian agriculture faces in not only of production but also that of distribution, and in our anxiety to concentrate on production problems, we should not forget the human and social implications of agricultural development (Rao, V.K.R.V. -1974).

Table 8
Percent Foodgrains Production by Group of States

(Triennial averages)

Region	*1960-62*	*1972-74*	*1999-2000 to 2001-02*
1. Northern States (Punjab, Haryan, U.P.)	25.2	28.5	40.3
2. Eastern States(Orissa, Bihar, Assam, West Bengal)	23.2	22.7	19.4
3. Rajasthan and M.P.	17.9	16.2	14.8
4. Western States (Gujarat & Maharastra)	11.3	8.8	7.3
5. Southern States (Andhra Pradesh, T.N., Karnataka, Kerala)	21.5	21.9	16.5
6. OtherStates/UTs	0.9	1.9	2.4
Total	100	100	100

Source: Economic Survey, Various Issues

FUTURE PROSPECTS OF GREEN REVOLUTION:

Green Revolution which was initiated in the 1960s yielded good results in giving a big boost to the production of wheat in the first stage and later to the production of rice. But recently it has been felt that high yielding varieties have reached to its saturation point and the scope for future increase in production appears to be very much limited. It is said that the seed-water-fertilizer technology has exhausted its potential. However, the Planning Commission has set a target of foodgrains production of the order of 300 million tonnes by 2007-08. Hence, the question arises that what are the prospects of realising this target. The most important challenge before us is to ensure adequate and sustained increase in food production to meet the nutritional needs of growing, healthier population. Our population has just crossed the one billion mark, and experts have projected that we would be overtaking China by 2035 as the world's most populous country. To feed this growing population, an additional 5-6 million tonnes of foodgrains will be needed annually. In order to tackle this problem scientists in India have been making efforts to develop hybrid varieties of rice and wheat so that the yield barrier operating at present can be broken. However, the only country that has so far really managed to adopt hybrid technology in any significant way is China. The hybrid rice has helped China to increase its rice production by over 300 million tonnes (Damodaran, H. 1999). To make hybrid rice more acceptable to the farmers, China provided seeds to farmers at subsidised prices. The fact is that the future prospects of the next phase of Green Revolution lies in hybrid seed technology.

However, the Tenth Plan is being formulated at a time when agriculture faces challenges from both domestic and external sources. The challenge before policy makers is not only to reverse the slowdown of agricultural growth in the 1990s but ensure that the gains of agriculture in alleviating rural poverty are not lost and the estimated 200 million under-nourished population get access to food.

The thrust areas during the Tenth Plan would include

- Increasing cropping intensity;
- Diversification to high value crops/activities;
- Development of minor irrigation and utilization of created irrigation potential;
- Rainwater harvesting and conservation for the development of rainfed areas-watershed approach;
- Timely and adequate availability of agricultural inputs like seeds, fertilizers, implements;
- Thrust on seed production-breeder, foundation and certified – to achieve the desired seed replacement rate;
- Reclamation/development of problem soils/lands;
- Encouragement to the private sector for effective extension and input support services;
- Promotion of a farming system approach;
- Cost effectiveness while increasing productivity;
- Briding the gap between research and farmer's yields;
- Utilization of unutilized/under–utilised wastelands and degraded lands by allocation/leasing;
- Emphasis on bio-technology for development of high-yielding seeds;
- Encouragement to organic farming;
- Strengthening of testing facilities for seeds, fertilizers, soil, water, pesticides etc.; and
- Development of facilities to import agri machines/ implements and study these for the development of models suited to Indian conditions (Tenth Plan, 2002).

CONCLUSION

It is apparent that the tasks of meeting the consumption needs of the protected population are going to be more difficult given the higher productivity base than in 1960s. There is also a growing realization that previous strategies of generating and promoting technologies have contributed to serious and widespread problems of environmental and natural resource degradation. This implies that in future the technologies that are developed and promoted must result not only in increased productivity level but also ensure that the quality of natural resources base is preserved and enhanced.

We also find that productivity gains during the Green Revolution era were largely confined to relatively well-endowed areas. Given the wide range of agroecological setting and producers, Indian agriculture is faced with a great diversity of needs, opportunities and prospects. Future growth needs to be more rapid, more widely distributed and better targeted. New technologies are needed to push the yield frontiers further, utilize inputs more efficiently and diversify to more sustainable and higher value cropping patterns. Detailed indigenous knowledge and greater skills in blending modern and traditional technologies to enhance productivity efficiency will be key to the farming success and sectoral growth. Most technological solutions will have to be generated and adapted locally to make them compatible with socio-economic conditions of farming community.

Since there is hardly any scope for further expansion of area under cultivation, the future production prospects depends largely on the improvements in the yield levels. Here what we need is to break the yield barrier and bridge the gap between the potential and actual yield through research and development efforts. So far the emphasis has been on the use of HYV seeds, but it loses its vigour with time. Therefore, new varieties need to be developed periodically to expand production possibilities. Hence, the country has to build up a vital research system, which is responsive to the changing needs and circumstances. Expenditure on agricultural research and education accelerated during the post-Green Revolution period of the 1970s, but slowed down since mid 1980s and it hovered around 0.49 per cent of agricultural GDP in the early 1990s, which was lower than the requirement of 1.0 per cent projected by the ICAR. Further, the level of research expenditure was sub-optimal or significantly lower than desired in states like Bihar, Orissa, Madhya Pradesh, Uttar Pradesh and West Bengal where productivity is low. There are two major areas on which research and development efforts are needed:

(i) Genetic resource management and biotechnology, and

(ii) Natural resource management and agro ecology.

These efforts may help us in breaking the yield barriers, especially in the unfavourable agro-climatic regions. It is also required to encourage private sector participation in frontier areas like natural resource management and biotechnology. For extending the scope of new agricultural strategy and optimization of it, it is desired that modern cultivation may be extended to new crops and new areas. Therefore, the extension of high yielding programme should also be introduced to other cereals, pulses and non-foodgrain crops like oil seeds, cotton, sugarcane, jute etc. Water is the basic input in the use of seeds and fertilizer and without it extension of Green Revolution is not possible. Therefore, there must be proper arrangement of irrigation facilities. Only then farmers find it to their advantage to seek more and more of other inputs.

REFERENCES

Abrol, I. P. (2004), "Agriculture", in R. K. Sinha (ed), *India 2025- Social, Economic and Political Stability,* Centre for Policy Research, Shipra Publication, Delhi.

Chadha, G. K. & Bhalla, G. S. (1982), "Green Revolution and the Small Peasant – A Study of Income Distribution in Punjab Agriculture", *Economic and Political Weekly,* May.

CMIE (2004), "Directory of Indian Agriculture", *Centre for Monitoring Indian Economy Pvt. Ltd.,* Mumbai.

Dantwala, M. L. (ed.) (1991), *Indian Agricultural Development since Independence,* Oxford & IBH Publishing Company Pvt. Ltd., Delhi.

Damodaran, H. (1999), "Green Revolution Fatigue – Have Yields Begun to Plateau?", *Business Line,* May 27.

Datt,R. & Sundaram KPM (2004), *Indian Economy,* S. Chand & Company Ltd., New Delhi.

Desai,B.M. (2002), "Policy Framework for Reorienting Agricultural Development", in Raj Kapila and Uma Kapila (ed), *Economic Developments in India,*Vol. 53, Academic Foundation, New Delhi.

Dhanagare, D.N. (1987), "Green Revolution and Social Inequalities in Rural India", *Economic and Political Weekly*, Annual Number, May.

Evenson, Robert, E. et at. (1999), "Agricultural Research and Productivity Growth in India", *Research Report 109, International Food Policy Research Institute*, Washington.

Government of India (2004), *Economic Survey-2003-04*, Ministry of Finance, New Delhi, Various Issues.

...........(2002), *Tenth Five Year Plan 2002-07*, Planning Commission, Government of India, New Delhi.

ICAR (1998), *National Agricultural Technology Project*, Indian Council of Agricultural Research, New Delhi.

Junankar, P. N. (1975),"Green Revolution and Inequality", *Economic and Political Weekly*, March 29.

Ladejinsky, Wolf (1987),"How Green is India's Green Revolution", *Economic and Political Weekly*, May.

Lekhi, R. K. & Singh, Joginder (2003), *Agricultural Economics*, Kalyani Publishers, New Delhi.

Misra, S.K. & Puri, V.K. (2004), *Indian Economy*, Himalaya Publishing House, Delhi.

Pant, K. C. (2001), "Planning for Agriculture: Challenges and Opportunities in the 21st Century", in Raj Kapila and Uma Kapila (ed), *Economic Developments in India*,Vol. 33, Academic Foundation, New Delhi.

Rao, C. H., Hanumantha (1992), "Agriculture: Policy and Performance", in Bimal Jalan (ed.), *The Indian Economy: Problems and Prospects*, Viking, New Delhi.

Rao, C. H. Hanumantha (1975), *Technological Change and Distribution of Gains in Indian Agriculture*, p. 178.

Rao, VKRV. (1974),"New Challenges Before Indian Agriculture", *Panse Memorial Lecture*, April.

Rao, V. M. & Jeromi, P. D. (2003), "Modernising Indian Agriculture", in Uma Kapila (ed.), *Indian Economy since Independence*, Academic Foundation, New Delhi.

Saini, G. R. (1976), "Green Revolution and Distribution of Farming", *Economic and Political Weekly*, XI (13).

Sawant, S. D. & Achutan, C. V. (1995),"Agricultural Growth across Crops and Regions", *Economic and Political Weekly*, March 25.

Part II

INDIAN ECONOMIC REFORMS

9

LIBERALIZATION, FISCAL DEFICITS AND ECONOMIC DEVELOPMENT IN INDIA

Vasudev Sedam H. and Mohammed Younus K.***

INTRODUCTION

The economic reforms in India attempted to clear the bottle necks for the larger private participation in the economy. The economic reforms meant, also, to liberalize the capital account of the economy letting a progressive in-flow of funds in the capital market of the country (Lahiri-2000). The public sector which had (and even at present has) a wide presence in the productive sector, mainly in capital industries, the economic reforms sought to initiate the process of disinvestment (Naib-2004) as a way to lay off the pressure from the Government budgets. Till date, the accumulative impact of economic reforms must have been to consolidate the fiscal reforms in terms of reducing fiscal deficits cutting public expenditures sharply and raising taxes (Jha-2003). This was sought to be achieved through substitution of private industries in the previously exclusive set of industries meant for public enterprise and greater participation of foreign investment in domestic economy.

However, the aim of containing fiscal deficits seems to have remained unfulfilled. The fiscal deficits have remained unchanged (see Table 1) except with few fluctuations. The pressure on Government treasury was expected to ease

* Reader, and

** Research Scholar, Department of Economics, Gulbarga University, Gulbarga-585 106, Karnataka, India.

following economic reforms. Therefore the continuation of higher fiscal deficits points to the fact that the sustainability[1] of higher (or critical) growth rates still lies with the government intervention (Gundlach-1999). Such intervention might be in institutional form and at expenditure levels. The institutional forms include, tax and customs incentives to stimulate private

Table 1
Central Fiscal deficits as percent of GDP

Year	*Fiscal deficits*
1992-93	5.47
1993-94	7.01
1994-95	3.70
1995-96	5.17
1996-97	4.9
1997-98	5.84
1998-99	6.5
1999-2000	5.4
2000-01	5.7
2001-02	6.1
2002-03	5.9
2003-04	5.6

Source: Reserve Bank of India Annual Report-2004

investment whereas a steady public expenditure helps allocation of investments in growth stimulating sectors (for example, infrastructure). A question, however, arises what was the economic reforms meant for ? Wasn't it to reduce government intervention and assume a laissez faire mode of economic policies ? And, why a developing country cannot have a classical fiscal policy i.e., to achieve a surplus or a balanced budget, at least? This paper attempts to deal with these questions.

THE GENESIS OF FISCAL DEFICITS AND ECONOMIC REFORMS

An understanding of the basics of our economic planning followed in India, would show that the budgets presented by the Governments of the day, were at once, a political manifesto, sometimes acknowledgement of social problems we faced and frequently the proposals for economic development. Given such a condition the fiscal policy might not be expected to be a pure exercise in ensuing a balance between the revenue and expenditure. The stabilization objective of the budget policies is not a tool only to make corrections in business cycles but also to arrange for rapid economic growth through engaging the unemployed resources in the economy. This is a paramount task in a developing country like India (Minhas-1988).

The Planning documents clearly state that:

"....the level of production and the material well-being a community can attain depends, in the main, on the stock of capital at its disposal, i.e., on the amount of land per-capita and of productive equipment in the shape of machinery, buildings, tools and implements, factories, locomotives, engines, irrigation facilities, power installations and communications." (GoI-1951).

Great importance has been given to capital stock. Further, the Plan documents state that:

"In under developed countries with low standards of living a rapidly increasing population, a rate of growth commensurate with needs cannot be achieved until the rate of capital formation comes upto around 20 percent of the national income."

The attainment of a high rate of growth has, therefore been a major goal of our Economic Policies. A coordinated programme with the State playing a leading role, was seen to be essential for raising the rate of savings, bringing an integrated, long-term view-point to bear on determination of sectoral priorities, and regulating the flow of scarce resources to areas of high priority if need be, by implementing key projects on its own initiative. As a role successive plans have sought to relate the level and composition of investment, especially in the public sector, to specified targets of aggregate income, keeping in view the volume of resources by way of domestic savings, external aid and export earnings which could be generated (Vaidyanathan-1984).

As a consequence of giving great importance to capital accumulation the investment sources had to be stretched as far as to invoke larger budget deficits. This was quite obvious in a situation where the economic policies gave highest priority to public sector. This was the only way to have import substituting industrial policy, since the private sector would not venture into where technological requirements needed huge investments. This was the reason why there had been a great

Table-2
Gross Capital Formation by type of assets with various sector as percent of Gross Domestic Product

Year.	*Construction*			*Equipment*		
	Public Sector	*Private Sector*	*Household Sector*	*Public Sector*	*Private Sector*	*Household Sector*
1	2	3	4	5	6	7
1971-72	4.0	0.4	4.4	1.9	1.2	2.7
1972-73	4.6	0.3	4.0	2.3	1.3	2.7
1973-74	4.1	0.3	3.3	2.3	1.4	2.7
1974-75	3.3	0.2	4.0	2.4	1.3	3.1
1975-76	3.3	0.3	5.0	3.4	1.9	2.0
1976-77	4.3	0.2	5.0	3.8	1.0	2.8
1977-78	4.5	0.3	5.1	3.3	1.3	2.6
1978-79	4.8	0.2	4.5	3.1	0.9	3.9
1979-80	5.2	0.3	3.7	3.3	1.3	4.0
1980-81	4.9	0.4	4.3	3.4	2.1	3.3
1981-82	5.1	0.6	4.2	3.8	2.9	2.4
1982-83	5.3	0.6	3.9	4.8	3.4	1.2
1983-84	5.2	0.5	3.9	4.3	2.6	2.3
1984-85	5.2	0.5	4.2	4.5	2.9	2.3
1985-86	5.6	0.6	4.5	4.5	3.1	2.4
1986-87	6.1	0.6	3.9	4.8	3.3	2.3
1987-88	5.6	0.5	4.6	4.4	2.5	4.0
1988-89	5.4	0.5	4.7	4.3	2.5	4.3
1989-90	4.6	0.4	5.6	4.6	2.8	4.3
1990-91	4.6	0.5	5.9	4.4	3.2	4.3
1991-92	4.7	0.7	5.7	4.5	4.7	1.8
1992-93	4.3	0.7	5.9	3.9	4.9	2.7
1993-94	4.3	0.9	5.1	3.8	5.1	2.4
1994-95	4.5	0.8	4.7	4.3	5.1	2.6
1995-96	4.4	1.3	4.5	3.3	6.8	4.0
1996-97	4.0	1.2	4.5	2.9	7.5	2.7
1997-98	3.6	1.4	5.4	2.8	6.7	1.9
1998-99	3.6	1.1	5.5	2.7	5.5	2.8
1999-00	3.8	1.0	5.5	2.5	4.9	3.7
2000-01	4.3	0.9	5.6	2.5	4.5	4.2

Source: National Accounts Statistic of India, EPW Research Foundation.-2001

controversy over the type of model to be adopted for planning.

The choice was to be made either for Mahalanobis capital goods model or for P.R. Brahmanand's wage goods model (Srinivasan-1985). However, our desire to achieve higher growth rates and economic self-sufficiency made capital goods model a base to our economic policies. This could be the reason why we see a progressive growth in capital formation by public sector is far greater than by private sector (see table 2).

Even when we compare household capital formation by assets, which is the residual after deduction of gross capital formation by public and private corporate sector, we see the public sector had to contribute more or equally for the development of economy. The importance of the public expenditure for the development of the economy stand more pronounced by the fact that capital in the form of machinery and equipment received huge attention by the public sector than in the private corporate and household sector. This points to the objective of State intervention to achieve growth rates through rapid industrialization, especially capital intensive. This is enough to indicate that the public participation in the economic activity proved quite decisive in the development of the economy. Correspondingly, the fiscal deficit of the government has increased. A comparison of total public capital formation and fiscal deficits (Table 3) would show the extent of pressure on public finances resulting from the planed economic policies giving priority to public sectors. Therefore, it could be postulated that, the mixed economic policy of economic planning and development lead to commit public finances for economic development. The fiscal policy of the government, hence, reflects it in the form of fiscal deficits.

However, capital formation in the economy was almost unsustainable, without steady increase in investment. The domestic private investment institutions were incapable of doing that. The earnings from trade were excessively negative as a result of protectionist trade policies. Neither, the government revenues could be increased nor the private sector realized better returns mostly on account of highest increment capital output ratio (Mohan-2003). As a result current account deficits by the year 1990-91 touched US $ 2.8 billion higher than the previous year.

Table 3
Gross Capital Formation and Gross fiscal deficit as percent of Gross Domestic product by the Centre

Year	*Gross Capital Formation*	*Gross Fiscal Deficit*
1971-72	6.0	3.3
1972-73	7.0	3.4
1973-74	6.3	5.0
1974-75	5.8	2.8
1975-76	7.0	3.0
1976-77	8.1	4.0
1977-78	7.8	3.5
1978-79	7.9	5.5
1979-80	8.5	6.5
1980-81	8.4	6.1
1981-82	8.9	5.4
1982-83	10.1	7.0
1983-84	9.5	6.2
1984-85	9.7	7.6
1985-86	10.1	8.3
1986-87	10.9	9.0
1987-88	10.0	8.1
1988-89	9.6	7.8
1989-90	9.2	7.8
1990-91	9.0	8.3
1991-92	9.2	5.95.6
1992-93	8.2	7.4
1993-94	8.0	6.0
1994-95	8.8	5.3
1995-96	7.7	5.2
1996-97	6.9	6.10
1997-98	6.4	5.6
1998-99	6.3	6.0
1999-2000	6.4	6.2

Source: Reserve Bank of India Annual Report-2001 Pg. 77

The major problem faced in 1990-91 was, how to finance the current account deficits ? With the fiscal deficits rising, the only way it could be met was by draining down the foreign exchange resources. As at the end of December, 1990, the foreign currency assets of the Reserve Bank of India stood at US $ 1.2 billion. This was despite the drawal of our reserve trance in International Monetary Fund of SDR 487 Million. The low level of resources in its turn triggered a number of consequences. India's recourse to the commercial borrowing totally dried up as the credit rating agencies down graded India (Rangarajan-2000).

The cumulative effect was low economic growth and low progress in poverty reduction and drought of new avenues of gainful employment. It is at this juncture that new Economic Reforms were introduced. The important aspects which directly or indirectly affected fiscal policy and reforms are as follows (GoI-1992).

(i) Tariff reduction and removal of quantitative restrictions

(ii) Elimination of most of the export restrictions, revamping of various export incentive schemes, streamlining of procedures and abolition of most of the sector specific direct export subsidies and export taxes.

(iii) Devaluation of the rupee and leaving the determination of exchange rate to the demand and supply in the foreign exchange markets.

(iv) Reforms in the system of personal taxation, customs duties and excise duties to increase revenues, reduce the cost of imported inputs and simplify and rationalize the excise duty structure.

(v) Public sector reforms, such as phasing out budgetary support in the form of non-plan loans to loss-making public sector units, disinvestment of public sector equity, allowing public sector enterprises to form joint ventures and raise fresh equity from the market, bringing public sector units within the jurisdiction of Board for Industrial and Financial Reconstruction and permitting greater flexibility in taking pricing decisions, particularly in the case of steel, petroleum products and coal.

vi) Reducing fiscal deficits by reduction of subsidies and in budgetary allocations to public sector units, expenditure control and tax reforms.

The anticipation was that, private investment would

increase. There will be a growth in output. The trade would shoot-up. The exchequer of the government would noι only become bigger but thought it would be replenished fast and frequently, consequently reducing fiscal deficits.

DEFICITS OF CENTRAL GOVERNMENT AND ECONOMIC REFORMS

The reforms introduced, made it inevitable for the government to show more responsibility towards fiscal policy and manage budgets better. This led to the passage of The Fiscal Policy and Budget Management Bill, 2000. This bill among other things contain the following broader fiscal reforms (GoI-2002)

(i) reduce revenue deficit by an amount equivalent to one-half per cent, or more or the estimated gross domestic product at the end of each financial year beginning on the 1st day of April, 2001.

(ii) Reduce revenue deficit to nil within a period of five financial years beginning from the initial financial year on the 1st day of April, 2001 and ending on the 31st day of March, 2001;

(iii) Reduce fiscal deficit by an amount equivalent to one-half per cent or more4 of the estimated gross domestic product at the end of each financial year beginning on the 1st day of March 2006;

(iv) Reduce fiscal deficit for a financial year to not more than two per cent of the estimated gross domestic product for that year, within a period of five financial years beginning from the initial financial year on the 1sdt day of April, 2001 and ending on the 31st day of March 2006;

(v) Prohibition of direct borrowings by the Central Government from the Reserve Bank of India after three years except by way of advances to meet temporary cash needs in certain circumstances.

We will take a pause here to discuss about the implications of economic reforms on the government exchequer. The Economic Reforms of 1991 took our economic policy closer to the *laisez faire* economic system. The non-intervention of the

State in the economic relationships of the market forces leads to the re-allocation of resources between the factors of production which give maximum output with the given technology. The Reforms we had introduced had in it embedded provision for the transfer of technology along with foreign direct investment under liberalized trade policy and capital account. A fresh flow of technology and investment in the economy, mired with higher capital-output ratio and obsolete production techniques, results in the increase of output. An aggregate increase in the output means, it might have preceded by proportionate capital formation in the private sector, ascribed to both domestic and foreign investors. It means there would be a flow of foreign investment in the form of foreign exchange and increased investment expenditures committed by the domestic corporate sector. In both the cases it leads to proportionate increase in government revenues through taxes on capital gains. Similarly, an increase in output not only increases domestic supply of goods and services, the trade in them, either imports or exports, also see an upward trend. In this case, the Government revenues should proportionately increase in the form of additional revenues collected through sales tax, excise and customs duty. Of course, the Reforms process started with the allowance of various fiscal exemptions offered to the private corporate world. But, these exemptions were only meant to provide incentives in the form of *low incidence of taxation,* taking into consideration both the ends of market wing, i.e. the producer and the consumer. The implication of all this could be seen in the form of increased personal incomes as a result of increase in employment and increase in tax revenues of the Government. Here we are concerned with the revenues at the level of Government exchequer, i.e. its fiscal position. Is there any decrease in the deficits of the Government. We also should keep in mind the fact that, the Reforms also initiated the process of disinvestment and voluntary retirement scheme, the famous *'golden hand shake'* policy which eases the pressure on the Government exchequer.

It does not seem the case that the Government is also the beneficiary of the Economic reforms. All types of deficits, revenue, primary and budgetary, have been stubbornly sustaining themselves. A peek into Table 4 would show this. Revenue deficit as a percent of gross domestic product on an average for the decade preceding Reforms was 1.88. In the period of reforms it has remained unchanged, nay raised, to an

Table:4
Growth of Deficits of the Central Government as percent of Gross Domestic product

Year	*Revenue Deficit*	*Fiscal Deficit*	*Primary Deficit*	*Budgetary Deficit*
1984-85	0.23	5.14	3.24	0.83
1985-86	0.69	5.64	3.55	0.88
1986-87	1.16	5.94	3.75	0.65
1987-88	1.72	7.09	4.66	1.53
1988-89	2.12	7.86	5.16	1.91
1989-90	1.30	8.47	5.49	2.65
1990-91	1.38	7.63	4.46	1.64
11991-92	2.49	7.34	3.95	1.34
1992-93	2.45	7.33	3.68	2.18
993-94	3.26	7.85	4.07	2.00
Decadal Average	*1.88*	*7.029*	*4.201*	*1.561*
1994-95	2.48	5.37	1.22	1.65
1995-96	3.81	7.01	2.74	1.28
1996-97	3.06	3.70	1.35	0.09
1997-98	2.50	5.07	0.86	0.83
1998-99	2.39	4.88	0.53	0.96
1999-00	3.05	5.84	1.53	0.06
2000-01	3.85	6.51	2.04	0.01
2001-02	3.49	5.41	0.75	0.04
2002-03	4.05	5.65	0.93	0.06
2003-04	4.36	6.14	1.46	0.07
Decadal Average	3.30	5.56	*1.34*	*0.47*

Source: Reserve Bank of India, Handbok of Statistis on Indian Economy: 2005

average of 3.30 percent for the decade 1994-2004. During the whole period, the revenue deficit fluctuated between a minimum of 0.23 percent and a maximum of 4.36 percent of GDP for the years 1994-95 and 2003-04 respectively. The primary deficit which is the residual of fiscal deficit after subtracting interest payments and debt servicing is decreasing. That is the lower primary deficit means a higher interest payments and debt servicing. In the period before Reforms it was low, whereas, in the period of Reforms this is increasing indicating that the Government has not been able to avoid going to foreign lending institutions, even after showing higher foreign exchange reserves.

Therefore, the gross fiscal deficit has sustained itself with increasing presence even after liberalization of the economy and a huge withdrawal of public investment from the market. As a percent of GDP the fiscal deficit for the decade preceding Reforms was on an average 8.2 percent, whereas, in the decade after liberalization has been still higher at 8.09 percent. The pressure on the government has not reduced. Still the responsibility lies on the State to see that the benefit of Economic

Table 5
Growth of Fiscal Deficit as percent of Total expenditure of the centre

Year	*Fiscal deficit as % of Total expenditure*
1983-84	34.30
1984-85	34.51
1985-86	36.67
1986-87	39.92
1987-88	41.50
1988-89	41.87
1889-90	39.63
1990-91	39.09
1991-92	38.35
1992-93	42.39
Decadal Average	*38.82*
1993-94	32.76
1994-95	42.48
1995-96	35.90
1996-97	33.79
1997-98	33.20
1998-99	38.33
1999-2000	40.58
2000-01	35.13
2001-02	36.49
2002-03	38.89
2003-04	40.50
Decadal Average	*36.89*

Source: Reserve Bank of India, Handbook of Statistics on Indian Economy-2005

reforms are reaped to the maximum by clearing the basic bottle necks like, underdeveloped infrastructure in the country . That's why even as percent of total expenditure, the fiscal expenditure is increasing (Table 5). It has been almost 39 percent of total expenditure in the period when the economy was being nurtured by the State, where there was a larger presence of public sector units always showing negative profits and savings. The Reforms, as has been indicated sought to begin disinvestment in the public sector, have not helped much in reducing deficits. For example, the fiscal deficit is still higher at

Table 6

Growth of Interest Payments as percent of total expenditure of the centre.

Year	*Interest payment as percent to Total expenditure*
1983-84	12.19
1984-85	13.42
1985-86	13.93
1986-87	14.42
1987-88	14.45
1988-89	14.88
1989-90	15.30
1990-91	17.23
1991-92	18.89
1992-93	19.88
1993-94	21.31
1994-95	24.65
1995-96	25.36
1996-97	25.93
1997-98	28.49
1998-99	28.73
1999-2000	30.76
2000-01	31.61
2001-02	31.05
2002-03	31.81
2003-04	31.73

Source: Reserve Bank of India A Handbook of Statistics on Indian economy-2005.

36.76 percent of total Government expenditure for the decadal period after liberalization and privatization of the economy. It could be the case that, the revenues of the Government are not increasing and at the same time interest payments and debt servicing obligations of the Government is increasing as usual.

As we can see in the Table 6, the interest payments have increased steadily from 13 percent in 1983-84 to 19.8 percent in 2003-04. There is an almost six percent of growth in interest payment obligations of the government through the periods of both pre-economic reforms and post. If the State have to meet its expenditure obligations more from borrowing, it means that

Table 7

Non-Development revenue expenditure as percent of total expenditure of the centre

Year	*Non-development Revenue expenditure as % of Total expenditure*
1983-84	34.92
1984-85	35.76
1-85-86	36.15
1986-87	35.84
1987-88	38.61
1988-89	38.34
1989-90	39.30
1990-91	40.41
1991-92	39.42
1992-93	41.49
Decadal Average	*38.00*
1993-94	42.13
1994-95	44.82
1995-96	44.90
1996-97	47.33
1997-98	48.72
1998-99	48.90
199-2000	49.55
2000-01	49.67
2001-02	50.91
2002-03	49.99
2003-04	*48.48*

Source: Reserve Bank of India, Handbook of Statistics on Indian Economy-2005.

the beneficiaries of Economic reforms are not paying its due share back to the State. This could be because of various exemptions given under the reforms in terms of taxes. A reason of other kind might also be there that the expenditure of the Government itself is not productive which means, the non-development expenditure might be increasing. The non-development expenditure of the Government is increasing (see Table 7). The combined figures for central and state non-development expenditures has been increasing rather fast. Where it was just 33.79 percent of the total expenditure in 1983-84 and increased to 38 percent in 1993-94. And, it increased to 52.05 percent in the year 2003-04 in the period of liberalization. On an average the decade preceding reforms has seen 38 percent of non-developmental expenditure and 48.48 percent in the decade after economic reforms where introduced. This clearly indicates that, the Government cannot shed its responsibility for shouldering the cause of higher economic growth in the country.

Table 8
Growth of revenue receipts of the Centre

Year	Tax GDP Ratio Direct	Indirect	Total
1983-84	2.0	7.08	9.17
1984-85	2025	7.15	9.40
1985-86	2.20	7.20	9.40
1986-87	2.05	7.39	9.44
1987-88	1.95	7.61	9.56
1988-89	2.02	8.29	10.31
1989-90	2.00	8.55	10.55
1990-91	1.91	8.72	10.63
1991-92	2.09	8.46	10.55
1992-93	2.06	8.56	10.62
1993-94	1.94	8319	10.31
Decadal Average	*2.05*	*8.01*	*10.06*
1994-95	2.42	7.55	10.16
1995-96	2.36	6.45	8.82
1996-97	2.66	6.45	9.11
1997-98	2.83	6.54	9.36
1998-99	2.84	6.57	9.41
1999-2000	3.17	5.97	9.14
2000-01	2.68	5.58	8.26
2001-02	2.99	5.87	8.87
2002-03	3.25	5.72	8.96
2003-04	3.22	5.35	8.57
Decadal Average	*2.84*	*6.21*	*9.05*

Source: Reserve Bank of India, Handbook of Statistics on Indian Economy-, 2005.

The Government is yet to realize higher revenues as a result of economic reforms. The revenue receipts of the Government have not increased, in fact after the reforms they dipped hugely as the ratio to gross domestic product (Table 8). There is a general perception in public economics that in developing countries indirect taxes constitute bigger part of the tax receipts of the Government. Whereas, the direct taxes which primarily includes income tax is low always (Rastogi-2004) It can clearly be seen that the tax revenues as ratios to GDP have not increased. They average tax-GDP ratio for the decade before reforms was 10.06 whereas in the decade after reforms it has been 9.05 percent a decrease of 10 percent. We, have to keep in mind that the reforms have helped the nation in achieved a growth rate of 6.6 percent on an average since the initiation of reforms. The, government revenues therefore, as a proportion of that increasing growth in the economy needed to show a positive gains. We are seeing that it has not happened.

CONCLUSION

An economic system is constituted by the Government, private corporate and the household sectors. The economic policies therefore, of whatever type or mix, affect all the sectors. Here, though, the Government stands as responsible to create institutions for the economic system as a whole it gets affected by its own policies, as we have seen, which very well reflects in its fiscal position. The public finances in India walked closely with the Five Year Plans. The budgetary allocations reflected the priority we gave to the economic growth. The development and non-development expenditures alike have shown that higher rates of growth could be achieved only with the help of State participation in the economy. It is considered as one of the agents of growth affecting the development of economy in a bigger way. But, where the Economic reforms could help the private sector in realizing higher investments and output while gaining larger profits as a result of globalization of the Indian market, the Government revenues have not increased proportionately. The State, as one of the agents of growth stands as a non-beneficiary of what itself introduced the Economic reforms in the form of liberalization of the trade and domestic market, privatization of industrialization and globalization of the economy. As a result of this the Government as responsible organization might fail in delivering the welfare services to its people. The way out of this impasse of static revenues could be i) larger liberalization of the economy and withdrawal of the Government participation from those economic activities which does not directly deal with the general welfare of the people and ii) to arrange for the effective implementation of taxation policies so that larger groups of income covered under it.

REFERENCES

GoI (1951) : "First Five Year Plan Document", GoI, Press, New-Delhi, P-16

GoI (1992) : "Indian Economic Survey" GoI Press, New Delhi,

Jha, Raghbendra (2003): "Fiscal Consolidation", Economic and Political Weekly, Vol.38, No.12 and 13, March 22-29.

Gundlach, Erich (1999): "The Economic Growth of Nations in the Twentieth Century" Economics, Vol. 60, No.99 P-17

Lahiri, Ashok K(2000): "Budget Deficits and Reforms" Economic and Political Weekly, Vol.35, No. 31, November-11, P-4050.

Minhas, B.S(1988): "The Planning Process and the Annual Budgets Sopme Reflections on Recent Indian Experience", Indian Economic Review, Vo.31, No.2, P-123.

Mohan, T T Ram(2003): "A more relaxed view of fiscal consolidation", Economic and Political Weekly, Vol.38, No.11, P-1014.

Rangarajan, C(2000): "India's Balance of Payments: Emerging dimensions", in 'Indian Economy since Independence', Edited by Uma Kapila, Academic Foundation, New-Delhi, P-706.

Rastogi, Anupam(2004): "Restructuring Public Finance", Economic and Political Weekly, Vol. 39,/June-26, P-2756.

Vaidyanathan, A(1984): "The Indian Economy Since Independence (1947-70)" in The Cambridge Economic History of India, Vol.II, Edited by Dharma kumar, Orient Longman, Cambridge University Press, Hyderabad, P-63.

NOTES

1. Reader, and
2. Research Scholar, Department of Economics, Gulbarga University, Gulbarga-585 106, Karnataka, India. *Economic and Political Weekly*, XI (13). Sawant, S. D. & Achutan, C. V. (1995),"Agricultural Growth across Crops and Regions", *Economic and Political Weekly*, March 25.

10

BUILDING STRATEGIC ALIANCES TO PROMOTE CONSUMER EDUCATION IN THE ERA OF GLOBALISATION

*Rameshwari Pandya**

We have experienced in the last decade of the twentieth century the process of globalization. This has resulted into a sea change in the way different societies are interacting because of opening up of boundaries across the nations. This breaking of the political/geographical borders began to be termed "globalization". However what do we mean exactly by globalization? Is it the unconsidered consequence of the free flow of capital or the result of a deliberate political process? In theory globalization means free flow of goods, ideas, individuals, capital and information.

The impact of globalization is only just beginning to be felt. The globalization that affect the future of Indian economy and Indian families as a particular are of two kinds. First and foremost there is a strong demand for more materials, by every one they may be living in village, kasba, town or big metros. Second due to change in the banking system and use of technology as a delivery tool to deliver goods anytime, anywhere just to promote marketing. The development of ATM machines, electronic cash registrars have become more and more part of everyday life.

* Senior Lecturer, Department of Home Science Extension and Communication, Faculty of Home Science, M.S. University of Baroda,Vadodar, Gujrat.

The social and cultural invasion is the result of globalized world. We find international brands easily in the market and in the popular T.V. serials. The impact of globalization is so drastic that it is fundamentally transforming our environment, the way we may look, work of the market and the society itself.

This is not easy as the new economic activities rubs shoulders with the old. There are tensions between established business and institutions and the new market.

The gap between the have and the have nots – those individuals and people that participate in the new economy they prosper and progress and those who do not lag they behind. This is a problem of unequal support system like education, road, bank and communication.

All over the world the revolution in communication technology has influenced our lives. Globalization is the result of this phenomena. It has changed the quality of product and even the value system of man kind. There are several reasons of this change earlier the consumer had to go to the market to buy the products but it is not necessary any more he can just put up on the net, and collect the information or the product of his choice. As the world has come closer is just the most cliched sentence we hear everyday. Communication ease has completely revolutionized the commercial arena with shop being in your house.

Shopping around the world today seems to be accessible, affordable and attainable with credit cards and bank loans; all aimed at attracting consumer. The other major impact of globalization is technologies are fuelling globalization, opening new markets and giving rise to new factors such as economic competition, empowerment and culture diffusion.

The easy access to city and information due to globalized market to the rural man has its impact on their overall life styles. Here it is important to mention that globalization to be successful it requires great foresight and systematic planning. Otherwise it may not yield good results. At the International scenario it may have worked but to make it work at grass root level a lot of initiatives and imagination is required.

The new concept calls for effective networking with the formal and non formal system as well as innovation because the knowledge that one gathers during formal education system also gets out dated and needs to be updated. In view of this modern mode of communication can play a vital role in imparting consumer education.

We know information is power. The arts and science of using information to one's advantage is one of the keys to widen influence and capture power in any society.

Different government agencies and NGOs, could generate necessary awareness among the masses. This can build important informed citizen to face the globalized world with confidence and ease. Following are some important strategies for promotion of consumer education.

PUBLIC EDUCATION

The education represents formal, non formal and informal approaches to learning for developing the knowledge base, aiming to help in

- Understanding the consumer laws, rights and responsiblities.'
- Forming independent opinion.
- Knowing relevant methodologies.

This is a long term procedure it is important that proper curriculum should be planned and implemented so that the globalization impact is well taken. As education is a key to development. For any development to be self sustaining it is very important that values, attitudes knowledge and skill also change. To bring this change education plays a very important role.

Today the educational and social demands have changed tremendously. We know that education helps in meeting the learner needs, societal expectations. However today's need is much more challenging as it needs to prepare the ground for accepting globalization and education can help as a catalyst for progress of the society by extending modernization.

TRAINING PROGRAMMES

Training involves a set of learning activities oriented to objectives of improving knowledge; skills and attitude of individuals to carry out specific tasks based on appropriate techniques. Thus it may include the short term training programmes and exchange of knowledge through seminars, conferences, workshops and group meetings. Training can help in moulding the mind of the next and current generation.

The globalization has permeated into the society as well as in the business environment. This development of Globalization has lead to several changes in the behaviour pattern of consumer and it is now important to have required competencies to cope up with the changing world. The competencies like make wise decision, critical thinking, communicating effectively. Well planned and designed consumer education can help cope with these situation of change.

The training and consumer education programmes aim at generating awareness/updating knowledge and skills of people at various levels. These programmes will not be very efficient and effective unless those who participate in these activities take very active interest in the related activities. Arrangement should be made to involve the persons who are active, failing which the spirit of the programmes will not gather momentum.

Entering the new world which has globalization as the pattern of life. It is important that it may have many disputes between groups of people having different values and beliefs and which may create problems in our rapidly changing societies. It is strongly felt need to give training and education so that problem does not arise.

EXTENSION PROGRAMMES

Community or village based out reach worker can be trained to provide consumer education. For the purpose of public information, radio, television and printed media with well designed and projected messages can be of great help. The process of training and education for living and working requires a continuous improvement and knowledge transfer between the various stake holders, like researchers, community leaders and volunteers. Training and education programmes in the area of consumer education are multidisciplinary and should have the following:

- Education and training programme must be an integral part of development planning.
- Oriented towards the most vulnerable sections of the society.
- Institutionalized as on going process.
- Based upon the outcome of training need analysis.

RESEARCH

The institute of higher learning which are involved in conducting research in traditional sciences and social sciences should include the area of consumer Education and Globalization. The research findings may form the basis for formulating policy and may also open certain commercial ventures.

Research programme are strongly influenced, if not completely determined by the choice of the path to development. Sustainable development is a concept heavily dependent upon science and technology, but which dictates that it be not assumed that there exists a "technological solution" for every problem.

It is important to have alternative path to sustainable development.

TECHNICAL ADVISES

Senior faculty members of reputed universities/ colleges can be consulted by various government, non-government public and private organizations for their expertise in the areas of consumer education as well as phenomena of globalization. We need a concentrated effort to use this vast human resource potential for conducting research and socio-economic analysis and globalization.

KNOWLEDGE TRANSFER

Course work in the subject consumer education can shape the minds of young people and also can accelerate their enthusiasm for working in this field. There is a major change in the government policy towards development. Since learning is essentially life long, an integrated, multisectoral approach would perhaps be most beneficial. While countries have been making efforts to bring about multisectorial coordination and integrate the functional literacy programmes with other developmental concerns, there is still a great opportunity to make consumer education a part of the agenda of other development agencies.

LITERATE ENVIRONMENT

It is important to develop a literate environmental to help sustain the literary and numeracy skills gained. This becomes particularly challenging in rural areas in multi-lingual societies.

Partnership with governmental and non-governmental bodies, to develop reading materials related to consumer education and make them widely available may be the most feasible approach.

The environment-building activities would involve massive use of media of different kinds, ranging from folk media to electronic media including radio, T.V., press etc.

NGOS AS AN INTERFACE

Voluntary organizations can significantly contribute to strengthening the capability of neighborhood groups and local communities more effectively through awareness campaigns participatory capacity building training programmes, media campaigns etc. It is important to choose approach on the basis of contextual characteristics. Successful interventions have always tried to incorporate people's choices as they have in evolved their coping strategies to several challenges facing their routine existence in adverse circumstances and globalization can be one of them.

STRENGTHENING THE CAPACITY BUILDING INITIATIVES

It is essential that the communities recognize that more effective approach will be preparedness; patience and feeling of brotherhood can reduce the damage to property and loss of lives disturbance in the value system takes place.

The capacity building efforts can be through sensitization, awareness campaigns, training programmes, printing and distribution of brochures and posters in regional languages etc. Print media and electronic media can be used to disseminate these messages. It is found to be effective if Street theatre and Folk art forms are used in the awareness campaigns for promotion of consumer education.

CAPACITY BUILDING IN THE COMMUNITIES

It is necessary that the feeling of dependency which the people have on government and the sense of helplessness and expectations of external support to meet local needs should be replaced by a strong sense of confidence, self-dignity and self respect among local communities. This is possible only by conscious efforts of activities for real development, the "beneficiaries" must be replaced by empowered stake holders who are able to assert their self respect and dignity rather than being treated like objects destined to stay in misery, starvation, illiteracy and abject poverty. The collective will of the people can radically transform the society and can march ahead keeping pace with the globalized world.

IMPORTANT ROLE HOME SCIENTIST CAN PLAY IN PROMOTION OF CONSUMER EDUCATION

Home is the first school that any child goes to. The learning's acquired by the children about the science of Home are therefore, the most fundamental in the entire education of the children. Home science in India is recognized is fundamental education because of three major reasons:

1. There is a cultural, philosophical and religious value placed on "home" in India, which makes all knowledge and services to home worthy of teaching and research. Home Science fulfills a role which is fundamental to Indian philosophy and culture, by its very virtue of specialized knowledge about improving the home and family living.
2. The industrialization in India has affected the structure and function of homes. The aspirations of

people about their standards of living, jobs and education have been so much elevated that the traditional home and family living have been rendered less contributory to the development of individuals. In the light of rising aspirations due to industrialization, a contemporary knowledge in home science has become necessary.

3. The social consciousness of Indian people is the highest in the current decade. The people have felt the need to make their own efforts to improve their health, education, clothing and shelter. Home Science gives knowledge to achieve better health; buy or make better garments and fabrics; and build or improve the house and its equipment and furnishings. The modern need of education is in addition, fulfilled by making home science a vocational education.

The broad objective of home science as stated by Thyagrajan (1977) as follows: To impart general education in preparing pupils for a satisfying personal living, developing a wholesome personality, acquiring happy human relationships and enriching one's life. At the same time it is also necessary to find the vocation for which one is most suited and getting the preparation for it.

Home Science is an interdisciplinary field of studies and has linkage with other subsystems in the family as well as at national perspective, it is important to interact with all these systems for pooling the resources. Because of the tremendous change in the political, social and economical scenario it is need of the hour to educate the prospective consumer as well as prospective employees also.

The home scientist can help in consumer producer interactions and can help as catalyst. We have already established our role for family welfare, other roles should not be under estimated but it should be tapped. Home Scientists have very successfully contributed in the various government programmes. In the same lines, it is high time that linkages should be established between developed and developing worlds to ensure an exchange of better understanding of different value system and culture, knowledge of technology will ultimately help in better quality life.

Today this society is no longer only the immediate village, town or nation, but the world as global political, economic, social and cultural trends are bringing sea changes in all the countries of the world and India is no special? No society remains static. A section of our society is already moving towards a so called "Western" culture as global changes and leading to a homogenized world society.

Home Science has a unique problem to be tackled. There is a change in the urban section, which is very fast while another large section which co-exist in the rural society which is tradition bound culture of oppression and exploitation. Bath modern as well as traditional families need intervention to cope up with this change.

Today the environment in which the families are attempting to meet their needs for food, clothing and shelter are constantly changing. So we need to constantly analyse the development opportunities and research possibilities relevant to the local situations.

In order to reflect the social and economic realities of current needs we must consider the following points. Life style issues and emphasis on training home based business for self employment, community based participation to develop skills to help poor households.

- Skills in formulation of public and family policy measures, which can help the policy makers.
- Consumer affairs, consumer advocacy and consumer protection issues.
- Economic development of families in this era of globalization.

With the world rapidly becoming a global village, the role of teacher becomes a more responsible one. They should reorganize and rearrange the curriculum to build the future generation more capable of utilizing the global network for the benefit of mankind.

RECOMMENDATIONS

- Appropriate strategies should be evolved for improving interaction between journalists and consumer forum.
- Success stories of consumer forum need to be published through involving eminent personalities.
- Reports on consumer education, should be made news worthy by highlighting their relevance to society.
- Research on consumer needs to be strengthened.
- On consumer Day, special supplements should be sponsored by advertisers in leading news papers.
- Out reach of folk media needs to be expanded through the involvement of Panchayati Raj Institutions and NGOs in the development and utilization of media.
- Notwithstanding all the attractions of the media, nothing can substitute the vital inter-personal contact of the teacher and taught (here the volunteer and learners) who are close to each other.
- Objectives of consumer education have to be carried to the people in the shortest possible time. This is a public relations functions.
- The massive training programme of consumer education personnel is to be reinforced by communication media.
- Interaction between media and civil society is an on going dynamic process and this new waves of technology especially digitalization and compression can be new binders on media and civil society.
- Students can play an important role in environment building like slogan writing, nukkar nataks etc. As they can provide an important service in creating awareness about consumer rights and responsibilities.
- The centers should have a good network with other organizations working in the promotion of consumer education in the country and abroad.
- The self help groups, consumer Association and Government officials should have good coordination for promotion of consumer education.

SUGGESTED CURRICULUM INPUTS

1. Non formal education packages for all to develop work skills, social awareness and information about consumer education.
2. Formation and management credit and marketing cooperative.
3. Communication technology especially to develop programmes on consumer education.
4. Media skills related to the many focal areas of the curriculum for use in mass media for promotion of consumer education.

CONCLUSION

It is important to know how change takes when local and global interface takes place. It is very important to understand how people in Asia need not be marginalized but can live with the market and yet have property rights of indigenous knowledge and have benefit from globalization.

Balanced development can only occur if we do not outright oppose the globalization yet find out ways to make people the stake holders in the change process and simultaneously gain from commercial exploitation of their resources. From the advent of globalization in 1991 it has affected the performance of all the major sectors of economy agrarian, industrial, banking and monetary, state, enterprises, trade and environment.

It is very important to understand globalization as a multi-dimensional process rather than as a project with a predetermined objective.

Thus it can be safely concluded that the globalization which is in a way result of new technology and communication which has tremendously shaken up the Indian psyche it has enlarged the horizon on one hand and on another it has diluted the concentration of quality. The globalization has given such a facelift that was not even dreamt of before. So it becomes very essential to concentrate at "Building strategic alliances to promote consumer education in the Era of globalization".

REFERENCES

Tuckelt, Alan (2003), "Global Citizenship Social Power" *Adults Learning* Vol. 15 No. 1. Sept. 2003.

Taylor Richard (2004), "The Market, Rules OK ?" *Adult Learning* Vol. 15. No. 8 April 2004.

APPEAL, Monitoring and Evaluation of Literacy and Continuing Education Programmes, Practitioners Manual, UNESCO – Bankok 1998.

Delors, Jacques (1996), Report to the International commission on education for the 21st century. Paris UNESCO Publication.

UNDP (1995), *Human Development Report 1995.* New York Oxford University Press.

Clarke, Arthur C. "New Communication Technologies and the Development World" *Media Asia,* Vol. 8 No. 1 Singapore 1981.

Chowld N. L. "INSAT, New Hopes, New Challenges". *The Times of India.* New Delhi 6th April 1982.

Maddison John, "Radio and Television in Literary" *Reports and Papers on Mass Communication* No. 62, UNESCO, Paris 1990.

Das, Selvie P. "Home Science for Better Child Development". In the Proceedings of Eleventh Biennial Conference of the Home Science Association of India. Pragati Art Printers, Hydrabad, 1973.

Hemaprabha, G. "Home Science in Secondary Education". In the Proceedings of the Twelfth Biennial Conference of the Home Science Association of India, Bagyam Printers, Coimbatore, 1974.

Kittrell, Flemmie P. "The Mission and Future of Home Science Today". Lecturer given at the Faculty of Home Science, Baroda, India, December 8, 1977.

Thyagarajan, Nirmala. "Home Science in Secondary Education and Higher Secondary Education". In Perspectives in Home Science, Silver Jubilee Celebrations Commemorative Volume of the Home Science Association of India, Vani Printers, Coimbatore, 1977.

11

ECONOMIC REFORMS AND INDIAN AGRICULTURE

N. Murali & Alamar***

Agriculture is the lifeline of sixty six per cent of the workforce in India and it is the foundation for national sovereignty. Development of agriculture is key to ensuring food security, eliminating hunger, eradicating poverty, generating demand for industrial goods, reducing unemployment and promoting overall development. India's long term economic prospects depend heavily on agricultural sector, which literally feeds the process of development. An increase in production and productivity in agriculture will create more jobs and raise the volume of work to be done. Besides direct employment in the sphere of crop raising, agricultural expansion also provides work in other spheres like agro-industries. In addition, large employment opportunities are created in many activities related to agriculture like storage, transportation, banking, etc.

Increased rural purchasing power caused by expansion of agricultural output and productivity will tend to raise the demand for manufactured goods and extends the size of the market, thereby making the growth process sustainable.

The demand for agricultural inputs – fertilizers, implements, irrigation etc – will lead to the greater expansion

* Faculty Member, Department of Economics, (Centre for Research), Arul Anandar College (Autonomous), Karumathur, Madurai e-mail : nmuralirbs@yahoo.co.in

** Reader, and Head, Department of Economics, (Centre for Research), Arul Anandar College (Autonomous), Karumathu, Madurai.

in the industrial sector. The long-run effect of the expansion of the secondary and tertiary sectors will be towards higher profits in them. These profits will tend to increase the rate of capital formation though their reinvestment. This is what Kuznets calls the 'market contribution' of agriculture when it trades with others. Hence a conscious and a serious look at the agricultural issues is, therefore urgently called for. Success or failure of economic reforms can be clearly judged as to what is happening in this sector on which the largest number of people are dependent for their livelihood which still has a significant impact on other sectors of the economy. There is no large country in the world which has attained the status of developed country without first developing its agriculture.

HISTORICAL PERSPECTIVE

The growth rate of agriculture before Independence was at 0.3 per cent which stagnated during 1900-47. In 1949-50 to 1964-65 we had a serious problem in food front. We imported 2.1 million tonnes of food grains in fifties and 4.5 million tonnes in sixties. A unique feature of economic turn around during 70's and 80's was growth in agricultural sector. The rural development strategy that centred around the green revolution had helped to achieve self-sufficiency in food grains production. In 2003-04, our food grains production was 213 million tonnes, the highest ever, for which we must thank our farmers. India's self-sufficiency in food is widely regarded as its greatest economic achievement since independence. Ever since the economic reforms were unleashed in 1991 the country has been facing the abysmal performance of agriculture in spite of normal monsoons. While India's population continues to grow geometrically, agricultural production has failed to keep pace. The Indian Economic Survey for 1996-97 already sounded the death-knell. The compound growth rate of food grains production between 1991-92 and 1996-97 was about 1.7 per cent which is lower than the annual population growth rate of 1.9 per cent for the same period. It is a matter of serious concern which indicates that the country is back in Malthusian words. (Devinder Sharma, 2001).

LOW PRODUCTIVITY

An unfortunate fact of Indian agriculture is the low productivity whether measured in terms of output per hectare of land or per worker. The low productivity in Indian agriculture is not due to nature's niggardliness. In fact, nature has been very bountiful. Arable land in India is 51 per cent of the total area whereas this percentage in the world as a whole is only about 11 per cent. We already have the largest irrigated area in the world which can be further extended. Our climate being moderate throughout the year, we can grow two to three crops in a year whereas in most parts of the world due to severe winters, only one crop can be grown in a year. In spite of these natural advantages, we are marginally self-sufficient in food front because of low productivity. Our average per capita annual availability of cereals even after the 'green revolution' is less than two thirds of the world average (Bhanu Pratap Singh, 2001).

After economic liberalization, contrary to expectations, agriculture has failed to show any buoyancy in its production. As a matter of fact there is a deceleration in the growth rates of food grains and non-food grains production during nineties as compared with eighties (Bhalla, 2000).

Table 1
Trend Growth Rate in the Indices of Area, Production and Yields of Foodgrains, Non-Food grains and All Crops during 1970-71 to 1999-00

	Food grains			*Non – Food grains*			*All Crops*		
Period	*Area*	*Production*	*Yield*	*Area*	*Production*	*Yield*	*Area*	*Production*	*Yield*
1970-71 to 1979-80	0.44	1.91	1.06	1.10	2.15	1.00	0.59	1.99	1.03
1980-81 to 1989-90	-0.22	2.81	2.71	1.11	3.70	2.28	0.09	3.13	2.12
1990-91 to 1999-00	0.07	1.98	1.30	1.29	2.77	1.08	0.41	2.30	1.19

Source: Report on Currency and Finance 2000-01

A reference to the above table reveals that there is a decline in the yield level of both food grains and non-food grains during 1970-71 to 1979-80 and 1990-91 to 1999-2000 but witnessed an increasing trend in the yield level during 1980-81 to 1989-90. The yield growth rate of good grains increased from 1.06 during 1970-71 to 1979-80 to 2.71 during 1980-81 to 1989-90 and in the case of non-food grains it increased from 1.03 to 2.28 during the same period. The yield growth rate of all crops taken together increased from 1.03 to 2.12 in the same period. The production and yield of both food grains and non-food grains suffered a major set back during 90's. The trend growth rate of production and yield of food grains declined to 1.98 and 1.30 and that of non-food grains it declined to 2.77 and 1.08 respectively during the reform era. It is disappointing that the alarming deceleration in agriculture sector after the reform period has not evoked any strong response from the policy makers beyond pious statements. This declining trend in the variable reflecting the agricultural growth of Indian Economy was due to supply side constraints arising from the squeezing of public investment in irrigation, soil and moisture conservation, agriculture research and extension and rural infrastructure in general. In the year 2000-01, the annual growth rate of agriculture was estimated to be a mere 0.70 percent and the growth rate for the last quarter in the same year was – 1.4 percent which is a worrisome feature (Ajit Karnik, 2001). But the agricultural sector revived and attained the growth rate of nearly 6 percent in 2001-02. One of the reason for this trend was the spatial distribution of monsoon rainfall in 2001 was one of the best in recent years.

TRADE LIBERALIZATION: A THREAT TO FOOD SECURITY

Food security is achieved, when all people, at all times, have physical and economic access to sufficient, safe and nutritious food to meet their dietary needs and food preferences for an active life (World Food Summit, 1996). In a country where there is mass poverty, where food consumption is low, where about half of the adults and children suffer from malnutrition and where expenditure on food accounts for the bulk of total family expenditure, it is essential to expand and strengthen – and not undermine or disband effective policies of food security.

Since India is an agricultural society, food security for most people is ensured through livelihood security in agriculture. Agricultural livelihood provides the entitlements that ensure access to food. Destruction of agricultural livelihood leads to entitlement failure and hence to food insecurity. The famines of 1877 and 1942 were also reflection of food insecurity faced by peasants (Vandana Siva, 2001).

The beginning of the nineties marked the introduction of a new policy framework for India. India launched its policy of economic liberalisation and integration with the world economy. Going more by the prescription being doled out by the Indian Industry, in league with World Trade Organisation (WTO), India is desperate in letting international trade determine its food security. Not realising that the pressure from WTO, backed by the US, European Union, Canada and Australia to force India to lift the quantitative restrictions and phase out the import barriers on agriculture is a recipe for destruction of livelihood on a massive scale. Singalling the end of an era of good self-sufficiency, cheap food imports are sure to drive out million of poor farmers from their meagre land holdings.

DISQUIETING TRENDS IN EXPORT AND IMPORT

The government is attacking the life standards of the rural people by allowing indiscriminate imports of even those goods in whose case India is perfectly self-reliant. Today our imports include number of consumer goods as well as agricultural products like coconut, rubber, sugar, tea, milk products and so on. The unfettered import of agricultural products are causing havoc to the life of the Indian peasants and thereby reducing the availability of employment for agricultural workers.

The new threat to our agriculture is now from international competition. The price of farm products in the international and Indian markets have been moving in the opposite direction. Prices of most farm products in the international market are on the decline due to rapid progress in the biotechnology and sophisticated farm machines which have considerably reduced the cost of production. For example the average yield per hectare of maize in US is about 8 tonnes whereas in India it is less than 1.6 tonnes. The productivity of apple in India is around 5.58 M.T. per hectare whereas the production in other major apple producing countries like U.S.A., stands at 25.45 M.T. per hectare. Indian farming sector which consists of small and marginal farmers is unable to take up agriculture on an economic scale. It is therefore difficult to think of integrating these farmers into the world trade and making them to reap the benefits of globalisation.

On the other hand, the prices in the Indian markets are on the upswing. This is because of low yielding seeds, primitive tools of production and higher input cost due to withdrawal of subsidies. But the farmers in the US and the other developed countries enjoy heavy subsidy provided by their governments added to their technical advantages. Agricultural subsidies in industrial countries hurt developing countries' ability to export. These subsidies are estimated to have reached 40 per cent of gross farm receipts making developing countries impossible to compete. The Economic Survey of the Government of India, 1998 observed that the share of agricultural exports fluctuated than that of manufactured exports. It declined during 1991-92 to 1994-95, rising in two subsequent years and again declining since 1977-98 Agricultural subsidies in industrial countries along with high trade barriers on agricultural products penalize developing countries where the majority of the poor live in rural areas (World Bank Bulletin, 2001). The free import of agricultural produce has resulted in sharp fluctuations and fall in the prices of cotton, rubber, tea, jute, coconut, tobacco and even food grains which has resulted in increasing hardships for the peasants and agricultural labourers. Free trade in agriculture destroys the livelihoods of poor, thereby increasing their vulnerability to food security. Hence the farmers are feeling insecure. The government's claim that India has achieved food self-sufficiency conceals a terrible reality. Even Planning Commission Statistics accept that 268 million people in our country do not have enough to eat and half the women in the age group of 15-19 and three-fourths of the children are anemic (Rajindar Sachar, 2001). There is a lot of discontent within the farming community and growing sense of frustration.

SHIFT IN CROPPING PATTERN

Another attack on food security due to trade liberalization is the shift from staples to cash crops. The goal of self-sufficiency in production is relinquished in favour of production for export and integration into world trade. Emphasis on export orientation in production alters cropping pattern and domestic production becomes dependent on patterns of international demand and changes in international markets. From 1960-61 to 2000-01, the area under nutritious grains called 'coarse grains' has gone down from 45 million hectares to 29.5 million hectares. The area under cotton has increased from 7.6 to 9.3 million hectares and sugarcane from 2.4 to 4.1 million hectares. Since the New Economic Policy introduced in 1990-91, the area under food grains has declined by 2 per cent and coarse grains by 18 per cent whereas the area under non-food cash crops such as cotton and sugarcane has increased by 25 per cent and 10 per cent respectively. The food production has gone down to 196.1 million tonnes in 2000-01 which was 208.9 million tonnes in 1999-2000 – a 6 per cent decline. Cash crops for sale in the international market will replace mass consumption crops leading to scarcity of necessities and increased vulnerability. For instance farmers grow tomato and potato for Pepsi in Punjab and maize and sun flower for Cargill in Karnataka (Chandakavate and Biradar, 2001). Whatever be the development in the new millennium, food continues to influence the world economy in no small measure. The policy of the Indian government is in a haste to catch up the developed countries where development is equated with Gross Domestic Product (GDP).

LOSS OF SEED SECURITY AND BIO-DIVERSITY

Ever since the Government of India opened up its economy for imports and foreign participation in agriculture many seed developing companies like Monsanto, Cargill, Pioneer Overseas, etc., set up shops in India and started influencing the Government of India to allow them market their seeds solely in their own interest which seriously damages the seed security of the farming community in India. These companies make the Indian farmers dependent on hybrid seeds produced by them. Added to this, the proposed changes in the patent laws and new seed technology like terminated seeds favours MNCs and big business houses to control over the Indian agriculture and thereby eroding the autonomy 'and self-reliance of Indian farmers (Surjeet, 2001), It is feared that the sterility-producing gene in the plant would contaminate other plants thereby causing unprecedented damage to the rich Indian ecology. The MNCs also try to transfer the biological wealth of the developing countries and cross breed them with some other varieties and secure patent rights.

PRICE FAMINE

In a developing country like India the government must take the responsibility of ensuring food to the people at a reasonable price. Though self sufficiency in food production has been achieved, the population lacks access to food at an affordable price. The per capita availability of food grains for human consumption in India is 180 kg. whereas the same figures for China and USA are 450 kg. and 900 kg. respectively. Hunger in our country is not related to availability of food in the market but is caused by inadequate opportunities for sustainable livelihoods resulting in insufficient purchasing power. It is claimed that India has achieved self-sufficiency in food production and the granaries of Food Corporation of India is overflowing with 60 million tonnes of food grains. But the offtake from the public distribution system has been consistently dropping even though large section of the population continue to suffer from malnourishment and hunger. The irony of starvation among plenty amply illustrates Prof. Amartya Sen's Price Famine' theory that famines are a result of lack of purchasing power and not a lack of food availability (Nidhi Nath Srinivas, 2001). Ironically, those who produce food for the nation themselves often go hungry. The real income of farmers and agricultural labourers has been eroding over a period of time because of crop failure in some parts of the country, pressure from imports and fall in the number of working days. The real agricultural wages which grew at 2.5 to 3 per cent per year in 1990's was slower than in 1980's when the real agricultural wages were growing at a healthy 4 to 4.5 per cent per year. For better purchasing power, the farmer needs steady income throughout the year, rising year by year, something which cannot be achieved without some fundamental and structural changes in Indian agriculture.

NO SHIFT IN WORK FORCE

One of the laws of economic development is that as an economy grows, there will be a shift in the workforce from agriculture to industry and then to services. A.G.B. Fisher in this connection writes that "... in every progressive economy there has been a shift in employment ... from the essential primary activities ... to secondary activities of all kinds and to a still greater extent into tertiary production". Despite a fairly high growth in GDP, the process of shifting away of the labour force from agriculture to non-agriculture has not gathered any substantial momentum since 1951. It is important to note that while the share of agriculture in total GDP has gone down remarkably, its share in work force has only registered a marginal decline. The share of agriculture in GDP declined from 55 per cent in 1950 to 22 percent in 2004-05, whereas the proportion of workers engaged in agriculture declined, only from about 66 per cent to about 58 in the meantime. This type of disproportional growth rate in GDP and labour force participation in agricultural sector is not a healthy phenomenon (Alamar and Murali, 2001).

LOW INVESTMENT IN AGRICULTURE

A higher growth rate of the economy cannot be achieved without giving due emphasis to agriculture. It requires a significant volume of investment in agriculture. But the evidence on public investment in agriculture is disturbing with National Accounts Data showing a steady decline in the real public investment in agriculture since 1980 (Montek Singh Ahuluwalia, 1996).

Table 2
Gross Capital Formation in Agriculture at 1999-00 Prices

	Investment in Agriculture (in crores)			*Investment in Agriculture*
Year	*Public*	*Private*	*Total*	*as a % of GDP*
1999-00	7754	35719	43473	2.2
2000-01	7018	31158	38176	1.9
2001-02	8529	38215	46744	2.2
2002-03	7489	38018	45507	2.1
2003-04	12809	35024	47833	2.0
2004-05	12591	30532	43123	1.7

Source: Economic Survey 2005-06

The above table clearly shows that the gross capital formation in agriculture had dwindled over the last few years. In the post reform period, there has been a huge withdrawal of the state's allocation of funds from the economic and welfare activities in the rural sector. Since public investment crowds in private investment there has been a continuous reduction in the gross capital formation in the agricultural sector. Another major reason for the decline in investment in agriculture has been fiscal compression, which mainly falls on investment in agriculture. The niggardliness of our policy makers is evident from the drastic cut in plan expenditure on agriculture and allied activities, rural development and irrigation from 37 per cent of the total plan expenditure during the First Plan to less than 20 per cent in the Ninth Plan. In similar situations Indonesia and other East Asian countries gave a high priority to agriculture and rural development and did not allow public investment to be cut for these sectors in the wake of fiscal stabilization in the eighties. (Hanumantha Rao, 1995).

The investment on agricultural research in India is only 0.2 per cent of the GDP whereas in the world as a whole this percentage is 0.8 and in countries such as US between 2-3 per cent. It is to be realized that compared to information technology, biotechnology is no less important for a country like India where two-thirds of the population is still dependent on agriculture for its livelihood (Bhanu Pratap Singh, 2001). While people are being denied food on the grounds of cutting back public expenditure, the Government is committing high public investment on airports and super highways. The declining trend in real public investment in agriculture needs to be reversed if we want to achieve a sustained growth in Indian economy.

THE ALTERNATIVE

Agriculture has suffered in the new era of liberalization and that it is this 'policy vacuum' that has taken a heavy toll of the incomes of farmers in recent times. In order to safeguard the interests of the farmers the government can take the following steps.

A reduction in farm subsidies is one of the objectives of Indian fiscal policy which hampers agricultural sector. Instead of cutting down farm subsidies, the government can explore different sources for augmenting revenues especially through taxes, which is roughly around 12 per cent of the GDP in 2004-05.

Our policy makers should understand that no country can make steady progress unless all the sector of its economy move ahead at the same speed. Stepping up public investment, strengthening input delivery mechanism, building rural infrastructure, disseminating market and price information to farmers, ensuring accessibility to institutional credit are some of the areas that need attention. Farmers have less access to institutional credit and unable to cope up with the dept and driven to distress. In spite of large Banking network the critical gap in the rural credit still exist. There should be a definite road map to meet the emerging needs in the rural credit.

The government can take immediate steps to tackle the problem of agricultural workers and provide employment by promoting cottage and agro-based industries. A comprehensive crop insurance scheme can be introduced to save the farmers against the natural calamities.

The government can impose import restrictions in the form of tariff protection, anti-dumping duties, quantitative restrictions and other measures on all products that cause prices to fall or change the cropping pattern to ensure remunerative prices for all products. Patent laws should not be changed against the interests of the peasants. Terminated type of technology and indiscriminate use of banned pesticides may be prohibited. The operation of MNCs in agriculture can be regulated with suitable legislation.

Because of the absence of any technological breakthrough there is stagnation in the yield levels of various crops. This can have very serious implications for food security in a country where the propensity to consume for food grains is higher. Hence serious effort should be made on scientific discoveries in genetic engineering and bio-technology.

A strong and effective system of procurement needs to be maintained to meet the requirements of an effective an expanded public distribution system (PDS). The prices of commodities supplied in PDS should be reasonable and affordable by the poor. The government effectively implement the food for work programme and National Rural Employment Programme which will accelerate the domestic demand for manufactured goods so that agriculture and industry will feed each other and drive the economic growth. Hence due importance should be given to the agricultural sector by the Government which goes with the Brundtland Report of 1987 that "the government intervention in agriculture is the rule in both developed and developing countries". Enhancement of agricultural growth is essential for achieving an overall GDP growth rate in the range of 8 to 10 percent. No progress is possible unless millions of farmers across the country can see a ray of hope on the horizon. Agriculture is not a question of Economics and Trade, but of dignity and survival. The importance of agriculture can be summed up "If agriculture survives India survives"

REFERENCES

Ajit Karnik, "Slowdown of the Economy: Which way out?", *Economic and Political Weekly*, Vol. 38(42), October 20-26, 2001: 3972.

Alamar, K and Murali, N., "Services Sector in India", *Loyala Journal of Social Sciences*, 15(2), July-December, 2001: 197.

Bhalla, G.S., "Emerging Crisis in Indian Agriculture – Causes and Suggested Remedies", *Mainstream*, December 23, 2000: 89.

Bhanu Pratap Singh, "Why are We still Poor?", *The Hindu*, July 2, 2001 : 12.

_______., "Managing Food Economy", *The Hindu*, June 16, 2001 : 10.

Chandakavate, M.S. and Biradar, R.R., "Economic Reforms and Indian Agriculture: Some Reflections", *The Asian Economic Review*, 48(2), August 2001 : 172.

Devinder Sharma, "Trading Food Security", Paper presented in the *National Seminar on Human Rights, Social Movements, Globalisation and Law*, at Panchgani (Maharashtra), December 24 January 1, 2001.

Economic Survey 2005-06.

Government of India, "Agricultural Statistics at a Glance", Ministry of Agriculture, 1998.

Hanumantha Rao, C., "Attack on Poverty and Deprivation: Role of Structural Change and Structural Adjustment" *The Indian Journal of Labour Economics*, 38(1), January-March 1995: 15.

Montek Singh Ahluwalia, "New Economic Policy and Agriculture: Some Reflections", *Indian Journal of Agricultural Economics*, 17(3), July-September, 1996: 412.

Nidhi Nath Srinivas, "Sow the Dream and Reap the Reality", *The Economic Times*, July 8, 2001: 7.

Rajindar Sachar, "Nation in Disarray", *The Hindu*, May 21, 2001: 12.

Raghuvendra Pratap, "Reforms Long Overdue in the Agricultural Sector", *The Economic Times*, 41(187), September 2001: 6.

Reserve Bank of India "Report on Currency and Finance 2000-01".

Surjeet, H.S., "National Agricultural Policy: Recipe and Disaster, People Democracy, February 11, 2001: 3.

Vandana Siva, "At the Mercy of Globalisation", *The Hindu*, September 23, 2001, Magazine: II.

Viyas, V.S., "Agriculture: The Second Round of Economic Reforms", *The Indian Economic Journal,* 48(3), January-March, 2000-2001: 24.

World Bank, "Prospects for Growth in Developing Countries", *Bulletin,* 12(2), April-June, 2001: 3.

World Food Summit 1996 in Madhura Swaminathan, *Weakening Welfare: the Public Distribution of Food in India,* Leftword Books, New Delhi, 2001:121.

12

TWELFTH FINANCE COMMISSION AND RESTRUCTURING INDIAN PUBLIC FINANCES

*Prakash S. Kamble**

INTRODUCTION

Finance Commission is an effective mechanism of maintaining fiscal balance, equity between union and sub-national governments in India and making the process of economic development as rapid as possible. It is the valuable gift of the Indian constitution (Article 280(1)). Hence after every five years the finance commission is appointed, and its recommendations are accepted and implemented by the Union government, Till date, in all, eleven Finance Commissions have been appointed and their suggestions have been attempted to enforce so as to get fulfill the pre-determined goals and objectives concerned with Indian Public Finances and socio- economic development of the economy. Recently the XIIth Finance (C. Rangrajan, Chairman) commission has submitted its report on November 30, 2004 covering the period 2005-10. The recommendations of the commission include a plan for restructuring of public finances of the centre and the state through improvement in revenue mobilization and brining down debt levels, and through enactment of fiscal responsibility legislation by states.[1] This necessitates to examine the recommendations of the XIIth Finance Commission concerning restructuring of Indian Public Finances necessary for fiscal balance, equity, justice and growth

* Reader, Department of Economics, Shivaji University, Kolhapur, Maharashtra.

of the economy. It is against this overall background, the present paper endeavours to review the recommendations of the commission with reference to restructuring of public finances of the Union and the State governments in India and also suggests measures and modifications in that direction.

RECOMMENDATIONS OF THE TWELFTH FINANCE COMMISSION (TFC) FOR RESTRUCTURING PUBLIC FINANCES

Indian Public Finance comprises of the finances of the Union, State and Local governments. But the present paper is only concerned with public finances of the Centre and States and their restructuring. The TFC has recommended the following recommendations[2] for the restructuring of Indian Public Finances.

Centre and States are to improve the combined tax- GDP ratio to 17.6 per cent by 2009-10. Combined debt- GDP ratio, with external debt measured at historical exchange rates, to be brought down to 75 per cent by 2009-10. Fiscal deficit to GDP targets for the Centre and States to be fixed at 3 per cent. Revenue deficit of the Centre and States to be brought down to zero by 2008-09. Interest payments relative to revenue receipts to brought down to 28 per cent and 15 per cent in the case of the Centre and States respectively. States to follow a recruitment policy in a manner so that the total salary bill, relative to revenue expenditure, net of interest payments, does not exceed 35 per cent. Each state to enact a fiscal responsibility legislation providing for elimination of revenue deficit to 3 per cent of State Domestic Product (SDP). The system of on-lending to be brought to an end over time. The long-term goal should be to bring down debt-GDP ratio to 28 per cent for the Centre and the States. The norm prevalent in the European Union (EU) countries under the Maastricht treaty for fiscal deficit and inflation, the fiscal deficit of 3 per cent of GDP and the debt-GDP ratio less than 60 per cent are the EU norms [3]

PRESENT POSITION OF INDIAN PUBLIC FINANCES:

To assess the recommendations of the TFC relating to restructuring of Indian Public Finances, it is of vital importance to review the finances of the centre as well as the states. This is useful in judging the suitability and applicability of the recommendations of the TFC. At the same time their possibilities of achieving and if modifications necessary. In this backdrop, it is essential to study and appraise the finances of India into three parts such as: A) Finances of the Union Government, B) Finances of the State Government, C) Combined Finances of the Union and States.

Finances of the Union Government.

The overall budgetary position of the Union government of India facilitates to assess the trends in its finances.

Table 1
Overall Budgeting Position of the Union Government

(Rs. in crore)

Sr. No.	*Items*	*2001-02*	*2002-03*	*2003-04*	*2004-05*	*2005-06*	**CGR%*
1.	Rev. Receipts	201449	236936	263878	300904	351200	11.75
2.	Cap. Receipts	161004	165204	207490	204887	163144	0.26
3.	Total Receipts	362453	410309	471368	505791	514344	7.25
4.	Rev. Exp.	301611	340482	362140	386069	446512	8.16
5.	Cap. Exp.	60842	69827	109228	119722	67832	2.19
6.	Total Exp.	362453	410309	471368	505791	514344	7.25
7.	Rev. Deficit	100162	95377	98262	85165	95312	-0.98
8.	Fiscal Deficit	140955	135524	123272	139231	151144	1.40
9.	Primary Deficit	33495	18134	-816	13326	17199	-12.48

Source: Budget Documents of Govt. of India.
*CGR: Compound Annual Growth Rate

Table 1 reveals that during the period from 2001-2002 to 2005-2006, it is the revenue receipts, which showed considerable growth (11.75% p.a.). The growth of capital receipts was (0.26%) meager. Growth of Revenue receipts led to the considerable growth in Total Revenue (7.25%) of the Union government during the period into our consideration. Total expenditure (7.25%) of the Union government was considerable, which was mainly due to the growth of Revenue (8.16%) expenditure. Growth in Capital expenditure (2.19%) was higher than the growth of Capital (0.26%) receipts which has been reflected in the growth of Fiscal (1.40%) deficit of the Union government. It is satisfactory thing that the government has succeeded in arresting the growth of Revenue as well as Primary deficit, which were- 0.98 and 12.48 per cent respectively.

The transactions of the government on revenue account play a vital role in performing its recurrent functions and providing services and facilities to the people.

Table 2
Transitions of Union Government on Revenue Account

(Rs. in crore)

Sr. No.	*Items*	*2001-02*	*2002-03*	*2003-04*	*2004-05*	*2005-06*	*CGR%*
I.	Rev. Receipts	201449	236936	253935	300904	351200	11.75
A.	Gross Tax Rev.	187060	221918	251527	306021	370025	14.61
1.	Transfer to NCCF	557	1600	3600	1600	1600	23.49
2.	States share	52841	56141	63758	78617	94959	12.43
3.	Net Tax Rev.	133662	164177	184169	225804	273466	15.39
B.	Non-Tax Rev.	67787	72759	69766	31538	25500	-17.76
II.	Rev. Exp.	301611	341648	366227	386069	446512	8.16
A.	Non-Plan Exp. of Which	239954	268979	289384	296396	330530	6.61
1.	Int. Payments	107460	115663	123223	125905	133945	4.50
2.	Defence	38059	41088	44347	33483	34375	-2.01
3.	Subsidies	31207	44618	49907	46514	47432	8.73
4.	Non-Plan Grants to States & UTs	15327	15010	18369	14828	33953	17.24
B.	Plan Exp.	61657	72669	76843	89673	115982	13.47
1.	Central Plan	42017	49483	52123	59817	83370	14.68
2.	Assistance for States & UTs plans	19640	23186	24720	29856	32612	10.67

Source: Same as of Table 1

As far as Revenue receipts mobilization by the Union government is concerned, it mainly relied on Tax revenue (14.61%) because Non-tax revenue registered a negative (-17.76%) growth. But its transfers to National Calamity Contingency Fund (NCCF) were significant (23%). Besides this, States share in Revenue receipts was considerable (12.43%), as a result Net Tax Revenue growth for the Union government showed a moderate growth of 15% p.a.

On the Expenditure side, Plan expenditure achieved the prominent place (14.68% p.a), in comparison with Non-plan revenue expenditure i.e. 6.61%. But Central government's expenditure on Non-plan grants was very rapid which registered 17.24 per cent growth. Subsides (9%) and Interest payments (4.50%) contributed significantly in the growth of Non-Plan revenue expenditure of the government. Defence expenditure showed negative growth (-2.01%) and plan assistance for states & UTs showed moderate growth of 11 per cent.

Table 3

Transactions of the Union Government On Capital Account

(Rs. in crore)

Sr. No.	Items	2001-02	2002-03	2003-04	2004-05	2005-06	CGR%
I.	Cap. Receipts	161004	167077	184860	270368	163144	0.26
1.	Market Borrowings	87724	112865	107194	111424	125310	7.39
2.	Small Savings, PPF	8755	8000	-	-	-	-
3.	State Provident fund	4173	8500	7500	4000	5000	3.68
4.	Special Deposits	8070	10280	9970	200	-	-
5.	Recovery of Loans & Advances	16403	18251	18023	-	-	3.18
6.	Disinvestments	3646	3360	13200	4091	-	2.92
7.	Ext. Borrowings	5601	-13496	3582	9034	9656	11.50
8.	Others	26632	27317	25391	25014	20047	-
9.	Securities against Small savings			-	34015	3010	-
10.	Draw down on cash balances			-	21025	3140	-
II.	Cap. Exp.	60842	62365	72568	119722	67832	2.19
1.	Non-Plan Exp. of which	21305	20945	28437	72008	40317	13.60
	Defence	16207	14912	20953	33483	34375	16.22
2.	Plan Exp.	39537	41420	44131	47714	27515	-6.99
a.	Central Plan	18193	18735	20028	22712	27015	8.22
b.	Assistance to states & UTs	21344	202685	24103	25002	500	-52.80

Source: Same as of Table 1

The Union government's transactions on Capital account reveal its growing dependence for Capital receipts on Market borrowings and External borrowings. But the government spent more on Non-plan expenditure, of which on defence. Its Plan Capital expenditure was negative (-6.99%) with considerable growth in Central plan (8.22%) expenditure. Growth in Capital expenditure on defence was rapid, which stood at more than 16% p.a. Table 3 presents transactions of the central government of India on Capital account.

The various fiscal parameters enable us in examining the state of the Union government finances in India.

Table 4
Fiscal Parameters of Centre and States (% of GDP)

Items	*2000-01*	*2001-02*	*2002-03*	*2003-04 (B.E)*	*2004-05 (*EFC Proj).*
Combined Finances					
Tax Revenues	14.6	13.7	14.9	15.2	16.7
Non-Tax revenues	3.5	4.1	4.7	4.4	3.2
Rev. receipts	19.4	19.1	20.9	21	20
Rev. Exp.	26.6	26.7	28.3	27.5	21
Cap exp.	3.1	3.2	3.9	4.4	6.6
Rev. Deficit	6.8	7.2	7	6.1	1.0
Fiscal Deficit	9.9	9.8	9.4	9.5	6.5
Centre					
Tax Revenues	9	8.1	9	9.2	10.3
Non-Tax revenues	2.7	3	2.9	2.5	3
Rev. receipts	9.2	8.8	9.6	9.3	13.3
Rev. Exp.	13.2	13.1	13.8	13.4	11.5
Cap exp.	2.3	2.7	2.5	2.7	4.0
Rev. Deficit	4.1	4.4	4.2	4.1	1.0
Fiscal Deficit	5.7	6.1	5.9	5.6	4.5
States					
Tax Revenues (own)	5.6	5.6	5.9	6.0	6.4
Non-Tax revenues (own)	1.5	1.4	1.5	1.4	1.5
Rev. receipts	8.8	8.6	9	9.2	13
Rev. Exp.	11.6	11.4	11.7	11.1	13
Cap exp.	3.1	3.2	3.9	4.4	2.9
Rev. Deficit	2.8	2.8	2.7	2.0	0.0
Fiscal Deficit	4.3	4.2	4.7	4.0	2.5

Source: RBI (2003a) RBI (2003b), Budget papers
*Eleventh Finance Commission Projections

The administrative ease of collecting taxes on goods crossing national borders has long been recognised, and is especially important for developing countries where administrative capabilities are limited.[4] Tax revenue of the Union government varied at the level of 9 to 10 pre cent of

GDP between 2000-01 and 2004-05 (Table 4). But the Non-tax revenue collection of the Centre was meager i.e. 3% of GDP. The level of revenue expenditure of the Union government could not match the level of Revenue receipts except 2004-05 (projections by EFC). There was about 4-percentage points gap between Revenue receipts and Revenue expenditure of the government. Its Capital expenditure remained at below 3% of GDP (Except 2004-05) during 2000-01 to 2004-05. Revenue deficit stood at 4% of GDP, but Fiscal deficit was about 2 percentage points higher of revenue deficit of the Union government.

On Expenditure front, it is the Interest Payments consumed the prominent share of the Revenue expenditure i.e. more than 5% of GDP (Table 5), followed by Pensions (0.7% of GDP as on average) and Economic services 0.5% of GDP. Revenue expenditure on Other General services (0.4%) and Social services (0.3%) was moderate. It is revealed from Table 5.

Table 5
Main Components of Expenditure

(% Of GDP)

Items	*2000-01*	*2001-02*	*2002-03*	*2003-04 (B.E)*	*2004-05 (EFC proj)*
Rev. Exp. Centre					
Interest payments	5.2	5.1	5.1	5.0	4.3
Pensions	0.8	0.7	0.6	0.6	0.7
Other General services	0.4	0.4	0.4	0.3	2.1
Social services	0.3	0.3	0.3	0.3	0.3
Economic Services	0.5	0.4	0.5	0.5	0.3
State					
Interest payments	2.8	3.2	3.3	n.a.	2.6
Pensions	1.3	1.3	1.3	n.a.	1.0
Other General services	0.2	0.2	0.4	n.a.	1.7
Social services of which	5.4	5.6	5.4	n.a.	5.8
Edu. Sport	3.1	3.1	2.9	n.a.	1.8
Primary health	0.8	0.8	0.8	n.a.	0.5
Water supply & sanitation	0.3	0.3	3.1	n.a.	2.3
Economic services of which	3.3	3.3	3.1	n.a.	2.3
Energy	0.7	0.8	0.6	n.a.	-
Cap Exp. Centre	2.3	2.7	2.5	2.7	4.0
Cap. Exp. States	3.1	3.2	3.9	4.4	2.9

Source: Same as of Table 4

Finances of the State Governments:

The worsening fiscal situation of the States has become a major cause of worry now days. The financial crisis faced by the States has reached to such an extent that several States are finding it very difficult to even meet the cost of the salaries of their employees.[5] It is observed that (Table 5) the States in India could not collect Revenue receipts in proportion of their Revenue expenditure. As a result, the gap between Revenue receipts (9% of GDP) and Revenue expenditure (12% of GDP) has been widening. Their Tax revenue collection was marginal, which stood at about 6% of GDP. But they failed in raising their non-tax revenue, which was just 1.5 of GDP. Hence the States did not become possible to enhance their capital expenditure necessary to speed up development. It was below 4% of GDP on an average. Revenue deficit of the states stood below 3% of GDP and their Fiscal deficit was about 5 of GDP, which indicates their growing dependence on loans for meeting Revenue expenditure. The negligible Non-tax revenue collections and higher levels of Revenue expenditure is a thing of serious concern.

Social services are the major item of State expenditure, which consumed the share of about 6 of GDP, followed by Economic services (3% of GDP) and Interest payments (about 3% of GDP). Education received considerable share (3% of GDP), but it is inadequate. Water supply and Energy could not get demanded expenditure, which remained below 1% of GDP. The States expenditure on Pension stood at on an average one per cent of GDP during the period into our consideration.

Combined Finances of the Centre and the States:

An important canon of tax reform is that as an economy develops reliance on indirect taxation, as a source of revenue should decline. This because indirect taxes typically have an excess burden associated with them. [6] The study of combined finances of the Centre and States helps in examining the extent of fiscal imbalance in Indian public finances. (see table 4).

Table 4 adequately reveals that Indian Public Finances (Centre and States) mainly relay on Tax revenues than the Non-tax revenues. Hence there is a huge gap between the Tax (15% of GDP) and Non-tax (below 5% of GDP) revenues. India's Revenue expenditure is at higher levels, but inadequate Revenue receipts (20% of GDP average) are increasing Revenue deficit i.e. 7% of GDP on an average. The level of Capital expenditure in India is significantly lower, which stood at below 5% of GDP due to increasing dependence of both the Centre and the States on Debt finance for their revenue expenditure. Hence we find higher and increasing Fiscal deficit, which stood at the level of about 10% of GDP during the period of our reference.

RESTRUCTURING OF INDIAN PUBLIC FINANCES:

In the light of the recommendations of the Twelfth Finance Commission (TFC) regarding restructuring Public Finances the foregoing analysis of Indian Public Finances highlights its need and the direction. The Government's objective to achieve fiscal consolidation is to be done through expenditure reprioritization and revenue argumentation [7] is the basic idea and principle to be kept in mind while thinking of restructuring Indian Public finances.

According to Twelfth Finance Commission (TFC) combined tax-GDP ratio of the Centre and the States is to be improved to 17.6 percent by 2009-10. It is not very difficult for the Centre and the States because in the past this ratio has improved by about one per cent during 2000-01 to 2004-05. If this trend is continued then easily and definitely the expected ratio can be improved before the stipulated period. Just the efforts should be made to improve tax collection efficiency continuously. It is expected to reduce the combined debt – GDP ratio to 75 per cent by 2009-10. This ratio has rose by on an average one per cent a year during 2001-02 (71.4%) to (77.5%) 2004-05. For this both the governments should endeavor to cut down this ratio by one percent of GDP a year to achieve this recommendation. A comprehensive Debt policy prepared and implemented by these governments is the need of the hour. The TFC recommends achieving the combined fiscal deficit – GDP ratio at 3 per cent by 2009-10. But it is very difficult for them because this ratio has declined from 9.9% in 2001-02 to just 7.9% is 2004-05, which was just by 0.5% a year. It will require to cut down in the debt ratio by one per cent a year strictly for which the dependence of the Centre as well as the States must be reduced on market borrowings, small savings and Budget deficit. For this new avenues of revenue should be discovered, existing sources should be exploited and utilized fully and expenditure reprioritization should be undertaken. External debt has not felt much burdensome during the period into our consideration. The TFC expects to bring down Revenue deficit of the Centre and the States to zero by 2008-09, which has declined from 7% of GDP in 2001-02 to 4% of 2004-05. For this the Union as well as the State governments must cut down Revenue deficit by one per cent of GDP strictly a year during 2005-06 to 2008-09. Their Revenue expenditure is growing rapidly and its proportion to GDP has stood at above 25 per cent in the last five years, which should be brought down consistently along with increasing Revenue receipts by giving stress on enhancing Non-tax revenue mobilization and control over Revenue expenditure through arresting expenditure on the items like Interest payments. The present state of Interest payments to Revenue receipts is 25 per cent in the case of States and 38% for the Centre is 2004-05 and 2005-06 respectively. It is expected to fall to 15 and 28%, for which by 2 per cent cut p.a. should be curtailment in interest payments by the States as well as the Centre till 2009-10. To achieve this target their dependence on the Debt liabilities should be reduced and Interest payments must be discharged regularly. To find out alternative revenue sources is a must for this. The Centre as well as the State governments already have banned recruitments as well as abolished the number of posts in their departments and undertakings. This will help in controlling their wage bill. But instead of recruitment ban and post abolishments this expenditure should be compensated through extravagance of money on elections, political functions and black money (40% of GDP). Some States have enacted fiscal responsibility legislation which should be enacted by all the States will facilitate fiscal discipline and correction of fiscal imbalance. No doubt, the attempts should be made by the Centre and the States to achieve debt- GDP ratio to 28 per cent. But it is very difficult task. Their rigorous efforts with positive approach may help in achieving this goal in the long run. The attempts in the desired direction should be undertaken by both of them.

It is challenging but desirable the restructuring of the Indian Public Finances (centre and state) in the backdrop of its necessity and urgency. But the efforts in the above said direction will definitely help and will be fruitful in restructuring Public Finances of both the Centre and the States in India. Political will with efficient administration coupled with due care of the welfare of the poor will enable in fulfilling this major and import goal of the Indian economy.

CONCLUSION

Fiscal health of the government plays a vital role in achieving the rapid and all-round economic development of the economy. It is the desirable fiscal discipline to achieve fiscal balance facilitates necessary fiscal health of the government of a country. But at the same time, it is difficult and challenging task in the developing countries like India. The recommendations of the Twelfth Finance Commission (TFC) are a concrete step in that direction. The TFC's suggestions for restructuring public finances are a definite and desired effort in that direction and goal. But in that attempt social welfare of the Indian people especially of the poor section of the population should not be neglected. The present paper is a little bit attempts to examine the need, urgency, appropriateness and possibilities of restructuring Public Finances of the Centre and the States. It is a fact that to achieve this goal is a tug of war between the unlimited and ever rising duties and responsibilities of the governments for social welfare maximization and limited but deficient financial resources. I could not get necessary and adequate data while preparing this paper.

REFERENCES

Government of India (2004-05), 'Economic Survey 2004-05', Public Finance, P.35.

Ibid, P.36.

Rastogi, Anupam (2004), 'Restructuring Public Finances', Economic and Political Weekly, June 26, 2004, (June 26 – July-2, 2004, volume xxxix No.26), P.2757.

Rajraman, Indira (2004), 'Fiscal Restructuring in context of Trade Reforms', Economic and Political Weekly, June 26, 2004, P.2788.

Mhaske, B.S.(2003), 'Finances of the States', in Jahagirdar & Deshmukh edited "Post Economic Reforms Scenario of Indian Economy", Centre of Economic and Social Studies, Amravati, P.149.

Jha, Raghbendra (2001), 'India's Public Finances at the Beginning of the 'Third Millennium', in Mungekar, Bhalchandra and others edited "Indian Economy in the New Millennium", Himalaya Publishing House, Mumbai, P.262.

Reserve Bank of India (2003), 'Finances of the Government of India: 2003-04,' RBI Bulletin, May 2003, P.264.

13

PERFORMANCE OF INDIA'S FOREIGN TRADE DURING POST REFORM PERIOD

*Zainab M. Khurram**

INTRODUCTION

Foreign trade comprises both visible and invisible[1] external transactions of the current account of the balance of payment of a country. The overall surplus in the current account enhances the foreign exchange availability enabling the country to import those products required for the implementation of various programmes of economic development meant for the benefits of the people. It also helps minimizing the magnitude of deficit on the capital account of balance of payment when autonomous capital outflows exceed autonomous capital inflows. Therefore, foreign trade policy should be directed to promote exports and allow imports merely of essential items needed for the economic progress of the country. Efforts should be made to search thrust markets for the thrust products both traditional and non-traditional exports. There may occur "Dutch disease"[2] if the exports of traditional items are ignored or paid less attention to their encouragement.

For long time since the inception of planning in India especially from Second Five Year Plan our government followed protective trade policy giving emphasis on import substitution trade policy. It was as a result of 1956 industrial resolution, which concentrated on the development of heavy and basic

* Zainab, M. Khurram teaches economics at Zakir Hussian College (evening), University of Delhi, J. N. Marg, New Delhi-2.

industries in order to build strong industrial base in the country and becoming self reliant in capital goods used for further production. Such policy made India high cost economy because of the diversion of resources to sub-optimal utilization causing higher inflation in the country and reducing our international competitiveness. It became the subject matter of academic criticism in late and early seventies. (Bhagwati and Desai – 1970) The World Bank also began imposing stringent conditions on the grant of "soft loan"[3] which compelled India to approach the international financial market involving higher interest rate and raising our external debt burden. The persistent deficit in India' balance of trade except the years 1972-73 and 1976-77[4], rising external debt and debt servicing charges, collapse of CMEA[5] bloc and Gulf war in August, 1990 reducing our exports to GCC[6] countries and the decline in remittances due to the large number of Indian workers returning home from there led to the economic crisis in our economy. The situation became so unfavourable by June 1991 that our foreign exchange reserves were hardly enough to meet more than a week import (R.B.I. Tarapore Committee Report, 1957, p. 5).

Reform measures in India began from mid sixties when first attempt was made devaluing Rupee on June 6, 1996 (Tarlok Singh, 2000-2001). In spite of several other policy reforms its effects on stimulating exports were negligible because of the countervailing duties imposed on our traditional products in which India enjoyed better prospects abroad. In late seventies, India appointed three committees one after the another – Alexander Committee (1978), Dagli Committee (1979) and the Tandon Committee (1980) to suggest reforms in the framework in India' foreign trade policy. The favourable impact of the reforms in foreign trade policy recommended by these committees were neutralized by the higher tariff structure in India.

Two more consecutive committees – the Abid Hussain Committee (1984) and the Narasimham Committee (1985) were instituted for rationalizing foreign trade policy. The former made recommendation for three years long term trade policy (1985-88)[7] and introducing gradual reduction in effective rate of protection rather than nominal tariff duties (Tarlok Singh, 2000-2001). The latter suggested several measures including the promotion only of those import substitution products, which require relatively lesser amount of foreign exchange. The measures also did not carry any discernible impact on our foreign trade due to prevailing tariff structure protecting high cost import substitution industries. When economic crisis in India reached its zenith in early nineties then government was compelled to adopt a comprehensive liberal trade policy on July 4, 1991[8]. This paper aims at analyzing empirically the impact of 1991 trade policy on the performance of India' foreign trade in terms of trend, composition, direction and its position in global economy.

IMPORTANCE OF FOREIGN TRADE

Foreign trade plays an important role in the economic expansion of a country as witnessed by the 19th century "new" countries[9] (Nurkse, R–1962). They were also known as "regions of recent settlement". In those days Great Britain was the "center" of economic growth and these countries were the "peripheral" areas where international trade played the role as "engine of growth" (Robertson, D.H-1938) because of the increasing demand from U.K. for the primary products of the then underdeveloped countries. The growth was further facilitated in these countries by the subsequent foreign private capital flowing from the center to these areas. These countries, which are now developed, took advantage of the demand for their products, greater investment among them, better educational and health facilities and infrastructure development. The role of foreign trade as engine of growth was multiplied by the working of foreign trade multiplier, which states that the national income of a country increases up to much greater extent due to the expansion of exports. The dynamic role of International trade is more conducive to those economies where socio-economic environment is more responsive to take advantage of the growing trade opportunities. Therefore, it has rightly been pointed that the role of foreign trade is "handmaiden" rather than "engine of growth" (Kravis, I.B.-1970).

It was the reason that the less developed countries[10] could not enjoy much gains from international trade both during 19th century as well as during 2nd half of 20th century. Where as they were neglected both by the center and peripheral areas in trade and investment their peculiar problems both on the demand side and supply side are also responsible for low benefits from trade to these countries. On the demand side, problems arose due to the price and income inelastic demand for their products, developments of synthetic substitutes and surplus production even of the primary products by developed countries and unfavourable terms of trade both for their traditional and non-traditional exports. Their problems on the supply side include rigid production structure, poor social and economic overheads and slow response to export order due to cumbersome export procedures involving numerous documents. These factors support the contention that the role of foreign trade in the economic development of a country is "handmaiden". Hence, the less developed countries should concentrate on the removal of the bottlenecks retarding them to take full advantage from growing world trade.

PERFORMANCE OF INDIA' FOREIGN TRADE

The liberal trade policy of 1991 has carried its impact on various indicators of India' foreign trade. India's exports, which amounted to US$ 18477 million in 1990-91, increased to US$ 32311 million in 1995-96 due to the various export-promoting measures introduced by the government. Our imports also rose due to the spurt in the various economic activities in the country and causing the increase in demand for raw materials and capital goods to be used for the production of exports products. Meanwhile, recession occurred in the developed countries in late Nineties reducing productivity in USA, Western Europe and Japan. It had unfavourable impact on our exports. The revival of world economy increased demand for our merchandise products, software exports and Business Process Outsourcing (BPO) brought stimulation to our exports and in the year 2003-04 our exports increased to US$ 64723 million.

India' trade balance has witnessed both the increasing and declining trend and there is persistent deficit in the current account (net) during post reform period up to the year 2000-01 but it is much below the level of 1991. It has occurred owing to our growing trade in services in the world market and remittances of Indian working abroad particularly in the Gulf

Appendix 1
Selected Indicators of India's Foreign Trade

(In US $ million)

Year/Item	Exports	Imports	Trade	Balance Invisible (net)	Current Account (net)
1985-86	9462.7	17297.7	-7835	2967.1	-4844.6
1990-91	18477	27915	-9438	-242	-9680
1995-96	32311	43670	-11359	5460	-5899
1996-97	34133	48948	-14815	10196	-4619
1997-98	35680	51187	-15507	10007	-5500
1998-99	34298	47544	-13246	9280	-4038
1999-00	37542	55383	-17841	13143	-4698
2000-01	45552	57912	-12460	9794	-2666
2001-02	44703	56277	-11574	14974	3400
2002-03	53774	64464	-10690	17035	6345
2003-04	64723	80177	-15454	26015	10561
As % of GDP at current market prices					
1985-86	4.4	8.1	-3.7	1.4	-2.3
1990-91	6.2	9.4	-3.2	-0.1	-3.2
1995-96	9.7	13.1	-3.4	1.6	-1.8
1996-97	9.4	13.8	-4	3	1
1997-98	8.7	12.5	-3.8	2.4	-1.4
1998-99	8.3	11.5	-3.2	2.2	-1
1999-00	8.4	12.4	-4	2.9	-1
2000-01	9.9	12.7	-2.7	2.2	-0.5
2001-02	9.4	11.8	-2.4	3.1	0.7
2002-03	10.6	12.7	-2.1	3.3	1.2
2003-04	10.8	13.3	-2.5	4.3	1.8

Source: Economic Survey, various issues.

countries. The share of India's software exports in its exports of major services increased from 10.2 per cent in 1995-96 to 48.9 per cent in 2002-03. It is heartening to note that the liberalization of trade policies and the removal of exchange restrictions current account of India's balance of payments enjoyed surplus during he successive years of 2001-02, 2002-03 and 2003-04. The surplus in the current account (net) during the year 2003-04 even reached to more than US$ 10 billion. Trends in selected indicators of India's foreign trade are given in appendix 1.

There are also structural changes in the composition of India's foreign trade. Regarding exports the share of agriculture and allied products both in terms of percentage share and percentage change shows the declining trend. Their share declined from 19.2 per cent in 1995-96 to 11.8 per cent in 2003-04. Exports of ores and minerals continue almost to be the same.

Appendix 2
Share and Percentage Change of India' Major Exports

Item/ Year	*Percentage Share*				*Percentage Change*			
	1995-96	*2000-1*	*2002-3*	*2003-4*	*1995-96*	*2000-1*	*2002-3*	*2003-4*
I. *Agriculture & Allied*	19.2	13.5	12.8	11.8	44.7	7.1	4.1	11.9
Tea	1.1	1.0	0.7	0.6	12.7	5.0	-4.7	3.7
Coffee	1.4	0.6	0.4	0.4	34.0	-22.0	-11.0	15.0
Cereals	4.7	1.7	3.0	2.4	264.0	2.8	65.2	-5.4
Fruits & Vegetables	0.7	0.6	0.6	0.7	23.9	18.6	14.2	51.0
Marine Products	3.2	3.1	2.7	2.1	-10.0	17.9	15.8	-7.2
II. *Ores & Minerals*	3.7	2.6	3.8	3.7	18.9	26.5	58.7	18.2
Iron Ore	1.6	0.8	1.6	1.8	24.5	31.9	104.0	29.7
III. *Manufactured goods*	75.2	78.0	76.6	76	16.5	16.9	21.1	20.0
Leather & Allied	5.4	4.0	3.1	3.1	14.3	35.1	.04	46.3
Gems & Jewellery	16.6	16.6	17.2	16.6	17.2	-1.5	23.9	16.8
Drugs etc.	3.2	4.3	5.0	5.2	27.4	15.7	28.6	24.8
Manufactures metals	2.6	3.6	3.5	3.8	17.1	31.3	16.6	29.8
Machinery	2.6	3.7	3.8	4.3	13.9	37.7	16.1	37.9
Transport Equipments	2.9	2.4	2.5	3.1	19.9	30.5	31.0	46.2
Iron & steel	1.7	2.0	3.1	3.4	24.7	20.8	122.0	32.5
Electronic goods	2.1	2.4	2.4	2.7	63.0	57.5	7.2	37.6
Cottonyarn, fabrics etc.	8.1	7.9	6.4	5.3	15.4	13.6	9.6	0.8
Readymade garments	11.6	12.5	10.9	9.8	12.0	17.0	14.6	8.6
Handicrafts	3.5	3.1	2.7	2.2	6.7	2.2	30.0	-4.8
IV. *Crude & Petroleum pds*	1.4	4.2	4.9	5.6	8.8	6213	22.0	38.1
V. *Others & Unclassified*	0.5	1.7	1.9	2.9	-22.0	35.9	-15.0	89.1
Total	100	100	100	100	20.0	21.0	20.3	21.1

Source: Economic Survey, various issues.

Among manufactured goods exports of gems and jewllery and readymade garments amounted to 16.6 per cent and 9.8 per cent in 2003-04 respectively. Our exports of pharmaceutical products, manufactured metals, machinery, iron and steel, electronic goods and crude and petroleum products have grown during the reform period.

There are also changes in the composition of India's imports. Food and allied products show an increase in their imports due to the continuous dependence of India on the import of edible oils due to lower domestic production. POL imports still occupy more than one fourth of India's imports. The large increasing prices of petroleum in the world market have brought strains and stresses on our economy. There is decline in the imports of capital goods especially project goods reflect the technological maturity and industrial capabilities of our country (Economic Survey, 2004-05). The increase in the imports of precious stones is due to the demand for India's gem and jewellery in foreign countries. (Appendix 2).

Appendix 3
Share and Percentage Change of India' Major Imports

Item/ Year	*Percentage Share* 1995-96	2000-1	2002-3	2003-4	*Percentage Change* 1995-96	2000-1	2002-3	2003-4
I. Food & Allied	3.6	3.7	4.6	4.6	-21	-35	22.2	27.3
Edible Oils	1.8	2.6	3	3.3	3.3	-28	33.8	40.1
II. Fuel	23	33.2	30.7	28.1	27.4	23	24.7	16.4
POL	20.5	31	28.7	26.3	27	24.1	26	16.6
III. Fertilizers	4.6	1.5	1	0.9	59.9	-46	-7.8	15.2
IV. Paper board etc.	1.3	0.9	0.7	0.8	92.2	1.1	0.6	46.3
V. Capital Goods	23.1	11	12.1	13.3	34.4	-7.3	5.9	40.3
Machinery	10.7	5.4	5.8	6.1	43.9	-0.9	20	33
Project goods	6.5	1.5	0.9	0.5	29	-23	-4.6	-27
VI. Others	23.5	29.8	28.2	29.8	25.7	-7.7	10.8	34.9
Chemicals	9.9	6.7	6.9	7.4	22.2	-15	8.7	34.9
Precious stones etc.	5.7	9.6	9.9	9.1	29.3	-11	31.2	17.6
Iron & steels	3.7	1.4	1.4	1.8	23.8	-13	11.9	60.2
VII. Unclassified Items	20.9	19	22.7	22.4	28.4	11.7	22.8	25.5
Total	100	100	100	100	28.	1.7	19.4	27.3

Source: Economic Survey, various issues.

Direction of India's foreign trade also reflects during post reform period. Growth of both exports and imports declined with OECD[11]. Exports to European Union (EU)[12] decreased from

Appendix 4
Direction of India's Foreign Trade

(Percentage Share)

Item/ Year 1	*Exports* 1990- 96	1995- 1	2000- 3	2002- 4	2003- 91	*Imports* 1990- 96	1995- 1	2000- 3	2002- 4	2003-
I. OECD	53	56	53	50	46.4	54	52	40	38	37.8
I.1 EU	28	27	22.7	21	21.1	29.4	26.7	19.8	19	17.3
I.1.1 Belgium	3.9	3.5	3.3	3.2	2.8	6.3	4.6	5.7	6	5.1
I.1.2 France	2.4	2.4	2.3	2	2	3	2.3	1.3	1.8	1.4
I.1.3 Germany	7.8	6.2	4.3	4	4	8	8.6	3.5	3.9	3.7
I.1.4 Netherlands	2	2.4	2	2	2	1.8	1.6	0.9	0.6	0.7
I.1.5 U.K.	6.5	6.3	5.2	4.7	4.7	6.7	5.2	6.3	4.5	4.1
I.2 North America	16	18	22.4	22	19.2	13.4	11.6	6.8	8.2	7.4
I.2.1 Canada	0.9	1	1.5	1.3	1.2	1.3	1	0.8	0.9	0.9
I.2.2 U.S.A.	14.7	17.4	20.9	20.7	18	12.1	10.5	6	7.2	6.4
I.3 Other OECD	10	8.3	5.1	4.6	3.7	11	9.7	5.9	5.3	6.9
I.3.1 Australia	1	1.2	0.9	1	0.9	3.4	2.8	2.1	2.2	3.4
I.3.2 Japan	9.3	7	4	3.5	2.7	7.5	6.7	3.6	3	3.4
II. OPEC	5.6	9.7	11	13	15	16	21	5.1	5.7	7.2
II.1 Iran	0.4	0.5	0.5	1.2	1.4	2.4	1.6	0.2	0.4	0.3
II. 2 Iraq	0.1	Neg.	0.2	0.4	0.1	1.1	Neg	Neg	Neg	Neg
II. 3 Kuwait	0.2	0.4	0.4	0.5	0.5	0.8	5.4	0.2	0.3	0.2
II. 4 Saudi Arabia	1.3	1.5	1.8	1.8	1.8	6.7	5.5	1.2	0.8	0.9
III. Eastern Europe	18	3.8	2.4	1.8	1.8	7.8	3.4	1.3	1.3	1.6
III.1 Russia[1]	16.1	3.3	2	1.3	1.1	5.9	2.3	1	1	1.2
IV. Others LDCs[2]	17	26	27	31	32.6	18	18	18	20	20.1
IV.1 Africa	2.1	3.4	3.2	3.2	3.3	2.2	2.3	1.7	1.8	1.3
IV.2 Asia	14.3	21	21.4	25	27.6	14	14.4	14.4	16	17.2
IV.3 Latin America & Caribbean	0.4	1.1	2.1	2.3	1.7	2.3	1.6	1.5	1.8	1.5
V. Others	6.2	5.1	7.3	4.2	4.2	3.5	5.1	36	36	33.3
VI. Total	100	100	100	100	100	100	100	100	100	100

1. Refers to former USSR before 92-93 2. Excluding member of OPEC.
Source: Ibid.

28 per cent in 1990-91 to 21.1 per cent in 2003-04. Similar is the case of imports, which decreased from 29.4 per cent to 17.3 per cent over the same period. Moreover, while India enjoyed surplus with EU in 1990-91 there occurred deficit in the years shown in the appendix 4. India's exports and imports declined with our important trade partners such as Germany and UK belonging to EU. India's efforts searching thrust markets for thrust products have given robust encouragement to its foreign trade with USA, OPEC, Asia and even Africa. India has maintained surplus with USA during all the years shown in appendix 4.

In spite of high-rise in petroleum price our exports increased to the OPEC countries and we succeeded enjoying surplus with this bloc since 2000-01. We are also enjoying comfortable surplus with Asia[13] due to our "look East" trade policy. In recent years, China has emerged an important trade partner of India. In 2003-04 it occupies the position as India's third highest trading partner after the US and UAE. If Hong Kong is also included with China then their combined trade account for 8.4 per cent of our trade making them our second highest trading partner (Economic Survey-2004-05, p. 125). Therefore, India's trade policy treating ASEAN + 3 (China, Japan and South Korea) a significant trading bloc has increased our merchandise trade with these dominating trading partners even more than EU and North America. In the year 2003-04, India's merchandise trade stood 19.9 per cent with ASEAN + 3 comparing with only 19.0 per cent with EU and 12.9 per cent with North America in the same year. (Economic Survey 2004-05, p. 125).

Performance of India's foreign trade may better be understood from appendix – 5. It provides an analysis of the impact of the changes in the unit value and volume of exports and imports and their impact on the net and income terms of trade. The deterioration in the price of exports relative to imports mainly, inter alia, due to the rise in international crude prices could not restrict our export growth in volume terms. The lower export prices increased demand for our products because of the improvement in their quality and thus international competitiveness. The higher export volume contributed much to the strengthening of export performance. It is also supported by the consistently improved income terms of trade, which measures the capacity to import as a result of the better export performance.

Appendix 5
Performance of India's Foreign Trade Sector

(Annual percentage change)

Year	*Export Value in Us dollar*	*Export Growth Volume*	*Unit Value*	*Import Value Us dollar*	*Import Growth Volume*	*Unit Value*	*Terms of Net*	*Income*
1990-2000	7.7	10.6	8.4	8.3	12.4	7.2	1.5	11.7
1990-95	8.1	10.9	12.6	4.6	12.9	7.6	5	16.5
1995-2000	7.3	10.2	4.3	12	11.9	6.9	-2	5
2000-1	21	23.9	3.3	1.7	-1.0	8.2	-4.5	18.3
2001-02	-1.6	3.7	-1.0	1.7	5.0	1.1	-2.1	1.5
2002-03	20.3	21.7	0.3	19.4	9.5	10	-9.4	10.3
2003-04	21.1	-	27.3	-	-	-		

Source: Economic Survey, 2004-05, Table-6.4, p. 113.

Appendix 6
Export Growth and Share in World Exports of Selected Countries

Country	*% Growth rate 1995-01*	*2002*	*2003*	*Share in world exports 2001*	*2002*	*20003*	*2003 value $ Billion*
1. China	12.4	22.4	34.5	4.3	5.1	5.9	437.9
2. Hong Kong	3.6	5.4	11.9	3.1	3.1	3	224
3. Malaysia	6.6	6	6.5	1.4	1.5	1.3	99.4
4. Indonesia	5.7	3	5.1	0.9	0.9	0.8	61.1
5. Singapore	4.1	2.6	15.2	2	1.9	1.9	144.2
6. Thailand	5.9	5.6	17.1	1.1	1.1	1.1	80.5
7. India	8.5	13.6	15.8	0.7	0.8	0.8	57.1
8. Korea	7.4	8	19.3	2.5	2.5	2.6	193.8
9. Developing countries	7.9	7.9	18.4	36.8	37.9	38.7	2878.1
10. World	5.5	4.8	15.9	100	100	100	7439.1

Source: Economic Survey, 2004-05, Table 6.5, p. 114.

Although, India's exports as per cent of GDP during post reform period has grown from 6.2 in 1990-91 to 8.4 in 1999-00 and 10.8 in 2003-04 yet its share in world exports was merely 0.8 in the year 2003. Even the share of smaller countries such as Malaysia and Thailand in world exports was more than one per cent (appendix 6) in the same year. The share of China was 5.9 per cent and China and Hong Kong together accounted for 8.9 per cent. Even Korea has improved much occupying 2.6 per cent share in world exports. It indicates that India is to go a long way to reform it trade policies further and improve he international competitiveness of its products in order to increase it share in world market.

IMPACT OF WTO

It was thought that after the establishment of World Trade Organisation (WTO) on January 1st, 1995 India's foreign trade would increase due the various reforms introduced in the world trading system. Regarding agriculture market access with predictability, reduction in domestic support to agriculture and export subsidies was imposed by WTO agreement on agriculture (AOA). Tariffs on manufactured products were also to be reduced and many other trade promoting measures under the provisions of TRIPS, TRIMS and GATS[14] were also to be implemented. India has certainly augmented its exports due to rule-based trade under WTO; yet the developed countries are still providing export subsidies to their farming community for the sake of keeping them engaged in agriculture and maintaining food security (Chadha, G.K.; 2000). This is retarding the accessibility of agricultural products from the developing countries like India.

There are also formation of regional trading arrangements (RTAs) bilateral free trade agreements (FTAs) violating the principle of non-discrimination in foreign trade (Bhagirath Lal Das, 2005). The developed countries are also restricting exports from developing countries like India by adopting antidumping duties (ADD) and countervailing duties[15] (CVD). They are also imposing measures like sanitary and phytosanitary (SPS)[16] and technical barriers to trade (TBT) like designing and labeling etc. in the name of labour standards and environments in order discourage exports from developing countries.

CHALLENGES AND TASKS AHEAD

There is no doubt that India has undertaken reform measures for export promotion and permitting essential imports but other countries in the world are much ahead of us. South Korea, China and the East Asian economies introduced reforms in their external sector much earlier, adjusted their resource allocation suiting to international standards and invited foreign investment much larger than us. These countries succeeded creating a place for themselves at the international level an improved the standard of living of their people. World market is competitive and nothing short of superior quality of our products enables one to compete there. It is not possible so long we improve the quality of our manpower through better education and health facilities. The governance in the country, which is poor, needs to be effective. We should improve our infrastructure and rationalize the export-import procedures and documentations so that foreign investment may be attracted in the country in order to fill-up the saving-investment gap.

After the introduction of WTO new challenges are to be faced abroad. The developed countries are imposing one type or the other measures discouraging exports from the developing countries. The idea of level playing field requires us to review both our strength and weaknesses. While maintaining strength weakness should be overcome through hard work and commitment by our people so that India could compete in the world market. At the same time, developed countries should not forget that their growth process has been facilitated by the exploitation of resources of underdeveloped countries for long time.

CONCLUSION

The protective trade policy adopted by Indian particularly after 1956 industrial resolution brought about strains and stresses in our economy. The resource allocation shifted to sub-optimal level giving rise to higher cost of production and inflation. Imports requirements continued greater than export proceeds due to low quality of our products having price and income inelastic demand in world market. The deterioration in Indian economy reached to its nadir in 1991 when foreign exchange declined to the extent that was not enough even to meet the cost of one week's imports. All these developments compelled

India to liberalise its economic policies not only to revamp its production structure but also to improve the performance of its foreign trade.

NOTES

1. Visible trade deals with the trade in merchandise and invisible trade include trade in services.
2. Dutch disease refers to the situation when a country discovers new resources and concentrates only on their development ignoring its traditional sector. The country begins earning substantial amount of foreign exchange from the exports of these resources paying little attention to the exports of traditional products. When the newly found resources are depleted such country catches Dutch disease. The concept became popular when Netherlands discovered gas and began relying only on the exports of the gas enjoying large market in Western Europe. The prosperity enjoyed by the Dutch led them to neglect the former items of exports. They did not realize the non-renewal nature of the gas availability and after sometimes they fell prey to the foreign exchange problems. It occurred because of their loosing the market of traditional exports and hence the Dutch disease.
3. Soft loan means the loans granted by the World Bank especially at a very low rate of interest.
4. Throughout since the inception of planning India enjoyed surplus in its balance of trade only in the year 1972-73 due to green revolution and 1976-77 due to the recession in Indian economy respectively.
5. Council for Mutual Economic Assistance (CMEA) operated as regional bloc for economic co-operation of East European Countries.
6. Gulf Co-operation Council (GCC) was formed in 1981 and includes six countries namely Bahrain, Kuwait, Oman, Qatar, Saudi Arabia and United Arab Emirates. The UAE comprises Abu Dhabi, Dubai, Sharjah, Ras al Khaimah, Umm al Qaiwain, Ajman and Fujairah Emirates. See the Middle East and North Africa (1992), London, Europa Publications Ltd. pp. 241 and 961.
7. Before 1985-88 trade policy India was pursuing annual trade policy.
8. On July 4, 1991 India undertook comprehensive trade reforms liberalizing its foreign trade policy.

9. During 19th century, UK (Center) dominated world economic scene and the now developed countries were known as "Periphery". There was classical trade pattern between the two meaning thereby the center was exporting manufacturing products and importing food-stuffs and raw materials from the then developing countries. Both the trade and investment by UK favoured the latter countries.
10. Less developed countries (exotic) known as tropical regions were discriminated by UK both in trade and investment during 19th century. During 2nd half of 20th century also these countries could not take much advantage from international trade except some East Asian economies.
11. Organisation for Economic Co-operation and Development (OECD) includes all the industrially advanced countries.
12. European Union (EU) comprises 25 countries as its members.
13. Association for East Asian Nations (ASEAN) + 3 which includes members of ASEAN, China Korea and Japan is emerging a significant regional trading bloc.
14. Trade Related Intellectual Property Rights (TRIPS) protects the inventor's rights and Trade Related Investment Measures (TRIMS) treats all the companies both domestic and foreign on equal level. General Agreement on Trade in Services refers to trade in services in non-discriminatory manner.
15. Countervailing duties (CVD) are being imposed by the developed countries on the products from developing countries for compensating low cost involved in the latter countries. It should be noted that where as the labour is cheap in the developing countries the quality of their products is also low combined with low productivity of their labours.
16. Sanitary measures are concerned with the health of animals and human beings while the phytosanitary measures deal with the health of plants.

REFERENCES

Bhagirath Lal Das, (2005), Multitude of Mini – WTOs, *Economic and Political Weekly*, Vol. XL, Nos. 44 and 45, October 29-November 4, 2005, p. 4668.

Bhagwati, Jagdish, N. and Padma Desai (1970), *India – Planning for Industrialisation, OECD, London,* Oxford University Press.

Chadha, G.K. (2000), Indian Economy under WTO Regime: Happenings, Non-Happenings and Missing Links, *IEA Conference (83rd) Volume of the Millennium*, Jammu.

Economic Survey, 2004-05, p.124.

Economic Survey, 2004-05, p. 125.

Economic Survey, 2004-05, p. 125.

Kravis, I.B. (1970), "Trade are Handmaiden of Growth: Similarities between the Nineteenth and Twentieth Centuries", *The Economic Journal*, p. 859.

Nurkse, R. (1962), *Patterns of Trade and Development*, Oxford, p. 13.

Reserve Bank of India (1997): *Tarapore Committee Report on Capital Account Convertibility*, p. 5.

Robertson, D.H. (1938), "The Future of International Trade", *Economic Journal*, p. 5.

Tarlok Singh, (July-September, 2000-01), "Balance of Trade, Exchange Rate and Trade Policy Reforms in India: Some Issues and Policy Perspective", *The Indian Economic Journal*, p. 73.

14

SOCIAL SECTOR EXPENDITURE IN INDIA: AN ANALYSIS OF CENTRAL AND STATE GOVERNMENT EXPENDITURE

Rekha Mehta and Pallavi***

INTRODUCTION

The term social sector was used to refer to social services and rural development. Expenditure on the budget head social services comprised expenditure incurred on education (including art and culture), medical and public health, water supply and sanitation, housing, urban development, the welfare of scheduled castes, scheduled tribes and other backward castes, labour and labour welfare, social security and welfare, nutrition and relief on natural calamities and others Two main approaches to the definition may be identified: one approach is social sectors from a human resource development and the other takes a human development approach.

Social sector development is a pre-condition for human development. And social sector development contributes to faster economic growth. Government investment in social sectors has a positive correlation to overall human development International experiences of Latin American and Sub-Saharan African countries have shown that unless governments take the responsibility of social sectors development, economic growth would be jobless, ruthless, voiceless, rootless and

* Asst., Prof., Dept. of Economics, J. N. V. University, Jodhpur.
** Research Fcv ellow, Dept. of Economics, J. N. V. University, Jodhpur.

futureless. Public spending on social services depends on the commitment governments are taken as the main indicators of development of social sectors. Reforming India's Social Sectors looks at an array of issues in relation to the four main themes of poverty alleviation, nutrition, health and education using theoretical and empirical analyses. The contribution of this themes, have collectively called for the reform of social sector policies in India.

The realisation that economic growth alone does not necessarily lead to an enhancement in the levels of social attainments of the population has been at the root of arguments that stress the need for an alternative yardstick to judge the development status of people. The evolution of concepts such as quality of life basic needs and the like as will as the more recent discourse on human development during the 1990s must be seen in this spirit. The protagonists of alternative norms of judging development have also been at the forefront in advocating an enhanced role for the state in ensuring that the linkages between economic growth and human development are strengthened and fortified. Thus, whereas earlier the rationale for public provision of education, health and nutrition is argued in terms of merit goods characteristics of these goods, recent debates have stressed varied causes ranging from enhanced growth prospects by investing in human capital to ensuring social security and human rights.

This paper attempts an analysis of social sector expenditure by central and state governments. I section deals with review of literature, Objectives and limitations of the study is discussed in Section-II, and Section-III gives Data and methodology. Social sector expenditure by central and state government are analysed in section IV and V. Section VI concludes the chapter.

REVIEW OF LITERATURE

A general scanning of the literature available in India from different published sources indicates that very few detailed studies have been conducted in the field of social sector expenditure. Mahendra Dev (2003) concludes, the budget has not addressed the major problems in agriculture, employment and the social sector. Employment creation, which is important for food security and poverty alleviation is not addressed at all in the budget. I.S. Hooda says that the social sector development is not possible unless more funds are allocated at the central as well as states level. But it is not mere total expenditure but it is the pattern of expenditure and efficiency of spending which is more significant. Abusaleh Sharrif, Prabir Ghosh and S.K. Mondal analysis that India, a developing economy of over a billion people recorded a relatively higher economic growth during 1980-2002, especially during 1990s, a decade known for noteworthy structural economic reforms.

S. Mahendra Dev, Jos Mooij (2002) examined trends in the social sector expenditure in the central and state budgets for 1990-91 to 2000-2001. In this analysis they included social services as well as rural development expenditure. They would like to conclude with two observations. First, there is an urgent need for stepping up social sector expenditure. Second, there is an obvious need for better utilisation of the allocated money. K. Seeta Prabhu (1994) analysis the structural Adjustment programme in the country is being implemented against a background of incomplete structural transformation, high level of poverty, low level of human development and distorted patterns of expenditure in education and health which are To analyse attuned more towards higher level facilities as compared to primary level institutions. Complicating the issue further is the fact that the bulk of expenditures on social sectors is incurred by the state governments which have pursued human development strategies with varying degrees of intensity.

OBJECTIVES

1. Had social sector expenditure declined/increased after economic reforms.
2. Has the share of social sector expenditure as percentage of GDP shown any change.
3. Whether there is any shift in Central Government expenditure on social sector.
4. To study the inter-state disparities of social sector expenditure.

5. To calculate the Public Expenditure Ratio (PER) and Social Allocation Ratio (SAR) suggested by UNDP.

LIMITATIONS

1. The paper is based on secondary data.
2. We are unable to calculate SPR and HER ratios because SPR is the proportion of Social Priority Revenue Expenditure and Social Services Revenue Expenditure and HER is the proportion of Social Priority Revenue Expenditure and NSDP. The SPRE included elementary education, public health, water supply and sanitation, maternal and child health and nutrition but we used CMIE, Public Finance for states data and they don't give broad classification of education and health.
3. All conclusions made in paper represent only quantitative aspects.

DATA AND METHODOLOGY

To analyse the above objective, relevant secondary data are collected from different issues of Public Finance, Centre for Monitoring Indian Economy and Economic Survey from 1981-2002. Tabular analysis and simple percentage statistical tools were used to analyse the data. UNDP (1991) computed four ratios, the Public Expenditure Ratio (PER), the Social Allocation Ratio (SAR), the Social Priority Ratio (SAR) and the Human Expenditure Ratio (HER). We calculate two ratios, PER and SAR, PER is proportion of total revenue expenditure and NSDP and SAR is proportion of social services revenue expenditure and total revenue expenditure.

In order to measure the growth rates semi log function of the type log $y_i = \beta_1 + \beta_2 t + u_t$ is used. In this model the coefficient measure the constant proportional or relative change in y for a given absolute change in the value of the regressor.

SOCIAL SECTOR EXPENDITURE BY CENTRAL GOVERNMENT

Expenditure is incurred by the central government either for satisfaction of collective needs of the citizens or for promoting the economic and social welfare. The central government is widening its activities in social and economic spheres to bring economic growth as early as possible. The expenditure on revenue account is on current items and is met out of current revenues. The important heads of revenue expenditure as shown in the budget of Government of India are General Services, Defence services, Social and Community services, Economic services and Grant-in-aid to States and Union Territories. The capital expenditure of the Union Government is expenditure met out of market borrowing, provident funds, reserve funds and other capital receipts. In government accounts it used to be classified into four categories: (i) developmental capital outlay; (ii) non-developmental capital outlay; (iii) loans and advances; and (iv) discharge of debt.

Table 1
Central Government Expenditure
Percentage of Total Expenditure and Social Sector in GDP

Year	*% Of Total expenditure in GDP*	*% Of Social Sector in GDP*
1980-81	15	0.8
1981-82	15	0.8
1982-83	16	0.9
1983-84	16	1.0
1984-85	18	1.2
1985-86	19	1.2
1986-87	20	1.5
1987-88	19	1.6
1988-89	19	1.5
1989-90	19	1.5
1990-91	19	1.4
1991-92	17	1.3
1992-93	16	1.3
1993-94	17	1.5
1994-95	16	1.5
1995-96	15	1.5
1996-97	15	1.4
1997-98	15	1.4
1998-99	16	1.5
1999-00	15	1.4
2000-01	16	1.4
2001-02	16	1.6
1981-90	18.1	1.6
1991-02	15.8	1.4

Source: Computed from the data of CMIE, Public Finance

Table 1 presents that before economic reforms, percentage of total expenditure in GDP was 18.1 percent and after reform it decreased (15.8%). As a percentage of GDP, Central Government spends around 15 to 20%. In 1991-92, the percentage of GDP was 17%. Only in 1986-87 a higher level was reached. After 1991-92, total expenditure, in terms of a percentage of GDP, was lower than that in the late 1989-90. As a percentage of GDP, Central Government spends between 0.8 and 1.6% on the social sector. Social sector includes social services and rural development. Table shows not major change in social sector expenditure after reforms.

Table 2
Central Government Expenditure Percentage Of Social Sector, Social Services And Rural Development In Total Expenditure

Year	*% Of Social Sector in Total Expenditure*	*% Of Social Services in Total Expenditure*	*% Of Rural Development in Total Expenditure*
1980-81	5.5	5.4	0.01
1981-82	5.6	5.3	0.3
1982-83	5.6	4.8	0.8
1983-84	6.5	5.4	1.1
1984-85	6.9	5.2	1.7
1985-86	6.4	5.1	1.3
1986-87	7.5	5.3	2.2
1987-88	8.5	5.8	2.7
1988-89	7.9	5.7	2.2
1989-90	8.1	5.1	3.0
1990-91	7.7	5.1	2.5
1991-92	7.3	5.3	2.1
1992-93	7.8	5.2	2.6
1993-94	9.0	5.8	3.3
1994-95	9.3	5.7	3.6
1995-96	10.2	6.5	3.7
1996-97	9.3	6.8	2.5
1997-98	9.3	6.9	2.4
1998-99	9.2	7.1	2.1
1999-00	9.2	7.5	1.7
2000-01	8.7	7.5	1.3
2001-02	9.5	8.0	1.6
1980-90	6.0	4.4	1.6
1991-02	9.1	6.9	2.2
1981-90	8.9	6.4	2.5
1991-02	8.7	6.6	2.1

Source: Computed from the data of CMIE, Public Finance.

Table 2 presents that there are three ways of examining trends in social sector expenditure. The first is to look at social sector expenditure as a percentage of Central Government total expenditure, the second is to calculate social services expenditure as a percentage of total expenditure and the third is to look at rural development expenditure as a percentage of total expenditure. As a percentage of total expenditure, Central Government spends around 5.4 to 10.2% on the social sector. After reforms, percentage slightly decreased as compared to before reform period. As a percentage of total expenditure, central government spends around 5 to 8% on the social services. Before 1991-92, the percentage of total expenditure was highest 5.8% in 1987-88, after that percentage declined till 1990-91. From reforms, percentage started to increase. The percentage of rural development in total expenditure was around 0.01 to 3.7% Above we want to find out the growth rate of our social sector expenditure. We use semi log model:

$$\log \quad y_i = \beta_1 + \beta_2 t + u_t \tag{1}$$

This model is like any other linear regression model in that parameters β_1 and β_2 are linear. Model like (1) are called Semi-Log models because only one variable appears in the logarithmic form. In this model the slope coefficient measures the constant proportional or relative change in y for a given absolute change in the value of the t. If we multiply the relative change in y by 100, will then given the percentage change, or the growth rate. We have use this model and find out growth rates of different social sector expenditure. The results are in Table 3.

Table 3 shows the growth rates of Central Government expenditure in pre and post reform. Growth rate of total expenditure was 16.16% in 1980-91 and 12.45% in 1991-2002, shows that total expenditure decreased after reforms. It means that central government reduced expenditure. Growth rate of social services was 16.42 in pre reform and 16.80 in post reform period, shows no major changes. Growth rate of education, sports and Youth affairs was 22.27 in pre and 17.31 in post reform period. Growth rate of health and family welfare, 14.31

in pre and also 14.31 in post reform period, shows that there were no changes. Growth rate of Water supply, housing etc. was 15.66 in pre and 19.61 in post reform period, that means expenditure was increased on water supply, housing etc. Growth of labour and employment was negative (-1.08) in pre-reform period and after reform it is positive (10.63), it shows major changes after reforms. Growth rate of economic services was 12.39 in pre-reform period and 8.06 in post reform period.. Central Government decreased expenditure on economic services. But growth rate of rural development was 47.63 in pre reform and 5.22 in post reform period, shows major change in central government expenditure pattern.

Table - 3
Growth Rate Of Different Parameters Of Central Government

Head	*Growth Rate from 1980-91*	*Growth Rate from 1991-2002*
Total Expenditure	16.16	12.45
Social Services	16.42	16.80
Education, Sports & Youth affairs	22.27	17.31
Health and Family Welfare	14.31	14.31
Water Supply, Housing etc.	15.66	19.61
Labour & Employment	-1.08	10.63
Economic Services	12.39	8.06
Rural Development	47.63	5.22

Source: Computed from the data of CMIE, Public Finance.

SOCIAL SECTOR EXPENDITURES BY STATE GOVERNMENTS

The revenue expenditure of the State Governments can be further classified under two convenient heads as (a) Developmental Expenditure and (b) Non-Developmental Expenditure. The first type of expenditure is one, which helps in the development of the states. The second one, as the name suggests, is of non-developmental type. The capital expenditure of the states has been increasing rapidly from the date of introduction of planning in our country. The capital expenditure is financed out of capital receipts, special loans and advances raised by the states along with advances and grants provided by the centre to the states.

Table 4 presents percentage of social sector expenditure in NSDP. In 1992-93, Orissa spends higher percentage of NSDP, and Punjab spends lowest percentage of NSDP from 1993-94 to 1999-00.From 1993-94 to 1999-00 Bihar spends higher percentage of NSDP. In 2001-02, Gujarat spends highest percentage and Maharashtra spends lowest percentage of NSDP.

Table 4
Percentage Share of Social Sector Expenditure in NSDP

	92-93	*93-94*	*94-95*	*95-96*	*96-97*	*97-98*	*98-99*	*99-00*	*00-01*	*01-02*
A.P.	14.8	13.2	13.3	13.0	12.6	12.5	12.1	11.6	13.9	14.6
Assam	15.7	15.6	14.9	15.3	13.5	13.9	14.0	14.7	24.5	19.9
Bihar	17.1	24.1	21.1	24.7	17.8	17.7	19.3	29.1	22.1	16.8
Gujrat	14.9	13.1	11.0	11.9	11.3	13.3	14.5	15.8	21.4	23.6
Haryana	12.0	10.5	12.9	11.7	11.2	11.3	13.7	11.5	12.5	12.6
Karnatak	15.6	14.5	13.8	13.8	13.8	12.9	12.3	13.2	13.4	15.1
Kerala	14.8	12.3	11.9	11.2	11.4	12.7	12.2	12.5	12.7	11.4
M.P.	16.4	17.8	16.1	16.3	18.1	17.3	16.3	16.2	16.5	13.1
Maharastra	11.2	10.5	11.8	10.1	10.6	10.6	9.4	9.3	12.2	8.7
Orissa	19.4	17.7	16.6	14.8	17.7	14.7	15.8	18.5	16.3	15.2
Punjab	1.1	1.8	9.4	9.4	10.9	11.7	10.1	9.1	12.5	11.9
Rajasthan	17.0	16.1	14.4	15.8	13.7	13.9	13.3	13.0	14.7	13.6
T.N.	17.3	12.9	11.9	11.3	12.0	11.7	11.2	11.0	11.6	12.2
U.P.	14.0	11.9	11.2	10.9	10.6	11.2	11.8	11.6	13.4	12.0
W.B.	9.7	9.7	9.7	9.4	10.3	7.9	8.3	10.4	11.3	10.4

Source: Computed from the data of CMIE, Public Finance.

Table– 5 gives and overview of State Government's Social Services Revenue Expenditure and Economic services Expenditure as percentage of State Government's Total Expenditure. In 1992-93, the highest ratio was 34.4 percent spends by West Bengal but in 2001-02, West Bengal's percentage decreased to 28.4 percent. Assam increase it's spending on social services as percentage of total expenditure from 1992 to 2002. In 2001-02, highest ratio was also spends by Assam as 38.2 percent, and Punjab spends lowest percentage of social services revenue expenditure as percentage of total expenditure in most

Table 5

Percentage Share In Total Expenditure

	Social Services										Economic Services									
	1992 93	*1993 94*	*1994 95*	*1995 96*	*1996 97*	*1997 98*	*1998 99*	*1999 00*	*2000 01*	*2001 02*	*1992 93*	*1993 94*	*1994 95*	*1995 96*	*1996 97*	*1997 98*	*1998 99*	*1999 00*	*2000 01*	*2001 02*
A.P.	30.5	28.0	27.6	32.7	32.1	30.8	32.1	32.2	27.8	27.4	25.4	23.9	23.2	15.9	30.4	23.7	18.8	16.9	23.3	21.5
Assam	31.4	33.6	32.8	33.2	36.4	34.8	37.7	33.6	34.6	38.2	18.9	17.7	23.9	20.2	16.3	14.6	16.3	14.1	14.0	15.2
Bihar	28.7	28.6	32.9	34.5	34.2	35.2	31.4	31.9	34.4	28.7	24.8	25.9	21.2	18.18	16.7	15.2	17.9	15.7	13.6	11.7
Gujarat	25.1	27.7	27.7	28.9	27.2	28.0	28.4	29.0	30.3	36.6	30.2	31.3	27.3	27.8	27.8	27.6	27.9	25.6	28.6	26.9
Haryana	27.5	21.3	16.9	25.9	17.8	20.2	24.3	27.0	27.0	25.8	27.3	21.3	23.3	19.5	21.7	22.8	25.4	21.4	23.2	23.6
Karnataka	29.3	29.4	31.1	31.2	30.9	32.8	31.3	30.8	32.4	29.5	23.7	22.3	23.3	23.5	26.7	23.0	22.4	22.5	22.3	24.4
Kerala	33.0	34.5	34.9	33.4	33.9	31.4	31.6	32.6	32.3	33.0	19.2	15.8	15.7	15.9	17.1	19.8	21.6	17.9	19.0	17.4
M.P.	30.4	30.1	32.4	32.2	30.9	31.5	34.9	34.6	32.7	29.6	25.2	29.0	22.9	24.7	28.6	21.5	21.7	22.5	18.8	18.1
Maha.	29.4	29.0	26.5	30.7	29.9	31.3	31.1	29.2	31.0	31.3	26.4	27.4	23.4	23.2	26.4	22.7	18.0	13.7	15.9	9.8
Orrissa	30.5	29.7	29.9	33.0	31.9	32.3	31.5	39.5	28.7	26.4	21.1	21.5	22.4	22.4	18.0	15.4	15.2	15.3	15.1	11.0
Punjab	24.5	22.0	16.4	22.7	21.7	21.8	24.1	22.7	24.5	23.2	21.6	18.5	12.8	13.7	30.6	21.7	11.7	15.4	13.7	12.7
Rajasthan	29.7	29.5	30.0	27.7	31.6	29.5	34.4	33.7	33.9	33.4	23.0	23.1	20.4	16.9	17.3	13.4	14.4	13.8	13.5	12.3
T.N.	32.4	35.6	33.7	34.6	33.3	32.3	35.7	33.8	32.7	31.5	31.6	25.6	24.4	23.6	22.8	22.1	18.5	19.1	19.6	17.9
U.P.	25.1	24.9	22.2	26.5	27.7	28.2	28.2	25.1	24.1	24.3	21.1	21.6	16.6	17.5	18.3	16.1	15.3	16.6	13.8	11.2
W.Bengal	34.4	33.8	32.8	32.1	31.2	32.4	32.9	36.1	31.1	28.4	18.7	19.9	18.0	17.3	16.9	15.2	14.7	13.3	15.1	13.2

Source: Computed from the data of CMIE, Public Finance.

of the years. In 2001-02 most of the states percentage declined as compared to 1992-93. In 1992-93, the highest ratio of Economic services as percentage of Total Expenditure was 31.6 percent spends by Tamil Nadu but after that it was decreased and the lowest was 18.7 percent spends by West Bengal. And in 2001-02, the highest ratio was 26.9 percent spends by Gujarat and the lowest was 9.8 percent spends by Maharashtra but percentage of both states has decreased from 1992. A comparison of economic services and social services of state governments shows a definite shift. Expenditure of most states on social services is same or increased but expenditure on economic services has declined. Some states like Maharashtra, Rajasthan, U.P., Orissa, it has declined very much

Now we calculated the UNDP suggested ratios of different states from 1992-2002. UNDP (1991), computed four ratios, viz., the Public Expenditure Ratio (PER), the Social Allocation Ratio (SAR), the Social Priority Ratio (SPR) and the Human Expenditure Ratio (HER) as indicators of the extent of political commitment of governments to social sectors. We calculated two ratios, PER and SAR. The PER is the proportion of state income that goes into public expenditure. The SAR is the percentage of public expenditure earmarked for social services.

Table 6 presents Public Expenditure Ratio. The Public Expenditure Ratio was 18.3 percent in 1992-93 0f A.P., which was much below the suggested 25 percent norm. The ratio was always lower than the norm suggested by the UNDP in Andhra Pradesh. The PER was 19.4 percent in 2001-02, which was also below the 25 percent norm. In Assam, the PER was below the suggested 25 percent in 1992-93 to 1999-00. But in 2000-01 and 2001-02, the ratio was higher (27.6 and 28.5 percent) than the suggested norm. In Bihar, the PER was 24.5 percent in 1992-93, which was below the 25 percent after 1992-93; the PER was always higher after 1993-94 till 2001-02. In Gujarat, 1992-93 to 1999-00, the PER was lower and in 2000-01 and 2001-02 the PER was higher than the 25 percent norm. In Haryana, 1992-93 to 1993-94 and 1995-96 to 2001-02, the PER was lower and in 1994-95, the PER was 27.1 per cent, which was higher. In Karnataka, Kerala, Maharashtra, Punjab, Rajasthan, Tamil

Table 6

Ratio Of Different States

	Public Expenditure Ratio (PER)										Social Allocation Ratio (SAR)									
	1992 93	*1993 94*	*1994 95*	*1995 96*	*1996 97*	*1997 98*	*1998 99*	*1999 00*	*2000 01*	*2001 02*	*1992 93*	*1993 94*	*1994 95*	*1995 96*	*1996 97*	*1997 98*	*1998 99*	*1999 00*	*2000 01*	*2001 02*
A.P.	30.5	28.0	27.6	32.7	32.1	30.8	32.1	32.2	27.8	27.4	25.4	23.9	23.2	15.9	30.4	23.7	18.8	16.9	23.3	21.5
A.P.	18.3	15.5	15.4	14.8	17.7	17.0	16.3	16.0	18.1	19.4	38.1	36.8	36.1	44.0	36.2	37.6	41.6	40.6	34.1	34.2
Assam	21.2	21.5	20.9	22.9	19.3	20.0	19.4	22.2	27.6	28.5	40.2	41.9	40.1	40.7	43.5	43.2	44.4	40.7	46.3	44.4
Bihar	24.5	35.2	32.7	38.7	28.0	29.6	30.6	42.1	34.3	28.1	33.8	33.0	36.4	38.4	39.0	40.1	36.0	38.6	40.6	34.6
Gujarat	17.7	16.3	13.5	14.2	13.8	15.7	17.4	19.3	25.2	27.5	32.3	33.6	34.8	35.7	33.4	34.9	34.8	35.6	37.0	42.4
Haryana	15.4	17.5	27.1	20.5	21.6	19.5	18.3	16.2	16.8	17.1	34.2	25.7	18.6	29.7	20.6	23.8	29.7	32.5	32.7	31.1
Karnataka	19.2	16.8	16.9	16.9	17.6	17.2	15.8	17.9	18.3	20.5	37.2	38.3	37.9	38.3	36.3	38.0	37.4	36.0	37.4	34.5
Kerala	21.3	18.0	17.5	16.5	16.7	18.4	18.1	20.3	19.9	18.7	39.4	41.4	41.1	39.7	39.6	37.4	36.3	36.4	36.5	36.8
M.P.	19.8	22.2	20.9	21.7	23.6	22.1	23.2	23.4	25.0	20.5	37.8	35.6	38.7	37.3	35.2	38.2	39.2	38.5	36.9	33.3
Maha.	14.1	12.9	12.7	12.2	13.1	13.3	13.5	13.6	17.1	15.1	35.7	35.3	35.8	38.3	35.8	37.9	36.7	37.9	37.3	36.1
Orrissa	22.7	21.5	20.7	19.7	22.6	19.8	21.8	24.7	27.1	27.2	39.2	38.0	36.9	39.1	39.4	40.0	39.9	47.3	35.0	32.7
Punjab	14.7	14.9	19.8	16.5	17.7	18.2	16.9	18.7	21.9	22.2	30.1	28.4	20.4	28.2	23.7	26.3	31.5	26.6	30.0	28.1
Rajasthan	21.1	20.4	18.4	20.0	16.5	15.8	17.7	19.3	21.6	20.5	37.7	37.2	37.4	36.3	41.2	41.7	42.5	40.9	40.5	40.3
T.N.	22.5	17.0	15.7	15.6	16.5	16.1	16.7	18.4	17.7	18.5	37.0	40.9	40.0	39.7	39.2	37.5	40.1	36.9	36.8	36.6
U.P.	20.4	18.7	18.6	18.9	17.0	18.6	19.6	19.7	22.0	20.8	31.7	30.5	30.4	31.3	33.2	33.8	34.1	30.2	30.7	30.7
W.Bengal	14.6	14.3	13.6	12.8	13.9	12.6	13.4	16.7	17.9	16.4	40.3	39.1	39.9	39.1	39.3	38.8	39.6	42.0	37.9	35.5

Source: Computed from the data of CMIE, Public Finance.

Nadu, Uttar Pradesh and West Bengal, the ratio was below the suggested norm 25 percent in 1992-93 to 2001-02. In Orissa, the ratio was higher than the norm in 2000-01 and 2001-02 (27.1 and 27.2) and in Madhya Pradesh, the ratio was equal the norm in 2000-01 (25%).

Table 6 also presents Social Allocation Ratio. In A.P., Social Allocation Ratio was between 36 to 38 percent, which was lower than the 40 percent norm suggested by the UNDP but in 1995-96, 1998-99 and 1999-2000, it was higher than the norm (44, 41.6, 40.6). In Assam, SAR was always higher than the 40 percent norm in 1992-93 to 2001-02. In Bihar, SAR was higher than the norm in 1997-98 (40.1) and 2000-01 (40.6) and rest of all 8 years SAR was lower than the norm. In Gujarat, SAR was higher in one year 2001-02 than the norm.

In Haryana, Karnataka, Madhya-Pradesh, Maharashtra, Punjab and Uttar-Pradesh, the SAR was lower than the suggested norm. In Kerala, SAR was higher in 1993-94 (41.4%) and 1994-95 (41.1%). In Orissa, SAR was equal the norm in 1997-98 (40%). In Rajasthan, SAR was higher than the norm, from 1996-97 to 2001-02. In Tamil Nadu, it was equal the norm in 1994-95 and 1998-99 and higher in 1993-94 (40.9). And in West Bengal, SAR was higher than the norm, in 1992-93 (40.3%) and 1999-2000 (42%).

Table 7

Growth Rates Of Social Sector Expenditure Of Different States

State	*1991-92 To 2001-02*	*Ranking Of State*
A.P.	12.82	6
Assam	12.16	8
Bihar	8.1	15
Gujarat	16.58	2
Haryana	14.22	4
Karnataka	12.37	7
Kerala	13.64	5
M.P.	8.79	14
Maha.	10.67	11
Orrissa	9.87	12
Punjab	23.63	1
Rajasthan	10.96	9
T.N	9.5	13
U.P.	10.95	10
W.Bengal	14.75	3

Source: Computed from the data of CMIE, Public Finance.

Above, we calculated growth rates of Social Sector expenditure of different states. Social Sector includes both social services and economic services expenditure. Table 7 presents Growth rate of social sector expenditure and ranking of states according to growth rate, From1991-92 to 2001-02. Punjab is at No. 1 with 23.63 percent and Bihar at No. 15 with lowest growth rate (8.1 percent).

CONCLUSION

In India the motto of development has always been 'Growth with social justice. 'The central and state governments always laid emphasis in their budget documents, on the importance of social sector development. It was repeatedly ensured that to carry the benefits of development to the poor highest priority would be given to social sector development programmes. But despite the big thrust to social sector development growth was always taken as a pre- condition for social justice.

We conclude that as a percentage of GDP, Social Sector expenditure has slightly decreased and as a percentage of total expenditure, social sector expenditure has also decreased after reforms as compared to pre-reforms. In a country like India with large size and diversity, there are limitations to what the governments even with the best of programmes can achieve. The year 1991 was the beginning of a fairly explicit phase of economic reforms in India. State governments also have a major role to play in developing infrastructure needed for accelerating growth. In fact, many of the critical areas are those where the primary responsibility is that of the state government. This includes investment in the social sectors, i.e., schools and health facilities and also investments in critical economic infrastructure such as the power system including especially rural electrification, the development of irrigation and water management systems, land development, state highways and district and rural roads. Larger investments are needed in all these areas to achieve higher rates of growth.

REFERENCES

Vaidyanathan- India's Economic Reforms and Development, Academic Foundation, New Delhi.

Ahluwalia, Montek. S. (2000), Economic Performance of States in Post Reform Period, EPW May 6.

Chakraborty, Achin (2002), Issues in Social Indicators, Composite Indices and Inequality, EPW March 30.

Dev, S. Mahendra (2003), Agriculture, Employment and Social Sector Neglected, EPW April 5.

Dev, S. Mahendra, Jos Mooij (2002), Social Sector Expenditures And Budgeting An Analysis of Patterns And The Budget Making Process in India In The 1990s, Working Paper No. 43, January.

.........Social Sector Expenditures in the 1990s, Analysis of Central and State Budgets, EPW March 2.

Dreze, Jean and Amartya Sen (1995), Economic Development and Social Opportunities. Oxford University Press, New Delhi.

Economic Survey– Various issues.

Guhan, S. (1992), 'State Finances in Tamil Nadu, 1960-1990.' In State Finances in India, pp. 239-318, eds. A. Bagchi, J. L. Bajaj and William A. Byrd, New Delhi, Vikas Publishing House.

Guhan, S. (1995), Social Expenditures in the Union Budget: 1991-96, EPW May 6-13.

Hooda, I.S. - Social Sector And Development, International Journal of Development Planning Literature Vol. 10 Nos 1 & 2.

Panchamukhi, P. R. (2000), Social Impact of Economic Reforms in India, EPW March 4.

Prabhu, K. Seeta (1994), The budget and 'Structural Adjustment with a Human Face' EPW, April 16-23

Public Finance, Centre for Monitoring Indian Economy-Various issues.

Shariff, Abusaleh, Prabir Ghose, S.K. Mondal (2002), State- Adjusted Public Expenditure on Social Sector and Poverty Alleviation Programmes, EPW February 23.

15

REGIONAL IMBALANCES IN THE DEVELOPMENT OF CONSUMBER CO-OPERATIVES IN INDIA

*W. N. Salve**

Co-operatives movement was introduced in the world in the form of consumer' co-operatives in the year 1844. Since then consumers co-operatives have made a tremendous progress in the western countries. (Bedi, 1996). In the world economy, consumers' co-operatives have developed in England, U.S.S.R., Sweden, and Garman, Japan, Canada countries. The United Kingdom and Union of Soviet Socialist Republics are home of the consumers' co-operatives, France and Germany for credit.

As agencies of technical and social progress, co-operatives have been regarded as an important for ameliorating the economic condition of millions of the downtrodden masses, both in the developed and developing countries. (Mamoria, 1983). In India, the first Co-operative Credit Society Act 1904 was enacted to encourge thrift, self-help and co-operation. (Goel, 1984). According to this act, the first consumers' co-operative society was organized in 1904 in Madras with the object of supplying necessities to its members (Bedi, 1996). Besides, Co-operative Societies Act 1912 was passed. This act also facilitated the registration of all types of co-operatives, including co-operative federations.

In the First World War period, it was a situation of inflation, when prices of essential commodities went up, the consumers

* Lecturer in Economics, Shri Venktesh College, Ichalkaranji, Kholapur District, Maharashtra.

co-operative movement began in India. It was necessary to stabilize the prices of essential in the market. During the Second World War, consumer's co-operatives have developed. After independence the Government of India accepted the Constitution of India. The preamble, the directive principles of state policy (article 42 & 48) as also the various plan documents further enjoin on the central/state government to provide an environment wherein co-operatives are fully imbued in the realm of social policy. (Goel, 1984).

Since 1951, the government of India has promoted consumers co-operatives as a strong alternatives to private trading. A specific attention was given on the growth of consumer's co-operatives in the five year plans in India. In the pattern of development envisaged in the five year plans, co-operation is expected to become progressively in principal basis of organization in several branches of economic life, notable in agriculture, small industry, marketing, processing, distribution, construction and provision of essential amenities for local communication. (Mamoria, 1983). The government of India has set up various institutions for the effectives functioning of co-operative based activities. Co-operation division in the ministry of food and agriculture was set up in the year 1955. Besides, the national co-operatives development corporation set up in 1963 has made its impact in terms of promotional and a periodic review to the programs. National Co-operative Consumers Federation (NCCF) was registered in August 1965 and its actual function started in September 1968. Today it is an apex organization in consumer's co-operatives. In almost, all states state co-operative federation of consumer's stores at state level was also organized. In recent years, a large number of national and state level federations like NAFED, IFFC, and NCCF in the sectoral fields have emerged. These federations provide leadership and support in administrative, technical, financial and other allied matters to the co-operatives at the state, district and local level in their respective spheres. (Goel, 1984). The central government employee's co-operatives society was established in 1963, with a view to encourage supply of consumer's goods to the employees. The society has a network of branches in different government colonies in the union territory of Delhi (Bedi, 1998).

Under the ministry of food and civil supplies, the department of civil supplies and co-operation was created in 1974, this promotes a consumes co-operatives movement as an integral part of the distribution system. Under the public distribution system, food grains are supplied to the rural, urban sectors of society. (Nagendra, 1999).

As a result of various steps taken by the government and the national and state levels federations of consumer's co-operatives in India, the consumer's co-operative movement made a good progress. At present, consumers co-operatives societies have developed in different fields like industry, railway, university, central and state level employees of the public sector, agro-based industries, co-operatives consumers societies have become new better instrument of national distribution in India. What is the present position of public distribution system in India? We shall try to know the position of P.D.S.

PUBLIC DISTRIBUTION SYSTEM

Under the public distribution system, essential items are supplied to the poor people through fair price shops/ration shops. The main objectives of the public distribution system in India are to provide essential consumer goods at cheap and subsided priced to the consumers. In addition to food grains, the public distribution system is also being used for the edible oils, kerosins, sugar and cloth. (Misra & Puri, 1997). Even through food grains and other essential items are supplied at reasonable rates to the poor through ration shop. However, the public distribution system does not benefit the poor at all. (Misra. 1997). Especially, Homeless migrant people, casual laborers on daily wages, migrant workers and those without proper residential addresses do not get facilities of PDS. Because most of the migrant people do not have ration cards. They are doubly disadvantaged because they are not only covered by the PDS but also have to pay higher prices for their entire purchases in the open market. The delivery system in fair prices shop/ration shop is not good. Even if the fair prices shop exists, food grains are not available in many places in rural as well as in urban areas. Instead of selling ration at subsided rates, shopkeepers sell the food grains in the open market at higher prices, pocketing the difference. Sometimes, they make bogus entries in the ration cards. (Misra, 1997). The consumers face various problems of ration shops like mismanagement, cold and curt behavior of the staff, and poor quality of fair prices shops, unsatisfactory services, shortage of materials. (Kulkarni, 1997). Today the main problem is rapidly increasing prices of food grains, which has made it more difficult for the poor to meet their essential food requirement from the market over a period of time. Some times, consumers face the problem of shortage of essential commodities in the market due to truckers strike. (The Sunday Times, 1999). In October 1999, prices of vegetables and other perishable items went up moderately in some parts of the country. Inter – state movement of goods continued to be affected on the fifth day of the nationwide truckers strike. It was observed that the movement of essential commodities was affected much by the agitation, and prices of vegetables and other perishable goods increased by an average 15 to 20 percentages in the market (The Indian Express, 1999).

According to 1991 census, about 48% of the population is illiterate in India. Therefore, traders and middlemen exploit the poor and illiterate people in the market by charging unreasonable rates of consumer goods. They indulge in various malpractices including the underweight of goods, charging of unreasonably high profit, adulteration, and discrimination between customers. As a result of this, the consumers are not able to get full value their money. (Bedi, 1996). Under this situation, the consumer's co-operatives stores play very important role in development of consumer's co-operatives movement in India. The consumer's co-operatives help to hold the price line in general. The consumer's co-operatives are also being encouraged to set up their manufacturing units. Some of the consumers co-operatives societies have installed their own manufacturing units in the field of dal milling, soap making rice polishing oil seeds processing, spice powdering, tailoring etc. co-operative marking societies can also easily and cheaply undertake the supply of input like seeds, fertilizers, pesticides, implements etc. and consumers goods related by farmers and others (Agarwal, 1996).

POSITION OF CONSUMER STORES

During the year 1993, there are 20,543 co-operative consumers stores and their memberships was 79.27 lakhs in India. It has been observed from table-1 that there are extremely uneven development of consumers co-operatives in different parts of the country. Table shows the over all picture of imbalances in the growth of consumers co-operative movement in India.

Table 1
Co-operative Consumers Stores and their Membership in India during the Year 1993 (31 March, 1993)

States		*Consumer Stores (%)*	*Membership (In thousand)*
Andhra Pradesh	1,145	(5.57)	669.89
Assam	474	(2.30)	157.90
Bihar	2,993	(14.59)	455.65
Dadra & Nagar Haveli	11	(0.05)	2.25
Daman & Diu	5	(0.02)	6.64
Goa	102	(0.49)	25.96
Gujarat	1,739	(8.46)	509.03
Haryana	66	(0.32)	73.18
Himachal Pradesh	265	(1.28)	35.96
Karnataka	1,778	(8.65)	796.76
Kerala	937	(4.58)	288.64
Madhya Pradesh	2,027	(9.88)	392.05
Maharashtra	3,459	(16.85)	1,944.93
Mizoram	28	(0.13)	1.24
Orissa	762	(3.70)	0.25
Pondicherry	24	(0.11)	49.94
Punjab	91	(0.44)	51.50
Rajasthan	588	(2.88)	293.01
Tamilnadu	3,921	(19.08)	2,160.14
Tripura	128	(0.62)	12.06
A. & N Islands, Arunachal Pradesh, Chandigarh, Delhi, Jammu & Kashmir, Lakshadeep, Manipur, Meghalaya, Nagaland, U.P. West Bengal.	N.A.	—	N.A.
Total	20,543	(100.00)	7,927.01

N.A.—— not available
Source: Doshi Ravindra, Arthasavand, 1977.

It has been seen from this table that out of 20,543 consumers store, Tamilnadu, Maharashtra, Bihar states accounted for 50.52% of the total number of consumer stores in India. Madhya Pradesh, Karnataka, Gujarat, Andhra Pradesh states together accounted for 32.56% of the total number of consumers stores. Kerala, Orissa, Rajasthan, Assam, Himachal Pradesh together accounted for 14.74% of the total number of consumer's stores.

If we consider the data of consumer's stores in the remaining states and union territories, it would be seen that the position of consumer's co-operatives stores is very weak. In terms of co-operatives consumer' stores and their memberships, Tripura, Goa, Punjab, Haryana, Mizoram, Pondicherry, Dadra & Nagarhaveli, Daman & Diu states and Union territories accounted for 2.18% of the consumers stores in the country. Inregards to memberships of consumers stores, it is observed from this table that Tamilnadu, Maharashtra, Karnataka, Andhra Pradesh, Gujarat states have accounted 76% membership of the total consumers stores in India.

Bihar, Madhya Pradesh, Rajasthan, Kerala, Assam states have accounted for 20% of the total membership of consumers stores. Tripura, Goa, Punjab, Haryana, Mizoram, Pondicherry, Dadra & Nagarhaveli, Daman & Diu, Himachal Pradesh states and territories have accounted for 4% of total membership of the consumers stores in India.

Due to lack of data, we could not give the relative position of co-operative consumers' stores in some states and Union Territories.

Although the relative position of certain states has improved and certain states have gone down the fact that there is inter regional imbalance in the development of consumers' stores in the country, which is undeniable. (P.B. Kulkarni, 1991). Even though, there is rapid quantitative progress, the primary co-operative consumers' stores are the weakest links in the consumers' co-operative movement. About 33 percent have ceased to function and are now dormant one. (Kulkarni S.K. 1990). However, co-operatives have developed in an uneven fashion leading to regional imbalances and friction among the member state. Though 45% of rural families are within the co-operative fold, the weakest sections ot the society are still not adequately represented in the member roll (Goel, 1984).

Consumer's co-operatives movement could not develop in rural areas due to lack of proper promoters and leadership in co-operative organizations. Therefore, consumer's co-operative movement must develop and strengthen it through consumers in rural and urban areas. Besides, consumer's movements are weak. Consumers are not aware of the provisions of consumer's rights.

In fact, traders, builders, contractors and private business agencies exploit consumers.

In 1962, president, John Kennedy defined four basic consumer rights, the right to be informed, the right to safety; the right to choose and the right to be heard. The consumer rights declared and recognized internationally add new dimensions to consumer protection. India leads the world in the number of laws it has enacted to protect the consumers. But their implementation is very poor. This is due to the loopholes at different levels in the implementation machinery. Above all, consumers themselves are not aware of the existing laws because of illiteracy and ignorance. In fact, the consumer movement is backward in India (Bose, 1998).

REFERENCE

Agrawal, A.N. Kundal Lal (1996), *Agricultural Problems of India.* Vikas Publications House Pvt. Ltd. New Delhi.

Bedi, R.D. (1996), Theory, *History and Practice of Co-operations,* R.L. Book Depot., Meerut.

Goel, B.B. (1984), *Co-operative Management and Administration,* Deep & Deep Publication, New Delhi.

Bose, Biplab S. (1998), *Handbook of Marketing Management,* Himalaya Publishing House, Mumbai.

Kulkarni P.B. (1991), *Distortions in Co-operations,* Himalaya Publishing House, Mumbai.

Kulkarni S.K. (1990), Co-operation, Phadke Prakashan Kolhapur.

Mamoria, C.B. (1983), *Rural Credit and Agricultural Co-operation in India* Kitab Mahal, Allahabad.

Mishra, S.K. Puri V.K. (1997), *Indian Economy*, Himalaya Publications House, Mumbai.

Nagendra, Ash (1999), "Consumers Protection and Analytical Atudy of the legal and Institutional Arrangements for Protection". The Maharashtra Co-operative Quarterly, Vol., No. 4. April-June.

Doshi, Ravindra (1997), Editor: "Statistical Data, (no. 26), Co-operative Societies in India" Arthsanvad, Vol. 21, No. 1, April-June, Marathi Arthshastra Parishad, c/o. Center for the Study of Social Change, Mumbai.

The Sunday Times, Oct., 24. 1999.

The Indian Express, Oct., 25, 26, 1999.

16

PARADIGM SHIFT IN LENDING PORTFOLIOS OF BANKS

Samkutty George *

INTRODUCTION

Banking industry in India is witnessing a transformational phase. The economic liberalization and its consequent changes in the economy have also reflected in the banking industry which compelled banks to seek safer avenues for their lending portfolio. Banks see great potential in retail lending and this become one of the most competitive segment and products in this sector are being continuously customised and regularly modified to attain a competitive edge. Banks are competing each other by offering tailor-made schemes with low interest and other offers for housing loans, vehicle loans, loans for consumer durables and other personal loans, for obvious reasons, which include: low rate of NPA, owing to the security attached and the emotional attachment the beneficiary holds towards the property which they pledged. The NPA under this segment is comparatively low when compared to the other segments where the banks used to lend money. The reason for the low rate of default is primarily due to the strong sentimental attachment to the property they pledged and does not want to fail the obligations; particularly in respect of housing loans as the beneficiary is considering it as his 'dream house' or car, which he consider more than an asset. Secondly, the securities

* Reader in Commerce, Henry Baker College, Melukavu, Kottayam District, Kerala.

involved in these sectors are comparatively high when compared to other sectors.

Since banks are flushed with funds and began to seek more profitable avenues due to the following reasons;

- There is a less off-take from the conventional lending portfolio of banks.
- More availability of funds consequent to the reduction in CRR.
- Banks began to seek for more secured avenues where there is low NPA existed.
- The demand from beneficiary is ever increasing

During the five-year period from 1999-00 to 2003-04, a major shift can be noticed in the lending portfolio of banks from their conventional segments to the personal loan segment. The total bank credit outstanding during 1999-00 stood at Rs. 460080 crores, which was increased to Rs.880312 crores showing a growth of 91.34 percent. During 1999-00, the credit to industrial sector outstanding was Rs.213779 crores, which was increased to Rs.334803 crores showing a raise of 56.6 percent. Even though the quantum of industrial credit outstanding increased during the reference period, a gradual decline can be seen during the five year period compared to total bank credit. The total industrial credit as a percentage of total bank credit during 1999-00 was 46.47 per cent, which was declined to 38.03 per cent during 2003-04, showing a difference of 8.44 per cent. The credit outstanding to trade sector has also decreased from 15.57 percent to 11.52 per cent. This was reflected in the personal loan segment which showed an upward trend during this period. In 1999-00 the loan to the personal segment outstanding stood at Rs.51638 crores, which tremendously increased during the five-year period and fetched to Rs.1,79,087 crores recording a hike of 246.8 per cent. In other words the personal loan increased from 11.22 per cent of the total bank credit showed an upward trend and recorded its highest percentage of 20.35 during 2003-04. Only minute changes can be noticed in other lending portfolios. This shows a paradigm shift of banks in their lending portfolios to the personal finance segment such as housing loan, vehicle loan and other personal loan, which they consider safer and where low NPA exists. The details are given in Table 1.

Table 1
Total Bank Credit and Credit Outstanding to the Various Lending Portfolios Outstanding and the percentage thereof

Amount: Rs in Crores

	1999-00		2000-01		2001-02		2002-03		2003-04	
Lending Portfolio	*Amount*	*%*	*Amount*	*%*	*Amount*	*%*	*Amount*	*%*	*Amount*	*%*
Total Bank Credit	*460080*	*100*	*538434*	*100*	*655993*	*100*	*755969*	*100*	880312	*100*
Agriculture	45638	9,92	51730	9,61	64008	9,76	75935	10,04	96245	10,93
Industry	213779	46,47	236430	43,91	271625	41,41	309827	40,98	334803	38,03
Transport Operations	8073	1,75	8700	1,62	9323	1,42	9409	1,24	11172	1,27
Professional services	14653	3,18	19232	3,57	27702	4,22	33908	4,49	43927	4,99
Personal Loans	51638	11,22	65940	12,25	82518	12,58	113942	15,07	179087	20,34
Trade	71618	15,57	89534	16,63	100872	15,38	104049	13,76	101438	11,52
Finance	21873	4,75	26455	4,91	37614	5,73	50645	6,70	58964	6,70
Miscellaneous	32806	7,13	40410	7,51	62330	9,50	58252	7,71	54675	6,21

Compiled from CMIE September 2005.

INDUSTRIAL LOAN

Since the major shift was noticed from industrial loan to personal loan segment, it would be interesting to analyze the same on institutional-wise. During 1999-00, the percentage of industrial credit outstanding to the total credit outstanding of SBI and its associates was 50.38 per cent. During the five-year period, a steady decline can be noticed and it fetched its lowest to 38.50 per cent during 2003-04. Similar pattern of decline can be witnessed among nationalized banks and foreign banks also. In nationalized banks, the percentage was declined from 43.56 per cent during 1999-00 to 37.02 per cent in 2003-04 recording a decline of 10.88 per cent. The highest percentage drop (15%) can be observed among the foreign banks. The corresponding figures under this group were 58.43 per cent in 1999-00, which was declined to 43.39 per cent in 2003-04. The nationalized banks showed a 6.5 per cent decline during this five-year period. It is interesting to note that a different picture can be noticed among the other scheduled commercial bank groups. The percentage was increased from 50.13 per cent during 1999-00 to 59.14 per cent during 2002-03 but was dropped to 42.7 during 2003-04. Thus it is clear that banks are gradually departing from the industrial finance segment. The details are given in table 2.

Table 2

Percentage of Industrial Credit Outstanding to Total Bank Credit Outstanding among various Bank Groups

Bank Groups	*% of Industrial credit O/s to Total Bank Credit O/s*				
	1999-00	*2000-01*	*2001-02*	*2002-03*	*2003-04*
SBI & Associates	50.38	47.34	38.9	38.23	38.50
Nationalised Banks	43.56	41.51	36.74	36.69	37.02
Foreign Banks	58.43	57.67	51.84	44.69	43.39
Regional Rural Banks	7.01	7.38	7.15	6.58	5.90
Other Scheduled Commercial Banks	50.13	45.39	58.81	59.14	42.70

Source: Compiled from CMIE September 2005

PERSONAL LOANS

The major shift in the lending portfolio of all bank groups was concentrated towards personal loans segment. The highest shift was noticed among the other scheduled commercial banks, which was increased from 7.89 per cent during 1999-00 to 24.81 per cent (16.92 % difference in 5 years) during 2003-04. The SBI and its associates also recorded a considerable shift from 10.69 per cent to 20.67 per cent (difference 9.99 %) during this period. The foreign banks also witnessed a major shift from 17.05 per cent during 1999-00 to 26.34 per cent during 2003-04 showing a difference of 9.29 per cent during the five-year tenure. The details are exhibited in table 3.

Table 3
Percentage of Personal Loans Outstanding to the Total Bank Credit Outstanding among Various Bank Groups

Bank Groups	*% of Personal loans O/s to Total Bank Credit O/s*				
	1999-00	*2000-01*	*2001-02*	*2002-03*	*2003-04*
SBI & Associates	10.69	11.97	13.72	17.22	20.67
Nationalised Banks	10.93	11.60	11.93	13.95	17.00
Foreign Banks	17.05	18.85	23.60	29.47	26.34
Regional Rural Banks	18.81	21.09	23.53	24.68	25.67
Other Scheduled Commercial Banks	7.89	8.96	6.30	8.20	24.81

Source: Compiled from CMIE September 2005

The personal finance segment was grouped into three viz., loans for consumer durables, loans for housing and other personal loans. During 1999-00, the total personal loans outstanding of the banks in India was Rs. 51,639 crores, which was increased to Rs. 1,79,087 crores in 2003-04. On a careful analysis, it is evident that the loan to consumer durables other personal loans were declined while the loans for housing was increased considerably. In 1999-00 the other personal loans were 58.74 per cent of the total personal loan amount outstanding, which was declined to 50 per cent during 2003-04, while the loans for housing has increased from 35.87 per cent to 47.66 per cent during the same period. The details are given in table 3.

Table 3
Personal Loan outstanding and its breakups among all bank groups (in %)

Items	*1999-00*	*2000-01*	*2001-02*	*2002-03*	*2003-04*
Personal Loans O/s (Rs in Crores)	51639	65940	82518	113942	179087
Break-ups thereof	%	%	%	%	%
Loans for consumer durables	5.39	5.25	3.89	2.83	2.35
Loans for housing	35.87	38.54	39.78	43.06	47.66
Other Personal loans	58.74	56.21	56.32	54.11	50.00
Total	100	100	100	100	100

*Source:*Compiled from CMIE September 2005

CONCLUSION

Credit to the Personal finance sector is a promising avenue for growth in banking industry today. The economic transformation was also reflected in the banking finance sector also, mainly in the industrial finance and trade sectors. These were the areas where banks and financial institutions had extended a large part of their retail loans. But now banks see great potential in marketing housing loans, vehicle loans and other personal loans where the default rate is comparatively low. The penetration of banks to retail lending has increased considerably which were under the control of specialized institutions. Increased consumerism, easy accessibility towards taking loans, and low rate of interest are the factors which are tempting people to avail loans. The increased security requirements and sentimental attachment towards the dream house or car, which are translated to lower rate of NPA among these sectors. Moreover banks are selective about customers i.e., people who are capable of proving their repayment capacity alone can avail loan from a bank. All these factors have resulted in increased competition among the banks, which has resulted in shifting from the conventional lending portfolio to the personal loan segment.

17

SUSTAINABLE DEVELOPMENT AND WATERSHED MANAGEMENT

–A Case Study of Managundi Project in Dharwad District of Karnataka

L. T. Nayak and B. Hymavathi Reddy***

INTRODUCTION

India has made significant strides in economic development including agricultural development and by 2015, it is poised to be the third largest economy in the world after U.S and China. The green revolution and extension of area under cultivation have made India self-sufficient in food from being a net importer in the past. Ironically however, the problem of poverty still persists. The government has initiated various poverty alleviation programmes to counter the problem but still every third Indian is below the poverty line.

Incidence of poverty is greater in rural areas as two thirds of the country's population is dependent on agriculture. With the increase in population the pressure has further increased on agricultural land.

Semi-arid lands constitute more than two thirds of cultivable land in India. They account for about 42 per cent of the country's food production. Hardly one fourth of the cultivable area is under irrigation and the remaining three fourths of the land is dependent on rainfall. Similar conditions exist in Karnataka state which has the second largest drought-

* Senior Scale Lecturer, Department of Geography, Karnatak Science College, Dharwad, Karnataka.

** Reader (Retd), Department of Studies in Geography, Karnatak University, Dharwad, Karnataka.

prone area after Rajasthan. Even if there is one year of drought crops fail and farmers are in distress. Continued drought over a period of 2 or 3 years leaves them in abject poverty.

Table 1
Poverty in India 1951-97 (head count-%)

Survey Period	*Rural*	*Urban*	*National*
Aug 51-Nov52	47.32	35.46	45.31
Julu 60-Aug61	45.30	44.65	45.27
July 65-June66	57.60	52.90	56.71
July 70-June71	54.84	44.78	52.88
July 77-June78	50.60	40.50	48.36
July 86-June87	38.81	34.29	37.69
July 90-June91	36.43	32.76	35.49
July 93-June94	36.66	30.57	35.04
Jan 97-Dec97	35.69	29.99	34.40

Source: World Bank 2000b: 149

In Karnataka the Kharif season contributes substantially to agricultural production and this depends largely on the southwest monsoon rainfall-its quantum, timeliness and its performance over time.

When the southwest monsoon fails there in very poor inflow into the tanks (an important source of irrigation) and some of them completely dry up. Even the ground water is depleted to very low levels. Karnataka has experienced consecutive droughts for the past three years and farmers, unable to pay the huge accumulated debts and feed their families resorted to suicide. Karnataka is also facing serious problems with regard to cattle fodder and it had to import it from, as far as Punjab and Haryana. Many of the farmers had to sell their cattle to slaughter houses and many of them migrated to other areas in search of livelihood.

The basic strategy needed to help the farming community is to inculcate farming sector from the vagaries of monsoons. Conservation of basic natural resources-land and water, flora and fauna are also necessary for agricultural development. All these and improvement in human resource development can be brought about by a well thought out and planned watershed development strategy.

Watershed development refers to the conservation, regeneration and the judicious use of natural resources including land, water, plants, and animals withina watershed, whereas a 'Watershed' is a geographical area that drains to a common point, making it an attractive unit for inputs and technical efforts in the conservation of soil and maximum utilization of surface and subsurface water for crop production (Palanisami).

Water-shed management tries to bring about the best possible balance in the environment between natural resources on the one side and human and other resources on the other, through proper planning strategies leadership training programmes and others (Reddy and Murthy).

The government of Karnataka has given a great deal of importance to watershed development and in fact has set up a separate department for watershed development to implement Karnataka Water Shed Development Programme and National water shed Development Programme for Rainfed Areas (NWDPRA). One of these programmes is the Sujala Watershed Development Programme (SWDP) under world Bank aid. The aims of SWDP are conservation of water through tanks, improving the existing ones by desilting, improving the ground water table, soil conservation, increasing agricultural productivity, area development through forestry, horticulture, bee keeping, fodder production and increasing grazing lands. SWDP also lays emphasis on non-agricultural activities, empowerment of women, formation of Self Help Groups (SHGs), development of tribals and vulnerable groups and above all poverty alleviation.

As people's participation is essential, the government has realized the importance of NGOs in the area and the SWDP has been entrusted to the India Development Service (IDS). The IDS has been working in the rural areas for community organization, Self Help Groups, human and animal health, waste land development, reutilizing local health traditions, agriculture, environment protection and related concerns, management, development education and net working and was considered as suitable and ideal for the achievement of the goals.

Earlier the approach was top down approach which did not have many success stories basically because the entire stress was on biophysical aspects without proper regard for socio economic aspects and community participation. Now, the approach is bottom up for successful implementation of the watershed programme.

As the Sujala water shed covers too a large area i.e. 4,26,968.58 hectares and 1270 villages therefore only Managundi sub water shed has been taken up for the present study.

OBJECTIVES

The broad objectives are:

1. To study the community participation and Self Help Groups, (SHG) Users Groups (UG) and Watershed associations (WA).
2. A detailed study of the protection and conservation measures of soil and moisture which include bunding, leveling, terracing, vegetation barriers, water harvesting structures such as ponds, nalla bunds, small dams, percolation ponds etc.
3. To Examine whether water level in the wells and tanks increased due to the water shed development.
4. To evaluate the impact of watershed development on irrigation development cropping pattern, forest, fodder, fuel, horticulture.
5. To assess the socio-economic status of the people in the village by watershed development programme.
6. To evaluate the impact of watershed development on animal resources.

HYPOTHESES

The following hypotheses have been framed to be tested in the field in order to achieve the objectives.

1. The protection and conservation measures of water harvesting increase the water level of the water bodies.
2. Community participation and self-help groups improve the socio-economic status of the agricultural labours, small and marginal farmers of the village.

3. Proper watershed management would enhance the area under irrigation and brings about changes in the cropping pattern.
4. The watershed development and management has its positive impact on the service sectors and also on animal resource of the region.

METHODOLOGY

The present study consists of primary and secondary data used to evaluate the impact of Sujala watershed project on dry forming. Secondary data has been collected from World Bank report-2000, Department of Agriculture, Census book 2001, Office of the Sujala water shed project. This helps to under stand the cropping pattern, horticulture, forest, animal resources, socio-Economic status of the beneficiaries, water levels of wells, tanks and small dams.

Primary data was collected from both beneficiaries and people involved with the project of 7 micro watershed projects and primarily IDS staff and farmers. The information was collected through personal interaction with individuals and, group discussion. The beneficiaries and non beneficiaries were contacted in the villages of the micro watershed. Further the structures/activities like check dams, nalabunds, vegetation bunds, agro forestry, horticulture etc, were taken in to account to assess their sustainability.

STUDY AREA

The Managundi sub watershed falls under Dharwad taluk in Dharwad district and located in the north western part of Karnataka with a geographical area of 5090 hectares, of which 3787.2 hectares of land is identified by the Sujala Water Shed project for development purpose. It consists of seven micro watershed namely Benakankatti, Managundi, Mansur Nigadi, Nuggikeri, Salakinkoppa and Yerikoppa with the total population of 12,823 residing in 2152 houses (Fig 1). The study area falls under semi arid zone. During the year 2000-2003 it had experienced a wide spread drought but in the year 2003-04 it recorded an average rainfall of 715 mm, the soils are red loamy in which cotton jowar, groundnut, sunflower and horticulture crops are grown.

Fig. 1

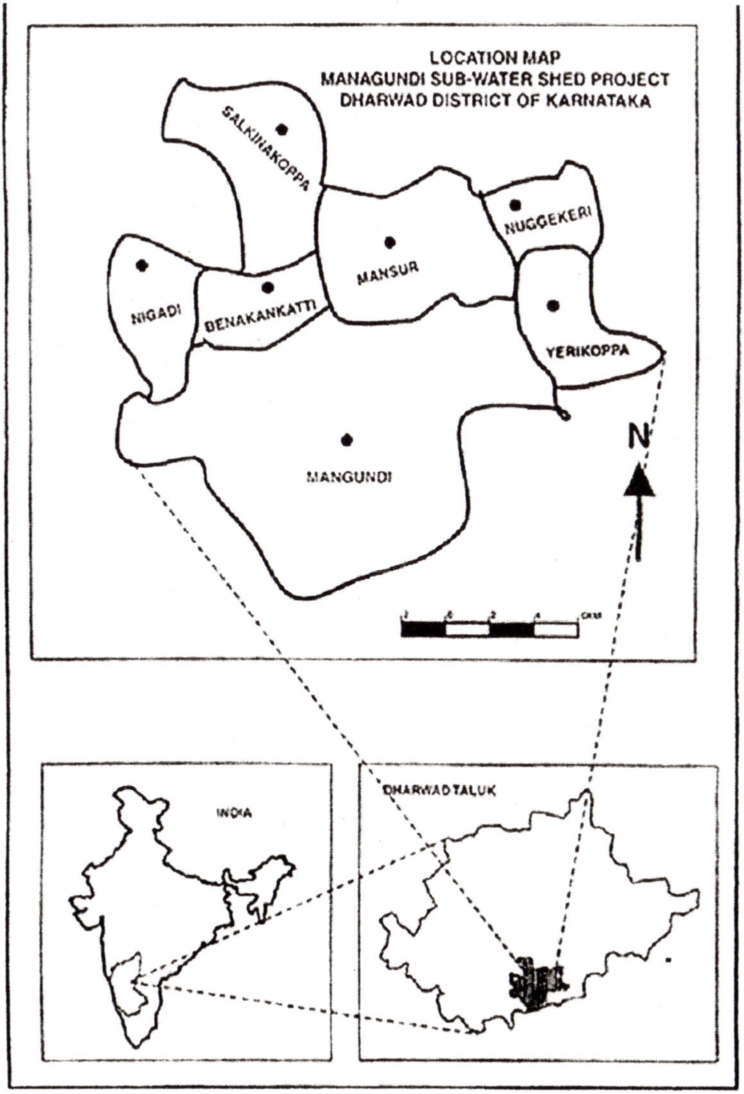

MANAGUNDI-ONGOING WATERSHED-DISCUSSION

Managundi wathershed implemented under Sujala Watershed project since 15-06-2002, covers seven villages. Out of the total

Table 2

General Information of Watershed Area

Sl.No. micro watershed	Name of the geographical area	Total Popu (2004) (in he)	Small land holders	Farmers: Marginal land holders	Farmers: Total	Land less labour	Land use in hectars: Dry land	Land use in hectars: Irrigated land	Land use in hectars: Barren
1. Benakankotti	1043.1	1276	95	72	167	54	895.1	88	60
2. Mangngundi	2896.0	2979	311	192	533	150	1945	88	883
3. Mansur	1841.34	2861	131	35	166	146	1384.11	3723	421
4. Nigadi	2009.3	2313	101	95	196	120	1038.15	121.15	944
5. Nuggikeri	444.48	888	70	41	111	57	396.28	8.2	40
6. Salkinkoppa	874.6	1214	60	31	91	136	423.6	11	230
7. Yerikoppa	729.0	1292	108	50	158	68	676	18	35
Total	9637.82	12823	876	516	1421	731	6757.4	4057.35	2593

Table 3

Area Under Sub Watershed (in hectares)

Arable Land under agriculture	Forest	Horticulture	Non-Avarble land	Area debated due to hillock, residential lay out, By pass and land occupied by K. University	Total
2983 (78.76)	145 (3.82)	659 (17.40)	433	870	5090

Source: Watershed project office-2004

watershed area about 870 hectors of land was deleted due to hillock land occupied by Karnataka University, residential layout, By pass and about 433 hectares of land non arable. Therefore the effective area fit for treatment is 3787 hectares. Out of the total watershed area 78.76 percent (2893 hectares) is for cultivation of crops, 17.40 percent (659 hectars) of land for horticulature and 3.82 per cent (145 hectars) of land for afforestration.

Changes in Cropping Pattern: The soils in the watershed area are red and medium black in which single crops are grown. It is interesting to mention that after the implementation of watershed project mixed cropping pattern has been practiced jowar with tur, groundnut with millets, cotton with sunflower, cotton with flowers and vegetables etc. The watershed area had 290 hectares of land under forest. It has been increased to 659 hectares due to horticulture plantations (Table 3). There are 1419 land holders in the watershed area, of which 63.77 per cent (905) belongs to small farmers and 36.22 per cent (514) marginal farmers (Table 2).

Socio-Economic Changes of Land less Labours: There are few people belonging to services sectors like carpenters (6) Dairy farmers (238) cattlegrazers/shepherds (95) incense stick makers (1) , Teastall owners (4), Tailors (23), grocery (19), fruit sellers (6) potters (6), Vegetable sellers (7) etc (Table 4). These people are helped and financed by the voluntary organizations conserved to watershed project. Like self help groups (SHG-83) and area groups (AG-40). As a result of these programmes their economic status has been improved.

Table 4
Service Sectors implemented by Watershed Project

Dairy farmers	*Cattle gazers*	*Tailors*	*Grocery*	*Veget able sellers*	*Pottery*	*Fruit sellers*	*Tea stall*	*Insense stick maker*	*Others*
238	95	23	19	7	6	6	4	1	14

Source: Watershed project office-Managundi

After implementation of watershed project in the Managundi village, the livestock population has increased to 6599 (Table 5).

Table 5
Livestock Population-2004

Bullock	*Buffalo*	*Goat*	*Cow*	*Sheep*	*Fowls*	*Total*
1873	1521	840	728	802	825	6599

Source: Watershed project office-Managundi

Under the training component the villagers are trained on various issues like arresting soil erosion, raising horticultural crops and other agricultural activities in the water shed area.

ARABLE LAND TREATMENT UNDER CONSERVATION MEASURES

As for the arable land treatment, various conservation methods have been introduced and adopted under watershed project such as earthern bund, farm ponds, divergent channels, bench terraces, Nalabund, Checkdam, percolation tank, repair of old tank, open wells etc. The earthen bund occupied prime project during the year 2003 and 2004 followed by divergent channels. The total expenditure under various heads is shown below. It is interesting to note that the expenditure on conservation measures and production system under arable land exceeds other activities in the water shed. The items covered under the production system are crop demonstration, agro forestry, dry land horticulture, home stead gardens etc.

Table 6
Conservation Measures-2004

Sl. No.	*Conservation measures*	*Total no's/length*	*Total expenditure incured*
1	Earthen bund	2,72,825*	55,57,109
2	Form pond	301	78,08,153
3	Diversion Channel	41,060*1	8,24,665
4	Bench terracing	305*1	2,60,971
5	Nala revitment	159	2,24,725
6	Check dam	5	5,43,795
7	Percolation tank	40	24026
8	Old tank repair	6	-
9	Nala bund	6	16,82,095
	Total		1,69,25,539

Note *1 figures in running meters

Augmentation in ground water: Before the implementation of the conservation measures there were many dug wells, wells, ponds and tanks of varying depth and width below ground level. Many of them were driedup. Similarly three borewells were drilled but there was no trace of water. But it has been noticed that after the implementation of various methods of conservation the same three failed old borewells received water of 2" and the water level of old wells, tanks and ponds has been raised.

Financial Achievements towards Different Activities: The major activities under taken in the watershed area are soil and water conservation, horticulture, Forestry, livestock and miscellaneous and the total expenditure incurred for these activities are Rs. 66,78,030, 14,72,708, 3,50,057, 1,03,200 and 15,180 respectively.

MAJOR FINDINGS

There is no doubt that the Mangundi sub watershed development programme has a visible impact on arable as well as non-arable lands, socio-economic condition of the people who have actively participated and availed the benefits of the programme.

1. Out of the total watershed area, 17.09 per cent of the area is not available for treatment due to hillock, residential layout, Bypass and land acquired by Karnatak University. Therefore, effective area for treatment account for 82.91 per cent of the total area of which arable and non-arable is about 78.76 per cent and 21.24 per cent respectively.
2. Out of the total landholdings 63.79 per cent belong to small farmers and 36.22 per cent marginal farmers.
3. Before the implementation of watershed programme, farmers were growing single crop like cotton, jowar, sunflower ground nut etc. But now mixed cropping pattern is practiced notably jowar with tur, cotton with sunflower, ground nut with millets.
4. About 500 people improved their socio-economic conditions by availing financial benefits from the

watershed programme by starting different service sectors.

5. Livestock population has been increased to 6599 and their producets ie. Milk mostly supplied to Dharwad city.
6. There are several conservation measures that have been adopted like earthern bunding, Diversion channel, Nala bund etc., for arable land treatment.
7. Water level of the earlier open wells, ponds small tanks and bore wells has been raised due to conservation of water in the watershed area.
8. In some villages few farmers already planted horticultural crops, like mango, agro forestration like teak, neem and further distribution is on in the other villages too and about 17 per cent of land is covered by horticulture crops.
9. The total expenditure made towards Horticulture is 35 per cent, Forest plants 30 per cent, soil and water conservation 20 per cent, water storage structure 10 per cent.
10. At the government level the commissioners are frequently changed or transferred this adversely affects the smooth functioning of the watershed programmes as each one gives different directions for implementation of the programme.
11. It has been noticed that people from different departments like agriculture, forest, horticulture etc, are not actively participating and co-operating with the representations of voluntary organizations of watershed development.

SUGGESTIONS

1. There should be co-operation between the various Govt. departments and the representative of the voluntary organizations.
2. Departmental people must visit frequently the watershed area are and examine the progress of the different sectors. For example forest department people

must inspect whether the seedling supplied have survived or not. Agricultural department people must examine the arable land taken for treatment.

REFERENCE

Agarwal S. K. (1997), Environmental Issues & Themes.

C. T. Pawar (2003), Assessment of watershed development programm: A Micro Level Empirical Analysis.

Dharwad District at a Glance 2004

Govt of Karnataka, Directorate of Economics and Statistics (2004), Socio- Economic Review and District Statistical abstract of Dharwad District.

Govt. of India, Irrigation and power Dept (2002), Report of the Irrigation Commission Vol. I & II.

Reddy and Murthy (1967), Regional Geography of Mysore.

Vrishali Deosthali (2003), Hierarchical Grouping of sub-watersheds in Bhima-Basin for Deepak Pillai soil conservation planning.

World Bank Report (2000).

18

SOIL RESOURCES AND SOIL EROSION PROBLEMS: A CASE STUDY OF BELGAUM DISTRICT

Suryakant N. Waghamare & S. I. Biradar***

INTRODUCTION

Soil is a natural medium for plant growth. Soil supplies nutrients for growing plants and plants in turn serve fodder for animal and food and fiber for man. Soils mainly being the resultant products of the parent rock materials have a high resemblance in matter of texture, colour and contents. Soil has been considered as one of the most valuable natural resource on which agricultural economy largely depends. It is the quality of soil that determines the capability of a land. Thus, soil alone can determine both land capability and land suitability. Such a valuable natural resource has been subjected to degradation due to soil erosion. The soil erosion particularly in agricultural fields has been the results of farm mismanagement and wrongful farm practices and unmanaged surface run-off etc., during the last many decades. Hence, the conservation of soil has become a greatest necessity to preserve the soil fertility.

STUDY AREA

Belgaum district is being located in the North – Western part of the Karnataka State. It extends between 15° – 23' to 16° – 58'

* Guest Lecturer, P.G.Department of Geography, Karnatak University, Dharwad, Karnataka.

** Reader in Geography, Karnatak University, Dharwad, Karnataka.

North latitude and 74° – 05' to 75° – 28' East longitude. The district consists 10 talukas and covers an area of 13, 415 sq. kms. Approximately 7 percent of total geographical area of Karnataka State. The total population of Belgaum district is 42,07,200 in the year 2001. The district generally receives heavy amount of annual rainfall. However, the district also experiences moderate drought conditions intermediately.

OBJECTIVES

The main objectives of this paper are 1 to analyse the distribution of soil resources and 2 the soil erosional problems in various parts of the Belgaum district.

Belgaum District Soil

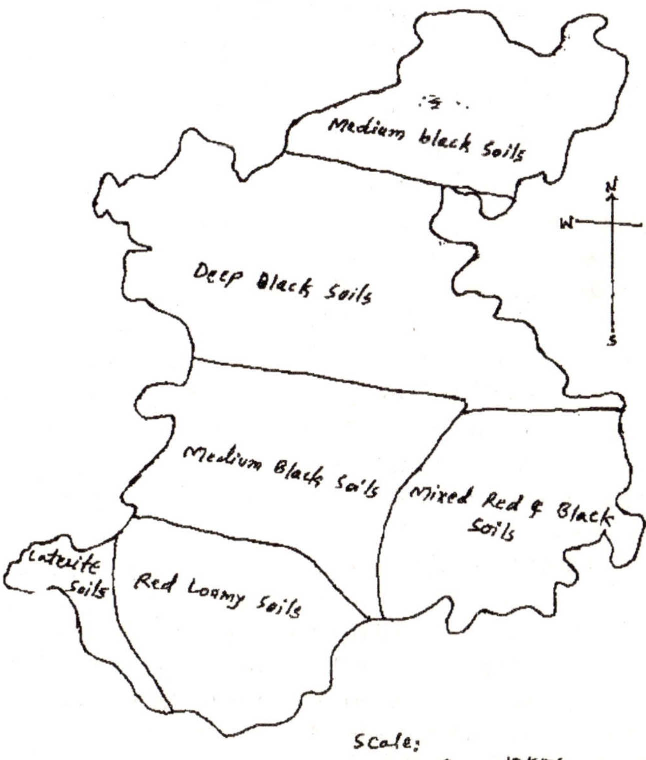

Source: Central Ground Water Board

METHODOLOGY

The present study has been mainly based on the secondary sources of information. The information has been collected from government and semi-government departments. The collected data has been analysed with help of maps and statistical diagrams. The analysis however also based on the field observation by the researcher.

ANALYSIS OF THE TEXT

The district consists rich soils like, medium black soils, deep black soils, mixed red and black soils, red loamy soils and literate soils etc.

Medium Black Soils: These soils are found in the Athani taluka and the central part of the district, i.e., Southern part of Gokak and Hukeeri taluka. Northern parts of the Belgaum taluka, North-East side of Bailhogal taluka and North-West side of Soundatti taluka of Belgaum district. These soils are moderately deep to deep, dark to very dark, grayish brown, dark reddish, brown or black in colour.

Deep Black Soils: These soils are distributed in the talukas of Chikkodi, Raibag and Northern side of Gokak and Hukkeri talukas. It occurs on very gently sloping to nearly level or flat topography in low lands of Deccan Trap and Limestone Regions. These soils are very deep, dark grayish, brown to very dark gray or black in colours. Deep black soils are also found occurring on a variety of (Geological) parent materials like genesis schist, sedimentary rocks of mixed origin including transported soils occurring in the basins of major river valleys.

Mixed Red and Black Soils: Generally, these soils occur in the talukas of Ramdrug and South-East part of Saundatti talukas. It is usually occurring on gently undulating plains or on complex geological materials comprising genesis, Dharwar schist and sedimentary rock formations. Usually the red soils resemble the red sandy soils of midland region in Physio-Chemical properties and black soils resemble the medium and deep black soils in Physio-Chemical characteristics.

Red Loamy Soils: These soils are found in Southern parts of Belgaum and North-Eastern side of Bailhongal and 1/3rd part of Southern side of Khanapur taluka. On hilly undulating land, granites, granitic, gneisses and Dharwar schist. These soils are very deep, dark brown to dark red, sandy loam to clay loam on the surface.

Laterite Soils: These soils are found in the western parts of Khanapur and occur on gently undulating, rolling and plain to hilly topography of peninsular gneiss's and Dharwar schist regions, occupying areas as a long ship along the western coast in the coastal high rainfall. These are deep to very deep, yellowish red to dark red, reddish brown or brown in colours.

SOIL EROSION PROBLEMS

The removal of organic matter and plant food from the top layer and its leaching by the agents of denudation is called soil erosion. Soil erosion is caused by running water on sloping lands, by winds over the drier areas, erosion is influenced by the nature of the soil, by the length and steepness of the slope, by the climate, especially by rainfall and by the crops grown. Some soils wash more easily than others. Erosion takes place with an accelerated rate on long slopes, particularly steep ones, also agricultural practices and the crops grown do have their influence on soil erosion, as the crops grown vary in the degree of exposure of soil. For example – Cotton, Maize, Beans, Tobacco, Potatoes, Cabbage and most of the other vegetables are soil exposing crops.

The severe soil erosion class is observed in 5.38 percent (107-326 sq. kms) of the Athani taluka area. This soil erosion class is found in the areas of Kotbagi, Bannur and Kannal of Athani taluka. In Bailhongal taluka 29.58 percent (332.00592 sq. kms.) of the total geographical area comes under the severe soil erosion class, which is found in areas of Dodawad, Godikatti, Govankop, Bidarguddi, Madanbhavi, Mutwad, Murkibhavi, Kakkunadi, Yadguddi, Hiremale, Marikatti, Hannikeri, Bharanatti, Sutgatti, Mattikop, Hogarati, Kuiynatti and Deshnur of Bailhogal taluka. The severe soil erosion class is noticed in

391.45 sq. kms. And it accounts for 37.74 percent of the Belgaum taluka. This severe soil erosion class is seen in the villages of Hosgenatti, Rajhangad, Yarmble, Munoli, Belvatti, Navage, Kattanbhavi, Bambarge, Handignur, Kednur and Kurihal of Belgaum.

Belgaum District Soil Erosion

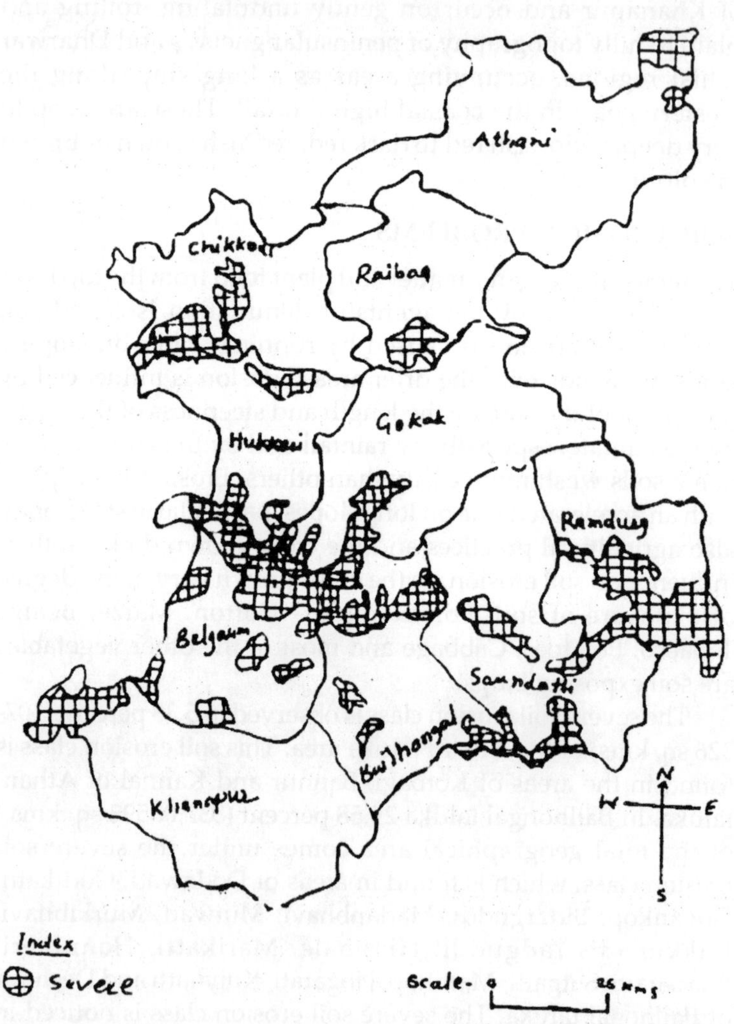

The Chikkodi taluka 26.6 percent (330.826 sq. kms.) of the taluka area come under the very severe soil erosion class, which is found in the villages of Boral, Hattarwad, Toranhalli, Nainglaj, Walki, Pattankudi, Kothali, Lakhanapur, Jatrat, Akol, Yemgarni and Galatga villages. In Gokak taluka (299. 68 sq. kms.) 19.46 percent of the taluka area is under the severe soil erosion class, which is found in the areas of Golkundargi, Ankalgi, Dumurbinatti, Kanageri, Kundargi, Pachapur, Kadabgatti and Urbinatti villages of the Gokak taluka. Severe soil erosion class is found in 12.87 percent (225.08 sq. kms.) of Khanapur taluka. This type of are is seen in the Hollund, Sade, chorla, Kankumbi and Kumbargi villeges of the taluka. An area of 9.82 percent (94.19 sq. kms.) of the Raibag taluka land is under severe soil erosion class. This class of soil is found in the areas of Kankanwadi, Devankatti, Bhendwad and Katakbhavi villages of Raibag taluka.

The Ramdurg taluka covered 29.83 percent (362.64331 sq. kms) of the taluka under severe soil erosion class, and it is found in areas of Chikkop, Kalhal, Jaulhal, Kittur, Mullur, Kallur, Jalikatti, Revdikop, Auradi, Tadsi, Hosker, Shavrikol, Kolchi, Halgatti, Turnur, Sunnal, Bannur, Godachi, Totagatti, Chandargi, Rokkadkatti and Murkatnal villages and Ramdurg town of Ramdurg taluka. Saundatti taluka has 22.66 percent (358.173025 sq. kms.) area under the severe soil erosion class, which is noticed in the Inam Hongal, Chikk Ulligeri, H. Ulligeri, Betsur, Yadahalli, Sanreskop, Marikatti, Sirsangi, Hallur, Basidone, Sindolgi, Tegihal, Mallur, Tallur Halki, Ramapurvatti, Sumapur, Sogal, Chachadi, Harugoppa and Guntur areas of Soundatti taluka.

CONCLUSION

The most serious forms of soil erosion in Belgaum district are sheet, rill and gully erosion. A cover of vegetation and soil granulation helps to prevent the detachment of soil particles and agricultural practices and the crops grown do have their influence on soil erosion, as the crops grown vary in the degree of exposure of soil. For example – Crops like grasses pastures and small grain crops are soil protecting. The schemes implemented under this head are contour bounding, terracing of land and afforestation for soil conservation. Moisture conservation in the soil assumes particular importance in low and precarious rainfall areas. Bounding is specially beneficial to the areas as it combines in it the triple advantage of prevention of sheet erosion of land, conservation of top soil moisture and augmentation of water supply to the water bearing strata in the underground, also mechanical measures consists of construction of mechanical barriers across the direction of water flow to retard or arrest the runoff and thereby reduce soil and water losses. Contour bounds, stone bounds, contour border strips and zing terraces are impounding type structures that retain the runoff while graded bounds, graded border strips, graded trenches and bench terraces are drainages type structure designed to drain runoff at none erosive velocity.

19

GLOBALIZATION AND ITS IMPACT ON BANKING SERVICES IN KERALA - A STUDY

Benson Kunjukunju* and Mohan P. Philip**

INTRODUCTION

Kerala can reasonably claim to have successfully tackled the first generation problems like illiteracy, low enrolment of girls in schools, high infant and maternal mortality rate, low expectation of life at birth and related indicators of under development. The National Geographic has referred to Kerala as one of the ten paradises in the world. The UN had projected Kerala as a role model for education, health care and social welfare. Kerala the "Gods own Country" was among the three finalists for best tourism spot in a survey conducted by the US based 'World Tourism Council'. In spite of the commendable position occupied by the Kerala in Human Development Index (HDI) it does not figure any where on the list of economically prosperous States. There are many people who have not benefited from the famous " Kerala Model of Development" and they remain very poor and deserve special support. They are the tribals, traditional fishermen, scheduled castes and people employed in traditional sectors like coir, cashew, handloom etc. Poverty among these groups is rampant. In the "Kerala Model of Development" social development has preceded economic development.

* P.G. & Research Department of Commerce, St.Thomas College, Kohencherry-689641, Kerala.

** P.G. & Research Department of Commerce, St.Thomas College, Kohencherry-689641, Kerala.

Today banks have become an integral part of our life. There was a time when only city dwellers alone were able to enjoy their services. The late sixties witnessed fundamental changes in commercial banking in India. Now banks offer services even to a common man and their activities extend to areas hitherto unbanked. Financial sector reforms, globalization and integration of world's financial markets have increased the level of competition in Indian banking industry. Improved customer service has become very important for banks to survive and to grow in the emerging deregulated financial markets. Consequently, banks are under increasing pressure to offer today what customers would expect tomorrow. Customers of banks are of varied types with different expectations and attitudes and come from divergent socio economic and cultural backgrounds. The customer will bank with the bank where they get satisfactory services. With out satisfying the customer no bank can grow in the competitive business world. The banks now compete with one another to offer value added services to customers to widen their client bases.

Following are some of the important products and services offered to the customers by the banks as a result of the financial sector reforms. ATM, Shared ATM networks, Any Where Banking, International Debit cum ATM Card, Home Banking, Mobile Banking, Internet Banking, Travel Currency Card, Credit Card, Corporate Credit Card, One window Service, Mobile Phone Recharge Facility, Priority Banking, Insurance Products, Investment and Financial Advisory Services, Demat Account, 24 Hour Tele- Banking, At Par Cheque Facility, Electronic Fund Transfer, Electronic Clearing Service, MICR Cheque Processing, Banking Ombudsmen Scheme, Computerized Statements, Payment of Insurance Premium , Utility Bills etc.

GROWTH OF COMMERCIAL BANKS IN KERALA

Kerala has an excellent banking network. As on 31st March 2005 there were 49 Commercial Banks and 2 Regional Rural banks (358 branches) having a total of 3044 branches spread across the State. During 1969 -2005, the growth of commercial banks branches was far below the national average (8 fold) and recorded only 5.5 fold increase with a compound growth rate of 5.8 per cent. It occupies the eleventh slot with respect to the number of bank branches (5.1% of total branches). Most of the branches in Kerala are in urban and semi urban areas, the rural areas having only 10.7 per cent of the branches. The rural branches in the State represent only 1.1 percent of the total rural branches in the country. It is estimated that about 5 per cent of the total deposits in the country are mobilized by the commercial banks of Kerala. The per capita deposits in Kerala is 50 per cent higher than the national figure. During March 2004 the total advance given by all commercial banks in Kerala was Rs.31,867 crores as against Rs.7,797 crores in 1995 and 15,941 crores in 2000. The growth of advances was 300 percent over a period of ten years while it was 450 percent at the national level. The credit deposit ratio of Kerala is 6 per cent less than the CD ratio at the all India level.

STATEMENT OF THE PROBLEM

The late sixties witnessed spectacular changes in commercial banking in India. The Indian banking industry has undergone major changes after liberalization and globalization reforms in the 1990's. In 1993, Reserve Bank of India allowed the entry of foreign banks in to India. The entry of new private sector banks and foreign banks posed a challenge to the monopoly hitherto enjoyed by the nationalized banks and old private sector banks. Economic liberalization, globalization, information technology revolution, changing customer requirements and increasing competition have posed a lot of challenges to the existing banking sector India.

E- Banking enables the customers to carry on basic banking transactions through PC or LAPTOP by remaining in their houses and offices. With E-Banking, the brick and mortar structure of the traditional banking gets converted into a click and portal model thereby giving real shape to the concept of virtual banking. Today's banking is no longer confined to branches. Customers are being provided with additional delivery channels which are more convenient to customers and are cost effective to the banks. The new private sector and foreign banks have expanded banking services through Automated Teller Machines, internet banking, telephone banking, mobile banking, home banking, electronic fund transfer etc.

Customers are the life blood of any business. Now the major objective of both private and public sector Indian banks is to attract a large customer base by offering more delivery channels, giving more importance to customer relationships by way of healthy maintaining customer relationships. In banking industry quality of customer services is of utmost importance. It is in this context that this study has been carried out to find out the level of awareness and satisfaction of customers on various banking services in the light of financial sector reforms in the country.

IMPORTANCE OF THE STUDY

Modern banking operations touches almost every segment of economic activity. The traditional Indian commercial banks at present faces major challenges in the form of competition from foreign banks and new generation private sector banks. The present study is an attempt to examine how far the old and new generation banks in Kerala have succeeded in popularizing their new banking services. The study also tries to evaluate the level of satisfaction of customers on banks and their various delivery channels. An increase in dealings between the bank and their customers shows the increased level of customer satisfaction. The customer will select bank only they are satisfied with its services. With out satisfying the customers no bank can survive when in the competitive business world. The present study will help the banks to understand awareness of customers on various banking services. The findings may also help the banks to widen their customer base and to detect the deficiencies in their present services. In view of the growing significance of banking services in the light of information technology revolution and globalization of financial activities the researcher feels that the present study can throw light on various problems experienced by both customers and banks and can be of use for policy formulation in this sphere.

OBJECTIVES OF THE STUDY

Following are the objectives framed for the study.

(1) To review the improvement in the functioning of commercial banks in Kerala in the pre and post liberalization period.

(2) To study and analyze the awareness of customers on various banking services provided by commercial banks in the post liberalization regime.

(3) To evaluate the level of satisfaction of customers on various services provided by the banks.

(4) To offer valuable suggestions on the basis of the study.

METHODOLOGY

The study is designed as an empirical one based on survey method. Data have been collected from both primary and secondary sources. The main thrust of the study is to understand the awareness of customers on new banking services and also to measure the level of satisfaction of customers on various services provided by commercial banks. For the purpose of examining the awareness and level of satisfaction on various banking services at the micro- level, a multi- stage random sampling technique was employed. In the first stage district were selected, in the second and third stages banks and customers were selected.

PRIMARY DATA

Primary data had been collected from 60 customers of Four Commercial Banks in Kollam city. Data had been collected by administering, a structured interview schedule.

SECONDARY DATA

Secondary data had been collected from text books, periodicals, newspapers, research journals, hypertext etc.

SELECTION OF SAMPLES

In Kollam city, there are 54 branches of commercial banks and four branches of district co operative banks. Of these 54 branches 15 are branches of private sector banks and 39 that of public sector banks. Of the 15 private sector bank branches 4 are branches of new generation banks and 11 are branches of old private banks. From the old private banks and new generation banks one branch each and from the public sector banks two branches were selected at random by using lottery method. In total Four Commercial Bank branches in the Kollam city were selected for the study. The banks selected for study are Federal Bank, UTI Bank, State Bank of India and State Bank of Travancore.

In order to elicit information from the customers about each of the selected branches fifteen customers were selected at random. The investigator waited in front of the branches to collect information from the customers. The customers were interviewed systematically, by the investigator in front of the branches at dates convenient to the researchers. The customers who were willing and ready to answer questions and prepared to spare sufficient time for this purpose were identified and interviewed.

MEASUREMENT OF VARIABLES

Measurement of Level of Awareness of Customers on New Banking Services Introduced as a Result of Financial Sector Reforms

For measuring the awareness level of customers about new services, Ten important banking services \ products were identified. The variables are identified by the researchers on the basis of available literature and discussions with banks officials. All questions in the schedule are qualitative in nature. Customers would mark '0' for no awareness, '1' for awareness and '2' for full awareness. The following are the variables identified by the researchers for the study.

(1) Automated Teller Machine (ATM)

An important modern technology which is gaining popularity among customers is the use of ATMs. This is a modern technology introduced by the banks to enable the customers to have access to money round the clock and also throughout the year. The ATM enables a customer to withdraw and deposit cash and cheque, check balance in account, print mini account statement, transfer funds between own accounts, payment of utility bills, recharge prepaid mobile card etc. By the end of 1990, Indian private and public sector banks have come up with their own ATM networks under the initiative of the Indian Bank Association in Mumbai. The Bank of India is the first nationalized bank to provide ATM facilities to the customers in Mumbai. Since the services are available 24 hours, the customers are fully satisfied. ATMs have brought about a great change in the quality of service rendered to the customers. It is against this back ground the researchers identified that it is an important variable to study the awareness and satisfaction level of customers.

(2) Any where Banking

Modern banking is more information based, speedy and border less due to the impact of E-Revolution. Any where banking is a modern technology introduced by connecting all branches of a bank through a net work to enable the customers to carry on banking transactions across the country. Earlier banking operations of a customer were restricted to the particular branch in which the account was maintained. With the introduction of this facility by banks customers can operate their account in any branch of the bank across the country during banking hours. This facility is also becoming immensely popular among customers and has been given due importance in this study.

(3) Internet Banking

E- Banking is basically internet based. With the internet banking facility the customer of the bank is just a click away from the bank. The customers can check their account status, fund transfer, make bill payments, place online requests for new cheque books, review term deposits etc. In addition, it enables the customers to conduct online trading, mutual fund purchases, online shopping, and payments to services such as insurance, electricity, telephone and mobile services across the country. Banking products and services such as deposits, remittances, credit card etc. as well as all important banking information's can be made available with easy access to customers on Internet. Customers can make use of these services with out being restricted by office hours, queues, tellers, and waiting. In view of the above facts, Internet banking facility is considered as an important variable.

(4) Credit Cards

Credit card or plastic money is a convenient medium of exchange. It enables its holder to purchase goods and services from the member establishments with out using hard money. Credit cards are made of plastic material and are designed to avoid the use of either cash or cheque. These cards also give the facility of credit to their holders. They can use them in all those establishments which have agreed to accept them. The credit card organizer makes payment to the concerned establishment once in a month and sends an invoice to the credit card holder for all his purchases of the previous month. Banks issue different types of credit cards and credit limit of each card varies. In India Central Bank of India was the first bank to introduce the credit card known as Central Card in the middle of 1981. Credit cards have found widespread acceptance in the metros and cities but are not popular in small towns and villages. This facility has become immensely popular since 1990 among all the customers and has been given due importance in this study.

(5) Mobile Baking

In traditional banking, customers have to visit the branch of the bank in person to carry on the basic banking transactions. E-banking is of great convenience to the customer. With Mobile banking, the concept of anytime, any where banking is literally at the fingertips of the customer. Mobile alerts such as debits and credits to the account, registered bill payment, inquiries like balance inquiry, last few transaction statements, demat account details, mobile banking password change etc. are made available to the customers through mobile phone at a nominal charge by the bank. It is against this background that mobile banking facility is taken as an important variable for measuring the level of awareness of customers.

(6) Bill Payment

E-banking opens new vistas of banking by way of providing enlarged, efficient, economic and quality service to the customers. With electronic banking, clients are able to deal with banks and get a lot of requests serviced through their desk top computers or through telephone. It facilitate the immediate payment of utility bills of customers such as electricity, water, telephone, mobile bills, payment of insurance premium, tuition fees, hostel fees of wards etc. Payment of utility bill is a novel technique adopted by banks since 1994 to attract customers. Hence it is considered as an important variable to assess the awareness level of customers.

(7) Banking Ombudsmen

Banking Ombudsmen Scheme was announced in June 1995 to protect the interest of customers and to redress their grievances. It is a quick and inexpensive facility. The main objective of this institution is to settle the complaints of customers with regard to banking services and to the satisfaction of customers. This scheme is applicable to all commercial and scheduled co-operative banks operating in India. The procedure for redressal starts with the lodgment of a complaint. Any person with a grievance against a bank can forward a complaint in writing to the Banking Ombudsmen either by himself or through his authorized agent. On receipt of the complaint as well as the information from the bank concerned, the Banking Ombudsmen will try to settle the complaint through an agreement between the complainant and the bank by way of conciliation or mediation. The concept of Ombudsmen is gaining importance and it is indeed a land mark institution in the history of Indian banking. Against this background the researchers take Ombudsmen scheme as an important variable.

(8) Insurance Products

Customers are being provided with additional delivery channels which are more convenient to customers and are cost effective to the banks. Commercial banks in association with insurance companies offer insurance products to its customers. It provides for coverage of insurance of personal accident, house-hold articles, jewellry, cash and other valuables against fire, robbery, flood, riots etc. and medical insurance product with cash less hospitalization and cash payment to meet incidental expenses, travel etc. This facility is also becoming very popular among the customers and has been given due importance in this study.

(9) Investment and Financial Advisory Services

Financial advisory services or personal finance solutions are provided by commercial bank to its customers. Through financial advisory services banks try to understand the investment requirements of their customers and prepare appropriate tailor-made financial solutions. Beyond merely advising the customers, the banks also help the customers to invest in a variety of instruments including mutual funds, RBI bonds, bonds of financial institutions, fixed deposits, insurance products, capital gain tax saving bonds etc. The banks also supply daily and weekly market roundups and quarterly newsletters to its customers. This is an innovative scheme introduced by commercial banks and the researchers considered it an important variable for study.

(10) Electronic Fund Transfer.

RBI started Electronic Fund Transfer (EFT) system in 1996. The system facilitated transfer of funds from one center to another across banks. The advantage of this system is that it facilitates transfer of funds on the next day of the day of transfer. At present an upper limit of Rs.25,000 has been set for individual transactions. This is also considered an important variable for study by the researchers.

MEASUREMENT OF LEVEL OF SATISFACTION ON BANKING SERVICES

For measuring the level of satisfaction of customers on various banking services, Ten variables were identified by the researchers. Five variables were selected from the new banking services (as a result of the financial reforms), (ranked 1st to 5th in Table I) and the five variables from the primary banking functions and services for retaining customers. Variables ranked 1st to 5th in Table I are (1) ATM facility, (2) Bill payment, (3) Financial and Investment Services, (4) Credit Card and

(5) Insurance products. Five other variables selected by the researchers for measuring the level of satisfaction are (1) Loan Processing Period (2)Cheque Processing Period (3) Employees Attitude, (4) Customer Conveniences and (5) Employee-Customer Relationship.

The customers of selected banks were required to indicate their level of satisfaction they derived from each variable. The customers expressed their level of satisfaction by stating as 'Excellent', 'Good', 'Satisfactory', 'Unsatisfactory' and 'No opinion'.

Loan Processing Period

The second important traditional function of a bank is advancing of loans to its customers. Loan processing period refers to the period taken by a bank for sanctioning loans. The period taken for sanction of loans vary from bank to bank and depends on the nature of loan, nature of securities offered, formalities and documents required etc. Customers expect speedy sanction of loans. But the bank take a reasonable time for sanction due to the procedural formalities. Undue delay in sanction of loans compels the borrower to follow up the loan application with frequent visits to the bank. Timely sanction of loan is considered as an important variable for measuring the customer satisfaction.

Cheque Processing Period

The commercial banks today enjoy the privilege of printing money in the form of cheques. The cheque currency is very popular in all places of commercial importance. In modern business world, the use of cheque to settle debts is found to be more convenient than the use of cash. A banker has an obligation to clear the cheque submitted by a customer with in a reasonable time. The variable 'cheque processing period' represent the time taken by the banker to clear the cheque submitted by a customer. Generally bankers take relatively more time for clearing the outstation cheques, but the customer expects a quick clearance. It is against this background that the researchers consider this variable as an important one for evaluating the customer satisfaction.

Attitude of the Employees

Each and every employee of a bank has a significant role to play in the success of the banking business. The attitude of the employees towards customers determines their ability to attract new customers, to retain existing customers and to create a goodwill about the bank among customers. The integrity, punctuality, loyalty and the way of interaction with the customers is of great significance in the present competitive world. Hence this variable is given due importance by the researchers to measure customer satisfaction.

Customer Conveniences

The customers of the bank expect some basic facilities at the bank premises at the time of availing banking service. These facilities are sufficient seating arrangements, furniture, pens, pins, drinking water, parking for vehicles, toilet, lighting, cleanliness etc. By availing these facilities customers can transact their business with out any hassles. Quality of customer convenience facilities are considered as an important variable by the researchers for measuring the customer satisfaction.

Employee-Customer Relationship

Today, the objective of a bank is to attract and retain a large customer base. This objective can be attained only by maintaining good customer relationship management, which implies the art of attracting, maintaining and enhancing customer relationships. Maintaining long term customer relationship is possible only by offering innovative and quality services to its customers . The researchers identified this variable as an important one for the growth of the banking industry and hence due importance is given to this in this study.

DISTRIBUTION OF RESPONDENTS ACCORDING TO THE LEVEL OF AWARENESS OF NEW BANKING SERVICES

Questions relating to the awareness of customers on banking services in the schedule are qualitative in nature. Customers would mark '0' for "no awareness", '1' for "awareness" and '2' for "full awareness".

The awareness level of customers about different banking services is ranked and depicted in Table 1.

Table 1
Awareness Level of Customers on New Banking Services

S. No.	Banking Services	State Bank of India Total Score	State Bank of India Rank	State Bank of Travan core Total Score	State Bank of Travan core Rank	Federal Bank Total Score	Federal Bank Rank	UTI Bank Total Score	UTI Bank Rank	Total Score Rank
1	ATM Facility	28	II	27	III	30	1	30	I	115(1)
2	Any Where Banking	12	III	11	IV	21	II	22	I	66(8)
3	Internet Banking	11	III	11	III	15	II	21	I	58(9)
4	Credit Cards	20	II	12	III	24	I	20	II	76(4)
5	Mobile Banking	6	III	5	IV	11	II	16	I	38(10)
6	Bill Payments	18	III	13	I	27	I	25	II	83(2)
7	Banking Ombudsmen	15	III	13	IV	18	II	21	I	67(7)
8	Insurance Products	22	I	16	III	18	II	I8	II	74(5)
9	Investment & Financial services	22	II	11	IV	19	III	25	I	77(3)
10	Electronic Fund Transfer	15	III	12	IV	20	II	22	I	69(6)

Source: Primary Data

From Table I it is clear that the customers of UTI Bank and Federal Bank are equally aware of "ATM facility" and ranked first. The second rank for awareness goes to customers of SBI and third to SBT. The survey further reveals that customers of new generation banks and private banks were more aware about ATM facility than the customers of nationalized banks. With regard to awareness of customers about "Any Where Banking" facility, the table shows that the customers of UTI Bank have the highest level of awareness followed by Federal Bank. SBI get rank number 3 and the least rank for awareness goes to SBT.

Table I shows the opinion of customers of selected banks about "Internet Banking". The customers of UTI Bank are to a great extent aware of this facility. Second rank for awareness of internet banking goes to customers of Federal Bank. But the customers of SBI and SBT are not well aware of this innovative facility. Regarding "Credit Cards" the customers of Federal Bank and SBI rank first and second for awareness. The customers of SBT are least aware of this service. It is clear from the table that the customers of all the selected banks are not well aware of the facility of "Mobile banking".

The awareness level of customers regarding the "Payment of various utility bills" the customers of Federal Bank are ranked first for awareness. The second rank for awareness goes to the customers of UTI and the third rank to SBI. The customers of SBT are least aware of this facility.

Table I further indicates the awareness of customers about the grievances and redressal mechanism. It is observed that customers of all banks are least aware about the "Banking Ombudsmen scheme". With regard to the awareness of customers about "Insurance products", the table shows that the customers of SBI have the highest level of awareness followed by customers of Federal Bank and UTI Bank. The least rank for awareness goes to SBT. Regarding "Investment and Financial Services" customers of UTI Bank and SBI are more aware than the customers of Federal Bank and SBT. The table further reveals the degree of awareness of customers about "Electronic Fund Transfer". The study discloses that the highest degree of awareness of customers about this facility is among customers of UTI Bank and second place goes to Federal Bank customers. The lowest degree of awareness goes to that of SBT customers.

Regarding the awareness level of customers about banking services, it is clear from Table I that the variable 'ATM' facility obtained a good response from customers and ranked first. The customers of both public sector and private sector banks are well aware about this facility. 'Bill payments' ranked second attract a good number of customers because of its high level of awareness. The third rank for awareness of new banking services goes to the variable 'Financial and Investment Services'. Variables viz. 'Credit Card' and 'Insurance Products' ranked fourth and fifth. 'Banking Ombudsmen' ranks sixth and 'Electronic Fund Transfer' ranks seventh due to the low level of awareness among customers about the services offered by the banks. 'Anywhere Banking' ranked 8th · 'Internet Banking' ranked 9th and 'Mobile Banking' 10th, also attracted only limited number of customers because of the low level of awareness of customers regarding these services.

DISTRIBUTION OF RESPONDENTS ACCORDING TO THE DEGREE OF LEVEL OF SATISFACTION OF CUSTOMERS ON VARIOUS BANKING SERVICES

For measuring the level of satisfaction of customers on various banking services ten variables were identified by the researchers. The customers of selected banks were required to indicate their level of satisfaction they derived from each variable. The customers expressed their level of satisfaction by stating as 'Excellent', 'Good', 'Satisfactory', 'Unsatisfactory' and 'No opinion'.

The responses of the sample customers of the selected banks on each variable were shown in Table 2

Table II reveals that the new banking services introduced since globalization, that all sample customers expressed their level of satisfaction relating to variable like 'ATM'. All customers also expressed their level of satisfaction on banking services like 'Loan processing', 'Employees attitude', and 'Employee-Customer Relationship'. Out of 60 sample customers 28 have ranked the variable 'ATM excellent',13 as good and 7 as satisfactory and 12 as unsatisfactory. Regarding 'Employees attitude' the scores are 27,16,11 and 6 and for 'Loan Processing' the scores are 25,13,9 and 13. Out of 60 customers 19 have no opinion on 'Credit Card' and 18 expressed as excellent and 10 as good. The variable namely ' Bill Payment', 18 customers have no response while 17 expressed as excellent. Twenty customers ranked the variable 'Insurance Products' as excellent and 11 have no opinion. Sixteen customers have no opinion on the variable 'Investment and Financial Services' because of the low level of awareness. On the variable of 'Cheque Processing' 53 customers, 24 expressed as excellent and 14 as good. 'Employee Customer Relationship' received a good response and 22 expressed as excellent and 14 as good.

Table 2
Variable Wise level of Satisfaction of Customers on various banking services

SL No.	Variables	Excellent	Good	Satisfactory	Unsatis-factory	No-opinion	Total Customers
1	ATM	28	13	7	12	-	60
2	Bill Payment	17	12	9	4	18	60
3	Credit Card	18	10	7	6	19	60
4	Insurance Products	20	13	8	8	11	60
5	Investment and Financial Services	19	12	6	7	16	60
6	Loan Processing Period	25	13	9	13	-	60
7	Cheque Processing Period	24	14	10	5	7	60
8	Employees Attitude	27	16	11	6	-	60
9	Customer convenience	21	13	9	14	3	60
10	Employee- Customer Relationship	22	14	12	12	-	60

Source: Primary Data

The survey further reveals (Table II) that among the ten variables selected for the study the biggest number of respondents identified the variable of ATM Facility as excellent (28), Employees attitude (27) and Loan processing period (25). Largest number of customers expressing no opinion on the variables like Credit card (19), Bill payment (18) and Investment and financial services (16). It may be because of lack of awareness of the customers on these services.

CALCULATION OF SATISFACTION INDEX

The customers of selected banks were asked to indicate their level of satisfaction they derived from each variable selected by the researchers to state as 'excellent', 'good', 'satisfactory', 'unsatisfactory' and 'no opinion'. For the purpose of further analysis, these qualitative grades were converted into quantitative terms. Researchers allot '0' point for 'No Opinion', 1 point for 'Unsatisfactory', 4 points for 'Satisfactory', 6 points for 'Good' and 8 points for 'Excellent'. These values when multiplied by the respective frequencies would give the total satisfaction level and the same divided by total frequencies would give the Total Satisfaction Index.

Table 3 depicts the variable wise Satisfaction Index and their Positional Ranks. The satisfaction index of the variable 'Employees Attitude' work out to 6.03 and received first rank. During the survey a good number of respondents opined specifically on the changes in the attitude of the employees of bank owing to financial sector reforms and the entry of new generation banks and foreign banks. The second rank for satisfaction index goes to the variable 'ATM' and third rank to 'Loan Processing Period'. Regarding 'Cheque processing period, customers give fourth positional rank. 'Employee customer relationship' is ranked 5th and 'Customer Convenience' ranked sixth.

Table 3
Variable Wise Satisfaction Index and Their Positional Rank

SL. No:	*Variables*	*Total Score of Satisfaction*	*Satisfaction Index*	*Positional Rank*
1	ATM	342	5.70	2
2	Bill Payment	248	4.13	9
3	Credit Card	238	3.97	10
4	Insurance Products	278	4.63	7
5	Investment and Financial Services	255	4.25	8
6	Loan Processing Period	327	5.45	3
7	Cheque Processing Period	321	5.35	4
8	Employees Attitude	362	6.03	1
9	Customer Convenience	296	4.93	6
10	Employee-Customer Relationship	320	5.33	5

Source: Primary Data.

DISTRIBUTION OF RESPONDENTS ACCORDING TO VARIABLE WISE LEVEL OF SATISFACTION, SATISFACTION INDEX AND THEIR POSITIONAL RANK

The Table further depicts that of the five new services selected for study, ATM attracted a good number of customers and the remaining four variables received only a token response. 'Insurance Products' (ranked 7th) 'Investment and Financial

Services' (ranked 8th) and 'Bill Payment' (ranked 9th) do not attract customers due to the general level of ignorance about the services offered by the banks or due to the non- availability of services in certain banks. The variable 'Credit Card' (10th rank) attracted only limited number of customers due to non-availability of the service in the bank or because of fear of customers on service charges, hidden charges etc.

SUMMARY OF FINDINGS

It is observed from the study that a good number of customers of banks in Kollam city are ignorant about the new services \ products provided by the bank to its customers as result of the financial sector reforms. Banks are not spending much time for educating the customers and popularizing these products among them. Some of the customers having only minimal awareness about these products are also ignorant of the features and benefits of the new facilities.

It is noted that staff of the public sector banks have only limited personal contact with its customers when compared to the new generation and private sector banks. Majority of the customers are satisfied with the cheque clearance facility and employees attitude. A section of the customers are not satisfied with the banker customer relationship and existing customer convenience facilities in the selected banks especially vehicle parking, drinking water facility, stationery etc. Customers also opined about the delay in sanction of loans.

SUGGESTIONS

While keeping in view the foregoing findings of the study, certain suggestions are hereby put forward by the researchers which would be of use to the bankers and their policy makers.

The customers of new generation banks and old private sectors banks are fully satisfied with the ATM facility. But the customers of nationalized banks are not fully satisfied with this facility because they are not provided with the facility of deposit of cash and cheque through ATMs. By extending these facilities banks can widen their customer base and also increase the scope for better utilization of banking services.

To make customers aware of the banking services and new products, it is advised to conduct customers meet or customer relationship programmes periodically, through which banks can interact with their customers and to educate and enlighten them about their new products and services. Besides the employees of the bank have to take the initiative for informing the customer about the new schemes even when though the customer does not inquire. The success of new services like internet banking, mobile banking, international debit cum ATM Card, home banking, Priority Banking, Insurance Products, Investment and Financial Advisory Services, Demat Account, 24 Hour Tele-Banking, etc is highly depends upon its usage by the customers. There for the bankers should educate its customers regarding the methods of using each service. Other wise these services can not be effectively implemented.

Many customers are ignorant and afraid of the interest rate, bank charges, service charges etc. applicable for the new services offered by the bank to its customers. Before launching a new service or product the banks should furnish necessary information to their prospective customers about the specialties and benefits of the scheme to them, charges applicable etc. by posting brochures to their customers and by displaying details on the notice board at prominent places in the bank.

In a competitive business environment in order to retain and widen the customer base, the banks should initiate steps to better personal contacts with their customers. The banks must concentrate on enhancing quality of its personnel and try to develop it further.

In nationalized banks some customers are concerned about the delay in their transactions and agitated over the need for standing in queue for long during peak hours for deposit and withdrawal of money. It is advisable for the banks to request the customers to use the ATMs for withdrawal of money up to a certain limit as far as possible and meaningful.

To avoid delay in sanction of loans necessary steps should be taken at the earliest or as and when they are noticed.

CONCLUSION

The study reveals that the strategies followed by the Indian banks are still far from adequate and have not obtained the expected results. Further research studies in this direction will definitely identify the real causes for low level of awareness and satisfaction about banking services among the customers. The systematic planning and introduction of customer oriented and customized products and services by the Indian banks will help them to compete and succeed in the contemporary competitive banking environment.

REFERNCES

Banking Statistics for Kerala, State Level Bankers Committee, Canara Bank, Thiruvananthapuram.

Benson Kunjukunju Dr. and Dr. S .Mohan, Institutional Finance and Rural Development, New Century Publications, New Delhi. 2002.

Economic Review, Kerala State Planning Board, Thiruvananthapuram, 2004.

Gordon. E (Prof.) and Dr. K. Natarajan, Banking Theory and Practice, Himalaya Publishing House, Mumbai. 2003.

Maheshwari S.N. and Dr. R.R. Paul Banking Theory Law and Practice, Kalyani Publishers, New Delhi, 2000.

Sathya Swaroop Deasish, Service Quality in Commercial Indian Banks in Delhi, Indian Journal of Marketing, pp. 41-50 March 2003.

20

PROBLEMS OF THE AGED

D. R. Albal Z. A. Pathan** A. V. Melvanki****
*M. B. Chalwadi*****

INTRODUCTION

Aging of population results from a change of the age structure of the population. This can take place either due to a decline in the proportion of the young population or due to an accelerated growth of the proportion of the population in the older age group.

The former is called aging from the base while the latter is referred to as aging at the apex (UN, 1956). Population of aging and the increased longevity of older persons are signs as well as consequences of socioeconomic development. In the developed countries population of aging has already taken place as a result of reduced fertility and mortality rates. In the developing societies, on the other hand, the number of aged persons is on the increase, even though they as a percentage is yet to become conspicuous. But the present situation cannot be ignored, if socioeconomic development is to progress effectively. In her efforts to transform herself into an economically and socially developed country, India has to consider population

* Reader in Sociology, Karnatak University Kittur Rani Chennamma P. G. Centre, Belgaum.

** Research Scholar in Sociology, Karnatak University Kittur Rani Chennamma P. G. Centre, Belgaum.

*** Research Scholar in Sociology, Karnatak University Kittur Rani Chennamma P. G. Centre, Belgaum.

**** Guest Faculty in Geography, Karnatak University Kittur Rani Chennamma P. G. Centre, Belgaum.

as an important variable to be reckoned with. The fertility of this country is declining, though slowly but surely.

Mortality rate has already decreased. Consequently, Indian population is in an intermediate stage of transition to aging and some time between 2010 and 2020 she will graduate into a full fledged aged society (Radha Devi, 1998).

Since India is a vast country with varying levels of development, be it social, economic or demographic, it is only natural to see that the different states in the country are in the different stages of population aging.

AGED DEFINED

The term "old" can be associated with physical incapacity, biological deterioration, or disabilities or even psychological factors. "A man ages *biologically* as a continuing process, *socially* as perceived by the members of the society, *economically* when retired from the work force and, *chronologically* one grows older with time" (Benyaklef, 1991). However, definitions other than the chronological one are difficult to operationalize, and hence chronological age is the most widely used indicator to define the aged.

Chronological age also is an important indicator of health, functional capacity, labor force participation, life cycle stage and income. But to assign a particular age at which a person becomes aged is a difficult proposition. However, at the World Assembly on held at Vienna in 1982, all persons aged 60 years and above were taken as the aged. Similarly, in the United Nations International Conference on Aging and Urbanization (1991) the term "elderly" is defined as the population aged 60 years and above. However, this definition of old age ignored the heterogeneous nature of a population group covering a range of at least 25 years in the case of less developed countries. Regrouping this population into smaller age categories, nonetheless, can solve this problem. The most commonly used groups are the 60-74 years, 75 years, and over. However, many of the more developed countries classify a person as aged only when he/she reaches the age of 65 years.

This cut off age has relation to the longevity of the people. When the life expectancy of the population was 40 years, a person aged 40 years was considered as aged. In the least and less developed countries of to-day the expectation of life at birth is hovering around 60 years and hence the 60 year demarcation is accepted for aged. This is true at the all-India level also. Hence, in this study, 60 years is taken as the lowest age to consider a person as aged.

Increase in the number of aged persons assumes importance as their needs and their problems are much different from that of the young or the adult persons. Aged persons will have to adjust to a new kind of familial and social situation. This adjustment is a kind of downward shift unlike the change from childhood to adulthood. In the latter situation it is an upward shift from an irresponsible care free child to a responsible adult with increase in recognition at home and society, making decisions for oneself and, more often than not, for the other members of the family also. Further, *ceteris paribus*, adults are healthy, mentally and physically, and upward move is much easier than downward move. With the downward shift, which in effect means making room for others, comes a series of mental, physical and emotional adjustments for which most of the aged often are not prepared for.

Until recently, aging has been a neglected subject in India by both administrators and academicians. But the socio-economic scenario of the country is changing very fast. This has far reaching consequences on the lives of the aged. The life expectancy of the population at every age is also increasing very fast. The increasing health and medical facilities in the country and improved standard of living helped to add years to life with the result that the elderly are living longer than they used to in olden days.

There are several factors that are acting simultaneously to make the situation of the elderly of to day different from that which prevailed in earlier days. Factors like changing values, changing family structure, changing status and roles in the family and urbanization and migration can have great impact on the aged.

LOCALE OF THE STUDY

Belgaum, a delectable mid-sized town nestling high in the Western Ghats, grew out of a village Venugram or the 'village of bamboo' over a course of 3,200 years at least. The Belgaum City was converted into Municipality in the year 1851. Belgaum has an enviable heritage and presents much to be discovered. It lies in the zone of cultural transition between Kamataka, Maharashtra and Goa with a known antiquity clearly traceable up to 2nd Century A.D.

Belgaum participated actively in the Freedom Movement with whole country. One of the prominent lady warriors Rani Channamma of Kittur along with Sangolli Rayanna and Babasaheb was first to start this movement. Belgaum was also chosen as the venue of the 39th session of Indian National Congress in December 1924 under the President ship of Mahatma Gandhiji. The then Shahapur Municipality which was near to Belgaum was merged in Belgaum Municipality on 4-7-1952.

The District Headquarters, Belgaum is a picture of contrasts. On one side is the old town area where the cotton and silk weavers still create magic with their fingers. And on the other side the modern, bustling, tree-lined Cantonment built by the British.

The specific objectives are:

1. To examine the general social, economic and demographic condition of the family in which the elderly lives.
2. To examine their living arrangement
3. To understand their health condition and health care.
4. To explore the extent of the familial and friendship network to which the aged relates themselves to.
5. To assess the expected and actual role and status of the aged
6. To examine the inter-generations attitudinal changes in giving care to the elderly.
8. To seek suggestions from the aged to improve the life situation of the elderly.

METHODOLOGY

The study is based on both Primary and Secondary data. Primary data is collected from 50 respondents belonging from different community, by employing random sampling method.

A pre-structured questionnaire prepared was administered to the respondents to obtain the data. Secondary data was obtained from published literature of the Government departments.

Table 1
Sex Composition of the Respondents

	No. of Respondents	*Percentage*
Male	35	70
Female	15	30
Total	50	100

Source: Field Survey.

Table No.1 reveals that out of the total respondents 70 percent of them are males and remaining 30 per cent are females. This shows that the majority of the respondents belong to the male category and here we can say that the percentage of the female respondent is less as compared to the male.

Table No. 2
Age Composition of the Respondents

Age Group	*No. of Respondents*	*Percentage*
60 – 65	13	26
66 – 70	15	30
71 – 75	10	20
76 – 80	05	10
81 – 85	02	04
86 – 90	03	06
91 – 95	00	00
96 – 100	01	02
Above 100	01	02
Total	50	100

Source: Field Survey.

Table 2 shows the number of respondents belonging from different age group. It is clear from the given table that 26 per cent of the respondents are in the age group of 60 to 65 years, 30 per cent are in 66 to 70 age group, 20 per cent are in 71 to 75 years, 10 per cent are in 76 to 80 years, 4 per cent are in 81 to 85, 6 per cent are in 86 to 90, there is none in the age group of 91 to 95 years of age, 2 per cent are in the age group of 96 to 100 and remaining 2 per cent are aged above 100 years.

Here we can conclude that the majority of the respondents are from either 61 to 65 or 66 to 70 years of age.

Table No.3
Religious Composition of the Respondents

Religion	*No. of Respondents*	*Percentage*
Hindu	32	64
Muslim	10	20
Christian	04	08
Others	04	08
Total	50	100

Source: Field Survey.
Note: Others include Sikhs, Buddhists, Jains, Parsi.

The religious composition of the respondents is shown in the table 3, the table disclose that 64 per cent of the respondents are Hindus, 20 per cent are Muslims, 8 per cent are Christians and the remaining 8 per cent comprises of the other religions. The information suggests that majority of the respondents are from Hindu community.

The Annual Income of the respondents as shown in the Table 4, informs that 24 per cent of the respondents have the annual income of less than Rs.10,000, 6 per cent of them have the annual income of Rs.10,001 to 20,000, 8 per cent have Rs. 20,001 to 30,000 and 6 per cent of them have Rs. 30,001 to 40,000, and the similar per cent have the annual income of Rs. 40,001 to 50,000 and Rs. 50,001 to 60,000.

Only 2 per cent of the respondents have the annual income of Rs. 60,001 to 70,000, 6 per cent have Rs. 70,001 to 80,000 and the remaining 24 per cent do not have any earning. It can be concluded that more number of the respondent does not have sufficient annual income.

Table No. 4
Annual Income of the Respondents(In Rupees)

Annual Income	*No. of Respondents*	*Percentage*
Less than10,000	12	24
10,001 – 20,000	03	06
20,001 – 30,000	04	08
30,001 – 40,000	03	06
40,001 – 50,000	03	06
50,001 – 60,000	03	06
60,001 – 70,000	01	02
70,001 – 80,000	03	06
Above 80,000	04	08
Not applicable	14	28
Total	50	100

Source: Field Survey.

Table No. 5
Marital Status of the Respondents

Marital Status	*No. of Respondents*	*Percentage*
Married	49	98
Unmarried	01	02
Total	50	100

Source: Field Survey.

Marriage being a Universal socio-religious institution, Table 5 exhibits that 98 per cent of the respondents are married and only 2 per cent of the total respondent is unmarried. Thus it is clear from the table that majority of the respondents are married.

Table No. 6
Educational background of the Respondents

Education	*No. of Respondents*	*Percentage*
Illiterate	07	14
Primary	09	18
High School	12	24
Pre-University	10	20
Graduate	08	16
Post-Graduate	04	08
Total	50	100

Source : Field Survey.

As revealed by the Table No. 6, about 14 per cent of the respondent are illiterate, 18 per cent have Primary education, 24 per cent have High School education, 20 per cent have attained education upto Pre- university level, 14 per cent are Graduates and remaining 6 per cent are Post-Graduate.

It can be concluded that majority of the respondents have attained education either upto Primary or High School or upto Pre-university. Thus we can say that there is very less representation of the illiterates.

Table 7
Nature of Marriage of the Respondents

Nature of Marriage	*No. of Respondents*	*Percentage*
Arranged Marriage	47	94
Love Marriage	02	04
Inter – Caste Marriage	01	02
Total	50	100

Source: Field Survey.

The institution of Marriage as observed by the respondents is exhibited in the Table 7. As per the table 94 per cent of the respondents had arranged marriage, 4 per cent had Love marriage and the remaining 2 per cent had undergone inter-caste marriage. The information reveals that majority of the respondents followed arranged marriage.

Table 8
Nature of Family

Nature of Family	No. of Respondents	Percentage
Joint Family	24	48
Nuclear Family	26	52
Total	50	100

Source: Field Survey.

The nature of family of the respondents can be understood with the help of Table 8. As shown in the table 48 per cent of the respondents have Joint family and 52 per cent are living in the Nuclear family. This shows that majority of the respondents live in Joint Family.

Table 9
Number of Children of the Respondents

No. of Children	*No. of Respondents*	*Percentage*
1 – 2	15	30
3 – 4	14	28
5 – 6	15	30
7 – 8	02	04
9 – 10	00	00
Above 10	00	00
Not applicable	04	08
Total	50	100

Source: Field Survey.

Table 9 exhibits that 30 per cent of the respondents have 1 to 2 children, 28 per cent have 3 to 4 children, 30 per cent have 5 to 6 children, 4 per cent of them have 7 to 8 children, none of them have more than 8 children and 8 per cent of the respondents do not have any child.

It can be stated that majority of the respondent have either 4 or less than 4 children.

Table 10
Occupational background of the Respondents

Type of Occupation	*No. of Respondent*	*Percentage*
Government	13	26
Professional	08	16
Business	05	10
Private Job	08	16
Agriculture	08	16
Any other	05	10
Not applicable	03	06
Total	50	100

Source: Field Survey.
Note: Other includes small vendors, mechanics and coolies.

Table 10 explains the occupational background of the respondents it shows that 26 per cent of the respondents are government servants, 16 per cent are professionals like Doctors, Engineers, Advocates and Teachers, 10 per cent in Business, 16 per cent in Private Jobs, 16 per cent followed agriculture and 10 per cent in the other occupations.

The aggregates of respondent has either Government or Private Job or are involved in Agricultural activities.

Table 11
Relation with the Family Members

Type of Relation	*No. of Respondents*	*Percentage*
Cordial	18	36
Non-Cordial	32	64
Total	50	100

Source: Field Survey.

The nature of relation with the family member of the respondents is revealed in the Table 11, it shows that 36 per cent of the respondents says that the relation with their family members is cordial and the remaining 64 per cent say that the relation with their family member is non-cordial.

The table exhibit that majority of the respondents have non-cordial relations with their family members.

Table 12
Reasons for Non-Cordial Relations

N = *50*

Reasons for Non-Cordial Relations	*No. of Respondents*	*Percentage*
Disobedient Children	22	44
Less contact of the family members	14	28
Lack of Co-operation	21	42
Too much freedom to Children	20	40
Children's demand to live separately	15	30
Lack of financial help	10	20
Mental tension	15	30
Irregularity in providing food & necessities	03	06
Lack of Medical facility	06	12
Disturbed relations with the relatives	03	06
Lack of love and affection	09	18
My own bad habits	03	06
Any other	00	00

Source: Field Survey.

The reasons for non-cordial relations in the family are explained with the help of Table 12. The respondents have more than one reason for the disturbed relations in the family. Out of the total respondents 44 per cent of the responses are that their children are disobedient, 22 per cent say that there is less contact of the family members, 42 per cent replied that they lack co-operation, 40 per cent says due to too much of freedom given to children, 30 per cent responded that their children demand to live separately.

And 20 per cent of them do not receive financial help from the family members, 30 per cent have mental tensions and only 6 per cent face the problem of provision of basic facility, 12 per cent do not get proper medical treatment and facility, 6 per cent of them have disturbed relations with the relatives, 18 per cent have lack of love and affection in the family and only 6 per cent respondent's bad habit is the cause of the non-cordial relations.

Table 13
Suggestions for a Happy Family

N = 50

Suggestions	*No. of Respondent*	*Percentage*
Respecting elders	47	94
Good values among Children	41	82
Respect and faith in Joint living	33	66
Sharing of Income	28	56
Celebrating functions altogether	30	60
Avoiding frequent quarrels	26	52
Any other	00	00

Source: Field Survey.

The suggestions for a happy family by the elderly are revealed in the Table 13. 94 per cent of the elderly suggests that the children must respect the elders, 82 per cent of them says that there must be good values among the children, 66 per cent opine that the family members must respect to live jointly, 56 per cent say the member must share their Income in the family, 60 per cent feels that the functions in the family must be celebrated altogether, and 52 per cent suggests that the members must avoid frequent quarrels.

Table 14
Respondents having friendship with their co-eves (aged)

Friendship with co-eves	*No. of Respondent*	*Percentage*
Yes	47	94
No	03	06
Total	50	100

Source: Field Survey.

Table 14 reveals that the respondents having the friendship with the people of their same age group with whom they share their emotions and sentiments, 94 per cent of the respondents say that they have friends of their own age and only 6 per cent said that they do not have friends of their own age group.

Table 15
Visiting Habit of the Respondent Children

Visiting Habit	*No. of Respondent*	*Percentage*
Yes	20	77
No	06	23
Total	26	100

Source: Field Survey.

Table 15, shows the visiting habit of the respondent's children to the house of the respondents. The table shows that out of the total 26 per of the respondent living in a nuclear family nearly 77 per cent of the respondent children visit the residence of the respondent and 23 per cent of the respondent's children do not visit the residence of the respondent.

Table 16
The reason for visiting to the residence of the Respondent

N = 20

Reason for visiting	*No. of Respondents*	*Percentage*
Good medical care	11	50
Provision of basic facilities	18	90
Love and affection	18	90
Entertainment	14	70
Any other	17	85

Source: Field Survey.
Note: Other includes occasion like festivals, marriage, rites etc.,

The respondent's children visit to the residence of the respondent due to one or other reason this is explained with the help of Table 16. The table reveals that 50 per cent of them visit because they receive good medical care, 90 per cent due to provision of basic facilities, 90 per cent for love and affection, 70 per cent for the sake of entertainment and 85 per cent visit due to other reasons i.e., on occasions like festival, marriage ceremonies or religious rite.

Table 17
Reason for not visiting to the residence of the Respondent

Reason for not visiting	*No. of Respondents*	*Percentage*
Love and affection of Grand children	5	83.33
Lack of medical facility	1	16.67
Resembles an old age home	3	50.00
Busy in their own family life	6	100.0
No response	2	33.33

Source: Field Survey.

Table 17 shows the reasons for not visiting to the residence of the aged. It shows 83.33 per cent of the respondent's children do not visit because they have too much love and affection towards their own children and they do not like to leave their children, 16.67 per cent do not visit due to non-availability of medical care, 50 per cent feels that the residence of the respondent seems like oldage home, 100 per cent of the respondent's children do not visit because they are busy in their own family life, and 33 per cent of the respondent do not have any response other then the mentioned.

CONCLUSION

The study "The Problems of the Aged" is a sociological analysis on various problems of the elderly in Belgaum city. From the ongoing analysis it is interesting to note that old people of Belgaum city are experiencing a range of problems, but the number, nature and type of the problems experienced differ according to their age, sex, marital status, place and economic status.The article is based on the intensive study of the governing factors and problems of old people and it also compile the suggestions given by the aged to solve their problems.

The study includes 50 respondents of which 70 per cent are male and remaining 30 per cent are females. Majority of the respondents fall in the age group of 60 to 80 years of age. As far as the religious composition of the respondents is concerned majority i.e., 64 per cent of them are Hindus. The annual income of the respondents shows that most of them have either less then 20,000 of annual income or they have no income at all, this suggest the poor state of the elderly and their education level shows that majority of them have education only upto high school level.

Marriage is the universal institution can be reflected by observing that majority of the respondents i.e., 98 per cent are married and in which most of them i.e., 94 per cent have undergone arranged marriage and more number of them are residing in nuclear family. Much number of them have upto 4 or less than 4 children. The aggregates of the respondents are engaged in professional, agricultural and private jobs.

As regards to the type of relations among the family members of the respondents 64 per cent of them said that their family relations are non-cordial because their children are disobedient and there is lack of co-operation and due to this they suffer from mental tension. Majority of the respondents suggests that the children or the family members must respect their elders and must have faith in joint living and they should also share their income with the family members and all this is possible if the family members have good values and are celebrating their socio-religious functions together.

The respondent who are living away from their children are often visited by their children on various occasions.

REFERENCE

Birren, James F., "The Psychology of Aging" Englewood Cliffs, N.J:Prentice Hall Inc., 1964.

Brocklehurst, John, "Aging and Health" in David Hobman(ed), The Social Challenge of Aging, London: Croom Helm.

Ram Ahuja, "Social Problems in India", Rawat Publications, Jaipur & New Delhi, 1992.

Ram Ahuja, "Indian Social System", Rawat Publications, Jaipur & New Delhi, 1994.

Singh, J. "Problems of elderly", Psychological Abstracts, p,2.

21

DEVELOPMENT OF CONSUMER'S CO-OPERATIVES IN KOLHAPUR DISTRICT

*W. N. Salve**

Today, it is no wonder that co-operation has permeated in nearly all fields and as a form of business organization it has been adopted in almost all countries of the world, whether capitalist; socialist or communist; whether small or large; whether agriculture or industrial. (Mamoria, 1983).

Co-operative organizations are the most important agencies for promoting economic and social welfare. It also helps in building up the moral and material strength of the people (Goel, 1984).

Kolhapur has been well known through the ages as one of the important towns of the southern Maharashtra. However, Kolhapur had been growing its importance as a center of trade, particularly after the opening of the Miraj-Kolhapur Railway Line and many traders and migrants had been settled in the town. The rivers in the Kolhapur district have perennial water and provide good scope for irrigation works. At present, Kolhapur district is the heart of the green revolution belt in southern Maharashtra, which is known as ideal center of the green revolution in India.

Co-operative movement had developed in then Kolhapur state due to Chhatrapati Shau Maharaja's economic policy, he emphasized on co-operative form in all sectors. Sugarcane is

* Shri Venktesh College, Ichalkaranji, Kholapur district, Maharashtra.

the most important industrial resource of the entire Kolhapur district. At present, there are 15 co-operatives sugar factories, which are located in various parts of district like Warana (Waranahagar), Panchganga (Ichalkaranji), Kumbhikasari (Kuditre), Bhogawati (Parite), Dudhganga, Vedganga (Bidri), Rajaram (Bavada), Gadhinglaj Ajara (Gavase), Jwahar (Hupari), Shri Datta (Shirol), Doulat (Halkarni), Shri Datta (Asurle-porle), Shau (Kagal). The sugar co-operatives established industries in rural area involving the bulk of the rural population in the process of peaceful and concurrent socio-economic development of all classes. They create socio-economic opportunities but also the much needed self-confidence in farmers. Therefore, Jagjiwan Ram Babu says, Co-operative sector in the sugar industry is an expanding sector, on the whole, the co-operative sector has done well, it will expand much more not only in sugar but in all other industries connected with agriculture. In Maharashtra, co-operative sector has developed from 1961, Table-1 is showing progress of co-operative movement from 1961 to 2004. Really, co-operative sugar factories in Kolhapur district encouraged to develop co-operative movement in various fields like agro-based ancillary industries, cotton spinning mills, dairy, poultry, paper mills, agricultural product processing, marketing transporting co-operative societies, credit co-operative consumer's co-operative, *mahila* credit societies, manufacturing, employees, co-operatives consumers societies etc.

These factories have been the brightest stars of co-operation on the horizon of India, and co-operative sugar industry is the prince of all the processing industries. Most of the co-operative organizations have set up consumers co-operative stores, Bazaars in order to provide marketing facilities to consumers, employees, farmers in the Kolhapur district. Marketing can be defined as the overall strategy or complex, which moves goods from services of production into the hands of the consumer (Bose, 1998). At present, Shetkari Sahkari Sangh Ltd. (Kolhapur), Warana Bazar (Waranahagar), Shau Bazaar, Vivid Karyakari Shetkari (Vikas), Seva Society Ltd. (Ichalkaranji), Jaysingpur Bazaar (Jaysingpur), Shri Hanuman Dairy Products Co-operatives Society Ltd. Yalgd. From the point of view of consumer's co-operative movement, consumer's co-operatives have changed the face of Kolhapur district. The main objectives of consumer's co-operatives are to organize supply of essential goods to the public and to expand benefits to members like price concessions and distributive patronage dividend to check the exploitation of consumers in the private business.

However, consumer's co-operative stores/Bazaars like warna, shetakari, janata Bazaar made a good progress in Kolhapur District.

For the purpose of case study, we tried to show the overall picture of warna bazaar and shetakari sangh ltd. in Kolhapur district as per annual reports of consumer's co-operatives.

WARNA BAZAAR

It has been observed from annual report of warna bazaar – 1998-99, that the total membership of warna bazaar was 1622 in 1980-81, which increased to 9695 in 1998-99. In 1998-99, out of 9695 members; 7481 (77%) were females and 2214 (23%) males. The proportion of the female members are more than male members. It is mainly because of developing other women's co-operative activities like Warna Bhagini Mandal, Shri Warna Mahila Udyog, Warna Poultry, Dairy, Warna co-operatives Bank, Warna Mahillas, Credit Society. The value of one share is generally Rs. 501/- for male and Rs. 251/- for female membership. The share capital increased from Rs. 7.02 lakhs in 1980-81 to Rs. 56.98 lakhs in 1998-99. During 1980-81, total sales amounted to Rs. 1.63 crores, which increased to Rs. 37.62 crores in 1998-99. The net profit was Rs. 55,509/- in 1980-81, which increased to Rs. 5,47,308 in 1998-99. There are 31 branches of the warna bazaar, which are located in rural and semi-urban areas in Kolhapur district. Warna Bazaar has started different schemes and programms in order to increase the membership of the warna bazzar.

SHETKARI SAHAKARI SANGH LTD.

Shetakari Sahakari Sangh Ltd. has been working since 1939 in Kolhapur district. There are about 100 branches of this sangh.

Most of the branches are concentrated into rural and semi-urban areas. There five division of this sangh.

(a) Agricultural Marketing.

(b) Agricultural Inputs and Development

(c) Consumer's Unit-Shetkari Bazaar, whole provision, cloth and sarees, utensils, households articles, foodgrains, spices, pulses, cereals and eatable, dryfruits, chocolates, boild sweets, cakes and biscuits, cosmetics, furniture, wrist watches, traveling, camera ornaments and jewellery, shoes, stationary, books, dress materials, medicines, cycles and electric appliances.

(d) Processing Units – furniture, chilly power, utensils, oil mills,

(e) Other – timber, press and printing, transporting unit.

According to annual report of shetakari sahakari sangh ltd. Kolhapur for the year 1997-98, the membership of shetkari sangh was 50,929 in 1980, it increased to 54,487 in 1998. The share capital was Rs. 39.10 lakhs in 1980, which increased to Rs. 121.12 lakhs in 1998. In the 1980 and 1998, the net profit was Rs. 8.46 lakhs and Rs. 19.16 lakhs respectively. The above statement shows an upwards trend in the business of shetakari sahakari sangh ltd. At all levels. Membership of shetakari sahakari sangh ltd. has increased. However, membership is open to the entire public and membership of consumer's co-operatives societies consists of wage earners, the professional classes residing in rural and urban areas. Consumer's co-operatives societies allow credit sales to employees from 60 to 75% of their earnings, on the conditions that their employers deduct the installments from the monthly salaries of employees. Members mostly receive the dividend 12% in the shape of share. The warna bazaar, shetakari sahakar sangh ltd., Kolhapur has also come to occupy an important place in the consumers co-operatives map of India.

Today, whether in urban market, semi-urban market or rural market, the consumer's behaviour is changing due to mass communication facilities, transport facilities, better availability of products and services and also due to government policies and if marking companies do not keep pace with such changing situations, the products services offered by them to consumers would become useless or obsolete. (Bose, 1998). The demand pattern of consumers is changed due to change in various factors like income Consumptions, saving habits, seasons, and festival etc. consumers try to purchase goods according to their desire due to self-service system. It is clear that consumers are becoming more aware about quality of goods and prices policy of consumers co-operatives.

Table 1
Progress of Co-operative Movement in Maharashtra

Sl. No.	Types of co-operative societies	30th June 1961	31st March 1991	31st March 2004
1.	Central Agricultural and non Agricultural Credit Societies	39	34	53
2.	Primary Agricultural Rural Credit Societies	21,400	19,565	21,000
3.	Non-Agricultural Credit Societies	1630	11,291	25,664
4.	Agricultural Marketing	344	931	1220
5.	Processing, Sugar Factories, Rice Mills	4306	28954	40881
6.	Other Co-operatives, Consumer's Housing etc.	3846	43,845,	90,035
	Total Units	31,565	1,04,620	1,78,853

Source: Lok Rajya-January-2006

Consumer's co-operatives stores like warna bazaar, shetakari sahakari sangh ltd., Janata bazzar have become popular with the consumer's. The ultimate aim is to provide goods to the consumers at the lowest possible prices. Goods are packed and sold cheap here and they are able to attract large number of consumers. Consumer's co-operative stores arrange to sell goods in various packages like small, medium and large size of packages. Package features communities product message and motivate the consumers to its products. Consumer's co-operatives stores/bazaars have their own central prepacking, cleaning and labelling facilities. Consumers try to observe the goods in stores regarding details of weight, prices, origin, content and producers name, address, date of manufacturing and batch numbers etc. consumers have freedom to choose and buy the goods in consumer's co-operatives stores. Consumers feel happy that their favorable brands are available in safe and attractive packages. This gives consumers extra satisfaction. (Bose, 1998). Consumers co-operatives stores arrange to sell goods according to consumers shopping habits. Consumer's co-operatives stores have adopted the sales promotion policy. Consumer can be motivated to buy products, if proper sales efforts are made (Bose, 1998), Private traders cannot provide such type of facilities to customers. In fact, the goods are under weighted at the time of sale and are not of the desired quality, the price level is raised artificially and consumers do not get full value of for what they spent (Bedi, 1996).

Although consumers co-operative stores made a good progress in Kolhapur district. However, consumer co-operative movement has not been developed in rural areas. It is necessary to set-up consumer's co-operative society for each village of Grampanchyat level. It should be formed on the basis of one village, one consumer co-operative society.

REFERENCES

Bedi, R.D. (1996), *Theory, History and Practice of Co-operation*, R.L. Book Depot., Meerut.

Bose, Bipla B.S. (1998), *Handbook of Marketing Management*, Himalaya Publishing House.

Ghuge, V.B. (1975), *Chhatrapati Shahu's Socialistic Economic Policies, 1884-1922*, Kolhapur Zillah Parishad Press.

Goel, B.B. (1984), *Co-operative Management and Administration*, Deep and Deep Publication, New Delhi.

Jagjiwan Ram Babu (1969), *Speech at the 10th Annual General Meeting of NECSF*, New Delhi, Co-operative Sugar, Vol. No. 4, December, 1969.

Keer, Dhanaajay, (1976), *Shri Chhatrapati Shahu, A. Royal Revolutionary*, Popular Bombay.

Kulkarni, S.K. (1990), *Co-operation, Phadke Prakashan*, Kolhapur.

Mamora C.B. (1983), *Rural Credit and Agricultural Co-operation in India*, Kitab Mahal, Allahabad.

Sovani, N.V. (1952), *Social Survey of Kolhapur City*, Vol. 111, No. 24, GIPE, Pune.

ANNUAL REPORTS

1. *58th Annual Reports of Shetakari Sahakari Sang Ltd.*, Kolhapur, 1997-98.
2. *23rd Annual Reports of Shri Warna Bazaar*, Warnanagar, 1998-99.
3. *Indian Co-operative Reivew*, Vol. II, No. 2, January, 1965.

22

MEASUREMENT OF RURAL POVERTY UNDER MICROFINANCING PROGRAMS AND SUSTAINABILITY OF MICROFINANCING INSTITUTIONS: A THEORETICAL FRAMEWORK

*Debnarayam Sarkar**

I

In order to live we must satisfy a variety of needs, and our ability to function adequately in society depends upon the extent to which these needs are met. When important needs are not met, individuals or families are said to be in 'Poverty' because the condition of their lives is not considered satisfactory. The problem in defining 'Poverty' is largely a cultural problem is determining what is, or what should count as, inadequate social functioning[1]. But social functioning must rest ultimately on the nutritional flows maintain life and health. Because nutritional flows are the basic flows on which all else rests, much of the writings on poverty has been confined to the problem of want.

Credit is important in the lives of the rural poor in a developing economy because much of their nutritional problem is confined to this credit. The majority of the rural population is left with an inadequate resource base for the skewed distribution of land in the countryside. Faced with a weak social security system to fall back upon, this section of landless or near-landless rural population is forced to depend upon credit for its livelihood (Chavan and Ramkumar, 2002, p 955). It was this understanding

* Professor, Centre for Economic Studies, Presidency College, Kolkata.

led various developing countries to make credit as an integral part of their poverty alleviation programmes. With increasing criticism of state-led formal credit system and its utilization for poverty alleviation, in recent years countries have moved towards new mechanisms of lending, such as micro-credit. Micro-credit has been claimed to be a solution to most of the problems that originated out of states efforts to alleviate poverty using the instrument of credit (Yunus 1999).

Assessing the impact of participation in a micro-credit programme has featured prominently in recent research studies and has become an increasingly important aspect of development activity, as agencies, and particularly aid donors, have sought to ensure that funds are well spent. A frequent question in whether or not Microfinance Organizations (MFOs) reach the poorest of the poor. In convention with this, the new paradigm of microfinance emphasises financial self-sustainability of MFOs. Thus, increasingly outreach and sustainability have been developed as the two main criteria used to assess the performance of MFOs. But the conceptualization and measurement of outreach and sustainability of the MFOs is not as well developed. This paper is an attempt to discuss the conceptual issues of micro-cried and represents simple tools used to measure the depth of outreach relating to the performance of the microfinance programmes among the rural poor and sustainability of the microfinance organizations (MFOs) involved in the programme.

II

CONCEPT AND FEATURES OF MICRO-CREDIT

The old paradigm of micro-credit envisaged credit to poor people basically residing in rural and semi-urban areas at subsidized rates of interest through public or government financial institutions with donar support in general but terminated with high default rates. Although, the new paradigm of micro-credit retains most of the old characteristics such as farm and non farm credit, target group being the poor, operating largely in rural and semi-urban areas and small borrowal account, it emphasises financial intermediation with self-sustainability of institutions and qualitative/quantitative outreach to the poor (Robinson, 1995). The new microfinance operates on the principal 'Borrorier knows best.' The operational strategy under the new microfinance involves several feature such as simple procedures for reviewing and approving loan applications; delivery of credit and related services at commercial rates of interest in a convenient and user friendly way; quick disbursement of small and short-term loan; clean recovery procedures and strategies; maintaining high repayment rates, incentives of access of larger loan immediately following successful repayment of first loan, organisational culture, structure, capacity and operating system that can support and sustain delivery to a significant and growing number of poor clients and encouraging and accepting savings in concert with lending programmes (Micro-Credit Summit 1997, Draft Declaration).

The implementation of any lending programme directed towards the poor is often beset by three important difficulties. The first is the problem of exact targeting, which would ensure that there are no type I, or type II errors[2] (Cornia and Steward, 1993). Secondly, it faces the screening problem of distinguishing the good (creditworthy) from bad (not so creditworthy) borrowers, because the poor borrowers do not generally maintain any account of the past business activity or furnish any documented business plan for which they are seeking loan. Thirdly, it faces the problem of monitoring and ensuring productive usage of the loan and enforcing the repayment of loan. The formal lending programme is often surrounded by these difficulties (Chavan and Ramkumar, 2002). But the scheme of micro-credit has been based on innovative financial practices in solving these problems. First, it attempts to resolve the problem of targeting the poor either directly by specifying the member's eligibility requirement on the basis of asset ownership or indirectly by making the loan amount small and laying down other conditions such as attendance at the weekly member meetings, so that the non-poor are discouraged from borrowing (Hulme and Mosley, 1996a). Secondly, it attempts to overcome the screening problem through group formation. (Yunus, 1999). The concept of group borrowing is driven by the idea that solidarity among like-minded people living in similar social and economic conditions is crucial to the success of this programme. Moreover, the loans are given or it turning into a bad investment (Hulme and Mosley, 1996a). Finally, the problem of monitoring the loan usage and enforcement is taken care of individually as well as through the group that helps in monitoring and enforcing repayment from each of the members. If any member defaults he/she faces penalty in the form of ostracism and loss of social standing. Though loans are offered without any personal collateral, they involve social collateral (Hulme and Mosley, 1996a). Further a repeat loan is not sanctioned till the accounts of all the group members are settled (Hossain, 1988). MFOs insist on putting the loans to the use specified by the borrower strictly within a period of seven days. It follows a system of weekly repayment of small amounts. This is done as "parting with large amount of cash at the end of a loan period is often psychologically trying for the borrower" (Yunus, 1999: 61). But the NGO-led micro-credit programmes with such innovative practices has risen to fame for their performance of credit provision in reaching the targeted poor population and repayment rates compared with state-led programmes (Chavan and Ramkumar, 2002).

Microfinance affects poverty through a number of channels, not only through borrowers' income (Mosley 2001). In the positive sense, it may enable the borrower to hire additional workers, who if poor will cause the level of poverty to fall. Secondly, the presence of new microfinance institutions in a particular market sector may have an effect both on the price of credit or on access to it. If poor people become less poor as a consequence of either effect, this will reduce the level of poverty independently of what happens to the income of borrowers. Finally, new economic activities stimulated by microfinance loans (both production and consumption) will, to the extent that they raise the purchasing power of poor individuals, influence the level of poverty. In the negative sense, microfinance, loans may expose a borrower to a higher risk of insufficient disposable income, which if it materializes may force her to sell assets in order to maintain her repayment, which may reduce her long-term income level. These 'general-equilibrium effects' of finance on overall poverty may swamp the effects of finance on the poverty of individual borrowers.

III

OUTREACH AND SUSTAINABILITY

Concept

Outreach: Outreach is the social value of the output of a microfinance organizations in terms of depth, worth to users, cost to users, length and scope. (Navajas et al, 2000) First depth of outreach is the value that society attaches to the net gain from the use of micro-credit by a given borrower. Since society places more weight on the poor than on the rich, poverty is a good proxy for depth. Deeper outreach usually increases not only social value but also social cost. But when a lender finds better ways to judge risk at a cost less than the savings from the better judgement, deeper outreach increases only social value and not social cost. For example, a lender that does not need physical collateral to judge credit worthiness could serve poorer users and thus have deeper outreach, all else constant, than a lender that requires physical collateral. Depth of the outreach reflects the social value attached to the net gain of a specific person. For example, $100 of net gain for a poor person may be worth more to society than $ 500 of net gain for a rich person. 2nd worth of outreach to users is how much a borrower in willing to pay for a loan. Worth depends on the loan contract and the tastes, constraints, and opportunities of the user. With the cost to the user constant, more worth means more net gain 3rd, cost to outreach to users is the cost of a loan to a borrower. Cost to users includes both prices and transaction costs. 4th, Breadth of outreach is the number of users. Breadth matters since the poor are many but the aid dollars are few. 5th, length of outreach is the time frame in which a microfinance organization produces loans. 6th, scope of outreach is the number of types of financial contracts. These six aspects of outreach – Depth is the social value of worth to users less cost to users, Breadth counts users, length counts types of contract – are useful because direct measures of the social value of microfinance are expensive. Outreach is worth minus cost, weighted by depth, summed across breadth of users and scope of contracts, and discounted through length of time. Outreach is commonly proxied by the sex or poverty of borrowers, the size or the terms of the loan contract, the price and transaction costs brone by users, the number of users, the financial and organizational strength of the lender, and the number of products offered, including deposits.

Sustainability: Sustainability is performance. (Navajas et al, 2000). The social goal is not to have sustainable microfinance organizations but rather to maximize expected social value less social cost discounted through time. In principle sustainability is not necessary nor sufficient for social optimality. In practice, however, sustainable organizations led to improve welfare the most (ibid). Sustainability is not an end in itself but rather a means to the end of improved social welfare (Rhyme, 1998).

Measurement of Sustainability of MFPs

A MFP is sustainable if it can pay for gross subsidy it enjoys. Let us consider the following:-

(i) A classical MFP provides two types of financial services – credit and saving.

(ii) Total fund is financed by borrowing (B), Grants (G) and Member saving (MS). It borrows from the banking system at a concessional interest rate; it receives grants from different donor agencies.

(iii) The programme mobilizes saving which is built-in within the system. Each member contributes every week a fixed amount of individual member savings.

(iv) Total income of the MFP comes from Loan given to the member borrower (L); investment to bank or other (I), and income grants for reimbursement of operating expanses (IG).

(v) Total expenditure of the programme is specified by (1) cost of total employment (Emp) (ii) Cost of borrowed fund (B) (iii) Fund of member saving (MS) (iv) Loss of loan (L) (v) Other operating expenses (OPE).

(vi) MFOs are donor driven, Sources of subsidy are cheap borrowed funds (B), grant (G), income grant (IG) and equity and reserves (EQE).

Hence the total Fund (TF) available to the MFP may be specified as

$$TF = B + G + MS \tag{1}$$

TR (Total revenue) of the programme is given by

$$TR = (r_1 L) + (r_2 I) + IG \tag{2}$$

r_1 = rate of interest of L; r_2 = rate of interest of I
Total expenditure (TE) of the programme is,

$$TE = W\,Emp + b_1 B + m_1\,MS + \lambda L + OPE \tag{3}$$

Where W refers to wage and b_1 and m_1 represent average borrowing interest rate on member savings respectively represent ratio of loan loss to loan.

Considering eqs. (2) and (3), profit π is denoted by,

$$\pi = [(r_1 L + r_2 I + IG) - (w\,Emp + b_1\,B + m_1\,MS + \lambda L + OPE)] \tag{4}$$

The reported profit (π) of MFP does not provide much information about its sustainability because these institutions are subsidized.

Gross subsidy[3] of the MFP may be specified as,

$$S = r_m\,(G + EQE)^4 + B\,(r_m - b_1) + IG \tag{5}$$

Where r_m is the market rate of interest reflecting opportunity cost of fund.

The MFP is financially sustainable if it can pay for gross subsidy and total operating costs out of it total revenue. Thus using eqs. (4) and (5) net subsidy of the MFP is

$$NS = S - [(r_1 L + r_2 I + IG) - (\varpi EMP + B_1\,B + m_1\,MS + \lambda L + OPE)]$$

If S is greater than the sum of the second and third parts, than there is positive net subsidy and vice-versa. Hence it is necessary to be sustainable for any MFP to have the ability to pay for the gross subsidy out of its profits.

Measurement of Outreach

Despite the existence of vast literature for the measurement of poverty, the literature that explores the outreach of the MFPs is not well developed. The following attempts may be of help in this respect.

(a) Index of Affluence (AI): An index of affluence (AI) is constructed to measure the relative level of poverty in various countries and also among different groups within a country.

Index of Affluence (AI) = (Per capita income of the particular segment of population ÷ Poverty line income) X 100

Where per capita income of the particular segment of population = (Total income ÷ Total population) of the particular group.

or, (share of the segment of income in total income x total income) ÷ (Share of the segment in population X total population).

Higher the value of AI leads to the lower incidence of poverty.

(b) Amartya Sen's (1976) General Class of Poverty Measures:

$$Ps = A(z, m, n)\sum_{i=1}^{m}(z - y_1)V_i \qquad (1.1)$$

Where m is the number of poor with income below poverty line z; n is the size of population; V_i in the weight (m+1–i) on the income gap $(z–y_i)$ of person i. A (z, m, n) is the normalizing parameters dependents on the size of population n, total number of poor m and the poverty line z. The normalized value of the measure when each y_i=Yp, specified by Sen (when all poor have the same income level), is

$$(m/n)\ z–Y_p/z) \qquad (1.2)$$

Where Yp in the mean income of the poor.

Therefore, $m/n = z–Y_p / z = A(z - Yp)\ m(m+1)/2$

[as $\sum_{i=1}^{m}(m+1-i) = m(m+1)/2$]

Thus A = 2/ (m+1) nz

Hence sen's measure of poverty can be written as

$$Ps = \{z/(m+1)nz\} \sum_{i=1}^{m}(z - y_1)(m+1-i) \tag{1.3}$$

(c) Alternative measure of Poverty (Khare and Tripathi, 2001)

Using Sen's (1976) (Poverty measure) Khare and Tripathi derived an alternative measure of poverty:

$$P = A(z, am, n) \sum_{i=1}^{m} U_i V_i \tag{2.1}$$

Where $U_i = z - Y_i$ and V_i are the weight on the poverty gap Ui of person i and A (z, m, n) is a normalizing parameter as specified earlier.

This measure of poverty does not require the income data to be arranged in any order. They define a simple measure of poverty for the it individual as $g_i = z/y_i$ and weight v_i as directly proportional to g_i i.e. v_i

$$= k.\ z/y_i \tag{2.2}$$

$$\text{or } \sum_{i=1}^{m} V_i = kz \sum 1/y_i$$

They assume that the sum of the weights is equal to unity.

$$\text{i.e. } 1 = Kz \sum_{i=1}^{m} 1/y_i$$

$$\text{or } K = 1/(z \sum_{i=1}^{m} 1/y_i) \tag{2.3}$$

From (2.2) and (2.3) we have

$$V_i = 1/y_i \ / \text{ or } \sum_{i=1}^{m} 1/y_i \tag{2.4}$$

They assuem that all the poor have zero income.

Then from (1.2) and (2.1) we have

$$m/n = A(z, m, n)\, z \sum_{i=1}^{m} V_i$$

$$\text{or } (A(z, m, n) = m/nz \qquad (2.5)$$

From (2.1), (2.4) and (2.5) we set the following experience of the measure of poverty

$$p = m/nz\,[\sum_{i=1}^{m}(z - y_i),\, 1/y/\sum_{i=1}^{m} 1/y_i\,]$$

Lower the value of Sen's or alternative index of poverty is an indicative of the lower the incidence of poverty.

(d) Relative measurement between borrower's group and control group.[5]

(i) Change in income and/or asset: Change in income of borrowers as a percentage of change in income of a control group (so as to be as similar as possible to the borrower group). If the change of average borrowers income is greater than that of the control group, if may suggest that for borrowers on the average the net impact of borrowing on income is positive. This measurement may be extended to the different types of borrowers' group and control group.

(ii) Head count Index: Head count index is the number of people below the poverty line [here, as a percentage of the total number of the sample (i.e. total number of people below poverty line ÷ total number in the sample) x 100].

Poverty Impact of Head Count Index: It is the number of people who crossed the poverty line as a percentage of those who did so within the control group [i.e. (Total number of people below poverty line under borrowers group ÷ total number of people below poverty time under control group) x 100].

(iii) Poverty Gap: The measure of poverty gap is:

$\sum_i (z_i - y_i)/z_i$, where yi are the individual incomes below the poverty line and z is the poverty line.

Poverty Impact of Poverty Gap: It is the change in the poverty gap deflated by the change in income of the control group.

(iv) Debt-service ratio: Microfinance in intended a risk-management tool (Masley 2000). Borrowers with very low incomes will seek at all cost to avoid exposing themselves to increased levels of risk, and as a consequence will make use of financial services essentially for purposes which protect their livelihood – protecting their consumption levels, protecting their savings, and insuring both of these against decline. If this strategy increases income on a substantial basis, this will enable the households to tolerate more risk in a serious way. If it fails, the assets are sold, risk-aversion increases and as a result the vulnerability increases. When the income in risk is a serious one depends, of course on the rate of return achieved on assets and whether this corresponds to the return expected. Whether or not it (vulnerability) actively represents a problem for borrowers depends on the debt-service ratio in relation to the growth of income of borrowers. We, thus, use this method to examine the extent of vulnerability imposed by credit (i.e. debt) on borrowers:

If we assume change in income from period t-1 period t,

$$D_t = d_t/T_t/\Delta y/y_{t-1}$$

{Where Dt = Debt Service ratio at period t in relation to the growth of income.

d = Total debt payment

y = total income

y = Change in income}

(e) Benchmark and proxy Indicators

In order to measure the depth of outreach relating to the performance of microfinancing programs Meyer et al (2000), Grosh and Baker (1995), chung et al (1997) used two types of poverty indicators – Benchmark and proxy. Per capita income or expenditure levels are the most commonly used benchmarks by policy makers who are interested in anti-poverty measures to raise incomes and command over resource use (Ravallion, 1995). Benchmark indicators, developed through comprehensive income or consumption surveys and representative surveying, are expected to accurately reflect the degree of poverty, found in a country at a particular point of time (Meyer et al, 2000). Proxy indicators are generally constructed from information that is readily obtainable through visual inspection or simple interview that collect data on household demographics, housing characteristics asset holdings and educational attainment.

The term benchmark indicator is used to refer to the indicator of poverty against which proxy indicators are compared. Efficiency in an important characteristics for proxies a household defined as poor or non-poor by a benchmark indicator should be defined the same way by a proxy. Therefore, the rank order of a group of individuals or households constructed with a proxy should be similar, if not the same, as the rank order obtained using the benchmark. The evaluation of the Benchmark and proxies, consist of two interrelated steps. The first involves statistic tests of association, while the second involves evaluating efficiency.

Undercoverage in measured as the number of households identified by the proxy as non-poor when in fact they are actually poor or extremely poor divided by the total number of poor and extremely poor identified by the benchmark. Leakage is measured as the number of household identified as poor by the proxy when in fact they are actually non-poor divided by the number of household identified as poor by the proxy. Positive predictive values reflect the percentage of household correctly defined as proxy while negative predictive values reflect the percentage of households correctly defined as non-poor by the proxy. Relative risk is defined as the positive predictive value divided by negative predictive value.

(f) The index of Fulfillment of Basic Need

The Index of Fulfillment of Basic Need is a simple common formula used for the measurement of poverty (Boltvinik, 1994; Navajas et al, 2000). This approach is common in Latin America. The index is computed not for individuals, but for households. It has four parts:

Housing: Type of material used for floors; walls and roof

Access to Public Services: Sources of water; Presence of an indoor toilet; Access to electricity; Type of fuel used to cook food.

Education: Years of School completed; Current attendance of school; Literacy.

Access to Health Service: Use of formal health care, use of informal health care.

The Index of Fulfillment of Basic Index (IFBI) is simple average of the ratio of the four observed indicators x_j to the norms x_j norm.

$$\text{IFBN} = (1/4) \sum_{i=1}^{n} x_j / x_j \text{ norm} \tag{1}$$

The range of the ratio of x_j to x_j norm depends on the range of answers in the nationwide assessment. The indicator for education is the average of indices for individual members of a household;

$$\text{IE} = (1/N) \sum_{i=1}^{n} (y_i + s_i/y_i \text{ norm} + S_i \text{ norm}) L_i \tag{2}$$

Where,

IE	=	Index of Education of the Household
N	=	Number of Members of the Household
Y_i	=	Years of Schooling for Person i
S_i	=	School Attendance Dummy for the age of Person i
Y_i norm	=	Norm of Years of Schooling for the age of Person i.
S_i norm	=	Norm for Attendance for the age of Person i; and
L_i	=	Literacy dummy for person i.

EVALUATION

As regards sustainability of MFPs, the most careful and comprehensive recent surveys shows that the programs that target the poorest borrowers generate revenue sufficient to cover just 70% of their full cost (Micro Banking Bulletin, 1998). While subsidy rates will surely fall as more programs gain age and scale, even many older, larger programs are far from being able to make both ends meet with their own revenues (Morduch, 2000; p. 618). Some donors believe that little more than 5% of all programs today will be financially sustainable ever (ibid). It is also claimed that financial sustainable programs can achieve greater scale than subsidized programs and then the subsidized programmes can make a bigger dent in poverty. But socially minded practitioners argue that the target households (termed here the "core" poor) can potentially benefit from microfinance service, even if average loan sizes are too small to allow the kinds of economies of scale that have delivered financial sustainability for well-known programs such as Bancosol and Bank Rakayat Indonesia's unit desa system.

In comparison with other anti-poverty measures, microfinance appears to be successful and cheaper at reducing the poverty of those close to poverty line, but inefficient, by comparison with labour market and infrastructural means, in reducing poverty (Paul Mosley 2001). A variety of lending models have achieved the reduction of income and asset poverty, but have little impact on extreme poverty. The vulnerability of microfinance clients on the liability side have often been increased by borrowings and the coping strategies which those clients use have often been especially risky in the case of poorest clients. As a consequence, a number of gaps still remain in the structure of microfinance. The tentative inference we draw in that Bolivian MFOs are relatively effective at reaching the poor, not the poorest. For a total survey of reality 200 non-poor, poor and extremely poor over six years, Paul Mosley (2001) finds a single case where a microfinancing organization had managed to reduce extreme poverty one that was in a indirect manner (ibid, p. 129). Navajas et al. (2000) analysed evidence of outreach for five MFOs in Bolivia. Most of the Poor households reached by the MFOs were near the poverty line – they were the richest of the poor. Although the average cost of reducing poverty through microfinance was cheaper than any of the anti-poverty modalities with the exception of rural health expenditure, the issue of appropriate insurance has not been resolved for poverty reduction. It is observed that microfinance clients, urban and rural, are highly vulnerable and open to risks of decapitalisation and a major reason for this is their lack of access to any viable insurance arrangements. For eight years Bancosol used a forced saving arrangement in which 20 percent of the interest charge was used as a group insurance premium to protect the repayment of loans, but this arrangement was done away with in 1994, so that the impact of negative shock on borrower's income[6] is now thrown on to coping mechanism such as reciprocal lending solidarity group. In rural areas where poverty is the worst, the insurance issue is particularly urgent because of the instability of income and high associated level of risk. Other studies (Hulme & Mosley, 1996; Mosley & Hulme 1998) argues that microfinance does not assist the poorest, as is so often claimed. Chavan and Ramkumar (2002) reviewed the available empirical evidence on the NGO-led micro credit programmes and institutions vis-a-vis the state-led programmes and institutions and observed that NGO-led micro-credit programmes and institutions such as Grameen Bank of Bangladesh, Bangladesh Rural Advancement Committee (BRAC) have been successful in reaching their target group of poor more effectively than state-led programmes and institutions such as IRDP and RRBs of India. However even these have not been free of the 'exclusion problem' in targeting; yet all micro-credit programmes have generated a positive change in the incomes of beneficiaries, but this change in marginal (Chavan and Ramkumar, 2002; p. 962).

Hence the question arises despite giving high subsidized credit by donar agencies to MFLs whether or not most of the MFPs reach the poorest of the poor. The result of the performance of different MFPs of the world are reasonably supportive of microfinance as an efficient means of reducing poverty, but not extreme poverty. But microfinance has emerged as a popular mode of finance for the poor and small scale producer in many countries (Khandkur, 20001; p. 49). Poor households are typically excluded from the formal banking system for lack of collateral, but the microfinance movement exploits new contractual structures and organizational forms that reduce the riskness and cost of making small, uncollateral loans. Contrary to the belief that the poor are bad credit risk, it is now established that the poor are creditworthy and that the loan repayment rate even higher among the poor than the non-poor (Khandker, 2000). Microfinance programs have also demonstrated that even poor households can save in substantial quantities. Success stories are being written around the world, from Jakarta to Dacca to Nairobi to Lapaz. Advocates have broadcast these successes widely, and donars have been quick to pledge billions of dollars to support the expansion of programs in the next decade. But at the same time donars face a challenge in that they need to demonstrate that they are supporting poverty programms that reach the very poor. They have been keen to assess the impact of these program.

MICROFINANCE SCENARIOS IN WEST BENGAL

Broadly there are mainly two different models which have emerged under the SHG linkage approach operating micro-financing activities in West Bengal. Each of the two different models are further classified into three linkage approaches in the following. (Sarker 2001):

- Model-I – NGOs are working as promoters and linking SHGs directly with the Banks [Example: Sree Ma Mahila Samity]
- Model-II – NGOs are working as intermediaries for channelising credit from Bank to SHGs [Example: Sish, 24 Parganas District.]
- Model-III – NGOs are developing as MFIs for Providing credit to SHGs with bulk supply from RMK/SIDBI/RASS/Different foreign institutions etc. [Example: Village welfare society/Tajmahal Gram Vikash Kendra]
- Model-IV – SHGs are being enrolled as members of PACS for saving and credit linkage [Example: Hooghly district, Howrah District]
- Model-V – SHGs are organized under state sponsored programs (SGSY/DWCRA) and linked with Banks for credit linkage [Example: Bagnan Nari Unnayan Samanya Samiti]
- Model-VI - Bank themselves promote SHGs and provide them credit [Example: United Bank of India/Allahabad Bank in 24 Parganas North District].

SHG Linkage Approach Operating in West Bengal

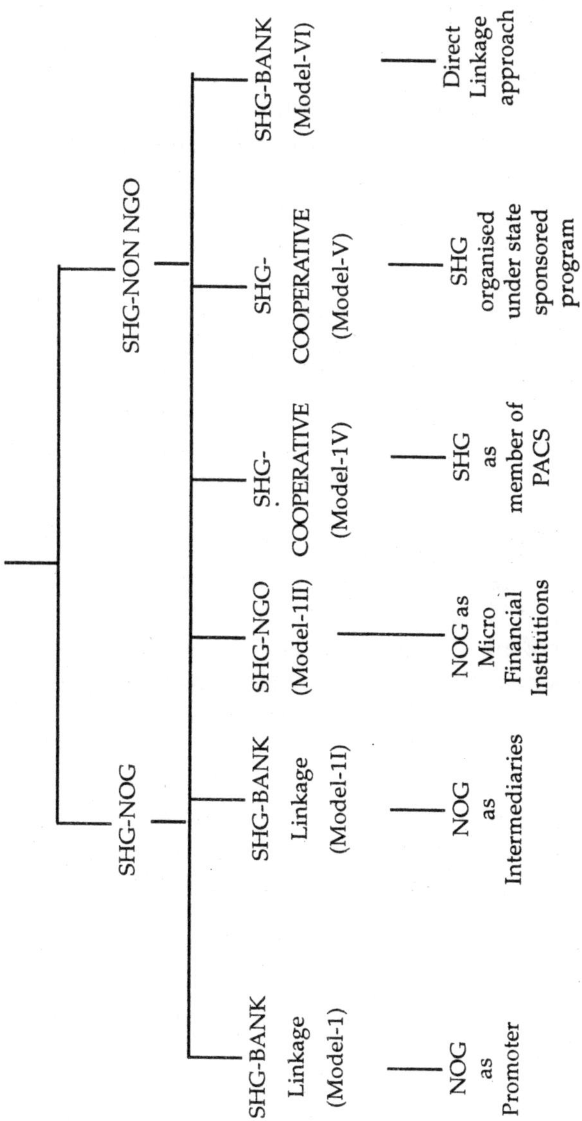

Few NGOs and Co-operative are the major MF practitioners working in West Bengal. Most of the NGOs in West Bengal are engaged in multi-sectoral development programs, where MF or saving and credit program is a part of that comprehensive intervention package which is executed through NGOs. Example: RMK, Mass Education, Seva Sangha. Swanirbhar, Sreema Mahila Samity, Indian Institute of Mother and child, TGBK etc. Various NGOs are engaged in implementing Rastriya Mahila Kosh (RMK) sponsored schemes and started their own operation through Micro-finance schemes. The prominent ones are Mass Education. TGBK, Seva Sangha etc.

Under Co-operative SHG linkage approach, West Bengal has established a few good examples such as in Hooghly and Howrah District. As a part of national strategy, all Indian MF Players are also in operation in West Bengal. Under SHG-BANK linkage of Commercial Bank, first linkage in West Bengal was established by Sagar Gramin Bank in Habra II Block in North 24 Parganas District (Sarkar, 2001). But the success of SHG - Bank linkages in West Bengal is not satisfactory in relation to other advanced states like Andhra Pradesh, Karnataka. Most of the MF activities are limited to Southern States namely A.P. Tamilnadu and Karnataka. West Bengal is a later starter in development of micro-finance and is in its early stage of growth.

In West Bengal, the members of SHGs promoted by different agencies like NGOs. Bank, Co-operatives, Panchayat etc. almost belong to female category. In DWCRA-SHGs linkage programme, all the members of SHGs usually belong to women category. About 90 percent SHGs are exclusively of women in SGH-BANK linkage programme in West Bengal. In SHG-NGOs linkage programme, more than 90 per cent SHGs belong to women. This is also true for SHG-PACS linkage project. As regard employment, SHGs of female category in West Bengal are almost working in self-employed traditional village and household/cottage industries which are agro-based like Khadi, handlooms handicraft, sericulture, coir, woolsilk, spinning, leather and leather product, tailoring, industries relating to the processing of cereals and pulses, gur, molasses, processing of fruits etc. These are labour intensive associated with limited economies of scale. Women employed in these industries are almost self-employed. These traditional village and household industries are very small and they are set-up mainly for primary product processing. No impact study that measures the depth of outreach of MFPs and sustainability of MFIs has in fact, yet been executed in West Bengal.

COMPLEXITIES

The question of whether or not an MFO should target the poor is complex on the ground of self sufficiency of MFOs. There are several reasons why MFOs might want a more heterogeneous group of clients that would occur if they limit themselves to just serving the poor. First, Hulme and Mosley (1996) fear that by striving to reach self-sufficiency, MFOs that exclusively serves the poor but relies on uncertain subsidies for their survival. Second, self-sufficient organizations serving heterogeneous clients may become larger, better able to withstand adverse shocks and develop a more diversified, less risky loan portfolio. Third, profits earned for serving larger clients may be used to cross-subsidize the costs of serving poor clients: so interest rate for the poor may be lower than if MFOs exclusively serve the poor. Fourth, incentives given to the non-poor may be necessary part of the well designed cost-minimizing programme to reduce poverty. In order to attain self-sufficiency of MFO, high rate of interest on loans is effectively a burden on the outcomes of the poor. Despite charging high rate of interest by NGO-led MFOs compared with the State-led institutions, most of the existing micro-credit programs are subsidized. In the case of State-led programmes their subsidy is borne by the government, while in the case of NGO-led institutions it is mainly borne by domestic and international private donors. During 1980s, if subsidies had been removed, Grameen Bank would have incurred losses (Hossain 1998); in 1986, the loss thus incurred on credit operations was 5.7 per cent of the outstanding loans. The majority of Bolivian MFOs, whatever their legal status, now see the achievement of financial self-sufficient as an overriding goal, and by contrast with many other countries, organizations on lending free or concessional credit at a concessional rate which dominated the NGO sector in the early 1990s, are now a small, rate and endangered spices (Mosley, 2001). Although the pressures of globalization have created almost universal pressures towards institutional self-sufficiency within the country, they have not succeeded in defining a "concessional model" of how to achieve that financial sustainability either in Bolivia or elsewhere and of how best to reduce poverty. Indeed, outreach and sustainability are the two issues not usually complementary to each other; they are basically substitute. If MFOs are more profit-oriented, they may be sustainable; but MFOs will not usually reach the poorest of the poor. The serious drawback of this system is that it might help the interest of the multinational corporations (MNCs) to augment the profit of their microfinancing programs throughout the world in general and the developing countries in particular as a result of which the agreement of TRIPS may be highly weighted in favor of them.

IV

CONCLUSION

The trickiest and largest issue of Micro-credit system is how the instrumentality of their credit system should be used relating to the context of the depth of outreach of the Microfinance programmes (MFPs) and self-sustainability of the MFIs involved in that programme. To this end, the relationship between microfinance and other anti-poverty strategies (like primary health care, primary education, agricultural extensions land-reform programmes, public sector expenditure in developing agriculture and rural infrastructure) is an urgent need in reducing rural poverty in general and extreme poverty in particular. There should be a review of performance of both NGOs and Non-NGOs Programmes and greater formal-informal collaboration of MFPs in different parts of the world. Delay in these would help in mushrooming of organizations with dubious credentials to indulge in financial services activities, which eventually would undermine the very potential of a powerful alternative development movement (Nair, 1998). Even more profit-orientation of the MFPs might induce the MNCs to be largely involved in this business as a result of which the agreement of TRIPS may be highly weighted in favor of them.

NOTES

1. In our particular society, aspects of social functioning that are considered important are being gainfully employed, maintaining a household, and engaging in satisfying personal and social relationship. If an individual has adequate nutritional flows and adequate amount of stocks, such as housing, clothing and education, his needs will be fulfilled and his social functioning will counts as satisfactory. But if there is a failure of needs fulfilment he will be in poverty (Jackson, 1972).
2. This implies that, under no circumstances are the poor excluded from the benefits of the programme (Type I) while the non-poor can become its beneficiaries (Type II).
3. There are two types of subsidy: financial and economic. If a MFP is not cost effective, the programme will require financial subsidy for effectiveness, the programme will require financial subsidy for its survival if the programme revenue can not cover its costs. Cost and financial efficiency, on the other hand, determine the degree of financial sustainability. However, financial sustainability of any MFP does not necessarily guarantee its economic sustainability if financial revenue is not sufficient to cover operating expenses and economic cost of cheap funds. An economic subsidy exists if the cost of resources for on lending are less than the opportunity cost of resources for on lending are less than the opportunity cost of these funds. Following Yaron (1992), economic subsidy can be divided into interest subsidy (financial cost-subsidy), equity subsidy and income subsidy (grants for revenue expenditure). If the profits of MFP is greater than the economic subsidy, the MFP/MFI receives no net economic subsidy implying zero social costs for its continuing operations. The programme is then both financially and economically sustainable.
4. Equity and reserve are considered as a source of subsidy on the ground that generally management does not have any equity ownership of the MFP, and in most cases grant funds or cheap borrowed funds, along with profit (surplus of income over

expenditure) are capitalized. Hence capital funds (equity and reserves) do have opportunity cost.

5. Control group consists of individuals so as to be as similar as borrowers group, have been approved for loans but have not had time to make much (any) use of them. The individuals of control group come from the same geographical catchment and occupational group as borrowers but lack experience of borrowing from the organization under examination.
6. Out of several income shocks, there is one type of shock which deserves special mention and this is the shock to farmer's income which occurs during the months before the harvest. An important role of microfinance in relation to poorer farmers is the provision of emergency consumption loan during the hungry season before the harvest.

REFERENCES

Adams, D. and Von Pischke. J.D. (1992), "Micro Enterprise Credit Programmes" Deja *World Development*, 20.

Amin, S. and Pebley, A. (1994), "Gender Inequality Households The Impact of a women's Development Programme in 36 Bangladeshi Villages." *Bangladesh Development Studies*, Vol. 22 No. 2 & 3; 121-154.

BIDS (1998), Bangladesh Institute of Development Studies: *The census Report of the BIDS study on PKSF's Monitoring and Evalution System.* Bangladesh Institute of Development Studies, Dhaka.

BIDS (1990), Bangladesh Institute of Development Studies, *Evolution of Poverty Alleviation Programs in Bangladesh,* (Mimco) BIDS, Dhaka.

Burkley, G. (1997), Micro Finance in Africa? Is it either a problem or a solution? *World Development.*

Chavan. P. & Ramkumar R. (2002), "Micro-Credit and Rural Poverty: An Analysis of Empirical Evidence" *Economic & Political Weekly,* Mar. 9.

Chowdhury O.H. and Khandker, S. (1995), "Targeted Credit Programs and Rural poverty in Bangladesh", paper presented at workshop on 'Credit Programs for the Poor: Household and Intrahousehold Impacts and Program Sustainability, '*World Bank and Bangladesh Institute of Development Studies, Dhaka.*

Concept of Microfinance I & II, (2000 and 2001), A study of West Bengal Credit, SHGs and Microfinance, *SIPRD Report*, prepared by Sen, Manab.

Copestake, J. Bhalotra, S. and Johnson, S. (2201), "Assessing the impact of Micro-Credit" A Zambian case study, *Journal of Development Studies*, Vol. 37, No. 4.

Copestake, J. (1995), IRDP Revisited (Mimco).

Cornia, G.A. and Stewert, F. (1993), "Two errors of Targeting", *Economic Policy Series*, UNICEF, International Child Development Centre Italy.

Chung et al. (1997), Kimberly Chung, Lawrence Haddad Jayashree Ramkrishna, and Frank Riely, *Identifying the Food insecure: The Application of Mixed-Method Approach in India*. International Food Policy Research Institute, Washington DC.

Ghate, Prabhu et al (1992), *Informal Finance: Some Findings From Asia*, Oxford University Press, Hongkong.

Govt. of India, (1997), *Ninth five year plan 1997-2002*, Volume-1

Grosh, M.E. and Baker, J.L. (1995), Proxy Means Tests for Targeting, School Programs: Simulations and Specialization LSMS Working Paper No. 118, World Bank, Washington DC.

Gujarati. D.N. : Econometrics. (Third Edition).

Hashemi, S.M., Sehular S.R. and Riley, A.P. (1996), "Rural Credit Programms and Women's Empowerment in Bangladesh," *World Development*, Vol. 24, No. 4:635-653.

Holcombe, S. (1995), Managing to empower: *The Grameen Bank's experience of poverty Alleviation*, London: Zed k Press.

Hossain, M. (1998), *Credit for Alleviation of Rural Poverty. The Grameen Bank in Bangladesh*, Washington DC; IFPRI.

Huda, S. and Mahmud, S. (1998), *Women's Control Over Productive Assets: The Role of Credit Based Development Interventions*. Working paper No. 28 BRAC-ICDDRB Joint Research Project at Matlab, Dhaka.

Hulme, D. and Mosley, P. (1996), *Finance Against Poverty*, Vol. 1 & 2, London : Routledge.

Hulme, D. (2000), "Impact Assessment Methodologies for Microfinance: Theory, Experience and Better Practice", *World Development*, Vol. 28 No. 1,

Jackson, D. (1972), *Poverty: Macmillan Studies in Economics.*

Kabeer, N. (1999), *The Conditions and Consequences of Choice: Reflections on the Measurement of Women's Empowerment.* UNRISD Discussion Paper Number 99.

Kaladhar, K. (1997), "Microfinance in India, Design, Structure and Governance", *Economic and Political Weekly,* October, 18.

Kaladhar, S.R. (1998), *"Fighting poverty with micro-credit: Experience in Bangladesh"* Washington, DC : Oxford University Press for the World Bank.

Kaladhar, S.R. (2000), "Savings, Informal Borrowing and Microfinance". *The Bangladesh Development Studies:* Vol. XXVI, July-September.

Khalily, M.A. (2000), "Efficiency and Sustainability of Formal and Quasi – formal Microfinance Programmes": An Analysis of Grameen Bank and ASA. *The Bangladesh Development Studies,* Vol. XXVI, July-September, Nos. 2 & 3.

Lalit, M.A. (2001), "Micro-credit and Savings of Rural Households in Bangladesh". *The Bangladesh Development Studies,* Vol. XXVII, March No. 1

Mahmud, S. (1994), "The Role of Women's Employment Programmes in Influencing Fertility Regulation in Rural Bangladesh." *Bangladesh Development Studies,* Vol. 22 Nos. 2 & 3 : pp. 9?-120.

Mahmud, S. (2000), "The Gender Dimensions of Programme Participation": Who Joins a Micro-credit Programme and why? *The Bangladesh Development Studies,* Vol. XXVI, July-September.

McClave, J.T. and Benson, P.G. : (1990), "Statistics for Business and Economies" (4th edition).

Meyer, R.L. *et. al.* (2000), "Measuring Depth of Outreach: Tools for Microfinance". *The Bangladesh Development Studies,* Vol. XXV June-September.

Mohana, S. (2000), "Microcredit and Empowerment of Women-Role of N.G.O.s", *Yojana,* February.

Morduch, J. (2000), "The Microfinance Schism". *World Development,* Vol. 28 No. 4.

Mosley, P. and Hulme, D (1998), "Micro Enterprise Finance ": Is there a Conflict Between Growth and Poverty Alleviation. *World Development,* Vol. 26, No. 5.

Mosley, P. (2001), *Microfinance and Poverty in Bolvia Journal of Development Studies*, Vol. 37, No. 4.

Mustafa, S. (1995), "Impact Assessment Study of BRAC's Rural Development Programme, Final Report," Research and Evaluation Division. BRAC, Dhaka.

Nair, T.S. (1998), Meeting the Credit Needs of the Microenterprise Sector: Issues in Focus. *The Indian Journal of Labour Economics*, Vol. 41, No. 3.

Navajas, S. (2000), "Micro-Credit and the Poorest of the Poor: Theory and Evidence from Bolvia." *World Development* Vol. 28 No. 3.

Nayyar, H. and Ramaswamy, P. (1995), *Globalization and Agricultural Marketing*, National Institute of Agricultural Marketing, Jaipur: Rawat Publication.

Otero, M. and Rhyne, E. (1994), *The New World of Microenterprise Finance*. London: IT Publication.

Pitt, M.M. (2000), The Effect of Non-agricultural Self-employment credit on Contractual Relations and Employment in Agriculture. The case of Micro-credit Programmes in Bangladesh. *The Bangladesh Development Studies*, Vol. XXVI, June-September.

Pitt, M. and Khandker, S. (1995), "Household and Intrahousehold Impact of the Grameen Bank and Similar Targeted Credit Programs in Bangladesh." Paper presented at Workshop on "Credit Programs for the Poor: Household and Intrahousehold Impacts and Program Sustainability," *Dhaka: World Bank and Bangladesh Institute of Development Studies.*

Proshika (1995), "Proshika Manobic Unnayan Kendra, Impact, Evaluation and Monitoring cell. *Impact Assessment Survey Report*" Dhaka.

Puhazhendi, V. and Jayaraman, D. (1999), "Increasing Women's Participation and Employment Generation among Rural Poor : An Approach Through Informal Groups" *Indian Journal of Agriculture Economics*. Vol. 54, No. 3, July-September.

Rahman, R. I. (1986), *Impact of Grameen Bank on the Situation of Poor Rural women*. Working paper No. 1. Grameen Bank Evaluation Project. Bangladesh Institute of Development Studies, Dhaka.

Rahman, R. I. (1996), "Impact of credit for Rural poor: An Evaluation of Palli Karmasahayak Foundation's Credit Programme," *Research Report No. 143*, Bangladesh Institute of Development Studies, Dhaka.

Ravallion, M. and Sen, B. (1994), *"Impact on Rural Poverty on Land Based Targeting."*

Remenyi, J. (1991), *Where Credit is due.* London IT Publication.

Robinson, M. (1995), "The Paradigm Shift in Microfinance: A Perspective from HIID", *Development Discussion Paper No. 10.* Harvard Institute of International Development.

Rogaly, B. (1996), Micro Financing Evangelism, Destitute Women and Hard Selling of a New Anti-Poverty Formula. *Development in Practice,* 6(2).

Sarkar, D. (2001), "A study of SGH-NGO and SHG-NON-NGO Models of Rural Micro Financing in West Bengal" *Indian Journal of Agricultural Economics,* July-September.

Schuler, S.R. and Riley, A.P. (1997), The Influence of Women's Changing Roles and Status of Bangladesh's Fertility Transition: Evidence from a Study of Credit Programs and Contraceptive Use. *World Development,* 25(4).

Steele, F. (1998), *The impact of an Integrated Micro-credit Program on Women's Empowerment and Fertility Behaviour in Rural Bangladesh.* Policy Research Division. Working Paper No. 115. The Population Council New York.

Wood, C. and Sharrif, S. (1997), *Credit : Where Credit is Due.* Dhaka & London VPL and Zed Press.

Yunus, M. (1998), *Bankers to the Poor.* The University Press Limited, Dhaka.

Yunus, M. (1999), "Bankers to the Poor – Micro-lending and the Battle Against World Poverty." *Pacific Affairs,* New York. The University Press Limited, Dhaka.

23

DEVELOPMENT ROLE PLAYED BY NGOS IN BARODA– A SURVEY PROJECT

Rameshwari Pandya and Megha Sidhpura***

INTRODUCTION

Voluntary action in India has been an inbuilt culture of Indian life and tradition. We all know that even prior to independence Voluntary Agencies were providing social services. During that period their main focus was on social reforms like spreading awareness against child marriages, *sati pratha* etc. However after independence there were policies and commitment which strengthened and supported the voluntary agencies and their movement.

The voluntary agencies have played very important role in the national development because of their direct rapport with the people. The voluntary organizations have an extra advantage as they can plan and execute their programme according to the local needs and resources and do not have to waste time in rigid bureaucratic red tapism. This is the reason people work with great motivation and commitment and spirit.

Much of importance is given to the NGOs and much written and discussed about their efforts; therefore it was necessary to uncover the facts and real picture of the NGOs.

* Senior Lecturer, Department of Home Science Extension and Communication, Faculty of Home Science, M.S. University of Baroda,Vadodar, Gujrat.

** Research Scholar, Department of Home Science Extension and Communication, Faculty of Home Science, M.S. University of Baroda,Vadodar, Gujrat.

The Department of Home Science Extension and Communication works in collaboration with the NGOs in various ways. Students of the department are also placed during their study and are also recruited by the different NGOs. We all know that administrators are the pillars and beneficiaries are the hearts of the NGOs, as they are the most appropriate people who can throw light on the following unanswered questions such as:

- What is the status of NGOs and their problems?
- Who are the beneficiaries of the NGOs?
- What is the opinion of the beneficiaries regarding programmes, staff members and timings of the NGOs?
- How much beneficiaries have improved and what problems do they face in the different NGOs?

Hence, it is in this direction study was undertaken regarding the beneficiaries of the three selected NGOs working for welfare of women in Baroda.

An attempt is made to study the different aspects of the NGOs and their problems. This study will throw light on the most crucial aspects of the NGOs namely their functioning and beneficiaries. Hence, the findings of the present study will add to the knowledge about the NGOs and their role which they play for the welfare of women leading to sustainable development.

Beneficiaries are the crux of the NGOs. They are raison deter of any organization. So, their opinion about the selected aspects of the organization, improvement found in them, the problems faced related to the organization and their valuable feedback for the organization will help for further improvement in planning and implementation of future programmes and services. The information related to all the above aspects will provide strategic guideline to the administrators of organizations and government policy planners.

OBJECTIVES OF THE STUDY

1. To study the *profile of the beneficiaries* of the selected NGOs working for the welfare of women in Baroda.
2. To study the *overall opinions* of the beneficiaries regarding the selected aspects of the NGOs:
    - Programmes

- Timings
- Staff members

3. To study the *overall differences* in the opinions of the beneficiaries regarding selected aspects of the NGOs with respect to the selected variables:
    - Age
    - Family Size
    - Marital status
    - Monthly family income
    - Educational qualification
    - Personality dimension
4. To study the *opinions* of the beneficiaries regarding the selected aspects of the NGOs with respect to the following variables:
5. To study the *improvement* found by the beneficiaries in them after joining the NGOs.
6. To study the *differences in the improvement* found by the beneficiaries in them after joining the NGOs with respect to the selected variables.
7. To study *problems* of the beneficiaries related to the NGOs.
8. To study the *differences in the problems* of the beneficiaries related to NGOs with respect to the selected variables.
9. To seek the *suggestions* from the beneficiaries for the improvement of the NGOs.
10. To collect the *profile* of the selected NGOs working for the welfare of women.
11. To study the problems of the selected NGOs related to the selected aspects.
    - Finance
    - Staff Members
    - Miscellaneous

DATA COLLECTION

Data was personally collected by interviewing the respondents. Thus extensive field work was done during December 2004 and January 2005. The total time taken to interview a beneficiary was 30-40 mins. To collect information related to the NGOs, 2-3 meetings were arranged with the administrators, almost 40-45 mins. Were taken for an interview.

SELECTION OF THE SAMPLE

The sample for the present study comprised of 100 beneficiaries of the three selected Non-Government Organizations working for the welfare of women in Baroda.

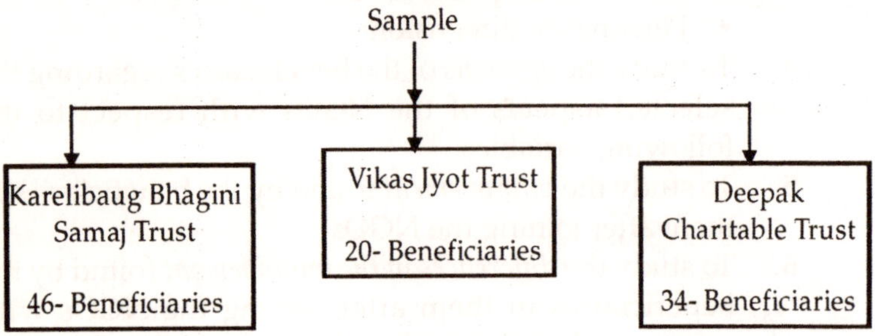

CONSTRUCTION OF THE TOOLS

For the quantitative data related to the beneficiaries, an interview schedule consisting of five sections was prepared. To collect the profile checklist and open-ended response system was used. For the personality dimension two point scale, prepared by V.S. Sahntamani and A. Hafeez (1978) was used. Further three-point scale was prepared, to study opinions related to the selected aspects like programmes, staff members and timings, improvement found after joining the NGOs and problems faced related to the NGOs. To collect the suggestions checklist and open-ended response system was used.

To collect the qualitative data regarding the selected NGOs, interview schedule was prepared; where in set of open-ended questions related to their profile, programmes, methods and problems were included. Problems were studied in detail under three selected aspects, viz. finance, staff members and miscellaneous.

PLAN FOR STATISTICAL ANALYSIS

In the present study data were analyzed through quantitative and qualitative methods.

SCORING PLAN AND CATEGORIZATION

Table 1
Categorization of the Variables under Study

Sl. No.	*Variables*	*Basis*	*Category*
1.	Age	≤ 20 years	Young
		21-30 years	Middle
		31-40 years	Upper Middle
		≥ 41 years	Old
2.	Marital status	————	Unmarried Married
		————	Others
		Divorcee } Widow }	
3.	Educational qualification	<10th standard	Low
		≥10th standard	High
4.	Family Size	2-3 members	Small
		4-5 members	Medium
		≥ 6 members	Large
5.	Monthly family income	≤1500 Rs.	Low
		> 1500 Rs.	High
6.	Personality dimension	0-10	Introvert
		11-20	Extrovert

FINDINGS OF THE STUDY

This section presents the discussion of the findings of the present study. The discussion has been divided into two parts:

1. Beneficiaries
2. NGOs

1. Profile of the Beneficiaries

Findings revealed that nearly one third of the beneficiaries belonged to young and upper middle age group whereas little above than one fourth were from middle age, that means beneficiaries approaching the NGOs hold from different age groups. The probable reason would be that the NGOs could cater to the needs of the beneficiaries of all age group.

It was also found that majority of the women were married. It is a known fact that married women have to shoulder greater household responsibilities than unmarried girls do, yet more married women are found to be coming to the NGOs to attend programmes. However, among them widows and divorcees were considerably less in number. The reason could be their widowhood or divorcee status that inflicted on them a lot of restrictions restrain their movement outside. Hence, problems related to single parenthood would cause further impediments preventing them to attend the programmes. Likewise, many parents did not prefer sending young unmarried girls to NGOs. They felt unsecured while sending alone to NGOs for participation in public activities.

Of the beneficiaries almost half of them belonged to families of medium size with 4 to 5 members in a family. To add to it majority of the families reportedly earned more than 1500 rupees per month. So, it is understood that per capital income in these families was too inadequate to survive particularly when the inflation rate is very high.

It was also reported that more than half of the beneficiaries were employed to support their families. It was because their family income was too low that women had to help their spouses to raise enough for their economic needs. These women are employed as anganwadi workers health workers, maid servants, farm–labourers or workers in catering businesses, etc.

Kaul (1990) and Bhatia's (2000) study too reveals similar findings about the beneficiaries with respect to their age, educational qualification and income level.

The findings reveal significant fact that a good majority of women possessed extrovert personality. The women could become open, free, practical and confident with readiness to work in groups. This made them more extrovert energetic and active participant to contribute significantly to the social cause.

Looking at religions composition among the beneficiaries it was found that a high majority of them were Hindu and very few of them followed the Islam faith. Compared to Hindu women, fewer of Muslim women approached NGOs and participated to earn benefits. The reason is that Muslim families are more conservative than Hindu families. Secondly, following the riots in Gujarat in 2002, the communal harmony was much disrupted and damaged heavily. As a result if NGOs were located preferably in Hindu dominated areas. In this light, Muslim families might not feel safe to send their daughters, wives or daughters-in-law to NGOs although it might earn them a number of benefits.

There are number of objectives that motivated the beneficiaries to join the NGOs one is that they felt a need of various kinds like training, legal advice, counselling, health related services etc. Secondly, some beneficiaries joined the NGOs for satisfying their own interests, which otherwise would not have due realization. Some of them were interested in *mahendi* art work, embroidery work, etc. So they joined the classes run by the NGOs.

Desire for self development was yet another reason that the beneficiaries' responses revealed. They joined personality development classes, Spoken English classes and mahila sangathan activities that the NGOs conducted.

It was revealed through the present study that the NGO's run various welfare programmes and provides need-based services to women. The findings of the study reflect that women participated in different programme according to their needs and expectations. They also availed benefits in view of their different problems and purposes from the services rendered by the NGOs. It is indicated that one third of the beneficiaries participated in awareness generation programmes which were mostly for HIV/AIDS awareness. The NGOs therefore seek to outreach workers to approach these women and make them aware of HIV/AIDS. It might be possible that some of these women have only heard the term HIV/AIDS but they do not have its knowledge. Hence, in order to know about HIV/AIDS they might have joined the programmes conducted by the NGO.

It was found that beneficiaries were more interested in vocational training programmes run by the NGOs. More than one fourth of the beneficiaries joined sewing classes thinking that they will be able to raise adequate livelihood with tailoring and stitching. Some of the beneficiaries attended embroidery classes and beauty parlour classes. While some other beneficiaries received training for anganwadi worker, some of them are working as anganwadi workers.

Banking is another area of public need that needs to be explored in remote rural areas. The NGOs initiated it by setting up Self Help Group called "Bachat Mandal". One fourth of the beneficiaries became members of Self Help Group (Bachat Mandal) that the NGOs constituted. While women joined saving banks they thought if they saved and deposited money in the saving bank they could at least secure some amount of money which could be useful as and when needed. It can provide for a secured future.

Women faced many problems related to their reproductive health. NGOs organized health camps. They also sent their health workers to visit door to door. The beneficiaries felt more comfortable talking to the health workers on their visits. Some of them even discussed freely their health related problems and got solution in terms of counselling and treatment. This contributed significantly to public education and awareness as regards health and hygiene of life and environment.

Some women approached the NGOs to get assistance for legal advocacy. Legal advocacy or counselling is yet another crucial area for the illiterate in remote rural areas particularly in problem areas like property ownership, divorce, mental and physical harassment, etc. Most women are not aware of their rights. On the other hand for their poor economic conditions they could not afford to hire a lawyer. Thus, they were unable to stand for their own rights. In this light legal assistance extended by the NGOs provded most precious to them.

Methods are the most important aspects of any welfare or developmental programmes. Beneficiaries were approached through various methods, such as home visits, discussions, demonstration, field tour, video shows, group level methods and mass level methods. More than half of the beneficiaries were approached through home visits. For programmes like HIV/AIDS awareness, literacy, saving banks, health services, etc. beneficiaries were contacted at their homes. They were also collected in a nearby place or a faliya or a lane for public meeting at which discussions were held. Discussion was the most frequently used method for the various programme. It proved very effective allowing participation of the beneficiaries in need and giving voice to their concerns and confusions. Beneficiaries also attended the demonstrations held for tailoring and embroidery, recipe of food items and even usage of condom. All these methods yielded good results in terms of good response of the beneficiaries in need.

Anganwadi workers, members of saving banks, members of mahila sangthans, etc. were taken to the field tours in order to have better insight into the respective fields. The NGOs also organized video shows that almost one third of the beneficiaries watched. It became a popular method and the most effective means to impart to people instruction with delight.

About one third of the beneficiaries also reported that during implemented of programmes different mass level methods were also employed. Mass level methods are helpful to cover large population. At the same time, they are helpful in causing awareness among people, specifically women, on their specific issues and concerns such as girls education, importance of balanced diet, care to be taken during pregnancy, prevention of AIDS, legal rights of women etc. They can be explained and understood with the help of posters, exhibitions, booklets, campaigns, etc.

Administrators at the NGOs, however, report that they do involve beneficiaries in different stages of the programme. At the planning stage beneficiaries may help NGOs to identify need based programmes that would suit their expectations. During the implementation they can be helpful in reaching them out to the other women. They also help NGOs to build a rapport with women. In the last stage of evaluation opinions and response regarding the effectiveness and benefits of the programmes may be shared among members of the NGOs and the women participant in order to have clear vision and insight into the goal to be achieved.

Suresh (1990) too reports in his study that the rate of participation was very low in selected organisations in Kerala. In these programmes, beneficiaries were hardly taken into confidence for monitoring, supervision, evaluation and follow-up.

2. Opinions of the Beneficiaries

Over a long association with the NGOs the beneficiaries from definite opinion about the NGOs. It would be interesting and also helpful to have a look at the opinions that the beneficiaries formed. They focus on three selected aspects, viz. programmes, staff members and timings. The beneficiaries' opinions may be held important when they throw light on the above stated aspects of the NGO. It would be encouraging to know that more than half of the beneficiaries, that is about 65 per cent of them hold favourable opinions regarding these selected aspects of the NGOs.

They expressed high opinions regarding each aspect. This shows that they might be highly satisfied with the programmes, the staff members involved in them and the timings of the NGO. However, there remained significant difference in the overall opinions of the beneficiaries with respect to a monthly income of their families.

Income of the beneficiaries' families may affect their priorities and needs significantly. It is the priorities and needs that motivate them to participate in different programmes. This allows them different experiences leading to different perceptions and insight into the selected aspects of the NGO. This further leads them to forming different opinions.

The findings also revealed that no significant difference was noticed in the overall opinions of the beneficiaries regarding the selected aspects of the NGOS with respect to their age, marital status, educational qualification, family size and personality dimension. Irrespective of difference in these aspects of the beneficiaries they found the NGOs equally useful to them. The beneficiaries might have received equal treatment from the NGOs. This might have encouraged similar and equally favourable opinions about the programmes, staff members and timings of the NGOs.

The studies presented by Sen's (1994), Bhatia's (2000), Kaul (1990), Brahmbhatt (1996), Mehta and Das (2003), Siwach (2004) too report almost similar findings that beneficiaries expressed favourable opinions about the NGOs. Thus, there seems to prevail unanimous opinion among women beneficiaries that the NGOs exert positive impact on their minds through various programmes and through motivated efforts to help them improve their life.

Opinions Regarding "Programmes"

The NGOs conducted various programme as detailed above for the benefit of women. The objective was to improve their lots, raise their confidence level and make them economically independent. Such welfare programmes received hearty response from the women beneficiaries. In order to check their opinions, responses were collected from them, the findings reveal that high majority of the beneficiaries held more favourable opinion about "Programmes" of the NGO.

The responses collected for the beneficiaries reflect that the NGOs offered various programmes including educational, vocational and the welfare kind to reach out to the maximum number of women. The responses meaning that programmes were need based and interesting were reported with very high intensity indices. The reason may be that the variety of programmes that the NGOs conducted might have addressed the demands and needs of the beneficiaries. It might have made them more focused and concentrated in spirit. This implies that NGOs modify programmes with the time and see to incorporate the changes that occur in the society. They also seek to focus on the needs of the people in view of the specific government policies and programmes announced from time to time.

The findings further report that programmes were well planned, organized, implemented and evaluated. It may be because the NGOs obtained collaboration of international and national level programmes and schemes that added high standard and qualify management to their programme with planning, implementation and evaluation patterns. There was more a touch of professionalism and bia-free approach reflected from among the organizers and workers involved.

Opinions Regarding "Staff Members"

"Staff members" form another crucial point in the triangular work area in which the NGOs have to work. They form a crucial link between planners of the programme and their beneficiaries. Thus they play a very important role to carry out any programme or services. They are the channels through which information is passed on to the beneficiaries. Hence, opinion about them again counts as significant aspect of the present study.

The responses collected from the beneficiaries reveal that a majority of the beneficiaries expressed more favourable opinions regarding "staff members" of the NGOs. Very high intensity indices have been reported for them stating that they were efficient enough to plan appropriate methods to suit the objectives of the programmes and needs of the beneficiaries. The more encouraging fact was that they were friendly considerate to deprived women of rural society who were very needy. This could be because NGOs hire qualified staff keeping in mind the jobs to be performed. Secondly, they provide regular training to their staff members. A good training enables a worker to plan appropriate methods to meet a particular objective with due efficiency and results. The findings reveals that at different stages of programmes, the staff at the NGOs employed different methods.

Further, the staff was working very well with their intrinsic motivation to help and serve people. This raised considerably among them a sense of involvement and commitment. The beneficiaries report that they established a very healthy relationship with the staff members and volunteers of the NGOs. They could approach them and talk to them freely. It allowed increased interaction between them. They could develop a personal rapport with the staff. They could share their concerns, problems and issues as well with due frankness.

Opinions Regarding "Timings" of the NGOs

"Timing" at which the NGOs would hold programmes required serious consideration because women who attend the programmes of the NGOs hail from rural and slums setups. As it has been discussed earlier a majority of them have to play a dual role as a care taker of a family and as a working woman. When they are employed anywhere it becomes clear that they have to manage their timings of households duties as well as work places. A good majority of the beneficiaries expressed a favourable opinion about timings at which the NGOS held various programmes.

The timings were suitable to the beneficiaries. The reason might be that the NGOS plans its activities and programmes keeping in mind the leisures or free hours that women enjoyed during a day in a village or in urban slums.

The intensity indices that reflect on the time that the beneficiaries utilized for the programmes was the highest. The programmes were organized regularly and timely. Today in fact NGOs have grown more punctual and regular in conducting programme because majority of the programmes are grant-in-aid and NGOs are accountable to the funding agencies in terms of timings and timely outcome of the programmes that they finance.

IMPROVEMENT FOUND AS REPORTED BY BENEFICIARIES

Any proejct or welfare programme has to be result-oriented. The result is visible through improvements affected in a target group of people. Further, its success can be measured through the feedback that can be obtained through responses or opinions of the beneficiaries. In order to obtain realistic picture of the success of the programmes the responses were collected from the beneficiaries and formulated in terms of the findings of the study through scrutiny and analysis.

The findings of the study reveal that after joining the NGOs a majority of the beneficiaries noticed more improvement in their conditions. The first change they noticed in them was that earlier they were not able to come out of their homes as there were many restrictions laid on them. It was because of the good efforts put in by the NGOs that women started coming out of their homes slowly and steadily to attend programmes. It increased their general awareness and also developed in them self confidence. This was reported by them in their responses with very high intensity indices. The women could overcome from their seclusive nature and break their isolation. As a result they could develop communication skills with which they can now share their thoughts, concerns and issues of common interests with their friends, relatives and family members besides the staff members of the NGOs.

Further they gained information, knowledge and also developed some skills because of different programmes and services. Through active participation they could enhance their educational level and also become more independent with awareness for their own rights. For instance, women initially joined the Self Help Group scheme launched by the NGOs, they did not know even an abc of the banking procedures. They did not have confidence to carry out transaction. But in the course of time they learnt about the formalities and the system and now they can go to bank and do all works independently. This finding can be supported by what Joshi (2004) observes in "The capacity building support and involvement in economic activity have helped the women to gain respect and self-confidence. They can now go to bank for deposit or withdrawals for loaning." On the other hand women who attended adult education classes learnt basics like alphabets, numbers, etc. to enable them to spell their names, or do simple calculations.

By attending programmes women became aware of their own legal rights. It was widely reflected by the beneficiaries that they would not tolerate any injustice or misbehaviour inflected on them. On the other hand, they also started involving themselves in decision-making process in their families as well as in a society or a community. They invited members of their community to form a community based women's activist group called Mahila Sangathan through which other beneficiaries are playing a significant role in the development of their own area and people.

Kaul (1990), Sen (1994), and Bhatia (2000) reported that the beneficiaries found improvement in them after attending programmes or receiving services offered by the NGO. Wadiwale (2004), Mehta and Das (1997) too observe similar trends. They report that beneficiaries could develop good ability to socialize with people, could make use of time more fruitfully by working and earning. They became more knowledgeable, confident, decision makers, planners, problems solvers and better organizers. Many personal attributes were gained by them.

The findings related to improvements experienced by the beneficiaries are also supported by Gaonkar (2003). She found that Self Help Group (SHGs) have made lasting impact on the lives of the women particularly in the rural areas of Goa.

While reviewing the experiences of watershed project in Uttaranchal, Joshi (2004) finds social, economic, political and administrative empowerment and leadership that developed in women who joined Self Help Groups (SHGs).

PROBLEMS FACED

Problems that arise in the course of imparting programmes and services by the NGOs and also that of receiving benefits and services by women form an inevitable factor that hardly can be ignored. However, the lesser the problems arise the higher stays the index of success. The present study reveals encouraging fact that majority of the beneficiaries faced fewer problems in relation to the NGOs.

Also for all the items low intensity indices were found. The highest intensity indices reported was for the items stated as "transportation is not provided to the beneficiaries". The reason may be that beneficiaries came from far away places to attend the programmes. So, it might be difficult for some of the beneficiaries to spend money on transportation. Another reason could be that if the transportation was provided to the beneficiaries then their family members would not feel tensed and concerned for them. And if no transport was made available to the beneficiaries they would walk down to the NGO, which is time consuming and tiring. A few beneficiaries faced another problem that was of delay in receiving services. The reason might be that most of the programmes or services of the NGOs are grant in-aid. The NGOs were also facing a problem of delay in receiving funds from government or funding agencies. As a result sometimes the beneficiaries faced difficulties.

Curiously enough, it was reported by the some of the beneficiaries that fees charged to participate in the programme were very high. The findings however reveal that the NGOs did not charge any fees for a majority of the programmes, however for programmes like sewing class, beauty parlour and computer literacy class etc. they charge very nominal fees. The beneficiaries coming from a poor section of the society might find it difficult to pay the fees for the course. On the other hand, those young beneficiaries who were not working had to be dependent on their father's or husband's salaries. It might cause problem for them as to how to manage the fees for a programme of her interest.

Difference in the Problems

It was further found that age and marital status of the beneficiaries marked significant differences in the problems faced by them in relation to the NGOs. Differences with respect to age may be for the reasons that needs and demands of an individual vary with her age. Medical science has demonstrated that the older can make new connections, absorb new truths, and acquire new skills. They are also ready for innovations. On the other hand, the younger mostly live in a fantasy world. They always expect something fantastic from life and every surrounding thing. The reason is that they hold less experienced, realistic and mature attitude than the older do. So, Hence beneficiaries too reported differences in the problems according to their age wise characteristics. Here, it was found that young people reported more problems than others.

Further, the findings also reveal that married women reported fewer problems than the unmarried ones and others. According to their marital status women confront different living conditions which may cause to them problems of varied dimensions and proportions. An unmarried woman may desire for self-development, while married woman may have educational or vocational interest in mind. A widow may have approached an NGOS looking for some kind of income generation activity. They might have preferred to participate in vocational courses or preferred to receive counselling from Women Guidance Centre (Mahila Margadarshan Kendra). The NGOs have also helped widows to register under widow pension scheme. So, in all these programme or services, widow might have faced some other kind of problems. Thus, differences were noticed in the problems faced by women with respect to their marital status.

SUGGESTIONS

A few suggestions may be worked out in view of change in women's aspirations and expectations in life with the changing time. If suggestions are accepted and incorporated with due sincerity, they may present any kind of stagnancy in the improvement affected and keep the efforts fresh and vital enough to render expected results. Beneficiaries suggested that new innovative programmes and services like personality development classes, spoken English; computer literacy classes etc. may be started. The beneficiaries may expect above programmes for the welfare of women keeping in mind today's demand. It indicates that now women living in rural and urban centers are becoming alert and more aware and more concerned about overall development of their personality. The Director of Deepak Charitable Trust reported that now women living in rural areas are now involved in dairy project, where they have to keep daily account on computers and hence, they want to learn computer operation. It was further suggested that NGOs should create awareness regarding its activities among the people and it should encourage more and more number of women to take benefits of the different services. It implies that some of the beneficiaries still found women who avoided coming to the NGOs, reason might be that either they were not aware of it or they were not free to move out of homes.

Further, majority of the beneficiaries suggested that innovative communication strategies should be devised and employed in the programmes and services. It shows that the methods used by the NGOs attracted beneficiaries and they found them interesting and meaningful. They may strongly feel that if new communication strategies will be used then programmes will be more successful. It indicates that the beneficiaries too felt the importance of communication strategies in welfare and development programmes.

Kapoor (2004) reports almost similar findings as Adult learners suggested that computer education should be provided;

more opportunities to express opinions, childcare center facility, adequate transport facilities, etc. should be provided to adult learners who come for adult education classes.

NON-GOVERNMENT ORGANIZATIONS

Profile of the NGOs

The three selected NGOs under study namely Karelibaugh Bahgini Samaj Trust, Vikas Jyot Trust, Deepak Charitable Trust based in Baroda were established during 1971–1982. In the Post independence time, the NGOs were flourishing in the country and their growth was tremendous. Under the socialistic democratic pattern of the state-nation, India was declared a welfare state and under it a number of schemes and policies announced for the growth and support of NGOs in the country. Lawani (1999) notes the reasons that the increase in the education level of public, proper canvassing of the provisions and schemes available, special enlargement by the concerned departments to take up the projects, encouragement for the grassroot level organizations like mahila mandals, youth clubs, etc. are the various reasons for the fast growth and development of voluntary organizations during the post-independent India.

Regarding growth and existence of NGOs, Gomes (1989), Narayana (1990), Maithani (1995) and Bhatia (2000) present similar observations in their studies. Their findings reveal that the NGOs under the study are operating at local level. These NGOs' area of work is limited either to a particular village/ villages or an urban community. It may be for the limitation of funds available and the staff employed. They may not be adequate to work for larger population.

It was further found that all the three selected NGOs work with the similar objectives of women welfare. Here, it should be noted that the objectives are formulated keeping in mind historical, socio-economic and cultural factors that prevailing at a time. Ideologies and personalities of founder members too play vital role to influence the objectives.

It is encouraging to state that the NGOs in question are working hard to meet all the objectives as stated in their constitution. Reasons can be many; one of the probable reasons can be availability of finance. In the present study it becomes evident that majority of the programme of the NGOs are funded by Government or other funding agencies. They also receive donations from foreign and local persons. Another reasons can be infrastructure facilities. The NGOs under study are found to be possessing good infrastructure.

Further the findings reveal that the NGOs have a well defined power structure. With a well-defined administrative hierarchy the responsibilities are divided, delegated and shared by the staff members down the line. This leaves hardly any chance for chaos or confusion. Lalitha and Kohli (1982) and Singhal (1998) present similar observation in their studies. They state that well defined formal organizational structure attribute a good shape to the NGOs and their programmes and services. These factors helped them to plan and run their programmes smoothly and efficiently.

The findings also indicate that the NGOs are well equipped and have good infrastructure facilities to carry out their programmes effectively and efficiently. It is obvious that a NGOS needs minimum infrastructure and facilities are to enable it to deliver welfare services to beneficiaries. And in this respect, the NGOs under study do not face any problems. Further, their location in an urban centre like Baroda is an added advantage to them.

In a political and economic exploitation developing country like India women are among the people who are the most vulnerable groups. Therefore, NGOs are expected to provide interventions to empower women. It is evident from the present study that the NGOs under study encompass all the important thrust areas through their programmes and services. They organize various programmes and extend services to improve overall status of women, whether educational, vocational, health, legal awareness and assistance etc. Therefore, it can be concluded that the objectives of the NGOs do not just remain on the paper. They all are converted into well planned programmes and services though collective will and efforts in order to benefit deprived women in the society.

It is further observed in the present study that the NGOs employ different methods like home visits, discussions, circular letters, campaigning etc. to inform the target group of women about the programmes and to attract them to come and attend the programmes. Even in the implementation of the programmes the NGOs employed various methods and materials to make them focused and effective.

It may be noted here that the NGOs do not use popular methods like folk drama and puppet show so frequently. The reason may be a lack of professionally trained staff members who would employ them efficiently. The administrators reported that they would like to provide training for the above mentioned methods so that more and more women can be attracted towards the NGOs and their activities to get the maximum benefits and improve their lots.

The present study throws light on the fact that the NGOs revise their programmes regularly. The project team prepares written reports which focus on negative and positive aspects that may further be taken up for discussion at the meetings with the director or the manager. Based on it the evaluation is carried out by the organization. Then the progress reports are prepared and submitted to the respective government departments or funding agencies. The reason is the NGOs stay accountable to those funding agencies. The reason is the NGOs stay accountable to those funding agencies that finance their projects and the funding agencies are much concerned about the proper utilization of funds as well as overall benefits rendered to the beneficiaries.

It is observed that the beneficiaries are hardly involved in the evaluation stage. This implies that beneficiaries are not granted opportunities to express their opinions or problems as regards the NGO's programmes and the other aspects. Lalitha and Kohli (1982) reported that periodic evaluation of programmes is essential to tone up the performance of these organizations with a view to incorporate suitable changes and modification therein.

The findings further reveal that in view of the selected NGOs no similar pattern of participation was noticed. It shows that the NGOs adopt different philosophies in different stages of programmes related to participation of beneficiaries. The reasons may vary. Sometimes the NGOs may provide opportunities but because the beneficiaries on their part may not be so willing and interested in the participation. The vis-a-vis situation may also be found. However social reformists and social-workers attach prime importance to the situation that the beneficiaries are allowed participation in the decision making process.

PROBLEMS

The findings of the present study further reflect on what the NGOs are lacking in some areas and what kind of problems they face related to those particular aspects. They have report on their weaknesses and problems related to different areas like finance, personnel and others to include co-ordination, identification and implementation of the programme. It was found that the NGOs are not facing similar problems and the extents of their problems too differ. Hence the problems may be discussed in the sections titled as finance, staff members and miscellaneous.

Finance

Regarding the finance aspect the administrators of the NGOs complain about delay in receiving funds. It is a major problem that the two NGOs except Deepak Charitable Trust confront severely. Because of delay in funds the NGOs face difficulties in starting and continuing a programme in time and running it smoothly. The administrator of the Karelibaug Bhagini Samaj further expressed that they have to pass through lengthy and tedious procedure to get funds and even after the utilization of funds unnecessary formalities have to be carried out. It is understood that as a part of their accountability the NGOs need to report back to funding agencies or the Government Departments that finance their projects and inform them about specific programmes. They also have to report on every single expenditure that they incur however small it may be.

The Deepak Charitable Trust, on the other hand, reported only one problem related to the finance. It is a different matter that the trust has its own funds which may be available to them as and when needed. Therefore they may not face many problems related to the finance. They in fact enjoy relative freedom. However, the administrator reported that they sometimes find difficulty in producing the utilization certificate because the appointed Chartered Accountants are not aware of the procedures and formalities as related to the NGOs.

Thus, from the findings it can be inferred that except one problem of delay in receiving finance the NGOs are not facing any other problems. It shows that the NGOs under study enjoy a good financial status. They get enough finance for their programmes through grants, funds or donations. Or it may be said that NGOs undertake only those programmes for which grants are available. Thus they do not have to worry about arranging funds for the proposed programme.

Staff Members

Since personnel form backbone of any organization their value cannot be undermined for its success. Qualities in personnel are a valuable asset to the organization. They give a touch of quality and efficiency to the working of an organization. Therefore, they count much for the success and fame that an organization achieves. The qualities of personnel working in NGOs include a sense of dedication and commitment and interest in the social services. In earlier times personnel were expected to have spirit of service and they did not require any special education or training. But now much importance is attached to professionally trained workers. Here, it should be noted that professionally trained workers expect high salaries, status and also opportunities for their own growth and development in their career. They would never want to confine their future in a service motivated organization operating in less challenging environment. They would rather dream for advancement and success that would give them a feel of accomplishment.

The NGOs under the study reported that they face problems to some extent in getting full time staff members, who are suitably trained and sincere and committed to work. For instance, the Bhagini Samaj faces a problem of stability of staff members to greater extent, as they keep on changing jobs.

Similar findings are reported by Chaudhary (1972), that voluntary agencies are under staffed and are inefficient. Because of lack of qualified staff the voluntary agencies are unable to maintain minimum quality standards of work.

CONCLUSION

The findings of the present study clearly depicts that the NGOs hold their definite objectives related to the welfare of women. They conduct many programmes and offer services through various methods in order to achieve their set objectives. But a review of available literature reveal that majority of the NGOs rely on government grants and funds from funding agencies for their programmes and services. They lack in independent source of funds. Thus they are heavily dependent on funds and support of the government as well as other funding agencies. When you receive financial support you fall to the obligation of the funding partners. Under obligation, you have to accept their policies and conditions. Rather they are imposed or dictated on you. In addition, you also owe accountability of what you do. The eventually restricts their innovativeness and freedom of planning and implementation.

The opinions of the beneficiaries regarding selected aspects such as programmes, staff members and timings and problem faced by them reflect that they are satisfied with the functioning of the NGOs. They report improvement in different aspects of their life. Here, it is worth to mention that the efforts of the NGOs towards welfare of women are greatly successful despite the fact that they face problems like delaying funds and unavailability of fulltime trained staff. Thus the efforts of the NGOs should be recognized and appreciated duly. The media are expected to carry out responsibility of motivating public opinion in the favour of selfless service that the NGOs render to the society.

The findings of the present study are directly applicable to the thrust area of the Department of Home Science Extension and Communication, as department is associated with number of NGOs in and around Baroda. Further, the findings might be helpful in fieldwork in collaboration with a number of NGOs.

To conclude it can be said that NGOs have undertaken many programmes and services through different approaches for the welfare of women. Considering the findings reported by the administrators of the NGOs as well as beneficiaries it can be concluded that NGOs just do not have plans on papers only but in reality they want to improve the status of women. Opinions and improvement found by the beneficiaries suggested that they are very satisfied with the programme and services offered by the NGOs. Therefore, present study implies that NGOs' efforts towards welfare of women are of great success and should be appreciated.

REFERENCES

Bhatia A. Women's Development and NGOs. Rawat Publication, Jaipur and New Delhi, 2000.

Brahmbhatt, U. Study of Marriage Counselling Service Provided by Karelibaug Bhagini Samaj Trust, Dissertation (M.S.W.)... M.S. University, Baroda, 1996.

Chaudhary, D. Paul Voluntary Social Welfare in India, Sterling Publication (P) Ltd. New Delhi, 1971.

Dhama, O.P. Education and Communication for Development, Oxford Publication; New Delhi, 1985.

Gaonkar, R. Role of SHGs in Empowerment of Women, Zuarinagar, Goa. Mimeographed paper read as ISTR Sixth International Conference, Contesting Citizenship and Civil Society in a divided world, Toronto, Canada, 11-14 July, 2004. (www.jhu.edu/nistr/conferences/toronto/abstracts/pdf)

Gomes, Lawrence Role of Voluntary and Other Organisations in Development. Yojana, Vol. 33, No. 23, pp. 28-31, 1989.

India, Department of Women and Child Development. Ministry of Human Resource Development. National Perspective plan for Women 1988-2000 A.D. Government of India, 1988.

Joshi, M., Women's Empowerment: Experience from Watershed Project. Social Welfare Vol. 51, No. 4, July 2004, pp. 32-37.

Kaul, A. Educational, Economic and Social Impact of Voluntary Training Agencies offering Income Generating Programmes on Low Socio Economic Status Women of Baroda City. Ph.D. (Thesis) ...., M.S. University, 1990.

Lawani B.T., NGOs in Development, Rawat Publication, Jaipur and New Delhi, 1999.

Maithani, B.P. Voluntary Organisations as Partners in Promoting Participatory Development, Kurukshetra, Vol. XLIII, No. 5, pp. 3-5, 1995.

Mehta and Das, NGOs and Women Empowerment in Pandya R. M., and Mathu, A.A. (Eds.), Imbibing value education – various perspectives, Kalpaz Publications, Gyan Book House, 2003, pp. 163-167.

Narayana, E.A. Voluntary Organisation and Rural Development in India. Uppal Publishing House, New Delhi, 1990.

Pandya, R. M. NGOs – Towards Self-Reliance. Social Welfare, Vol. 43, No. 5, August 1996, pp. 22-24.

Rana, K., People's Participation and Voluntary Action. Dimension, Roles and Strategies. Kanishka Published, Distributed, New Delhi, 2001.

Robson, Lacke and Dawson, User Involvement in the control of Voluntary Organizations, 1997 (www.irf.org.uk).

Sen, S. Voluntary Organisations and Women Development, Dissertation (MSW)..., M.S. University, 1994.

Singhal, C.S. Assam: Survey of NGO Activities. Social Welfare, Vol. 45, No. 10, January 1998, pp. 24-29

Siwach, R.K. Perspective Role of Vos in Tenth Plan. *Social Welfare,* Vol. 50, No. 11, February 2003-pp. 13-15

Suresh, K.A. Participation of Beneficiaries in the Developmental Programmes of NGO in Kerala, *Journal of Rural Development,* Vol. 9, No. 5, September 1990, pp. 911—915.

Wadiwale, Role of SHGs in Empowerment of Women, *Social Welfare,* April 2004, Vol. 54, No. 11 pp. 20-25.

24

HUMAN RESOURCE DEVELOPMENT IN ORISSA, ESPECIALLY IN THE FIELD OF EDUCATION

*Bibekananda Mishra**

Education is one of the important aspect of Human Resource Development. Education is life and life is education. In our state, the Human Resource Development is not mark-worthy. Therefore, our state Orissa is called as the poorest state in the country. In our state 45 persons are living under poverty line.

In the year 1990-91, the Government of Orissa was estimated expenditure to the extent of 16.45% in education out of the total budget. Similarly, in the year 1995-1996, the budget allocation was 18.5% for the field of education. Again, for the session 1999-2000, the education share of this province was 20.67%. In the same way, during the year 2004-2005, the education share of Orissa was estimated at 9.74%. During 2005-2006 Financial Session, the financial allotment was 08.016%. So, the estimated budget provisions of the current year is not remarkable for the wide field of education, considering on percentage basis that is 08.016%.

In numerical figures, during the year 1999-2000, the total education budget was Rs. 11,201.91 crore a out of which 01.9% i.e. Rs. 218.02 crores was allocated for Higher Education. Similarly, in the year 2004-2005, the total amount of the budget for the education sector was Rs. 19,040.56 crores out of which

* Lecturer in Economics, Konark Bhagabati Mahabidyalaya, Konar, Puri-752111, Orissa.

01.48% i.e. Rs. 282.26 crores was spent for Higher Education. In the same context during the fiscal year 2005-2006, the aggregate budget of education in the state was Rs. 26,576.86 crores and out of that 1.15% i.e. Rs. 308.62 crores has been spent in Higher Education.

Now, in our State 42,205 primary schools, 3,640 M.E. Schools, 5, 360 High Schools, 254 + 3 Aided Degree Colleges, 500 Un-Aided Colleges, and 58 Government Colleges as well as 9 Universities level to the University level.

Another aspect is that 1,000,00 Teachers of Primary Schools got Government Cadre in the month of September-1989. 30,000 Teachers of M.E. Schools' of Orissa declared Government in the last part of the year, 1989. In the same context, near about 20,000 teachers and employees of High Schools in Orissa declared Government Employees status in 1994.

Now, in our state, 254 Degree Colleges, 610 High Schools, 609 M.E. Schools are not yet declared as Government Institutions due to continuous budget deficit.

The posts which have been fallen vacant after the retirement or death of the employees are not being filled up by the Govt.

From 1991 onwards, due to retirement and death reason, 17,715 posts have fallen vacant in the school and mass education Department. In the same line, 742 Class-I Posts, 799 Class-II Posts, 1,413 Class-III Posts and in this way totally 2,956 Posts have fallen vacant in the Higher Education Department of Government of Orissa.

Another demerit is that in many M.E. Schools and U.P. Schools in which only 2 classes are functioning, in that case only single teacher has been appointed. If that teacher is taking leave or suffering from illness, then the classes are ultimately being hampered. Again, it has been seen in many High Schools and secondary Training Schools' teachers are imparting teaching through deployment basis. In this connection he/she may visit 3 Schools within two days or 3 Schools in three days or in man cases, the deployments have given for some months.

Demonstrators of the colleges, those who have been rendered more than 13 years of service are also not receiving their grant-in-aid. Similarly, many lecturers those who have sacrificed for a long i.e. above 20 years are also not getting grant-in-aid. Many High School teachers and College Lecturers are now receiving "Block Grants", which is just like contractual payments.

As per 1994 G.O., the Government has abolished the Tutorial system from the colleges. In result, many higher qualified lecturers did not come to the grant-in-aid fold due to the shortage of work-load. Again, the vital fact is that, the students are being deprived of to clear their doubts of general classes due to non existence of Tutorial Classes in the Colleges. To solve this problem, recently the hon'ble minister of Higher Education has announced to implement the tutorial class system again. Another problem is that in this year the Government was proposed to withdraw some sanctioned subjects from the different Government and Aided Colleges of the State due to enrolment of less number of students. This issue was widely debated. My points is that, if the different subjects from the colleges will be abolished then the lecturers of the concerned subjects will go where? What will be their fate?

Another aspect is that, lecturers teachers and employees are not getting regular salaries at the end of the month. Sometimes they are getting their arrear salaries after 4 months, 5 months or 11 months.

In case of Administrative affairs is concerned, it is observed that many governing Boards of many colleges and the managing committees of many High Schools and some employees of the institutions have intentionally and arbitrarily doing illegal works in appointments and approval matters of the employees. Again, at Directorate and Government level, many employees have been indulged in doing blackmailing works. Therefore, the employees of the Educational Institutions are suffering lot.

Again, according to the G.O. of 1994 it was stated that, the teachers and the employees of all the High Schools, M.E. Schools, + 2 Colleges and Degree Colleges will get grant-in-aid. But practically that venture has not been finished. In the meanwhile, Government has circulated a notice to all the Private

Colleges not to appoint any lecturers after the date 31-12-1998. Previously, the Government has validated the post of lecturers of Aided colleges upto 31-12-1992. Therefore, 69 M.L. As of different Parties of Legislative Assembly have requested to the Hon'ble Minister of Higher Education to validate the posts of the lecturer those who have got appointment by the College Managing Committee w.e.f. 01-01-1993 to 31-12-1998.

Further, the Government has also appointed 28,000 "Sikshya Sahayakas" in the State to check up drop-outs and to educate all children. They are now getting Rs. 1500/- each per month.

During the year-1990, at the World Education Conference held at Jamitien of Thailand, there was a declaration that "Education for all". The declaration paper contains that "Investment in Education, fields the highest dividends in both social progress and economic growth and is an investment on Development of Human Resources of any nation..........".

SUGGESTIONS

1. The surplus lecturers those who are coming under validation rule, they should get grants from the Government. Further those surplus lecturers should be adjusted in the Government and Non-Government Colleges of the State in vacancy Posts.
2. The Government should allocate more funds in budget for the Development of Education.

25

REPRODUCTIVE HEALTH: AN UNFINISHED AGENDA

Dilip Kumar Ghosh *

INTRODUCTION

The issue of empowering women is closely interwoven with the reproductive health of women. In the International Conference on Population and Development (ICPD) held in Cairo in 1994 it was recognized that the health agenda of women should receive high priority in their empowerment process. ICPD programme of action defined reproductive health in following words :

> "Reproductive health is a state of complete physical, mental and social well being and not merely the absence of disease or infirmity, in all matters relating to the reproductive system and to its functions and processes. Reproductive health, therefore, implies that people are able to have a satisfying and safe sex life and that they have the capability to reproduce and freedom to decide if, when and how often to do so. Implicit in this last condition are the rights of men and women to be informed and to have access to safe, effective, affordable and acceptable methods of family planning of their choice, as well as other methods of their choice for regulation of fertility which are not against the law, and right of access to appropriate health-care services that will enable women to go safely through pregnancy and childbirth and provide couples with the best chance of having a healthy infant. In line with the above definition of reproductive health,

* Senior Research Officer, State Institute of Panchayats and Rural Development, Kalyani, Nadia.

> reproductive health care is defined as the constellation of methods, techniques and services that contribute to reproductive health and well being by preventing and solving reproductive health problems ... (United Nations, 1994)".

Health status of any person is a complex process depending on biological, social and cultural factors. These factors are highly interrelated but they affect men and women differently. For example, biological and social factors have cumulative effects throughout their entire life cycle. Unlike men, women exclusively are subject to the risks related to their pregnancy and child bearing. Frequent pregnancy coupled with scarce maternity care makes women vulnerable to different risks of pregnancy related causes. In general, reproductive health is found to be worst among the poor and women are subject to more deprivations within the deprived families. In the empowerment process, reproductive health care in favour of women is an important component. But most often this issue remains uncared for leaving women in disadvantaged position within family and within society. The situation can be described from a World Bank Study :

> "Women's disadvantaged social position, which is often related to the economic value placed on familial roles, helps perpetuate poor health, inadequate diet, early and frequent pregnancy and a continued cycle of poverty. For example, women in many parts of the world receive medical treatment less often when sick, and then only at a more advanced stage of disease. In countries where women are less educated and have less control over decision making and family resources, they are also less apt to recognise health problems or to seek care" (Tinker, Anne and others, 2000).

The same study also found that "more than one-fifth of the disease burden among women aged 15 to 44 results from reproductive health problems which can be prevented or treated cost effectively". The burden of disease in females aged 15 to 44 years in developing countries as delineated in this study (2000) is like this - injuries (15.6%), other communicable diseases (7%), STD and HIV (6.3%), maternal causes (16%), malnutrition (4.1%), tuberculosis (4.9%), depression and other neuro-psychiatric condition (24.6%) and other non-communicable diseases (21.5%). But detailed statistics are not available for disaggregated level (district or sub district level). World Health Organisation Statistics show that complications of pregnancy and childbirth are major causes of death among the women of reproductive age, particularly in developing countries. Therefore, any empowerment process in favour of women should take care of ensuring safe motherhood. Safe motherhood not only includes adequate healthcare for women in their pregnancies and delivery but also the prevention of unwanted ill-timed pregnancies. It is generally accepted that women's education and their participation in economically productive work have negative correlation with fertility. The logic is expressed by researchers in following words :

> ".... there is probably little reason to doubt that when women have greater autonomy, decision making power, control over their own and household resources, access to adequate services, and freedom from violence and coercion, they also exercise greater power in their sexual and reproductive relations. In such a context, they tend to make decisions which result in delaying marriage, having fewer children, spacing pregnancies and even remaining unmarried or childless by choice" (Sen and Presser, 2000).

In this backdrop, the present article is developed with district-disaggregated data available for West Bengal. West Bengal is considered because of its unique feature that the Left Front Government under the leadership of Communist Party of India (Marxists) has been administering the State uninterruptedly since 1977. The main problem is data limitation in respect of all the components of reproductive health of women and the services provided for them. The major source of health related data is the publication 'Health on the March' by State Bureau of Health Intelligence, Government of West Bengal. On the basis of availability district of disaggregated data, article is divided into three sections. Section I deals with family welfare programmes and fertility behaviour among married women. Section II presents the scenario related with safe motherhood. Data of Reproductive and Child Health Survey conducted by the Department of Health and Family Welfare, Govt. of West Bengal are mainly used here. Section III presents the nutritional status of women in West Bengal. In addition to these official data of the Department of Health and Family Welfare, Govt. of West Bengal, National Family Health Survey reports for West Bengal provide macro scenario of the state in respect of reproductive health. State policies and their execution are culled from different issues of 'Economic Review' made by the State Government.

SECTION I

Reproductive health services are recognised as vital components in the process of empowering women. The supporting view is expressed in following words (Barroso and Jacobson, 2000) :

> "Such services are empowering to the extent that they assist women and men in meeting their own fertility goals safely and effectively, provide a wide range of choices and information, raise consciousness of and address broader reproductive and sexual health issues and actively promote individual rights, respect and dignity. With this context, the role of contraceptive delivery efforts is to assist women and men in reducing unwanted fertility". (ibid)

Though no district wise data on unwanted fertility is available for West Bengal, NFHS1 (1992) and NFHS2(1998-99) throw some light on this issue taking the state as a whole. In the words of NFHS2 :

> "The impact of unwanted fertility can be measured by comparing the total wanted fertility rate with the total fertility rate (TFR). The total wanted rate represents the level of fertility that theoretically would result if all unwanted births were prevented. A comparison of the TFR with the total wanted fertility rate indicates the potential demographic impact of the elimination of all unwanted births ... In this case, a birth is considered unwanted if the number of living children at the time of conception was greater than or equal to the ideal number of children reported by the respondent at the time of the survey..."

In table 1, total wanted fertility rate (TWFR) and total fertility rate (TFR) for women with selected background characteristics are given. These data are taken from NFHS1 and NFHS2 survey reports. The difference between total fertility rate and total wanted fertility rate is the unwanted fertility.

Table 1
Wanted fertility rates by selected background characteristics: West Bengal

Background Characteristics	*NFHS1*			*NFHS 2*		
	TWFR	*TFR*	*Unwanted fertility rate*	*TWFR*	*TFR*	*Unwanted fertility rate*
Residence						
Rural	2.43	3.25	0.82 (25)	1.90	2.49	0.59 (24)
Education						
Education						
Illiterate	2.76	3.73	0.97 (26)	2.10	2.79	0.69 (25)
Literate but not	2.11	2.82	0.71 (25)	1.75	2.30	0.55 (24)
Completing Middle School Middle School	1.37	1.77	0.40 (23)	1.53	1.71	0.18 (11)
Complete						
High school complete and above	1.35	1.50	0.15 (10)	1.31	1.42	0.11 (8)
Religion						
Hindu	1.96	2.52	0.56 (22)	1.63	2.02	0.39 (19)
Muslim	3.17	4.59	1.42 (31)	2.25	3.29	1.04 (32)
Other	1.74	2.30	0.56 (24)	1.38	1.68	0.30 (18)
Caste/tribe						
Scheduled caste	2.74	3.52	0.78 (22)	1.89	2.34	0.45 (19)
Scheduled tribe	2.22	3.05	0.83 (27)	1.81	2.31	0.50 (22)
Other	2.15	2.85	0.70 (25)	1.68	2.21	0.53 (24)

Source: NFHS 1 and NFHS 2 Survey Reports.
Note: Unwanted fertility rate = TFR – TWFR percentage figures are in brackets.

From table 1 it can be seen that most women with the exception of illiterate women and women of Muslim Community, want to have fewer than two children on an average (NFHS 2 Survey). According to NFHS 1 Survey, caste classification of women shows that women irrespective of castes/ tribes wanted to have more than two children – but this scenario changed totally in NFHS 2 Survey. No woman whatever be their caste/ tribe would want to have more than two children. Even rural women do not want more than two children. This certainly is the outcome of expanding educational opportunities. However, the difference between TWFR and TFR is found to be very large in rural areas and in case of illiterate women and women of Muslim Community. NFHS 2 Survey found that for the state as a whole TWFR was 1.78 against TFR 2.29 – thus difference was 0.51 children i.e. 22 percent of TFR. If unwanted births could be avoided, then it can be said that West Bengal can achieve below – replacement fertility. Here comes the role of family planning programmes and education of women in particular. In urban areas, the difference between TWFR and TFR is low (only 18 percent of TFR). According to NFHS 2 Survey report, in West Bengal "knowledge of contraceptive methods is universal with virtually all currently married women recognizing at least one method of contraception and at least one modern method of contraception". Methods of contraception are classified into two groups e.g. modern method and traditional method. Modern methods consist of pills, IUDs, injection, condoms, female sterilisation and male sterilisation. Traditional methods are normally of two types viz. periodic abstinence or the rhythm method and withdrawal. National Family Health Survey conducted during two periods (1992 and 1998-99) collected information on current use of family planning methods in the state. As district disaggregated data for current use of family planning methods are not available, for presenting the pattern of use, we have to boast upon NFHS data. In table 2, both NFHS 1 and NFHS 2 data are given for getting an overview of changes occurred during the period.

From table 2 it can be seen that contraceptive prevalence is very low among women of scheduled tribe communities and Muslims. Literacy is positively related to the use of contraceptive method. Women completed middle school level of education are found to use any contraceptive method more than illiterate women. Thus girls' education has a major impact on population control in the state.

NFHS data for the two survey periods show that mostly used contraceptive method is female sterilization. The use of condoms is more prevalent in urban and among the literate women. Sterilization is preferred by women as it is mostly done in hospitals and government clinics and is less expensive. This method is adopted by more illiterate women than women having some educational attainments. The results of NFHS

Table 2
Current use of family planning methods in West Bengal

Background Characteristics	NFHS1				NFHS 2			
	Any method method	Any modern method	Any traditional	Other method	Any method method	Any modern method	Any traditional	Other method
Residence								
Rural	55.7	37.6	18.2	0.5	64.5	47.5	15.9	1.0
Urban	61.8	36.5	25.3	0.7	73.4	46.4	26.6	0.4
Education								
Illiterate	49.1	35.9	13.2	0.4	62.2	49.4	11..8	1.0
Literate but not Completing Middle School	61.6	41.8	19.8	0.7	68.7	47.9	19.7	1.1
Middle School Complete	66.9	36.2	30.7	0.3	75.1	45.9	28.9	0.3
High school complete and above	75.1	31.9	43.2	1.1	72.5	37.8	34.1	0.5
Religion								
Hindu	61.4	41.2	20.1	0.4	69.8	50.2	19.0	0.7
Muslim	43.0	23.3	19.7	1.2	56.3	37.6	17.5	1.2
Other	60.7	37.3	23.4	-	64.6	44.3	14.6	5.7
Caste/tribe								
Scheduled caste	54.5	38.8	15.7	0.3	68.2	53.1	14.0	1.1
Scheduled tribe	44.8	36.4	8.4	0.8	52.8	41.3	9.6	1.9
Other	58.4	37.2	21.3	0.6	66.9	44.9	21.2	0.7

Source: NFHS1 and NFHS2 Survey Reports.
Note: Figures are in percentage.

Table 2 (a)
Current use of some modern contraceptive methods in West Bengal

Background Characteristics	*NFHS1*			*NFHS 2*		
	Female Sterilisation	*Male Sterilisation*	*Condom*	*Female Sterilisation*	*Male Sterilisation*	*Condom*
Residence						
Rural	27.4	5.1	0.9	33.5	2.0	1.6
Urban	23.3	2.1	4.3	27.0	1.2	7.1
Education						
Illiterate	28.3	5.5	0.2	39.5	2.7	1.0
Literate but not Completing Middle School	29.3	4.5	1.4	30.0	1.2	2.4
Middle School complete	23.2	2.3	2.4	23.2	0.8	4.4
High school complete and above	10.8	-	10.6	12.9	1.1	11.4
Religion						
Hindu	30.0	4.4	2.1	35.9	1.9	2.8
Muslim	13.1	3.8	1.2	18.7	1.9	3.5
Other	27.8	6.8	-	30.2	0	2.1
Caste/tribe						
Scheduled caste	30.9	6.0	0.7	43.6	1.7	1.3
Scheduled tribe	30.2	4.5	-	31.1	2.9	0.5
Other	25.5	4.1	2.1	27.3	1.8	3.7

Source: NFHS 1 and NFHS 2 Survey Reports.
Note: Figures show distribution of currently married women and are in percentage.

for the two survey periods in this respect are given in table 2(a).

Table 2(a) shows that, in between NFHS 1 and NFHS 2 there occurred a substantial increase in female sterilisation in rural areas (22.26 percent). Among illiterate women also there occurs a increase of about 39.57 percent increase in adoption of sterilisation method for contraception. The sterilisation as a technique is simple, safe and effective and can be administered in local health centres. Tenth Five Year Plan also puts stress on adopting this terminal method of contraception :

> "... Currently, age at marriage is very low and a majority of the women complete their families during early 20s. In the current Indian milieu of stable marriages, sterilisation is the most appropriate method of contraception for such couples".

Tenth five year plan, however, keeps the door open for the couples to take decision in the matter of choosing the method of contraception – the main objective is to reduce unwanted pregnancy substantially. If unwanted births can be avoided it would be easier to achieve replacement level of fertility. In the words of Tenth five year plan :

> "... It is imperative that all the unmet needs are fully met within the Tenth Plan period and a substantial reduction in unwanted pregnancy is achieved. Making a balanced presentation of advantages and disadvantages of methods, improving counselling, quality of services and follow up care will enable couples to make appropriate choices regarding contraception, increase couple protection rates and continuation rates and enable the country to achieve the goal of replacement level of fertility by 2010".

The evolution of family welfare programme in India shows that in 1960s and 1970s vasectomy was the most widely used method of contraception. Thereafter male sterilisation declines sharply. Tenth five year plan emphasizes re-popularisation of vasectomy for effective male participation in planned parenthood :

> "...It is essential that efforts to re-popularise vasectomy are intensified. Ample data exists to show that vasectomy is safer than tubectomy. Every effort will be made to repopularise vasectomy by improving access to vasectomy services. These

services will be made readily available to all at convenient times as an outpatient procedure in all primary, secondary and tertiary care institutions."

In West Bengal, the same trend is noticed. For example, during 1960s, of total sterilisation performed, male sterilisation was to the extent of 89.67 percent while female sterilisation was to the tune of 10.33 percent. Similarly, in 1970s the proportion of male sterilisation was 70.91 percent while female sterilisation was around 29.09 percent. Since 1980s, this trend reversed and the burden of sterilisation fell on the women as if they are the sole controller of decisions regarding childbirth. In table 3, percentage of male and female sterilisation are given – this indicates that female have no option but to accept the burden of family planning.

Table 3
Year wise progress in sterilisation programme : West Bengal

Year	*Total sterilisation*	*Male sterilisation*	*Female sterilization*
1990-91	320480	4668 (1.46)	315812 (98.54)
1991-92	327115	4414 (1.35)	322701 (98.65)
1992-93	312959	3163 (1.01)	309796 (98.99)
1993-94	354909	3102 (0.87)	351807 (99.13)
1994-95	361191	2046 (0.56)	359145 (99.44)
1995-96	331060	1754 (0.53)	329306 (99.47)
1996-97	326398	1321 (0.41)	325077 (99.59)
1997-98	321969	1677 (0.52)	320292 (99.48)
1998-99	269861	1173 (0.44)	268688 (99.56)
1999-2000	289076	1338 (0.46)	287738 (99.54)
2000-01	313817	1209 (0.39)	312608 (99.61)
2001-02	296969	1532 (0.52)	295437 (99.48)
2002-03	245258	1873 (0.76)	243385 (99.24)

Source: Health on the March, 2002-2003.
Note: Percentage figures are in brackets.

From table 3 it can be seen that since 1990-91, in every year proportion of female sterilisation increases over the previous year till 1996-97. However, from 2001-2002 it falls marginally. Table 3 indicates that even there is option for male sterilisation, onus of planned parenthood is shifted on the shoulders of women.

In West Bengal, family planning services are primarily provided through a network of government hospitals, family welfare centres and primary health centres (for the rural areas). According to NFHS 2 survey, the relative importance of various sources of contraceptive methods shows that the public sector, comprising government/municipal hospitals, government dispensaries, primary health centres and other government health infrastructure are the sources of providing contraceptives to 76 percent of current users of modern methods. Rural – urban break up of this coverage shows that in rural areas, 83 percent of current users depend on government sources and in case of urban areas this percentage is 60 percent only. Thus, dependence of rural people for getting the benefits of modern contraceptive methods is relatively higher than the urban people.

For getting the coverage of family planning programme, couple protection rate is widely used as an indicator. Couple protection rate (CPR) is simply the ratio of total current contraceptive users and number of eligible couples multiplied by 100. In West Bengal seven contraceptive methods are found to be in vogue – these are pills, condoms, IUD (Intra-Uterine devices), female sterilisation, male sterilisation, rhythm or safe-period method and withdrawal. In table 4, district wise couple protection rate for the period 1998-99 to 2002-2003 is presented.

From table 4, it can be seen that except in Howrah, Uttar Dinajpur, Malda and Darjeeling, in all other districts, CPR declines over the period. CPR and female literacy rate are highly correlated as increase in female literacy leads to increase in the users of varied contraceptive methods. The Economic Review 2001-2002 of the Govt. of West Bengal makes observation in this line :

> "... with the spread of education, social and personal values of the common people have become less tradition bound and more receptive to new ideas, specially in the sphere of family welfare ... the spread of education has considerable influence on the acceptance of family welfare measures is indicated by the high percentage of literates among acceptors of family welfare measures..."

Here, CPRs are for those availing of the facilities of contraceptive method given from government sources only. The actual users of family welfare measures are certainly far greater – according to NFHS 2 Survey, in West Bengal, CPR is 66.6 percent. The crux of this achievement is portrayed in Economic Review, 2002-2003 of the State Government :

Table 4
Couple Protection Rate

District	*1998-1999*	*1999-2000*	*2000-2001*	*2001-2002*	*2002-2003*	*Growth Index*
Burdwan	54.93	54.27	54.26	53.77	51.78	0.942
Birbhum	45.48	44.64	42.77	42.52	38.63	0.849
Bankura	44.33	43.73	43.75	43.81	42.90	0.967
Midnapur	39.08	38.11	37.40	36.33	34.41	0.880
Howrah	26.20	26.30	29.15	29.75	28.72	1.096
Hooghly	37.05	35.40	34.49	34.33	31.74	0.856
North 24 Parganas	25.70	25.03	24.29	24.42	21.14	0.822
South 24 Parganas	21.13	20.63	20.53	20.00	17.66	0.836
Kolkata	41.25	39.86	38.11	36.35	39.14	0.948
Nadia	37.37	35.84	36.69	33.57	31.21	0.835
Murshidabad	34.54	34.40	36.85	37.50	32.97	0.954
Uttar Dinajpur	22.67	21.59	19.30	21.20	32.56	1.436
Dakshin Dinajpur	26.21	27.34	28.50	29.60	25.83	0.985
Malda	21.02	20.26	21.24	21.11	24.11	1.147
Jaipaiguri	40.68	39.71	38.52	37.99	34.22	0.841
Darjeeling	44.27	42.82	41.59	38.84	65.32	1.475
Cooch Behar	50.90	49.39	41.10	50.32	48.31	0.949
Purulia	44.81	43.91	45.12	42.30	41.58	0.928
West Bengal	36.25	35.43	35.34	34.82	33.62	0.927

Source: Different issues of Health on the March.

Note: (i) Estimation based on performance data from government sources only.

(ii) CPR figures are in percentage.

(iii) $\text{Growth index} = \dfrac{\text{Value of CPR in 2002-2003}}{\text{Value of CPR in 1998-99}}$

"West Bengal has been successful in involving the common people through the Panchayats and Municipalities and NGOs in the implementation of family welfare programmes in the state. The involvement of these agencies has not only increased the reach of the family welfare programmes but has also created the awareness among the poor about the need for family welfare measures."

Management of unwanted pregnancy is also necessary along with broadening the periphery of contraceptive users. Unsafe abortion accounts for a sizeable number of maternal deaths. Definitive data on this issue is not available to make in - depth study. "Health on the March" publication by the Health Department of the State Government provides data on cases of MTP taken place in the districts. As no estimation on illegal induced abortion is found in this publication, it is not possible to give any indication to what extent women become prey to unwanted pregnancy and have to face the adverse consequences, even death. According to Tenth five year plan document :

> "The estimated number of illegal induced abortions in the country is in the range of four to six million. There has not been any substantical decline in the estimated number of illegal abortions, reported morbidity due to illegal abortions or share of illegal abortions as the cause of maternal mortality. The management of unwanted pregnancy through early and safe MTP services as envisaged under the MTP Act is an important component of the ongoing RCH programme" (Chapter 2.10).

The dimension of the problem of unwanted pregnancy and consequent abortion can also be revealed from the observations of the Tenth Plan. The prime reason for each unwanted pregnancy is profound inequality of gender in the society. Dixon-Mueller and Germain (2000) explained unwantedness in following words :

> "By unwanted sex we mean any sexual act or relationship in which a person is forced by threat or social pressure or by economic circumstance to participate against her or his will. The unwantedness may refer to the particular partner (a spouse or lover, an acquaintance, a stranger) or to the fact, timing or nature of a given sex act. Pressure to acquiesce results from gender ideologies and behavioural norms in the environment such as those requiring the early marriage of girls to protect their modesty, with or without consent. Unwantedness also results from the use of physical force or force-threat in the relationship in general or at the time of the sexual act; emotional abuse; or the more subtle

> but no less compelling coercion of economic and social dependency in which the more vulnerable partner (e.g. a wife or girl friend, an abused child or adolescent, an employee, even a commercial sex worker) believes that she or he simply cannot refuse".

In India Medical Termination of Pregnancy (MTP) Act was passed in 1972 to enable women with unwanted pregnancy to seek and obtain services for safe abortion. According to Tenth FYP till the end of Ninth Plan, women get little benefit of the provisions of this Act.

> "In spite of these efforts, there has not been any increase interms of coverage, number of MTPs reported and reduction in the number of women suffering adverse health consequences of illegal induced abortions".

Abortion has a welcome effect on population growth – but it must be safe and legal. According to Henshaw and Morrow (1990), about 20 to 25 percent of all recognised pregnancies worldwide are terminated every year by induced abortion, including 25 to 40 percent in China, Singapore and Turkey and 40 percent or more in Cuba and South Korea. In table 5, data on medical termination of pregnancy in West Bengal districts for a consecutive period of five year are given to have an overview of the progress of MTP. These data are taken from different issues of Health on the March, a publication of Department of Health, Govt. of West Bengal.

Table 5 shows that Kolkata and its adjacent two districts viz. North 24 Parganas and Howrah account for major share in MTP performed in the State – in 1998-99 their share is 79.74 percent in total MTP in the state, in 1999-2000 it becomes 75.83 percent, in 2000-2001 it declines to 66.99 percent. In general, the districts with high proportion of urban population, have higher share in total MTP performed. With this discussion, we shall now shift to discuss delivery care services availed by women. Limited availability of district disaggregated data very much restricts us from undertaking a detailed study. For this reason, section II is developed with NFHS reports and RCH survey results of the State Government.

Table 5
Progress of MTP in districts

District	1998-1999	1999-2000	2000-2001	2001-2002	2002-2003	Share of urban population (%)
Burdwan	466	663	701 (2.15)	640	655	37.18
Birbhum	1303	91	79 (0.25)	191	98	8.58
Bankura	198	139	85 (0.26)	98	68	7.37
Midnapur	1403	1224	1461 (4.50)	1582	1937	10.49
Howrah	1977 (4.84)	2213 (6.08)	1970 (6.06)	1487 (3.46)	1447 (3.43)	50.39
Hooghly	1556	1684	1999 (6.15)	1425	905	33.48
North 24 Parganas	7878 (19.30)	7608 (20.92)	10338 (31.83)	5966 (13.89)	2529 (6.00)	54.30
South 24 Parganas	229	318	537(1.65)	922	1584	15.77
Kolkata	22687 (55.60)	17753(48.83)	9451 (29.10)	20915 (48.70)	24105 (57.18)	100.00
Nadia	1452	1486	1411 (4.35)	2371	2094	21.27
Murshidabad	232	763	55 (0.17)	99	79	12.49
Uttar Dinajpur	NA	3	208 (0.64)	735	748	12.06
Dakshin Dinajpur	50	NA	86 (0.26)	472	1017	13.09
Malda	2	222	279 (0.86)	2275	1499	7.32
Jalpaiguri	84	368	1376 (4.25)	1144	1393	17.74
Darjeeling	665	761	793 (2.45)	726	765	32.44
Cooch Behar	212	407	310 (0.95)	806	601	9.10
Purulia	406	651	1340 (4.12)	1087	630	10.07
West Bengal	40800	36354	32479	42941	42154	28.03

Source: Different issues of Health on the March.
Note: Percentage figures in brackets. Share of urban population as in 2001 Census.

SECTION II

Women's health in reality is influenced by number of factors emanating from cross-section of disciplines. For providing a comprehensive definition of women's health, The National Academy of Women's Health Medical Education in Philadelphia published (in 1996) a resource guide for their faculty. The definition is quoted here from Levison and Levison (2001) :

> "Women's health is devoted to facilitating the preservation of wellness and prevention of illness and includes screening, diagnosis and management of conditions which are unique to women, are more common in women, are more serious in women and have manifestations, risk factors or interventions which are different in women".

Motherhood is unique to women and has many risks to women at the same time. According to India Health Report (2003), "... more than 1,00,000 Indian women die of pregnancy related causes every year, which is about 18 percent of total global maternal deaths". This signifies the importance of antenatal and delivery care for pregnant women. Since 1996, the Government of India introduced the Reproductive and Child Health (RCH) programme for integrating maternal health, child health, fertility regulation interventions with reproductive health programmes. RCH programme has some important elements for taking care of pregnant and lactating mothers. These are reproduced below from NFHS 2 survey report.

(i) provision of antenatal care, including at least three antenatal care visits, iron prophylaxis for pregnant and lactating women, two doses of tetanus toxoid vaccine, detection and treatment of anaemia in mothers, and management and referral of high risk pregnancies;

(ii) encouragement of institutional deliveries or home deliveries assisted by trained health personnel;

(iii) provision of post-natal care, including at least three postnatal visits; and

(iv) identification and management of reproductive tract and sexually transmitted infections.

The performance of RCH programme, however, is not encouraging during Ninth five-year plan. Tenth five year plan narrates the performance in following words :

> "Under the RCH programme, efforts were made to improve the coverage, content and quality of antenatal care in order to achieve substantial reduction in maternal and perinatal morbidity and mortality. Data from the rapid household survey, 1998-99 indicates that at the national level, 67.2 percent pregnant women received at least one check-up but only 10.6 percent had three antenatal checkups"

According to the RCH programme, as part of the antenatal care, women should receive two doses of tetanus toxoid vaccine, adequate amount of iron and folic acid tablets or syrup for preventing and treatment of anaemia and at least three antenatal check-ups that include blood pressure checks and other procedures to detect pregnancy complications. NFHS 2 provides the components of antenatal check ups carried on in West Bengal. Rural-urban break up available from this survey report reflects the deprivation of rural women in respect of getting antenatal checkups. Table 6 presents the rural-urban divide.

From table 6 it can be seen that except in case of ante-natal advice on diet, in all other components, rural women are more deprived than their urban counterparts. Sonography or ultra sound component is least availed by rural women. Between blood test and urine test, in case of rural women, testing of urine is less than urban women. The effectiveness of antenatal care depends on the tests and measurements made and advices given to the pregnant women.

According to NFHS 2 survey, neo-natal tetanus is an important cause of death in infancy. This is caused by newborn infants becoming infected by tetanus organisms, usually at the umbilical stump. The chances of attacking from neo natal tetanus increase in case of children delivered in unhygienic environments and when unsterilized instruments are used for cutting the umbilical cord. Death is certain if immediate medical help is not available in rural areas this is very much common as the health service network is not sound there. In the opinion of experts, neonatal tetanus is a preventable disease. To quote:

"Two doses of tetanus toxoid vaccine given one month apart during early pregnancy are nearly 100 percent effective in preventing tetanus among both newborn infants and their mothers. Immunity against tetanus is transferred to the foetus through the placenta when the mother is vaccinated" (NFHS 2 Survey Report).

Table 6
Components of Antenatal check-ups : West Bengal

Components of antenatal check ups	*Urban*	*Rural*	*Difference*	*Rural-Urban ratio*
Antenatal measurements/tests				
Weight measured	87.6	56.3	31.3	0.642
Height measured	35.2	17.2	18.0	0.488
Blood pressure checked	84.3	55.6	28.7	0.659
Blood tested	80.1	38.2	41.9	0.477
Urine tested	72.5	30.2	42.3	0.416
Abdomen examined	77.5	49.1	28.4	0.633
Internal examination	42.1	14.7	27.4	0.349
X-Ray	13.6	4.0	9.6	0.294
Sonography or ultra sound	23.4	3.2	20.2	0.136
Amniocentesis	1.2	0.1	1.1	0.083
Antenatal advice Diet	83.8	70.0	13.8	0.835
Danger signs of pregnancy	70.1	50.9	19.2	0.726
Delivery care	58.5	40.3	18.2	0.688
New born care	49.6	39.2	10.4	0.790
Family planning	22.9	23.4	0.5	1.022

Source: NFHS 2 Survey (1998-99) Report, Table 8.5.
Note: (i) Urban, Rural figures are in percentage,
(ii) Difference = Urban – Rural.
Difference is expressed in percentage point.

Tetanus Toxoid immunization programme for expectant mothers was introduced in our country way back in 1975-76. Government of India in Ministry of Health and Family Welfare introduced Universal Immunization Programme in the year 1985-86 with an objective to vaccinate all pregnant women against tetanus by 1990. This immunization programme was initially taken up as a National Technology Mission and later on in 1992 it was made a component of Child Survival and Safe Motherhood programme. In 1997, Government of India initiated the Reproductive and Child Health (RCH) programme for providing integrated health and family welfare services to women and children. Immunization programme for expectant mothers was brought under this newly introduced RCH programme. As noted in NFHS 2 Survey report, "according to the National Immunization Schedule, a pregnant women should receive two doses of tetanus toxoid vaccine, the first when she is 16 weeks pregnant and the second when she is 20 weeks pregnant". NFHS 2 Survey shows that the coverage of women receiving two or more tetanus toxoid injections is positively correlated with level of education. In case of illiterate women, because of their unawareness, the coverage of tetanus toxoid vaccination is comparatively less than the literate women or women with formal education. In spite of the best intention of the programme, full coverage of tetanus toxoid vaccine could not be achieved – NFHS 2 survey data for West Bengal shows the coverage of 82.4 percent of pregnant women with two or more doses. In NFHS 1 this coverage was to the extent of only 70.4 percent. Health on the March publication gives year wise coverage of tetanus toxoid vaccination to the pregnant women. This publication, however, does not make reflection on the doses of vaccination. In general, the trend is better coverage in urban areas than in rural areas. For example, according to NFHS 2 survey data, in urban areas, 87.5 percent pregnant women were covered under tetanus toxoid vaccination. The coverage is only 81.2 percent in the rural areas. In table 7, year wise coverage in the state since 1991-92 is given.

Table 7 shows that in spite of increase in the coverage of tetanus toxoid vaccination, all pregnant women could not be covered under the programme. Certainly this enhances risks for both mothers and the newborn babies. For providing sufficient antenatal care, West Bengal has a network of 17 district hospitals, 40 sub divisional hospitals, 36 state general hospitals, 923 primary health centres, 250 Block Primary Health Centres (BPHC) and 8126 subcenters (Health on the March, 2002-2003). Under the action plan of mother and child health and family welfare services, antenatal care, in general is provided by female health workers during their regular field visits. For consolidating the existing services, the State Plan of Action for

Children (2003) published by Govt. of West Bengal recommends strengthening of the First Referral units :

Table 7
Coverage of tetanus toxoid vaccine to pregnant women

Year	*Coverage in percentage*	*Change over the previous year*
1991-92	75.28	-
1992-93	76.84	2.07
1993-94	80.01	4.12
1994-95	88.78	10.96
1995-96	81.28	8.45
1996-97	86.36	6.25
1997-98	91.85	6.36
1998-99	90.43	1.54
1999-2000	84.86	6.16
2000-01	90.41	6.54
2001-02	88.44	2.18
2002-03	83.58	5.49

Source: Health on the March, 2002-2003.

"The First Referral Units to be identified at sub-district level, i.e. one for 3 – 5 lakh population and to be strengthened to handle obstetric emergencies. This will necessitate the posting of the specialists and providing facilities for operations, especially facility for anaesthesia. List of such First Referral units are made available in each village, so that there is no delay in referring the patients to appropriate health facility ... This will require the participation of panchayat members as well as motivation of the community to plan for emergency transportation wherever required..."

For getting district disaggregated data on antenatal care provided to pregnant women, we have the lone source in reports on important indicators of RCH released by the Department of Health and Family Welfare, Govt. of West Bengal. Total assessment of antenatal care provided thus is not possible because of non-availability of component wise data . One important task in antenatal care is early registration of pregnancy (12 – 16 weeks). But in West Bengal, out of the estimated number of pregnant women for a year, ANC (antenatal care) registration was possible in 79 percent cases during 1999-2000. In 2000-2001 it was possible to make ANC registration in 90 percent cases, in 2001-2002 this registration was possible in 89.51 percent cases and in 2002-2003 this figure rises to 94.41 percent. In West Bengal three antenatal checkups of pregnant women cannot be ensured to all in the target group. The shortfall in this respect can easily be comprehended from table 8 where district wise coverage of pregnant women having three antenatal checkups are given.

Table 8
Coverage of antenatal care in West Bengal

District	*1999-2000*	*2000-2001*	*2001-2002*	*2002-2003*	*Ranking by the latest year*	*Growth Index*
Burdwan	31.78	52.63	52.71	62.13	7	1.95
Birbhum	34.57	42.86	44.80	48.28	14	1.40
Bankura	65.95	56.68	71.85	71.60	3	1.08
Midnapur	58.16	43.30	49.18	64.04	10	1.10
Howrah	37.19	43.50	50.52	58.93	8	1.58
Hooghly	54.28	43.64	59.46	65.37	5	1.20
North 24 Parganas	29.19	28.64	33.90	45.88	16	1.57
South 24 Parganas	24.48	33.32	51.88	53.38	11	2.18
Kolkata	137.79	48.44	57.65	169.16	1	1.23
Nadia	49.58	52.34	54.18	66.11	4	1.33
Murshidabad	41.15	49.44	50.73	52.63	12	1.28
Uttar Dinajpur	35.71	35.92	21.80	37.55	18	1.05
Dakshin Dinajpur	26.92	39.05	44.97	41.42	17	1.54
Malda	32.47	44.65	43.93	47.15	15	1.45
Jalpaiguri	76.36	33.64	44.74	52.42	13	0.686
Darjeeling	105.00	101.51	91.75	83.67	2	0.796
Cooch Behar	61.91	56.45	59.12	55.89	9	0.902
Purulia	49.25	58.86	54.92	63.68	6	1.29
West Bengal	49.21	44.97	50.85	57.43	-	1.17

Source: Reports on important indicators under RCH programme for different years, Department of Health and Family Welfare, Govt. of West Bengal.

Note: (i) Figures of different years are in percentage.
(ii) Growth index=(Coverage in 2002-2003/Coverage in 1999-2000)

From table 8 it can be seen that except in three districts of North Bengal, in all other districts, antenatal coverage increases in 2002-2003 in comparison to the year 1999-2000. This has been possible because the State Government is making all out efforts to involve the local bodies in execution of Health Department programmes. The female health workers posted in subcenters and primary health centres are supposed to pay regular field visit for ANC registration and services. The anganwadi workers (AWW) of Integrated Child Development Services (ICDS), trained birth attendants and voluntary health guides are required to collaborate with female health workers of the gram panchayats (State Plan of Action for Children, Govt. of West Bengal, 2003).

DELIVERY CARE

An important component of RCH programme is to encourage deliveries under proper hygienic conditions and under the supervision of trained health professionals. On this issue, Tenth five year plan document makes the following observation :

> "During the Ninth Plan, it was envisaged that efforts will be made to promote institutional deliveries both in the urban and rural areas. Simultaneously, in districts where a majority of the deliveries were taking place at home, efforts were made to train the traditional birth attendants (TBAs) through an intensive Dai Training Programme and to increase the availability of disposable kits" (Chapter 2.10).

NFHS 1 and NFHS 2 surveys provide information on delivery care and delivery characteristics. On this basis, the Tenth Plan comments that "there are a large number of districts in many states where the situation with regard to safe deliveries is far from satisfactory". NFHS 1 and NFHS 2 provide data on place of delivery categorizing it into two broad categories viz. institutional deliveries (taking place in public institutions like government operated hospitals in district, town, block, municipalities and primary health centres having infrastructure to render delivery services and private institutions) and non-institutional deliveries (taking place in women's own home or their parent's home). In table 9, the percentage distribution of births on the basis of place of delivery and some selected background characteristics are given in respect of NFHS 1 and NFHS 2 data.

Table 9
Distribution of births on the basis of place of delivery: West Bengal

Background Characteristics	NFHS 1		NFHS 2		Absolute change	
	Institutional	Non-Institutional	Institutional	Non-Institutional	Institutional	Non-Institutional
Residence						
Rural	21.4	78.3	31.3	67.6	+46.26	-13.66
Urban	66.0	33.1	79.7	19.3	+20.75	-41.69
Education						
Illiterate	16.3	83.3	26.6	72.3	+63.19	-13.20
Literate but not Completing Middle School	35.9	63.3	38.7	59.9	+7.80	-5.37
Middle School complete	63.5	36.0	65.9	34.0	+3.78	-5.55
Middle School complete	63.5	36.0	65.9	34.0	+3.78	-5.55
High school complete and above	89.5	10.5	89.0	9.2	-0.55	-12.38
Religion						
Hindu	40.4	59.2	51.2	47.5	+26.73	-19.76
Muslim	11.8	87.6	15.9	83.5	+34.74	-4.68
Caste/tribe						
Scheduled cast	21.9	78.0	43.5	56.1	+98.63	-28.07
Scheduled tribe	16.0	83.0	20.2	76.9	+26.25	-7.35
Other	33.2	65.9	40.2	58.6	+21.08	-11.07
Total	31.5	68.0	40.1	58.8	+27.30	-13.53

Source : NFHS 1 and NFHS 2 Survey Reports.
Note : All figures are in percentage.

NFHS 1 and NFHS 2 figures show that institutional deliveries increase both in rural and urban areas and across all other background characteristics. Education has tremendous effect on place of delivery. As literacy level increases and women have the exposure to formal education, the mothers are more likely to give birth under institutional arrangement than the illiterate women. Overall, in West Bengal, deliveries in institutions increase from 31.5 percent during the time of NFHS 1 survey to 40.1 percent in NFHS 2 survey. This has been possible to a great extent through awareness generation among rural women in particular. The panchayati raj institutions are playing pertinent role in this matter. In West Bengal under the provisions of West Bengal Panchayat Act, 1973 along with its subsequent amendments, in panchayat samiti (the middle tier at the block level) and in Zilla Parishad (the tuppermost tier at district level) there is a standing committee in the name of Janasasthya-O-Paribesh (Public Health and Environment). This standing committee is composed of elected representatives and government officials – they are taking care in implementing the family welfare programmes through existing infrastructure.

Next to place of delivery, assistance available during delivery is also important in ensuring safe delivery of pregnant women. District disaggregated data for West Bengal are not available in published form. So discussion here is restricted to data available from NFHS 1 and NFHS 2 survey. The arrangement of delivery care is described in NFHS 2 survey report in following words:

> "In rural areas, a female paramedical worker, called an auxiliary nurse midwife (ANM), is posted at a sub centre to provide basic maternal health, child health, and family welfare services to women and children either in their homes or in the health clinic. Her work is overseen by a lady health visitor (LHV) posted at the PHC. With regard to safe motherhood, the ANM is responsible for registering pregnant women, motivating them to obtain antenatal and postnatal care, assessing their health throughout pregnancy and in the postpartum period, and referring women with high-risk pregnancies. The ANM is assisted by a male health worker whose duties include motivating men to participate in the family welfare programme and educating men about reproductive tract and sexually transmitted infections".

NFHS 1 categorised attendant during delivery into four categories viz. doctor, nurse/ midwife, traditional birth attendant (TBA) and relative/ other. In NFHS 2 survey one additional attendant viz. other health professional was specified. In table 9 (a), percentage distribution of births on the basis of attendant assisting during delivery is presented for NFHS 1 and NFHS 2 separately.

From table 9(a), it can be seen that irrespective of background characteristics, more births are attended by health professionals in NFHS 2 than NFHS 1 survey – the increase is from 33 percent in NFHS 1 to 44 percent in NFHS 2 survey. The absolute change is to the extent of 33.33 percent only. In case of illiterate women, this increase is to the extent of 75 percent. Table 9(a) also shows that, literacy status of women is positively correlated with proportion of birth attended by health professionals. Muslim women depend more on TBA and others for assistance during delivery. Dependence on TBA reduces by almost 25 percent in case of Hindu women in between the period of NFHS 1 and NFHS 2 survey. In case of Muslim women, this reduction is to the extent of 4.23 percent only. One important reason may be less propagation of education among Muslim women. Within women of scheduled tribe communities also dependence on TBA and others (friends, relative and other persons) for assistance during delivery is quite high. Here also, less exposure to education is a determining factor.

The Ninth Five Year Plan (1997-2002) document of the State Government reiterates that "the special efforts to improve the reach and quality of immunization for mother and child care programme and ensuring safe motherhood will continue to receive priority attention in the State". The report on important indicators under Reproductive and Child Health Programme (RCH) released by Department of Health and Family Welfare, Govt. of West Bengal in different years shows that the coverage of institutional deliveries is not substantial. In table 10 district wise share of institutional deliveries for the years 1999-2000 to 2002-2003 are given.

Ranking of the districts by the latest year data available (table 10) shows that districts in the lower echelon are South 24 Parganas (rank 18), Malda (rank 17), Uttar Dinajpur (rank 16), Cooch Behar (rank 15) and Murshidabad (rank 14). Of these five districts, except Cooch Behar, all have high proportion of Muslim communities. According to Census 1991, the proportions are 29.94 percent in South 24 Parganas, 47.49 percent in Malda, 36.75 percent in Uttar Dinajpur and 61.39 percent in Murshidabad. Except Darjeeling, most of the districts located in northern part of the state have very high proportion of non-institutional deliveries. As rural-urban disaggregated data are not available in published form, rural-urban

Table 9 (a)
Percentage distribution of births on the basis of attendant assisting during delivery

Background Characteristics	*Doctor*		*ANM Midwife etc.*		*TBA*		*Other*		*Total Health Professionals*	
	NFHS1	*NFHS2*	*NFHS1*	*NFHS2*	*NFHS1*	*NFHS2*	*NFHS1*	*NFHS2*	*NFHS1*	*NFHS2*
Residence										
Rural	12.7	28.5	10.4	7.2	40.5	33.8	34.4	29.8	23.1	35.7
Urban	45.1	66.3	21.4	15.4	22.2	10.4	10.0	7.8	66.5	81.7
Education										
Illiterate	9.4	23.3	7.9	7.0	42.8	34.6	37.5	34.5	17.3	30.3
Literate but not Completing Middle School	19.1	31.2	19.4	12.5	35.2	34.8	25.1	20.8	38.5	43.7
Middle School complete	41.6	60.5	22.9	8.4	25.1	13.6	9.7	17.5	64.5	68.9
High school complete and above	79.8	86.9	12.1	5.8	5.7	3.1	1.5	4.2	91.9	92.7
Education										
Illiterate	9.4	23.3	7.9	7.0	42.8	34.6	37.5	34.5	17.3	30.3
Literate but not Completing Middle School	19.1	31.2	19.4	12.5	35.2	34.8	25.1	20.8	38.5	43.7
High school complete and above	79.8	86.9	12.1	5.8	5.7	3.1	1.5	4.2	91.9	92.7
Religion										
Hindu	25.2	43.5	16.7	11.5	33.4	25.0	23.0	19.4	41.9	55.0
Muslim	8.8	17.3	4.8	2.9	42.5	40.7	41.8	39.1	13.6	20.2
Caste/tribe										
Scheduled caste	11.1	32.0	11.3	13.8	38.2	29.3	36.5	24.0	22.4	45.8
Scheduled tribe	8.5	21.6	8.2	2.9	45.9	33.2	36.2	39.3	16.7	24.5
Other	21.9	37.0	13.4	7.5	35.5	29.9	27.4	25.4	35.3	44.5
Total	20.1	35.3	12.9	8.7	36.3	29.6	28.8	25.8	33.0	44.0

Source: NFHS 1 and NFHS 2 Survey Reports.
Note: (i) All figures are in percentage, (ii) Total health professionals mean doctor, ANM, Midwife, LHV all taken together.

differentials cannot be studied here. Kolkata having no rural segment has full coverage of institutional births (table 10).

Table 10
Share of institutional deliveries in total deliveries

District	*1999-2000 (in %)*	*2000-2001 (in %)*	*2001-2002 (in %)*	*2002-2003 (in %)*	*Growth Index*	*Ranking by the latest year*
Burdwan	54.75	58.59	60.87	63.86	1.17	5
Birbhum	53.28	52.89	50.71	49.29	0.925	9
Bankura	58.15	64.30	65.56	67.02	1.15	4
Midnapur	43.92	45.74	44.17	34.83	0.793	13
Howrah	61.31	59.42	63.15	63.60	1.04	6
Hooghly	62.37	65.54	68.56	69.66	1.12	3
North 24 Parganas	52.97	52.45	50.91	53.55	1.01	8
South 24 Parganas	15.54	21.90	27.40	21.49	1.38	18
Kolkata	100.00	100.00	100.00	100.00	1.00	1
Nadia	66.72	62.51	57.16	60.85	0.912	7
Murshidabad	37.30	18.27	28.82	33.25	0.891	14
Uttar Dinajpur	27.75	28.18	35.41	24.23	0.873	16
Dakshin Dinajpur	50.91	44.75	43.88	46.42	0.911	11
Malda	25.00	23.01	23.79	23.72	0.949	17
Jalpaiguri	44.70	46.23	51.47	46.63	1.04	10
Darjeeling	73.66	64.47	67.40	71.05	0.964	2
Cooch Behar	29.54	29.56	31.37	32.63	1.10	15
Purulia	40.64	34.56	36.06	35.81	0.881	12
West Bengal	48.85	48.04	47.60	49.31	1.01	-

Source: Reports on important indicators under RCH programme for different years, Department of Health and Family Welfare, Govt. of West Bengal.

Note: (i) $\text{Growth Index} = \frac{\text{Share in 2002-2003}}{\textit{Share in 1999-2000}}$

On the basis of coverage of antenatal care (table 8) and share of institutional deliveries (table 10), we develop safe motherhood index (SMI) in the line of Krishnaji and James (2002). A safe motherhood index is constructed for each district by taking the simple average of these two proportions and presented in table 11. As location specific data are not available, it is not possible to construct SMI separately for rural and urban areas of the districts.

Table 11
Safe Motherhood Index of districts in West Bengal

District	*1999-2000 (in %)*	*2000-2001 (in %)*	*2001-2002 (in %)*	*2002-2003 (in %)*	*Growth Index*	*Ranking by the latest year*
Burdwan	43.26	55.61	56.79	62.99	6	1.45
Birbhum	43.92	47.87	47.75	48.78	12	1.11
Bankura	62.05	60.49	68.70	69.31	3	1.12
Midnapur	46.07	38.60	41.31	49.43	11	1.07
Howrah	49.25	51.46	56.83	61.26	7	1.24
Hooghly	58.32	54.59	64.00	67.51	4	1.16
North 24 Parganas	41.08	40.54	42.40	49.71	9	1.21
South 24 Parganas	20.01	27.61	39.64	37.43	16	1.87
Kolkata	118.89	74.22	78.82	134.58	1	1.13
Nadia	58.15	57.42	60.67	63.48	5	1.09
Murshidabad	39.22	33.85	39.77	42.94	15	1.09
Uttar Dinajpur	31.73	32.05	28.60	30.89	18	0.973
Dakshin Dinajpur	38.91	41.90	44.42	43.92	14	1.13
Malda	28.73	33.83	33.86	35.43	17	1.23
Jalpaiguri	60.53	39.93	48.10	49.52	10	0.818
Darjeeling	89.33	82.99	79.57	77.36	2	0.866
Cooch Behar	45.72	43.00	45.24	44.26	13	0.968
Purulia	44.94	46.71	45.49	49.74	8	1.11
West Bengal	49.03	46.50	49.22	53.37	-	1.08

Source: Table 8 and 10 of this chapter.

From table 11 it can be seen that SMI in four north Bengal districts out of six, declines over the period 1999-2000 to 2002-2003. As the antenatal coverage and proportion of institutional deliveries in total deliveries are highly correlated, any decline in SMI indicate fall in any of these two components or fall in the both. Whatever be the case, both situations indicate adverse health care for pregnant women. Out of 18 districts in the state, only in 4 districts downward trend in SMI is noticed. This requires utmost care for improvement. Data sets of RCH programme for different years show that in 1999-2000, proportion of deliveries by untrained personnel is 11.62 percent of total deliveries – in absolute terms, the number of deliveries by untrained personnel is 131506 out 1132006 deliveries. Figures for subsequent years are given below :

Year	*Total number of deliveries*	*Number of Deliveries by untrained personnel*	*Percentage delivery by untrained personnel*
2000-2001	1290491	142790	11.06
2001-2002	1328273	169994	12.80
2002-2003	1352972	164043	12.12

In this backdrop, the State Government pledged in its Tenth Five Year Plan document to enhance institutional delivery proportion to 80 percent by 2010 from 47 percent at the end of March, 2002. Unsafe motherhood is always a source of concern in the overall health spectrum. Tenth Five Year plan (2002-2007) of Government of India also emphasizes on this issue in following words:

"The prevailing high rates of maternal morbidity and mortality have always been a source of concern, and antenatal and intrapartum care aimed at reducing these have been components of the National Family Welfare programme since its inception. Although data on state/ district specific maternal morbidity/ mortality is not available, available figures from the SRS and the Survey of causes of death provide sufficient information on mortality rates and causes of death so that rational programmes could be evolved to combat major health problems in women ... During the 1990s, there has not been any decline in MMR and more than 100,000 women continue to die each year due to pregnancy-related causes".

The survey of causes of death by Sample Registration System (SRS) in 1998 showed that the major causes of maternal mortality are anaemia, obstructed labour, unsafe abortions, antepartum and post-partum haemorrhage, hyperintensive disorders and post-partum sepsis (Tenth Five Year Plan, Govt. of India). Health on the March, 2002-2003 of Govt. of West Bengal provides a break-up of causes of maternal death for 2001-02 and 2002-2003. The information is very much limited, as it is based on hospital admitted cases only and for the state as a whole. In spite of this limitation, the figures give a reflection on maternal death in the state. The causes of death and their share in deaths (in percentage) are given below :

Causes of death	*Share in 2001-2002*	*Share in 2002-2003*
Anaemia	20.37	24.36
Haemorrhage	15.77	16.48
Puerperal sepsis	3.83	4.76
Toxaemia	26.80	28.39
Tetanus	2.76	2.20
Obstructed labour	5.82	5.13
Other causes	24.65	18.68
	100.00	100.00

India Health Report (2003) discusses the source of the causes in detail. For clarity and assessing the gravity of the causes, it is relevant to quote here from this report :

> "Post partum haemorrhage is sudden, unpredictable and most dangerous in an anaemic women. Hence it is important to screen for anaemia and high-risk conditions, and ensure access to emergency obstetric care (EOC) including blood transfusion. But in the current safe motherhood initiatives, screening for complications and EOC are still inadequate
>
> ...Puerperal sepsis is most often a consequence of poor hygiene during delivery ... clean deliveries and quick detection, and the management of infection during the post-natal period, can substantially reduce mortality due to puerperal sepsis...
>
> Obstructed labour is often associated with a woman's age (very young mother), parity (first births), and short stature. Such cases need to have deliveries in institutions... The recording of blood pressure during antenatal check-ups and treatment for hypertension could substantially reduce mortality due to toxaemia ... Anaemia is a major contributing cause of deaths ... NFHS 2 revealed disturbing levels of anaemia among women – as many as 52 percent had some form of anaemia. Moderate and severe anaemia among pregnant women (28 percent) is almost double that of non-pregnant women (16 percent)".

For reducing maternal death, adequate antenatal care and enhancement of the coverage of institutional births are very much urgent to reduce maternal mortality rate to below 100 per one lakh. Tenth Five Year Plan of Planning Commission, Govt. of India makes the following recommendation :

"Deaths due to anaemia, obstructed labour, hypertensive disorders and sepsis can be prevented by improving the access of essential obstetric care, universal screening for detection of obstetric problems, referral and timely treatment of complications of pregnancy, promoting institutional delivery and postnatal care. Emergency obstetric services will help saving lives of women with haemorrhage during pregnancy or complications during deliveries. The Ninth Plan envisaged universal screening of all pregnant women, identification of women with health problems, problems during pregnancy and appropriate management including referral to centres where appropriate care is available. This, however, has not been operationalised; highest priority will be accorded to operationalise this during the Tenth Plan".)

As anaemia is found to be a major cause of maternal death let us now discuss nutritional status of women in section III. Non availability of district disaggregated data very much restrict serutiny of the situation. However, efforts are made to give some reflection through NFHS2 survey data.

SECTION III

NFHS 2 survey report describes the prevalence of anaemia in following words :

"Anaemia is characterized by a low level of haemoglobin in the blood. Haemoglobin is necessary for transporting oxygen from the lungs to other tissues and organs of the body. Anaemia usually results form a nutritional deficiency of iron, folate, vitamin B12 or some other nutrients. This type of anaemia is commonly referred to as iron-deficiency anaemia. Iron deficiency is the most widespread form of malnutrition in the world, affecting more than two billion people. In India, anaemia affects an estimated 50 percent of the population.

Anaemia may have detrimental effects on the health of women and children and may become an underlying cause of maternal mortality and perinatal mortality. Anaemia results in an increased risk of premature delivery and low birth weight. Early detection of anaemia can help to prevent complications related to pregnancy and delivery as well as child development problems...".

For preventing anaemia during pregnancy, in RCH programme, iron and folic acid tablets are delivered to pregnant women. According to NFHS 2 survey, overall, around 63 percent of women in West Bengal have some degree of anaemia. In table 12, proportions of ever-married women having anaemia are given according to the selected background characteristics. It can be seen that there are differences in prevalence of anaemia by background characteristics of women.

Table 12

Percentage of ever-married women having anaemia : West Bengal

Background characteristic	*Percentage of women with*				*Percentage with BMI below 18.5 kg/m2*
	Any anaemia	*Mild anaemia*	*Moderate*	*Severe anaemia*	
Residence					
Rural	64.2	45.9	16.9	1.4	49.8
Urban	57.8	43.1	12.9	1.8	24.5
Education					
Illiterate	67.1	45.7	19.5	1.9	53.0
Literate but not Completing Middle School	59.7	44.9	13.4	1.4	41.5
Middle School complete	57.4	46.1	10.6	0.7	34.3
High school complete and above	55.3	43.4	11.3	0.6	15.3
Religion					
Hindu	63.3	45.4	16.4	1.5	42.2
Muslim	59.2	43.9	13.7	1.5	47.6
Caste/ tribe					
Scheduled caste	67.1	46.6	18.6	1.8	49.4
Scheduled tribe	80.6	44.7	32.8	3.1	64.2
Other	59.1	44.9	12.9	1.2	39.9
Total	62.7	45.3	15.9	1.5	43.7

Source: NFHS 2 Survey (1998-99) : West Bengal.

Note: (i) The body mass index (BMI) is the ratio of the weight in kilograms to the square of the height in metres (Kg/m2).

(ii) All figures are in percentage.

From table 12, it can be seen that prevalence of anaemia is higher for rural women than for urban women – the gap is by 6.4 percentage points. Again, the prevalence of anaemia is found to be higher within illiterate women than women with education. It can be seen from table 12 that the prevalence of anaemia reduces with the level of education of women. For indicating nutritional deficiency, percentage of ever-married women with BMI less than 18.5 Kg/metres squared is also given foı each background characteristic. Percentage ɔf women in rural areas with BMI below 18.5 kg/m2 is higher than percentage of women in urban areas. Again, it can be seen from table 12 that there exists high prevalence of nutritional deficiency among illiterate women and scheduled tribe women. With the increase in the level of education, the proportions of women with BMI below 18.5 Kg/m2 get reduced.

Women's food consumption is closely related to their nutritional status. However, no reliable data are available for making any study on this issue. For making reflection on women's food consumption pattern we again have to depend on NFHS 2 survey data. In view of NFHS 2 survey report "the consumption of a wide variety of nutritious food is important for women's health". The details of food items are as follows :

> "Meat, fish, eggs and milk, as well as pulses and nuts, are rich in protein. Green, leafy vegetables are a rich source of iron, folic acid, vitamin C, carotene, riboflavin, and calcium. Many fruits are also good sources of vitamin C. Bananas are rich in carbohydrates. Papayas, mangoes and other yellow fruits contain carotene, which is converted to vitamin A. Vitamin A is also present in milk and milk products, as well as egg yolks".

NFHS 2 survey report observes that women of West Bengal consume green and leafy vegetables most often. In table 13, percentage distribution of ever married women is given on the basis of type of food and frequency of consumption. Fruit consumption is very rare by women.

Table 13
Percent distribution of ever-married women by frequency of consumption

(figures in percentage)

Type of food	*Daily/Weekly*	*Occasionally*	*Never*
Milk or curd	16.9	8.1	49.4
Pulses or beans	33.8	42.4	21.3
Green, leafy	55.0	36.4	8.0
Other vegetables	92.3	6.4	1.2
Fruits	4.2	10.8	66.0
Eggs	5.7	37.9	46.8
Chicken, meat on fish	23.3	45.7	28.7

From table 13 it can be seen that in case of 25.6 percent ever married women, milk or curd is not included in the list of their food items. This may be due to their unsound pecuniary conditions as poverty has a strong negative effect on the consumption of nutritious foods (NFHS 2).

For supplementing the nutritious consumption, in West Bengal, the pregnant women are given iron and folic acid tablets under Mother and Child Health programme. Different issues of Health on the March provide data on distribution of folifer to mothers but do not give any information on percentage an assessment on achievement of the health sector in supplementing nutrition of the expectant mothers of pregnant women receiving at least 100 IFA tablets.In table 14 we present estimated number of pregnant women from the report on important indicators under RCH programme for the years 1999-2000 to 2002-2003 and distribution of folifers to mothers during this period.

Table 14
Distribution of folifers

Year	*Estimated no. of pregnant women*	*No. of women covered*	*Percentage of coverage*
1999-2000	1936040	1430064	73.86
2000-2001	1864540	1831625	98.23
2001-2002	1886427	1636460	86.75
2002-2003	1863000	1393141	74.78

Source: (i) Health on the March of different years.
(ii) Report on important indicators under RCH Programme for different years.

From table 14 it can be seen that the coverage is short of the target number of pregnant women – of course this distribution of folifers include only the government sector hospitals and health centres only.

CONCLUSION

From the discussions above, it can be understood that the extent of reproductive health services provided to women in West Bengal so that much extensive. There is enough room for further improvement. For example, more or less half of the deliveries taken place in the state still remains out of the reach of institutional arrangements. For achieving a target to reduce the present maternal mortality rate of 264 per 1,00,000 live births to 100 by 2010 requires enhancement of the institutional capacity of the health sector infrastructure. India Health Report (2003) makes following recommendations for improvement of the existing situation :

> "Antenatal care must move from Tetanus Toxoid immunization and distribution of IFA tablets to comprehensive care. Every pregnant women must be seen at least once by a doctor and screened for anaemia, hypertension, diabetes, urinary and reproductive tract infections, malaria and TB. If laboratory support is not available in the facility, private services must be contracted and funds provided in the RCH programme. Antenatal care and immunization sessions at PHCs should be so organised that every woman is screened step by step and comprehensively – height and weight, urine and blood tests, followed by screening by the doctor. This can easily be organised, with specific duties at every counter being allotted to PHC personnel, including the supervisory cadre".

The Govt. of West Bengal is taking steps for optimum utilization of the public health infrastructure at the primary level by bringing all health programmes under a single field administration. Tenth Five Year plan of the Govt. of West Bengal proposes to integrate all societies implementing different health programmes, under the District Health and Family Welfare society to avoid implementation of different programmes at cross purposes. For ensuring better services to the people of the state and women in particular, the State Government has started a reform process by making health service providers at the village, block and district level accountable to the community leaders of the panchayati raj institutions. It is expected that the state can register significant achievements in the field of health services. In the Tenth Five Year Plan (2002-2007) document, the State Government affirms this process in following words :

> "The State Government has initiated a reform process based on the principles of transparency, accountability, decentralization and community participation. The process would be strengthened and deepened to reduce the present distortions in the manpower deployment, increase accountability and responsiveness of the health service providers and improve the monitoring and evaluation of the health service infrastructure at various levels".

With regard to reform process being undertaken by the State Government, the strengthening of village level health care activities should get utmost priority. This is natural, because of 38733477 women in the State, 28128662 live in rural areas – in percentage 72.62 percent of total women. Again, the differentials between rural women and urban women must receive adequate attention of policy makers. Otherwise, the gravity of the problems of reproductive health services would be lost in whirl of activities without any substantial amelioration of their sufferings which they are destined to bear.

REFERENCES

Barroso, Carmen and Jacobson, Jodi L. (2000), "Population Policy and Women's empowerment : Challenges and opportunities" in Harriet B Presser and Gita Sen edited book Women's empowerment and Demographic Processes : Moving beyond Cairo published by Oxford University Press, London, 2000.

Dixon – Mueller, Ruth and Germain, Adrienna (2000), "Reproductive Health and Demographic Imagination" in Presser and Sen (2000).

(a) Govt. of West Bengal (b) Govt. of West Bengal (c) Government of West Bengal (d) Govt. of West Bengal Ninth Five Year Plan prepared by Development and Planning Department, 1997Economic Review 2001-2002 and 2002-2003Tenth Five-Year Plan, Vol. I prepared by Development and Planning Department, 2002State Plan of Action for Children, 2003.

International Institute for Population Sciences (2001), National Family Health Survey (NFHS2) India, 1998-99 : West Bengal.

Levison, Julie H. and Levison, Sandre P (2002), "Women's Health and Human Rights" in Women, Gender and Human Rights : A global perspective ed. by Marjorie Agosin published by Rutgers University Press, London.

Misra, Rajiv, Chatterjee, Rachel and Rao, Sujatha (2003), India Health Report, Oxford University Press, New Delhi.

Planning Commission, Govt. of India, Tenth Five Year Plan, Vol. II.

Tinker, Anne and others (2000), Improving Women's Health : Issues and Interventions published by the World Bank, June 2000.

United Nations (1994), Report of the International Conference on Population and Development, Cairo, September 5-13, 1994.

26

INDIAN BANKING SECTOR-DYNAMIC PRESENT AND CHALLENGING FUTURE

*G. N. Joshi * and V. Aditya Srinivas***

INTRODUCTION

The Banking system is one of the pillars on which the sound financial systems rests. The functioning of any economy to a large extent depends on the working of the banking sector. The banking sector in India has seen lot of sea changes in the past one decade especially after the Indian economy was opened up in 1991. The Central Bank of India which is the Reserve Bank of India has always played a crucial role in the development of the banking sector and strengthening the banks to face the challenges of the dynamic scenario. The major events that changed the banking sector outlook came in 1969 when 14 banks were nationalized and 6 other banks were nationalized in 1980. The primarily role of the banks which even today has not changed is that of giving loans and accepting deposits. This was the only functions for which the banks were formed. But today this scenario has been changing rapidly with the banks now providing a variety of functions and services according to the needs of the customers. Today banks are focusing on variety of activities like Portfolio Advisory services, Wealth Management services, Custodial services to Institutional clients. Even the role of the RBI which was more of a regulator has changed to that of a development side. The RBI has scrapped the PLR (Prime Lending Rate) concept and now banks have

* Professor, Department of Economics, Veer Narmad South Gujarat University.

been given autonomy regarding deciding the lending rates and deposits rates. Indian banking systems has now also been recognized at the global level with banks like the SBI, ICICI opening up offices in various countries. ICICI bank has opened up its branches in London, Singapore, UAE, Shan Ghai etc while SBI recently acquired bank in Mauritius and Indonesia. The NPA (Non performing Assets) which is the prime concern in any banking sector of any country has been down to the standards of the global level. The NPA of the Indian banking sector is at below 3 % which makes Indian banking sector at par with the developed countries. The Securitization Act passed in 2002 gave the Indian banks the much needed powers to acquire the assets of the defaulters if they do not pay their dues to the banks. This has helped Indian banks to considerably reduce their NPAs and clean their balance sheets. The creation of the ARCIL (Asset Reconstruction Company of India) which is created by banks like ICICI, UTI, IDBI and HDFC has also contributed to reduce the NPAs as the ARCIL purchases the bad loans of the banks and then it takes up the responsibility of collecting the dues from the defaulters. Recently Kotak Mahindra Bank has also started the business of purchasing the bad loans from other banks and then collecting the dues from the debtors. The Indian banking systems has now realized the strengthen of economies and hence there are mergers and acquisition which has given the banks the required strengthen and resources to deal with the global competition. The merger of ICICI and ICICI Bank and that of IDBI and IDBI Bank signifies the fact that the consolidation is now being realized by the Indian banking sector. The entry of foreign banks like Standard Chartered, ABN AMRO, Citi Bank have also created lot of stiff competition in the banking sector.

Thus the Indian banking sector has witnessed various phases of business and growth as well as depression in the past 50 years. The cooperative banks which were the main sources of finance for the lower and middle class of the society has also seen various banks falling like pins due to the unethical practices of the top management, rising NPAs and liquidity problems. The scams in the Co operative banks like Madhavpura Mercantile Cooperative bank have shaken the faith of the investors and has also shaken the working of the whole financial system. The coming years are yet to witness many more dynamic changes in the banking sector with Bank of International Settlement (BIS) which is the Reserve Bank of World prescribing higher risk management measures for the banks in terms of higher base of capital. The capital adequacy ratio would have to be raised to 12% from the current 9% prescribed by RBI. The deadline for the Indian banking sector has been set at 31st March 2007.

Thus the present Indian banking sector has made a place for itself in this globalization era but the future is more competitive and requires strong reforms in the banking sector to make it more competitive which would make it at par with the global standards.

NPAs of the 20 State Owned Banks

Name	*Net NPA (%)2004-05*	*Net NPA (%)2003-04*
All Banks	1.28	2.34
Andhra Bank	0.28	0.93
Bank of Baroda	1.45	2.99
Bank of India	2.77	4.5
Bank of Maharashtra	2.15	2.46
Canara Bank	1.88	2.89
Central Bank	2.98	5.57
Corporation Bank	1.12	1.8
Dena Bank	5.23	9.4
Indian Bank	1.35	2.71
Indian Overseas Bank	1.27	2.85
Oriental Bank	1.29	0
Punjab and Sindh Bank	NA	NA
Punjab National Bank	0.20	0.98
Syndicate Bank	1.59	2.58
UCO Bank	2.93	3.65
Union Bank	2.64	2.87
United Bank	2.43	3.76
Vijaya Bank	0.59	0.91
State Bank of India	2.56	2.65

Source: The Economic Times, 5th June 2005 Mumbai

PRESENT SCENARIO

The present scenario of the Indian Banking sector is highly encouraging with the banks performing well and their NPAs reducing to the significant level. In a remarkable turnaround from the mid 1990s when a bad loan crisis hung over the financial sector, banks have managed to bring down the net Non- performing assets to below 3% on an average. Of the 20 state owned banks, 19 have reported their NPA below 3%. Ten banks have NPAs below 2% of which three banks – Andhra bank, Pujab National Bank, Vijaya Bank have net NPAs less than 1% of their loans.

The recent report of the RBI on the trend and progress in baking in 2003-2004. The NPAs of the banking sector in India as a whole fell from 4.4% in 2003 to 2.9% in 2004. The following table makes the picture more clearly about the NPA in different sector banks.

Item	*Gross NPA*	*GrossNPA %*	*Net NPA*	*Net NPA %*
Public Sector	51,538 crores	7.8	18,860 crores	3
Old Private	4,392 cr	7.6	2,140 cr	3.8
New Private	5,963 cr	5	2,717 cr	2.4
Foreign	2,894 cr	4.6	900 cr	1.5
Scheduled Commercial	64,786 cr	7.2	24,617 cr	2.9

Source: Economics Times dated 29th November, 2004

Of the total loans and advances aggregating Rs. 8,59,092 crore, the impaired credit as a per cent age of total outstanding at 7.4 %. However, as a per cent age of retail loans which is Rs. 1,89,041 crore impaired retail loans stood at 2.5%. Of the total retail loans, impaired housing loans constituted 1.9% while it was highest in the consumer durable segment at 6.6%.tis was followed by credit cards receivables at 6.3%. In the monetary policy for the second half of 2004-05, the RBI had, as a temporary counter cyclical measure, put in place risk containment measures. The risk weight age was raised from 50-75% in the case of housing loans and from 100-125% for consumer credit including personal loans and credit cards. The retail segment share in total loans stood at 21% with housing constituting 48% of the retail portfolio. The share of the housing loan portfolio in the total loan book has grown from 3% in 1993 to 7% in 2004. The banks in India have made substantial progress in cleaning up NPAs. Gross NPAs declined from 23% in 1992-93 to 7.8% in 2003-04. During 2003-2004, the share of NPAs from the priority sector in the total NPAs of PSU banks increased marginally. Though there as a decline in the share of NPAs from the agriculture sector and small scale industries, but an increase in the share from other priority sector. RBI has identified 203 urban cooperative bank as Grade IV banks and out of which 51 are in Ahmedabad and 31 in Mumbai.

BANKS PROFITABILITY AT THE GLOBAL LEVEL

Indian banks have been second in the world in terms of the net interest margin after the USA banks as the Indian banks have net interest margins of 2.8% while the US banks have it at 3%. The following table gives the world wide picture.

Countries	*Net interest margins of Banks (%)*
USA	3
India	2.8
Spain	2.4
Italy	2.1
Canada	2
UK	1.8
Sweden	1.4
France	0.9
Germany	0.8
Japan	0.6

Source: Economic Times dated 2nd December, 2004.

MANAGERIAL AUTONOMY

The recent Managerial Autonomy given to the Public Sector Banks will also played a vital role in the development of these banks. The managerial autonomy criteria for the banks have been laid down as under:-

1. Net worth of the banks must be more than Rs. 100 crores.
2. Three years continuously profitability
3. NPA less than 9%.
4. Capital Adequacy Ratio more than 9%

The managerial autonomy consists of allowing the banks to take independent decisions regarding the mergers and acquisitions, regarding the opening and closing of the branches and also about recruiting the professionals in the banks. These would enable them to take the market related decisions and make their working more professional and more transparent. The recent credit and monetary policy of the RBI has initiated the much needed reforms in the banking sector to make it compatible with the competition of the global level. The managerial autonomy would provide the PSU banks the required professional work force just like that in the private sector which would help the Public sector banks to improve their business and also provide better customer satisfaction. This type of autonomy would also help them to attract the right type of human capital required for the quick growth of the banks. The autonomy issue would also give the banks the much needed level playing field with the private sector banks in terms of mergers, acquisitions, opening and closing of branches and also acquiring the professional human capital.

CO-OPERATIVE BANKS

The beginning of co-operative banking in India dates back to about 1904 when official efforts were initiated to create a new type of institutional based on the principles of co-operative organization and management, which were considered to be suitable for solving the problems peculiar to Indian conditions. In rural areas, credit, was woefully inadequate, and unorganized money market agencies, such as money lenders, were providing credit often at exploitatively high rates of interest. The Co-operative backs were conceived in order to substitute such agencies, provide adequate short term and long term institutional credit at reasonable rates of interest, and to bring about integration of the unorganized and organized segments of the Indian money market.

In a effort to streamline the cooperative banking sector, the RBI has asked 100 loss making Urban Cooperative Banks to either surrender their banking licenses, merge with a healthier bank or face closure. There are only eight UCBs in the country having a deposit base of more than Rs. 1000 crore. The number of UCBs strong enough to take over the loss making banks could be even fewer. Thus a handful of big UCBs like Saraswat, Cosmos and Shamrao Vithal will be faced with the near impossible task of acquiring liabilities of close to 100 loss making UCBs. For banks in the Grade III category which are in a marginally better shape, the RBI has given six months time to improve performance and graduate to the next level. The RBI moves comes six months after thousands of depositors burnt their fingers in South Indian Coop Bank and Maratha Mandir Coop Bank. In Maharashtra alone the 658 UCBs have deposit base of RS. 55,000 crore. Total advances stand at Rs. 30,000 crore. India has 2,104 UCBs of which over 85% are confined to five states that are Maharashtra (658), Gujarat (359), Karnataka (321), Andhra Pradesh (169) and Tamil Nadu (136).

The Gross NPAs of 50 scheduled urban cooperative banks as a percentage of their gross advances dipped to 28.8 per cent in March 2004 from 30.2 per cent in March 2003. The net NPA to net advances ratio was 17.1 per cent, versus 19.3 per cent in March 2003. The NPA of the urban cooperative banks were Rs. 11,922 crores, while that of Central cooperative banks were 13,862 crores and that of State cooperative banks were 6284 crores as on March 31, 2003. The total NPAs of these three cooperative banks was Rs. 32,068 crores that amounts to the 50 per cent funding of the Golden Quadrilateral Road project.

INTEREST RATE RISK

The interest rate risk is the risk which always affects the banks in their management of the treasury operations and maintaining of the portfolios. The recent rise in the interest rates in the banking sector especially the home loans where ICICIBank and HDFC bank have raised the home loans by 0.5% has raised concern over the maintenance of soft interest rates. Though the Government has declared that the Public Sector banks would not be allowed to raise rates, but the Global hardening of the interest rates has caused lot of worry among the bank managers who are worried about the treasure management. The FED rate in the USA which has been raised six times in the past one and half years and has been raised from 1.25% to 3% has clearly given the signals that the interest rates world over are likely to harden. That clearly means that the Indian banks have also to raise the interest rates on the deposits and on the loans given. This would adversely affect the credit off take in the banks which again would reduce the assets of the banks which in turn would reduce the income of the banks.

INTEREST RATE RISK MANAGEMENT

The banks in the modern era have to deal with the sophisticated risk management instruments like the Interest Rate Derivative. This is the most important and widely form of derivatives all over the world. In the world of derivatives, which has the market of $155 trillion, the interest rate derivatives account for 54 % of the total turnover which takes place in the derivatives market whereas equity derivatives account for 17 % of the total turnover in the world. In India the interest rate derivatives has been started from 24 June 2003. There are three products, which the Indian interest rate derivatives provide. They are as follows:

Sr. No	Symbol	Description
1.	NSETB91D	Futures Contract on Notional 91 day T Bill
2.	NSE10Y06	Futures contract on Notional 10 year coupon bearing bond
3.	NSE10ZC	Futures contract on Notional 10 year zero coupon bond

The National Stock Exchange of India is the exchange that provides the trading of the interest rate derivatives. The lot size is 2000 and value of the contract is minimum Rs. 2 lakhs. This derivatives product is listed on the Wholesale Debt Market segment (WDM), which is used by the banks to hedge their debt portfolio. In the beginning when the products were launched there was no response from the banking sector for which the products were launched as above products were based on zero coupon bond curve while in the reality the banks deal on the basis of yield to maturity concept and so these products were not useful to the banks. But now SEBI has realized this problem and has converted the products on the basis of yield to maturity, which would now make the sense for the banking sector to use this product for their purpose. The banks can hedge their positions in this market and thus can protect the value of the debt portfolios by taking short positions in the interest rate derivatives instruments.

CAPITAL ADEQUACY

The Capital Adequacy Ratio required for the banks in the present scenario as per the RBI guidelines is 9% but this would be increased to 12% once the Basel II norms comes into existence. The banks are required to raise the capital base in order to be able to withstand any type of risk like the market risk, business risk and also the operational risk. This has caused the lot many banks to go to the market and raise the money in the form of the pubic issue. The ICICIbank recently raised Rs. 3500 crores through the pubic issue.

Suggestions for the Banking Sector:

1. **Foreign Direct Investment limit be raised:** The limit for the Foreign Direct Investment should be raised form the present 49% to 74%. This will enable to bring more foreign capital investment in the banking sector which would bring more competitiveness and encourage more healthy competition. This will also bring more foreign banks into the country and result into more employment opportunities for the educated class. The existing banks would also be forced to enhance its capabilities and will force them to give their best to the customers. The ultimate result would be more and enhanced satisfaction for the customers.
2. **Voting Cap of 10% be scrapped:** The voting cap of 10% in the foreign banks should be removed as this will enable more participation of the foreign banks in the management of the banks and their operations. This would increase the efficiency of the working of the Indian banks. This would also motivate more foreign banks having stake in the Indian banks. This would also provide strategic association between the Indian

banks and the participating foreign banks. This would also make the top management of the banks more transparent.

3. **CRR and SLR be reduced:** The present system when the minimum level of CRR is 5% and that of SLR is 25% should be reduced to minimum of 3% and 10% so that the banks have more funds at their disposal. This would enable banks to lend in those areas which were previously neglected.
4. **Priority sector focus:** The minimum lending norm for the agriculture sector should be increased from 18% to about 30% so that the much needed thrust is given to the agriculture sector. This would give the economy the required growth rate which is not possible without the agriculture sector growth as still to day 70% of the total population is dependent on agriculture for the purpose of livelihood. The other sunrise sector like the biotechnology sector should also get more focus in terms of increased lending so that more of new entrepreneurs are cultivated.
5. **One regulator for Co-operative banks:** There should be only one regulator for the cooperative sector rather than the present system where the RBI and Registrar of the Cooperative society jointly perform the role of the regulator. This has resulted in the buck passing and many of the banks have collapsed. Registrar of Cooperative Society should be given more powers to check the malpractices of the cooperative banks. The "whistle blowing policy" should be adopted and whenever there is even the slightest possibility of the liquidity problem, immediately the required action should be taken.
6. **Credit Information Bureau:** As the developed country has the Credit Information Bureau which provides information at the international level about the defaulters who take loan from one bank to repay the loan to other banks. Same is the case with the Cooperative banks where often defaulter of one bank

would take loan from other bank to repay the loans. The formation of Credit Information Bureau would provide information to the cooperative banks about the defaulters who have defaulted in their payments and this would prevent other cooperative banks from giving loans to those defaulters.

7. **Ban on loans to Director and family members:** The RBI should put a ban on the banks so that they cannot give the loans to the Directors of the banks and also to the family members. As these type of loan of are never paid off and ultimately results into creation of the NPA for the banks. Such ban would put a stop for the misuse of public money. This would prove more effective step for the cooperative banks as most of the loans which are not paid are from the Directors or their family members.

POLICY IMPLICATION

Banking sector is the one of the pillars of the economy and if one has to have the economy perform well, the banking sector has to be made strong and effective in terms of risk management, operational efficiency and more professional management. The cost of operations cannot be forgotten and hence consolidation is now the name of the game. By allowing more FDI, more autonomy to banks and making provisions for effective regulations and development of the banks, not only the banks would be made more competitive but also would sustain growth and development in the long run. As the Basel norms would be applicable by March 2007, it is imperative now that the whole banking system is geared up to face the stiff competition in this post liberalization era. An open banking system would not only provide more efficient operations to the customers but also increase the employment opportunity for the educated class. This would also help in attracting more foreign banks into the country which again would bring improved technology in the banking sector operations and also provide an opportunity for the Indian to become more competitive.

CONCLUSION

The Indian Banking sector has assumed significant growth in the last one decade with the reforms taking the right shape. But still there is lot of things which needs to be done for making the banks more competitive and growth oriented. The Public sector banks and the Private sector banks have shown tremendous improvement in their operations and have controlled NPAs to a very significant level but the threat is from the Cooperative banks which have many times failed to protect the interest of the deposit holders and have caused panic in the whole financial system. This part of the banking sector needs to be taken care off immediately otherwise it would nullify the growth in the banking sector by its repeated failures in the past and future. The coming two years would be very crucial for the banking sector as the Basel II would be made applicable and the banks would have to increase their capital base in order to deal with market risk, business risk, operational risk.

Thus, the Indian banking sector has made progress in the past few years but the best for the sector is yet to be achieved and this could be done only if the Government has the strong will and the reforms are actually implemented.

BIBLIOGRAPHY

(1) Banking Annual Magazine, October 2004 pp 32,33,34

(2) "Sector lights"- source Economic Times dated 2nd December, 2004.

(3) "Report on trends and progress of banking in India 2003-04"- source Economic Times dated 29th November, 2004.

(4) "Finmin wants RRB to merge with PSB banks"- source Economic Times dated 1st December, 2004.

(5) "Banks spruce up books, reduce NPAs to below 3%"- source Economic Times dated 5th June, 2005.

Part III

WOMEN EMPOWERMENT

27

HIGHER EDUCATION AMONG SCHEDULE CASTE GIRLS

D. R. Albal Z. A. Pathan** A. V. Melvanki*** M. B. Chalwadi*****

INTRODUCTION

The women of any country have an important contribution in the progress of the country. It is the women who are capable of building such children who may lead the country to the path of progress and prosperity. Educated women makes the family and the society cultured. Manu has therefore remarked that God resided at the place where women are worshipped, by worship he means where women are respected.

The utmost expansion of women education is necessary for the achievement of all sided development of India.

HISTORY & DEVELOPMENT OF WOMEN EDUCATION

Ancient Period

In ancient India, education of women had made a great progress. Women not only studied the vedic literature, but famous women such as Maittreyee, Gargi, Ghosha, Lopamudra

* Reader in Sociology, Karnatak University Kittur Rani Chennamma P. G. Centre, Belgaum.

** Research Scholar in Sociology, Karnatak University Kittur Rani Chennamma P. G. Centre, Belgaum.

*** Research Scholar in Sociology, Karnatak University Kittur Rani Chennamma P. G. Centre, Belgaum.

**** Guest Faculty in Geography, Karnatak University Kittur Rani Chennamma P. G. Centre, Belgaum.

etc., had themselves composed vedic verses. Women of ancient India had acquired great knowledge in different Shastras (learned discourses) equal to those of men but also acted as judges or mediators.

Education of women received encouragement during the Buddhist period also. The Buddhist who have the credit of making the first organized effort in the field of women education because they made proper provision of education for the Buddhist female monks. But this condition of women education could not continue for a long time. After the decline of Buddhism, when the revival of Hinduism started, women education received a major setback because Shankaracharya, the leader of the revival of Hinduism, was against the education of women.

Medieval Period

After the establishment of the rule of Muslims in India, Parda system became prevalent both among the Muslims as well Hindus. The system of Child Marriage also became very much prevalent among the Hindus. Thus most of the women were deprived of higher education. There was however, the provision of education for the women of royal families and rich persons at their houses. That is why, only a few famous women such as Razia Begum, Noor Jahan, Jahan Ara, Muktabai, Zebunissa, Jijabai etc., could acquire higher education and learning.

Buddhist Period

After the Muslims, East India Company established its rule over India, since the company did not require educated women in its offices, it showed an indifference towards education of women.

Only some individual efforts were made for expansion of women education, there are evidences to show that in 1851, 371 girl's schools were being run by Protestant Missionaries and total number of girls studying in these schools was 11,293. Nearly 2,274 girls were also living in hostels.

Likewise Roman Catholic Missionaries also organized some schools. Some Government and non- government educational institutions has also been established. Among such schools, a girl's school started by Sri. J.E.D.Bethune, President of the education Board of Bengal in 1849, deserves special mention. Despite all these efforts, government was till indifferent and apathetic towards the education of women. Hunter Commission of 1888 did not make any important suggestion in regard to the education of women.

Lord Curzon, the Governor-General laid emphasis on the establishment of some ideal schools with a view to reform and improve the education of women in accordance with the education policy of 19193. This led to some progress of women education in Primary, Secondary and also higher education. In 1904 Annie Besant established Central Hindu Girl's school at Banaras and Professor Karve established S.N.D.T. women's University at Poona.

Independent India

Independent India made special provisions towards the expansion of women education in the country.

In article 15 of the Indian constitution, it is written, "The State shall not discriminate against any citizen on ground only of religion, race, caste, sex, place of birth or any of them".

Radhakrishnan Commission of 1948, Mudaliar Commission of 1952 and National Committee of Women's education made useful recommendation for the expansion of women education.

National council of Women's education under Mrs. Durgabai Deshmukh in 1959, Hansa Mehta Committee in 1962 and Kothari Commission made useful recommendations for women at all stages.

EDUCATION OF WOMEN AND ITS IMPORTANCE

Education has been considered as an important instrument of bringing socio-economic development. Basic education has been regarded as the foundation of education system, whereas higher education is its pillar. Today higher education has become the part of every person's life. Basic education is the essence of human life, whereas higher education is the mobiliser of social life. Education is regarded as an important agent of social mobility and an instrument of social change.

The development of Higher education and women of any country/Nation depends on the education of its people. This is truer in case of women where they have been neglected for centuries together. This holds more in case of SC, ST & OBC categories of women. No nation can progress and develop without giving education to the women. It has to utilize the talents and abilities of women, who constitute about half of the total population; otherwise country will not progress. It is very important to note that for the overall development of women, higher education is a must. Higher education is the source of empowerment, because the better-educated women can easily take decisions and play vital role in every aspects of human life. Higher education helps the women to understand the world rationally and play the role accordingly.

With regard to education of women it is disheartening to know that they are not enjoying the fruits of Higher education. The attitude that giving higher education to the girls is a waste and thus the number of girls in higher education is less. But nowadays the girls are entering into the field of higher education. But most of the girls can be seen doing the traditional courses like, B.A, M.A., B.Sc., M.Sc., B.Com., and M.Com. The girls pursuing higher education belong to either upper caste or class. Even among them majority belonged to urban area. Religionwise percentage of Christian girls is higher compared to Hindus, Muslims and Jains. Percentage of Higher education among SC/ST/OBC is lowest. Hence there is the need for giving higher education to these sections of society.

OBJECTIVE OF THE STUDY

The main objective of the present study is to know various Problems of Scheduled Caste Girl Students of the Post-Graduate Centre, Belgaum.

METHODOLOGY

The study is based on both Primary and Secondary data. A case study method was employed to study all the 15 Scheduled Caste

Girls studying in Post-graduate center, Belgaum, in the month of November 2005. A pre-structured questionnaire was prepared and administered to the respondents to obtain the data. Secondary data was obtained from published literature of the government and academicians.

LOCALE OF THE STUDY

In June 1982 the University opened a new campus at Belgaum where facilities are available for post-graduate studies and research leading to both master's and Doctorate Degree programs in seven disciplines, viz., Kannada, Marathi, economics, commerce, Geography, Sociology and Mathematics. It is proposed to start PGDCA courses during 98-99.

The University has provided basic facilities on the campus. About 200 acres of land has been acquired on Poona-Bangalore highway No. 4. It is 20 Kms. away from Belgaum City. The University has constructed academic building at the estimated cost of Rs. 75.00 lakhs. A hostel for students and a furnished GuestHouse with well-laid roads and independent water supply is provided. About 3 Crores of rupees are invested to develop the campus and created academic facility on the campus.

Belgaum, a delectable mid-sized town nestling high in the Western Ghats, grew out of a village Venugram or the 'village of bamboo' over a course of 3,200 years at least. The Belgaum City was converted into Municipality in the year 1851. Belgaum has an enviable heritage and presents much to be discovered. It lies in the zone of cultural transition between Kamataka, Maharashtra and Goa with a known antiquity clearly traceable up to 2nd Century A.D.

Belgaum participated actively in the Freedom Movement with whole country. One of the prominent lady warriors Rani Channamma of Kittur along with Sangolli Rayanna and Babasaheb was first to start this movement. Belgaum was also chosen as the venue of the 39th session of Indian National Congress in December 1924 under the President ship of Mahatma Gandhiji. The then Shahapur Municipality that was near to Belgaum was merged in Belgaum Municipality on 4-7-1952. The District Headquarters, Belgaum is a picture of contrasts. On one side is the old town area where the cotton and silk weavers still create magic with their fingers. And on the other side the modern, bustling, tree-lined Cantonment built by the British.

Table 1
Age composition of the Respondents

Sl.No	*Age*	*No.of Respondents*	*Percentage*
1.	20	1	6.66
2.	21	4	26.66
3.	22	6	40.00
4.	23	3	20.00
5.	24	1	6.66
	Total	15	100

Source: Field Survey.

Table shows the age composition of the respondent, 6.66 per cent of the respondent are of 20 years of age, 26.66 per are 21 years of age, 40 per cent are 22 years of age, 20 per cent are 23 years of age and remaining 6.66 per cent are 24 years of age.

The information suggests that majority of the respondents have the age of either 21 or 22 years.

Table 2
Marital Status of the Respondents

Sl.No	*Age*	*No.of Respondents*	*Percentage*
1.	Married	03	20
2.	Unmarried	12	80
	Total	15	100

Source: Field Survey.

As marriage is a Universal socio-religious institution the Table No. 2 explains the marital status of the respondents. It is clear from the table that 20 per cent of the respondent are married and remaining 80 per cent i.e., the majority of the respondents are unmarried.

Table 3
Nature of Family of the Respondents

Sl.No	Nature of Family	No. of Respondent	Percentage
1.	Nuclear	4	26.33
2.	Joint	11	73.33
	Total	15	100

Source: Field Survey.

Table 3 explains the nature of family of the respondents, 26.33 per cent of the respondents live in Nuclear family, and 73.33 per cent live in Joint Family. The number of respondents living in Joint family is more as compared to Nuclear family.

Table 4
Native place of the Respondents

Sl.No	*Age*	*No.of Respondents*	*Percentage*
1.	Rural	4	26.66
2.	Urban	11	73.33
	Total	15	100

Source: Field Survey.

The native place of the respondents is depicted in the Table 4. The table suggests that 26.66 per cent of the respondents are from rural background and remaining 73.33 per cent of the respondents are from urban background.

Thus we can say that majority of the respondents are from Urban background.

Table 5
Sub-Caste Composition of the Respondents

Sl.No	*Sub-Caste*	*No. of Respondents*	*Percentage*
1.	Chalvadi	10	66.6
2.	Madar	01	6.6
3.	Lambani	03	20.0
4.	Samgar	01	6.6
	Total	15	100

Source: Field Survey.

The sub-caste composition of the respondents who are receiving higher education is shown with the help of Table 5. Of the total respondents 66.6 per cent belong from Chalvadi sub-caste, 6.6 per cent from Madar sub-caste, 20 per cent are Lambanis and remaining 6.6 per cent are Samgar.

It can be concluded that the majority of the respondents are either from Chalvadi or from Lambani sub-caste.

Table 6
Educational qualification of Respondents Father/Guardian

Sl.No	*Educational qualification*	*No. of Respondents*	*Perentage*
1.	Illiterate	2	13.33
2.	Primary	3	20.00
3.	High School	1	6.66
4.	Pre-University	2	13.33
5.	Graduate	7	46.66
6.	Post-Graduate	0	0
	Total	15	100

Source: Field Survey.

The educational qualification of the respondent's father/Guardian is shown in the Table 6. Out of the total respondent 13.33 per cent are illiterate, 20 per cent acquired primary education, 6.66 per cent High School education, 13.33 per cent Pre-university, 46.66 per cent upto Graduation and there is none who acquired Post Graduation.

Majority of the respondent's Father/Guardian has either received education upto Primary level or Graduation.

Table 7
Department of Pursuing Education

Sl.No	Department	No. of Respondents	Percentage
1.	Sociology	6	40
2.	Economics	1	6.66
3.	Kannada	0	0
4.	Mathematics	1	6.66
5.	Commerce	4	26.66
6.	Social Work	3	20
	Total	15	100

Source: Field Survey.

Table 7 depicts the Department in which the respondents are pursuing their Higher studies. 40 per cent of the respondents are acquiring higher education from Sociology department, 6.66 per cent from Economics department, 6.66 per cent from Mathematics, 26.66 per cent from Commerce, 20 per cent from Social work department and there is none from Kannada department.

It can be said that majority of the respondents are pursuing their higher education either from Sociology department or Commerce department.

Table 8

Occupational Background of the Respondent Father/Guardian.

Sl.No	*Occupational Background*	*No. of Respondent*	*Percentage*
1.	Government Service	8	53.33
2.	Private Service	7	46.66
	Total	15	100

Source: Field Survey.

The occupational background of the respondents father/guardian is depicted in the Table 8, it shows that 53.33 per cent of the respondents Father/Guardian are in Government Service and remaining 46.66 per cent are in Private Service.

Thus it can be said that majority of the respondent's father/guardian are government servants.

Table 9

Annual Income of the Respondents Father/Gaurdian.

Sl.No	*Income (In Rupees)*	*No. of Respondents*	*Percentage*
1.	0 – 4,999	2	13.33
2.	5,000 – 9,999	1	6.66
3.	10,000 – 14,999	2	13.33
4.	15,000 – 19,999	6	40.00
5.	20,000 and more	4	26.66
	Total	15	100

Source: Field Survey.

Out of the total respondents 13.33 per cent of the respondent's father/guardian have the annual income of Rs.0

to 4,999, 6.66 per cent Rs. 5,000 to 9,999, 13.33 per cent Rs. 10,000 to 14,999, 40 per cent Rs.15,000 to 19,999 and remaining 26.66 per cent earn more than Rs.20,000.

The table reveals that majority of the respondent's father/ guardian earn more than Rs.15,000.

Table 10
Details of Agricultural land

Sl.No	Agricultural Land(in acres)	No. of Respondents	Percentage
1.	Not applicable	04	26.66
2.	1 – 5	10	66.66
3.	5 – 10	01	06.66
4.	10 – 15	00	00.00
5.	15 and above	00	00.00
	Total	15	100

Source: Field Survey.

Table 10 gives the detail about the agricultural land possessed by the respondent. 26.66 per cent of the respondent does not have any land, 66.66 per cent have 1 to 5 acres of land, 6.66 per cent have 5 to 10 acres of land, and there is none possessing the land above 10 acres.

Table 11
Medium of Instruction in Examination

Sl.No	Medium	No. of Respondent	Percentage
1.	Kannada	10	66.66
2.	English	5	33.33
	Total	15	100

Source: Field Survey.

The medium of Instruction or writing the examination by the respondent is shown in the Table 11, it can be seen that 66.66 per cent of the respondent are from Kannada medium and remaining 33.33 per cent are in English medium.

This suggests that majority of the respondents are from Kannada Medium.

Table 12
Opinion about English Language

Sl.No	*Opinion*	*No. of Respondent*	*Percentage*
1.	Easy	4	26.66
2.	Difficult	8	53.33
3.	Very Difficult	3	20.00
	Total	15	100

Source: Field Survey.

As most of the respondents are from Kannada medium the opinion of the respondents about English language is reflected in the Table No.12, Out of the total respondent 26.66 per cent of the respondents feel that English language is an easy language, 53.33 per cent take it as difficult and remaining 20 per cent feel that it is very difficult.

This can be concluded that majority of the respondent opine that English language is difficult to them.

Table 13
Languages known by the Respondent

Sl.No.	*Languages Known*	*No. of Respondent*	*Percentage*
1.	Kannada	02	13.33
2.	Kannada, English	00	00.00
3.	Kannada, English, Hindi	07	46.66
4.	Kannada, Hindi.	02	13.33
5.	Kannada, Marathi.	04	26.66
6.	Kannada, Marathi, Urdu.	00	00.00
7.	Kannada, Urdu.	00	00.00
8.	Others	00	00.00
	Total	15	100

Source: Field Survey.

Table 13 depicts the languages known by the respondent, 13.33 per cent of the respondent know only Kannada, 46.66 per cent know Kannada, English and Hindi, 13.33 per cent know Kannada and Hindi, 26.66 per cent know Kannada and Marathi, Thus we can say more number of the respondent have knowledge of three languages.

Table 14
Educational Standard of the Respondent

Sl.No.	Educational Standard	No. of Respondent	Percentage
1.	Good	10	66.67
2.	Normal	2	13.33
3.	Better then other caste	3	20.00
4.	Less then other caste	0	00.00
	Total	15	100

Source: Field Survey.

Table 14 explains the educational standard of the respondent, 66.67 per cent of them are good in education, 13.33 per cent are normal, 20 per cent are better then other caste student and there is none who feels that they are less then other caste students.

On the basis of the above table it can be concluded that majority of the respondent are good in their education.

Table 15
Participation in Co-curricular activities

Sl.No.	Participation in Activities	No. of Respondent	Percentage
1.	Yes	9	60
2.	No	6	40
	Total	15	100

Source: Field Survey.

The participation in the Co-curricular activities by the respondents is reflected in the Table 15. Out of the total respondent 60 per of the respondent participate in the co-curricular activities along with their academic education and remaining 40 per cent said that they don't participate in the co-curricular activities.

It can be derived that majority of the respondents participate in the co-curricular activities for the all round development of their personality.

The source of encouragement received by the respondent for pursuing the higher education is depicted in the Table 16. It shows that 73.33 per cent of the respondent receives encouragement from their Father, 13.33 per cent from Mother,

6.66 per cent from Brother and remaining 6.66 per cent from sister and there none who receive encouragement from their relative.

Table 16
Source of Encouragement to Pursue Education

Sl.No	*Source of encouragement*	*No. of Respondent*	*Percentage*
1.	Father	11	73.33
2.	Mother	2	13.33
3.	Brother	1	6,66
4.	Sister	1	6.66
5.	Relative	0	0
	Total	15	100

Source: Field Survey.

The conclusion can be drawn on the basis of the table that majority of the respondent are encouraged by their Father.

Table 17
Reason for not Pursuing Technical Education

Sl.No.	*Reasons*	*No. of Respondent*	*Percentage*
1.	Lack of Proper Guidance	1	06.66
2.	Poverty	3	20.00
3.	Lack in English Language	11	73.33
	Total	15	100

Source: Field Survey.

As none of the respondents are pursuing technical education, here the reason for not pursuing the technical education by the respondents is studied. Table No.17 reveals that 6.66 per cent did no pursue technical education due to Lack of proper guidance, 20 per cent due to poverty, 73.33 per cent due to lack of English knowledge.

Thus we can say majority of the respondent did not pursue technical education because they lack good English knowledge.

The aim of the respondents in their life is depicted in the Table 18., 26.66 per cent of the respondent aim to become a Government servant, 6.66 per cent wants to become Lecturer,

6.66 wants to have business, 60 per cent of the respondents aim to become a Social worker after receiving their Higher Education.

Table 18
Aim of the Respondent

Sl.No	Aim	No. of Respondent	Percentage
1.	Government Service	4	26.66
2.	Lecturer	1	6.66
3.	Business	0	0
4.	Politician	1	6.66
5.	Soc-worker	9	60.00
	Total	15	100

Source: Field Survey.

The information discloses that majority of the respondent wants to become a social worker.

Table 19
Source of Expenditure for Pursuing Education

Sl.No.	Source of Expenditure	No. of Respondent	Percentage
1.	Govt.Scholarship	1	6.66
2.	Family	14	93.33
3.	Self Income	0	0
4.	Others	0	0
	Total	15	100

Source: Field Survey.

Table 19 reveals, the expenses for pursuing higher education by the respondent, 6.66 per cent of the respondent meet their expenses with the help of Government scholarship and majority of the respondents i.e., 93.33 per cent through family.

The Table shows explains that 66.66 per cent of the respondent are admitted to pursue higher education through their merit, 26.66 through caste based reservation, 6.66 per cent through donation.

Thus we can say that majority of the respondent are admitted to acquire higher education through their merit.

Table 20
Mode of Admission in Higher Education

Sl.No.	*Mode of Admission*	*No. of Respondent*	*Percentage*
1.	Merit	10	66.66
2.	Caste basis	4	26.66
3.	Donation	1	6.66
4.	Other	-	-
	Total	15	100

Source: Field Survey.

Table 21
Whether availed the Reservation facility

Sl.No.	*Reservation*	*No. of Respondent*	*Percentage*
1.	Yes	9	60.00
2.	No	6	40.00
	Total	15	100

Source: Field Survey.

The benefit of the reservation facility whether received by the respondents or not is reflected with the help of Table 21. It says that 60 per cent of the respondent availed the reservation facility provided to their community and the remaining 40 per cent did not availed the reservation facility.

But here we can say that majority of the respondent have availed the reservation facility for acquiring education.

Table 22
Fulfillment of respondent's requirement through Scholarship

Sl.No	*Extent of Fulfillment*	*No. of Respondent*	*Percentage*
1.	Some extent	9	60.00
2.	Fulfilled	0	00.00
3.	Not fulfilled	6	40.00
	Total	15	100

Source: Field Survey.

It is clear from the Table 22 that 60 per cent of the respondent feel that the scholarship fulfills their requirement at some extent and remaining 40 per cent feels that their requirements are not fulfilled, and there is none who says that their requirements are fulfilled.

Thus the conclusion can be drawn that most of the respondents fulfill their requirement with the help of scholarship only at some extent.

Table 23
The quality of education received by the respondent in the Department.

Sl.No.	*Quality of Education*	*No. of Respondent*	*Percentage*
1.	Normal	2	13.66
2.	Good	7	46.66
3.	Excellent	6	40.00
	Total	15	100

Source: Field Survey.

Table 23 gives the information about the standard of education provided to the respondent in their respective departments. 13.66 per cent of the respondents say that the quality of education is normal, 46.66 per cent say that it is good and remaining 40 opines that it is excellent.

Here most of the respondent opines that the quality of education is either good or excellent.

Table 24
Problems solved by the respondent in the Department

Sl.No.	*Problems Solved By*	*No. of Respondent*	*Percentage*
1.	Self	8	53.33
2.	Administrator	5	33.33
3.	Parents	2	13.33
	Total	15	100

Source: Field Survey.

Various problems faced by the respondents are solved by various sources; Table 24 shows that 53.33 per cent of the respondent solve their problem by themselves, 33.33 per cent through Administrator and 13.33 per cent through Parents involvement.

Thus it can be concluded that majority of the respondent's problems are solved by self or by the Administrator and there is very less involvement of parents.

Table 24
Respondents relationship with the Teachers

Sl.No.	*Type of Relationship*	*No. of Respondent*	*Percentage*
1.	Normal	2	13.33
2.	Friendly	7	46.66
3.	Non-secular	1	6.66
4.	Secular	5	33.33
	Total	15	100

Source: Field Survey.

Respondents relationship with their Teacher are revealed in the Table 24. It shows that 13.33 per cent of the respondents have normal relations, 46.66 per cent have friendly relations, 6.66 per cent of the teachers are not secular minded and 33.33 per cent are secular minded.

Table 25
Behavior of Non-SC students with the Respondents.

Sl.No.	Behavior of the Non-SCs	No. of Respondent	Percentage
1.	Good	11	73.33
2.	Lacks co-operation	2	13.33
3.	Discrimination	2	13.33
	Total	15	100

Source: Field Survey.

Table 25 reveals the behavior of non-scheduled caste students with the respondents. 73.33 per cent of the respondents say that they have good behavior, 13.33 feels that they lack co-operation, 13.33 say that their behavior is discriminative.

Majority of the respondents feels that the behavior of the non-scheduled caste students is good with them.

The behavior of the library staff with the respondent is shown in the Table 26. It can be observed that 46.67 per cent of the respondent think that the behavior of the Library staff with them is co-operative, 13.33 per cent feels that they have friendly behavior and the remaining 40 per cent of them say that it is non co-operative.

Thus we can conclude that majority of the respondents feel that the behavior of the Library staff with them is either co-operative or friendly.

Table No.26
Library Staff's behavior towards the Respondent

Sl.No.	Type of Behavior	No. of Respondent	Percentage
1.	Co-operative	7	46.67
2.	Friendly	2	13.33
3.	Non-cooperative	6	40.00
	Total	15	100

Source: Field Survey.

CONCLUSION

On the basis of the study made on the subject "Higher education among the Schedule Caste Girls" the conclusion can be drawn that most of the respondent are unmarried and are in the age of 21 or 22 years and live in Joint family. Aggregate of respondent are having Urban background the number of Chalvadi and Lambani sub-caste is more as compared to others.

The parents of the respondent are qualified and there is very less representation of illiterates. Much of the respondents are pursuing higher education either from Sociology or Commerce department. Majority of the respondents father/ guardian are government servant and have the annual income of more than 15,000 Rupee. The number of respondent from Kannada medium is more and they find English language difficult to study, their educational standard is good but on the other hand their participation in the co-curricular activities is less.

The respondents are encouraged by their Father and their aim is to become social worker. They meet their expenditure through their family and most of them are pursuing the higher education on the merit. They are well behave by the non scheduled caste friends and the teaching and non teaching staff of the Institute.

REFERENCE

Banks, Olive, "The Sociology of Education", Routledge and Kegan Paul, London, 1969.

B. C. Rai., "History of Indian Education & Problems", Prakashan Kendra, Lucknow, 2003.

Chitra, M. N., "Higher Education and Society in Mysore under British rule" Sociological Bulletin, 21(2), 1972.

Kirpal, V., "Higher Education for the Scheduled Castes", Economic and Political Weekly, 13 (4 and 5), 1978.

28

HUMAN CAPITAL VS WOMAN CAPITAL

*Jayashree Dam P. Choudhury**

INTRODUCTION

Under present economic scenario a great deal of attention has been given for development of "Human Resources" as it brings necessary changes in knowledge, skill, capabilities, creative abilities and aptitude of the people, who are supposed to adjust with on going changes in global arena. While human resource development (HRD) is a holistic approach, human capital (HC) is only partial picture of the situation as it deals with productive aspect of human being who are engaged in economic activities of the country.

As such human capital/ woman capital studies economic efficiency of the people who through their productive capacity accelerates economic growth rate of the country. Long back the importance of human-capital or human –skill was appreciated by the economic thinkers like Petty, Smith, say, senior, List, van-Thusen Roscher, Bagehat, Earnst, Engel, Sedgurick, Wales and Fisher[1]. So present discussion on significance of human-capital is acknowledgement of human-skill with new dimension.

MEANING OF THE TERM

According to Adam Smith it is the acquisition of talent that makes a person fortunate like flourishment of trade that depends on acquisition of machine or instrument[2].

Commonly human capital is defined as an individual's productive skill, talents and knowledge. It includes "Abilities

* Sr. Lecturer, Department of Economics, K.C.Das Commerce College, Guwahati.

and know-how of men and women that have been acquired at same cost and can command a price in the labour-market because they are useful in the productive process[3]. Thus it is measured in term of the value (price multiplied by quantity) of goods and services produced. Thus when value of goods and services rises, the value of human-capital rises and vice-varsa[4].

In economics capital is defined as produced means of production and process of creating capital is called investment. Investment is carried out to get return over it and it can be both public and private. However, investment in human resources is something different from investment in physical resources. This is because the end result of investment in case of former is permanent and holistic whereas in case of later it is materialistic concept. The argument can be supplemented by the examples of developed and developing countries where concept of economic development differs diagonically. The developed countries could fasten their economic growth rate because of speedy growth of science and technology, which is simply brainwork of superior quality of human resources. The controlled growth of population has made those countries qualitatively superior to that of developing countries where " Population Policy" is yet to be strictly followed. So it is a great privilege for a country to have quality population rather than having qualitative physical resources. For example – India is supposed to have rich physical resources, but most of them remained unutilized because of lack of technical hands and skilled workers. To balance between the physical and human resources the country thus needs more skilled workers for which amount of investment in human resources must go up.

Adam Smith has included skills and useful abilities of human beings in the category of fixed capital. He says that skill of a man is to be regarded as machine that has a genuine cost and returns a profit. He not only has aptly included materials and tools in the category of fixed capital but also human-capital, because acquired skills of labourers are in no way natural skills but are acquired after proper investment. In other way it is being produced[5].

Ricardo considers "capital" as that part of the wealth of a country, which is employed in production and consists of food, clothing, tools, raw materials, machinery etc. necessary to give effect to labour[6]. J. S. Mill on the other hand thinks that material progress of the society depends on size of the national wealth. By wealth he means tools, machines and skill of the labour force; thus he distinguishes between productive and unproductive labour. By productive labour he means those labour who spend time in acquiring skill and protecting property[7].

Of all, Karl Marx who advocated against labour exploitation exceptionally opines that increase in capital accumulation is only possible by increasing the productivity of labour, which involves technological improvement since capital-intensive technique increases surplus value. Surplus value converted into capital induces to take full advantage of advanced technology and in turn increases labour productivity. By labour he means productive human activity, which aims at transforming natural objects to satisfy human wants, while acting on nature he acquires knowledge and skill and introduces improvements into the process of labour[8].

DISTINCTION BETWEEN HUMAN RESOURCES AND HUMAN-CAPITAL

Everyone knows that population of a country is technically called human-resources and it is the quality of population that contributes towards growth of the country. Before showing the marked differences it would be appropriate to define the following terms in order to have in depth study of the chosen topic.

The term "Resource" means any product which is useful to man and society. Resource again denotes useful thing and it has a function in relation to man. The functional ability differs from time to time and from place to place. It increases with the advancement of scientific knowledge and with the development of means of transport[9].

Of the three resources– (a) natural, (b) man-made and (c) human-resources the study on third is both fascinating and confusing. It is fascinating as it involves several dimensions of human resources; it is confusing as it is interdisciplinary in nature.

Human Resource study thus comprises wide-range discussion on demographic pattern of the country, education, urbanization, size of rural settlement; occupational structure etc. which again depends on amenities like education, medical facilities, nutrition, roads, communication, income and etc; to be more specific, "quality of population" measures (their) social and political organization, (their) cultural values (their) economic efficiency or productivity and level of (their) growth in science and technology. However, the importance of human-resource development cannot be overemphasized, but there must be urgency to develop human-resources on priority basis.

Once the two terms "resource" and "quality of population" are defined, it is also necessary to define "development" in relation to human resources. By "development of people" it means advancement of knowledge, skills, competencies and improved behaviour of people within the organization for their both personal and professional use.

Human Resources	*Human Capital*
1. The term is multi dimensional in. approach	1. The term is unidimensional in approach.
2. It means whole-some development of the person i.e. cultural, educational, political and economic.	2. It deals only with economic aspect/ productivity of the person.
3. Quality of HR can be improved by lowering birth rate.	3. Quality of HC can be improved by training and education.
4. Better HR means improvement in HC.	4. Vice-versa is not true.
5. Improvement in HDI reflects Country's achievement and this helps the country to get better ranking in international arena.	5. Human Development Report projects only total picture of HR not HC. If quality of HR is satisfactory, it will automatically be reflected in economic development of the country. For example – economic growth rate of developed countries is high because of improved quality of HR.

Human Resource Development thus focuses on – individual development, professional advancement leading to career development performance and improvement to organizational development. In simple word, human resource is the holistic view of the "Human Resource Process".

Very often it is found that the terms human-resources and human-capital are interchangeably used. But there are some differences which are laid down below:-

Thus the two concepts HR and HC should not be mingled up. The term is to be used technically and deliberately depending on the requirement of subject matter, other wise it will be layman's interpretation.

NEED FOR HUMAN-RESOURCE DEVELOPMENT

While economic growth rate measures prosperity, human development index indicates quality of human resource of the country. Increase in National Income does not assure that people of the country are enjoying basic amenities of life. The fact is true otherwise how poverty, unemployment, gender-disparity, environmental degradation and illiteracy could be global issues specially in Third World countries! Appreciating the challenges of 21st century, the world leaders in September 2000 accepted, the UN Millennium Delaration for making the "World" a better living place for posterity. The Monterrey conference attended by both rich and poor countries is significant as it shows deep commitment and participatory feeling among the signatories.

To quote from HDR 2003 –

"We recognize that, in addition to our separate responsibilities to our individual societies, are have a collective responsibility to uphold the principles of human dignity, equality and equity at the global level. As leaders we have a duty therefore to all the world's people, especially the most vulnerable, and in particular, the children of the world, to whom the future belongs".

UN Millennium Declaration, is quite interesting and significant because from the day of launching of Human Development Report great emphasis has been put on improvement of quality of life of people in terms of income, health, education, nutrition, longevity, freedom, dignity, choices and so on. It is the deprivation that forbids one to enjoy creative life and compels him/her to live below poverty level. Such situation is mostly found in under development countries where economic development/ HDI ranking is dissausfactory. This is the reason why majority of Asia and Africa continents live substandard life. So it is due to publication of Human Development Report attention has been diverted from economic development to human development process.

Over the decades country's prosperity was measured in term of per capita income, is no more accepted as reliable parameter as it does not focus people's choices and welfare in true sense. The alternative dependable variables as proposed by Mahbub-ul Haque and endorsed by UNDP are education, nutrition, health and sanitation and they altogether measure quality of life. To enjoy such benefits while personal income is taken into consideration on the other hand state investment in social sector is also to be recorded; of course in recent time Prof. Amartya Sen emphatically has laid importance on this issue time and again.

WHAT IS GDI ?

Human Development Index (HDI) while gives general impression about quality people of the country, Gender Development Index (GDI) measures degree of gender-disparity practiced in the country. No doubt Gender-discrimination is a global phenomenon but with reference to India and SAARC countries the study is most urgent as female population in this region is around 50 percent. As such Gender Development Index (GDI) and Gender Empowerment Measure (GEM) are evolved to study the situation of gender-disparity in relation to HDI. The values of these two indicators make one understand the real deprivation the women accept for no fault of themselves. Wider is the accessibility to resources narrower is the gap between HDI and GDI. The following tables gives bird-eye view of gender-disparity expressed in terms of gender development index (GDI) and gender empowerment measures (GEM).

Table 1
Magnitude of Gender Disparity in Leading Development countries.

Countries	*HDI*	*GDI*	*GEM*
Bangladesh	0.440	0.428	0.304
Bhutan	0.459	0.444	n/a
India	0.545	0.525	0.240
Maldives	0.716	0.711	0.342
Nepal	0.463	0.441	n/a
Pakistan	0.508	0.472	0.176
Sri Lanka	0.721	0.712	0.321
South Asia	0.532	0.511	0.241
Developing Countries	0.637	0.630	n/a
World	0.706	0.700	n/a

Source: Human Development in South – Asia – 2000, "The Gender Question"

The table shows that Sri Lanka and Maldives with comparatively small size of population occupy first and second place respectively while India with vast sea of population ranks third. In this case recent observation of Prof. Asish Bose seriously has to be taken into consideration since he thinks that size of population is a vital factor while making HDDI ranking for a country (convocation speech – University News – vol. 44, No. 11, Mar – 13-19, 2006). However in 1997 out of 92 countries India's position in terms of GDI and GEM was 75 and 86 and in 1998 out of 102 countries the position was 88 and 95 respectively[10]. Again for 2005 GDI rank is 98 (Human Development Report 2005).

Comparing the status of women of SAARC countries with the highly developing and the world as a whole, it is seen that women of SAARC region are more deprived leading to less empowerment.

Again out of 176 countries India's latest HDI ranking is 127 and women's representation in Parliament is 9.3% against China's ranking of 104 and 21.8%[11]. This, on the one hand reflects male chauvinism and on the other rate of women's participation in political activities. Between the two giants India and China and also among Asian countries China's HDI value and women's political empowerment is better which may be due to preaching's of Buddhism. It is obvious that high HDI ranking countries like Norway (1), Holland (12), USA (7),

Canada (8), Japan (9), UK (13), France (17) Germany (18), Russian Federation (64) have better GEM value and more women representation in the parliament[12].

The GDI and GEM values of India suggest that efficiency of women resources/ women capital is far beyond satisfaction. However, the economists Mill and Taylor unlike other economists are of opinion that women are not less productive than men. So given the same opportunity, there is scope to improve GDI and GEM values for all the countries including the developed ones.

A CASE STUDY WITH REFERENCE TO ASSAM

Assam being in North-Eastern region (NER) of the country is yet to reap benefits of industrialization. There is no dearth of natural resources and fund flow through North-Eastern Council (NEC) is satisfactory, but desired impact is not realized. The economists like Dr. Manmohan Singh and Dr. Jayanta Madhab feel that development of NER may be accelerated through proper development of human resources. The fact is true when HDI value of Assam is compared with some leading states of the country. The HDI ranking for the state of Assam is of lower rank, i.e. the state achieved only 31 percent in human development. Among the districts Jorhat tops the list in HDI value 0.462, followed by Dibrugarh (0.422), Golaghat (0.396) and Sivsagar (0.392). Dhubri lies at bottom with HDI value 0.184. The indicators used in this case are education, health and income, and the state of Assam yet to achieve "education for all" "health for all" etc. Poverty level in fact is higher than national level. On the contrary Kamrup tops the list in term of education (0.616) and Dhubri is at the bottom (0.359) and for state as a whole is 0.495.

The health index is also dissatisfactory. It is only 39 out of 100 points in the scale. Jorhat again shows better position (0.6867) followed by Dibrugarh (0.6600) and Golaghat (0.5933) and Dhubri at the bottom (0.1467) [13].

The poor performance in health and education sector is due to poor budgetal allocation, which has mainly slowed down the process of human development. According to secondary source of information, the proportion of expenditure on education and health during 1973-74 was 21.55 percent and 6.96 percent and 1999-2000 it marginally increased to 28.88 percent and 7.91 percent respectively whereas for sustainable human development together they should not be less than 50 percent.

GENDER DEVELOPMENT INDEX (GDI)

When overall HDI value of the state is dissatisfactory, it may be assumed that GDI rank for the state will also be low. The GDI for the state of Assam is only 30 percent against Jorhat GDI value 0.449. On the other hand among the North-Eastern States Manipur (0.815) leads in GDI, followed by Meghalaya (0.807), Arunachal Pradesh (0.776) and Mizoram (0.77) [14].

Here question may be asked why so much importance has been attached to women-capital? The answer is simple.

The separate discussion is needed on the basis of the past experiences, whereby one comes to know about continuation of social injustices even after 59 years of independence. The World Development Report 2006 is also vocal about development through equality.

Moreover, in India 94% women are engaged in unorganized sector and only 6% are in organized sector for which specific strategy is to be adopted to improve overall condition of the social sector. The women with poor-skill and literacy level earn poor wages for which their health aspect mostly remains neglected; with poor health they are not in position to contribute efficiently towards economic development of the country hence GDI and GEM are the most effective tools to bring changes in women-capital.

IMPORTANCE

Human- capital which is partial study of human resources determines of quality of product, specially in a labour intensive country. In underdeveloped countries people are in general deprived of basic needs as per capita is below $2 (in some cases it is even less than $1) having direct impact on standard of living. The importance of human-capital is more sincerely felt after the New Economic Policy (NEP) as globalization has boosted up the quality concept rather than simply increase in production. In today's world production means qualitative production with less costing. The developed countries with high technology and superior man power/ human-resources are in position to produce goods at lesser price whereas in case of developing economy; it is not possible because of poor performance of domestic economy. So these undeveloped countries being labour intensive are in confronting situation under "Produce or Perish" regime. Unless more amount is spent on health, education and nutrition people will always have subhuman life and percentage of poor people will increase in absolute term. Moreover, post analysis of green revolution gives an impression that technological accessibility was available only to rich farmers resulting into bumper production whereas on the contrary it widened the gap between rich and poor farmers. The Third World countries basically are agrarian, so if condition of poor farmers does not improve in real sense level of poverty will increase and in that case HDI ranking will deteriorate further. In practice one blames the government for its failure of population policy, but policy will never be successful unless people are educated and in this case Kerala is the best example. So "Education" is the prime tool to bring change in health sector, food sector and etc. etc. Here it may be pointed out that village women mostly suffer from "Permanent Pregnancy", so if they are made literate through "Adult Literacy Scheme" maternal mortality (MMR) and infant mortality rate (IMR) will decline resulting into improved health status and small family will have better nourishment. The overall change will definitely bring permanent change in domestic economy and how it will ultimately raise per capita income is shown hereunder.

So there is no doubt in admitting that spending on education will bring cumulative benefits in the economy and in order to get better quality of human capital HDI value of a country must improve. The developed countries are in position to dictate the world economy because of their supremacy in human resources. The country strong in human resources (HR) is definitely strong in science and technology having its strong impact in primary and secondary sectors; the tertiary sector too will expand at tremendous rate and they altogether will accelerate economic growth rate of the country.

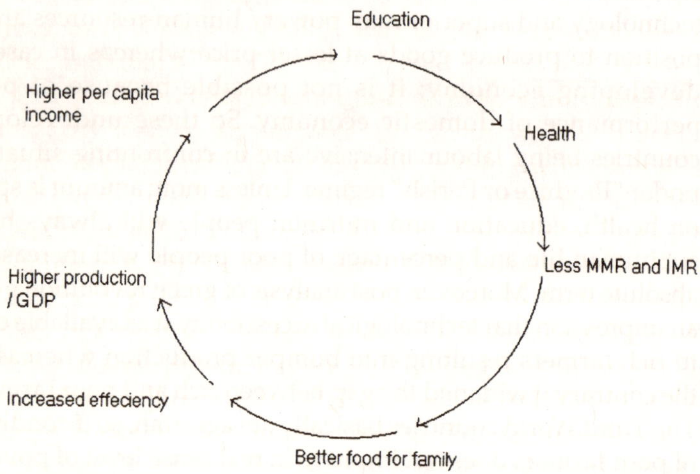

From above discussion it is clear that India under present scenario should have development of human resources with human touch. The size of population instead of considering as liability should be converted into assets. India has the advantage over those countries where population growth rates is frozen or negative. In near future where there is possibility of having crisis of manpower, India in that case may take lead as it is happening in the field of IT.

CONCLUSION

The success stories of advanced countries make the developing countries to accept the fact that ultimately it is the quality of population, which determines the fate of the country. Prosperity of the country does not depend on the stock of the resources (both physical and human) but how best it is being scientifically harnessed by the skilled workers and technocrats. Till 1990, development of the country was calculated in term of annual growth rate of the country, but when the United Nations for the first time published Human Development Report (1990), every country even the developed ones could understand their actual place in international field. The three parameters of HDI - education, health and income actually measure the rate of development with human touch. But even if the government spends more on education and health, the success rate may be slow because of malpractices. So application part of any scheme is more important than the objectives of the scheme. It has now become a global discussion that everyday India introduces new scheme but in term of corruption she is deteriorating her status day by day. If this is the impression about a country, which claims champion of civilization, what can be the quality of population can easily be estimated.

So, if proper care is not being taken even after observation of Prof. Sen, then it would really be difficult to produce healthy human capital for rapid industrial development of the country. Moreover to contain rural poverty, the country needs renovation of farm sector in order to enhance farm income. Since there is close relationship between income and consumption mere income does not assure minimum/ decent standard of living, so income of the family is one of the important factors to determine quality of life. It is generally believed that people with higher income would spend more on health, education nutrition and etc. Once the standard of living is raised, people will prefer more urban style of living and rate of urbanization ultimately will lead to subsequent changes thereby they will enjoy "quality of life".

To conclude, potentiality of workers can be increased through adult education and training and this will produce better quality of human-capital for primary and secondary sectors. The overall development of human resources will again bring desired change in the quality of women-capital, and minimize problems of social sector

Lastly, since excess population is the root cause of many of the problems of the underdeveloped/ developing countries and how it aggravates the situation further is depicted through the following flow chart.

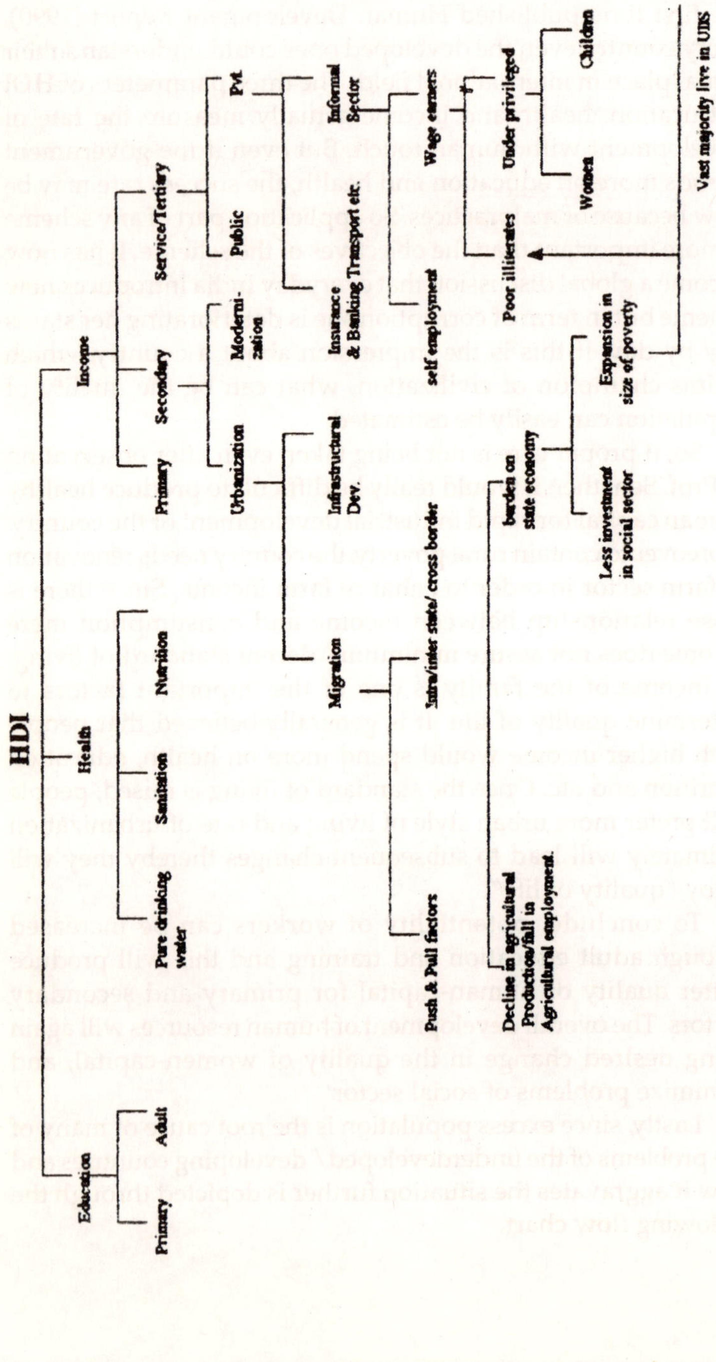
HDI
Education
Primary
Adult
Health
Pure drinking water
Sanitation
Nutrition
Income
Primary
Secondary
Service/Tertiary
Urbanization
Moderni-zation
Public
Pvt
Migration
Infrastructural Dev.
Insurance & Banking Transport etc
Informal Sector
Push & Pull factors
Intra/inter state/ cross border
self employment
Wage earners
Decline in agricultural Production/fall in Agricultural employment
burden on state economy
Poor illiterates
Under privileged
Less investment in social sector
Expansion in size of poverty
Women
Children
Vast majority live in UHS

SUGGESTIONS

Adequate measures are to be taken to stop the leakages so that there is proper utilization of fund and benefits are enjoyed by the targeted groups. Moreover instead of having highly ambitious schemes it is suggested to have concrete one with pragmatic approach.

REFERENCE

Wykstra, Ronald A. (ed. 1971), Human capital Formation and Manpower Development. P-3.

Sirageldin, Ismail (1979), Research in human capital and development vol. 1. P-VII.

Herbert, S. Parnes (1984), People, Power, Elements of Human Resource Policy, P-132.

Thurow, Leder C. (1976), Investment in Human capital P-3.

Paul, R.R. History of Economic Through P-120.

ibid p. 200.

ibid p-255.

ibid pp. 332-353.

Singh J.P. (1982), Human Resources ot North – East India p-1.

Human Development Report 1997. p-4. Oxford.

Human Development Report 1998 p-33.

Human Development Report 2003. p-316.

The Assam Tribune Sept. 19.2002.

The Assam Tribune Aug. 11.2002.

In addition following are also consulted:-

Towards Equality.

World Development Report- 2003 & 2006.

Human Development Report 2004 & 2005.

Yojana- Dec. 2005.

29

EMERGING LEADERSHIP AMONG DALIT WOMEN

(A Case Study of Village Panchayats In Bijapur Taluk)

*Vijaya B. Korishetti**

Indira Gandhi had said "To be liberated, a woman should feel free to be herself, not in rivalry to man, but in the context of her own capacity, Women should be more interested, more alive and more active in the affairs of the society, not because they are women, but because they comprise half the human race."

The restriction of women's roles to the private realm of home and family had an obvious external manifestation: their exclusion from public life and particularly from participation in decision making in the public sphere. This was only slightly less true for women from laboring households, whose income and participation in productive work was vital to the economy in general and the survival of their families in particular. With rare exceptions, women were thus historically absent from leadership roles in the community at large.

The freedom struggle changed this dramatically, as hundreds of thousands of women from all classes were strategically mobilized to participate in the mass movements of the 1930s, and took an active part in satyagrahas, political rallies and the Swaraj movements. The women of Karnataka were no exceptions. After independence however, the emphasis

* Senior Scale Lecturer, Department of Studies in Sociology, Karnataka State Women University, Bijapur.

on women's political participation became diluted and narrowed, with the focus mainly on voting. Few women entered the formal political sphere, and the proportion of women contesting elections and becoming political representatives in the state gradually declined.

In Indian constitution there are provisions for equal rights for all citizens irrespective of their social and economic status. However such provisions exist only in pen and paper for millions of economically and socially disadvantaged groups of people of India. The Scheduled Caste (SC), Scheduled Tribes (ST) people and the women are included in these groups. These people are underpowered economically, socially and politically.

In India women are in a much worse position than men not only in terms of sex ratio, life expectancy, literacy rate, nutrition, work force participation, wage earnings and work time disposition, but also in terms of their access to power structure which controls and guides the development programmes of a society. Since access to political opportunities and participation in political decision making process are important components of capability and autonomy, discrimination in this respect leads to wastage of women's talent and efficiency which are necessary for an all round development of a country. One of the three variables used in the construction of Gender Empowerment Index (GEM) is the relative share of women in administrative and managerial position. Women need to be involved in the decision making process in order to bring their demands in the national agenda. The entry of the women in the decision making bodies will ensure restructuring of the institution and lead to a solution of issues related to women's rights.

In order to ensure empowerment of women in political arena, the issue of reservation of one – third of the seats for women at grass – root level organization was taken up by different women's organizations and social thinkers. Accordingly, the Government of India passed the 73rd constitutional amendment which was followed by the 74th amendment mandating reservation of one – third of the seats for women in all village, block and district level elected bodies.

There is also the same reserved quota for women in the position of chairpersons and deputy chairpersons in these institutions. Since the Panchayat Raj Institution (PRI) plays a vital role in ensuring people's participation in the development process, it is felt that political empowerment of women through reservation of seats in PRI will train them up in exercising their power in decision making and remove social and economic discriminations against them.

MAIN FEATURES OF THE 73RD AMENDMENT:

1. **Imparting Constitutional Status to the PRIs' Functioning:** According Constitutional status to the PRIs provides an inherent check on the State not to tamper with the life of these institutions. This is supposed to facilitate their functioning as instruments of vibrant. The 'Gram Sabha', consisting of all eligible voters, has been made the soul of the PRIs to discuss and decide their own problems and to further people's participation.in various development programmes in a democratic way. This is also expected to foster maximum accountability and transparency of administration and public awareness.
2. **Direct Election:** This provision is expected to boost local people's initiative and enhance their involvement in the system.
3. **Powers and Functions:** The PRIs now have the power and authority to function as institutions of self-governance. Such laws may also contain provisions for the devolution of powers and responsibilities to Panchayats for preparing plans and to implement schemes for economic development and social justice on various subjects.
4. **Recognition of the Need for Women and Members of the Scheduled Caste to Contribute to Governance:** Representation for women's SC and STs is through reservation of a minimum of 1/3rd of the total seats at all three levels. The political empowerment of Women by providing this reservation means that about 7 to 8

lakh women will be participating in and contributing directly to the development process, and about 15 to 20 lakh women will be office bearers at all levels of Panchayats. Similarly the other disadvantaged groups of SCs and STs will get the opportunity to enter into the system through reservations in these bodies.

5. **Opportunity for Emergence of a New Leadership:** Allowing persons who have attained the age of 21 years to be eligible for contesting elections in PRIs is expected to provide opportunities to the youth to participate actively in the process of development and share power. A new leadership will emerge which will be more energetic and enthusiastic in the task of nation building.
6. **Financial Matters:** PRI's can now levy, collect and appropriate such taxes, duties, tolls and fees as may be laid down by the State Government. To review the financial position of the Panchayat, the Act provides that the Governor of a state shall constitute a Finance Commission of the State.
7. **Provisions of a State Election Commission and Bar to Interference of Courts in Electoral Matters:** The provision is expected to solve most of the problem relating to elections in the PRIs. Restricting interference of courts in electoral matters is also expected to reduce frequent litigation on flimsy grounds and avoid unnecessary delays in the electoral process. This will ensure regular and fair elections to the Panchayat bodies.

On the basis of her study, Dr. Mohanty concludes "...the 73rd Amendment has created an opportunity for large number of rural women to take part in public institutions. In many places, women have been functioning well and have engendered the development process, although in a limited sense." She also feels that the family has accepted the new role and even the relationship between husband and wife has been altered. She goes on to claim that the elected women prove to be the role model for the village women and argues that the entry of women into politics in such a big way is in itself a radical change. At the same time she also concedes that the constraints are many.

PANCHAYAT RAJ IN KARNATAKA

Karnataka was the first state to pass a new law as Panchayat Raj in accordance with the 73rd Constitutional Amendment. This new law called the Karnataka Panchayat Raj Act, 1993, provides for a three-tier Panchayat Raj system with direct elections to all three-tiers: reservation for women, Scheduled Caste (SCs) Scheduled Tribes (STs) and Backward Classes (OBCs): devolution of powers, functions and duties: creation of State Election Commission for election to the three-tiers and State Finance Commission for allocating funds to the Panchayat bodies.

Prior to the enactment of the Karnataka Panchayat Raj Act, 1993, there was a two-tier system of Panchayat Raj. These two tiers were the Zilla Parishad at the district level and the Mandal Panchayats, which comprised groups of villages. The Taluka Samithi was an ex-officio body. However, in accordance with 73rd Constitutional Amendment, the new Karnataka Act of 1993 establishes a three-tier system. Zilla Panchayat at the district level, Taluk Panchayat at the Taluk level and Gram Panchayat at the village level.

Under the 1983 Karnataka Act, 25 percent seats were reserved for women. The reservation of seats for the SCs and STs was in proportion to their population. The new law of 1993 reserves one-third seats for women and one-third for backward classes, besides reservation of seats for the SCs STs in proportion to their population (26). The report of the commission on the status of women in India was the first to document that woman are not being represented adequately in the decision-making position. Therefore, a recommendation was made demanding 30 percent reservation for women. With the introduction of the 33 (1/3) percent reservation, women have moved out of private domain into the public sphere.

RESERVATION FOR WOMEN, KARNATAKA

Historical Background

In 19th century Indian Women had begun to appear on the national scene in public and political activity. Women were not only being accepted in public activity but were organizing themselves to fight for their rights in different Walks of life.

At this stage important roles were being played by three note worthy Irish women. They were Margaret Noble, later known as Sister Nivedita, Annie Besant and Margaret Cousins. Annie Besant joined the Indian National Congress in 1914 and later in 1917 became its first women President.

Situation After Independence

Though women constitute nearly half of the population of the country, it is only after independence that efforts were made to promote women's participation in public life. Though the Constitution of India provides for the Government to make special provisions to safeguard the interests of women as detailed in Article 15(3) and Article 39, it has not made any provision for reservation for women in respect of jobs and political offices. As a consequence of this lapse, women have not advanced much politically and economically.

In the first General Election (1951-52) there were 27 women in the Lok Sabha. In the second General Election (1957), there were 25 women in the Lok Sabha. They constituted 6.2 percent of those elected. There were 196 women elected to 13 State Assemblies. The largest numbers were in Bihar, which elected 33 women. Madhya Pradesh elected 30, U.P. 25, Bombay 24 and Karnataka 18 women respectively.

But from 1962 onwards the number of women members in Parliament went on the decline. This is not because women were not participating in elections as voters-they were as active as men. The reasons for such situation developing are many.

Karnataka Experience

In the old Mysore State, Women's voices were scarcely heard within the portals of the legislature. As a result, in the princely state of Mysore there were demands that women be permitted to vote and be allowed to stand as candidates in election and seek nomination in the local bodies and representative assembly. For the first time in the history of the old Mysore, two women members Smt. Kamalamma Dasappa and Smt. Sakamma entered the Mysore representative assembly in 1930. The number of women representatives remained almost contained till Independence. In 1931 a significant effort was made to amend the Hindu law regarding the rights of women, and the widow's ability to adopt children. This resulted in the passing of the Mysore Hindu Widow Remarriage Act 1938 and Mysore Maternity Regulation Act, 1937.

Experience of Reservation for Women in Karnataka

The number of women legislators in Karnataka has declined from 18 in 1957 (8 percent) to just 8 (3.4 percent) in 1991. In the present Assembly, there are hardly 6 women that too in the State Legislative Council. So far no women except Smt. Yeshodamma Dasappa (that too for a short period) has been elected as the President of any political party in Karnataka. The number of women members of Parliament from Karnataka is just four which works out to 10 percent of the total number of Parliament members elected from Karnataka. The representation of women in the Council has been inadequate and at no time it has crossed three. Many a time positions such as Deputy or State Minister with an insignificant port-folio, was considered good enough for the women representatives in the State Minister. The situation is in no way better for women in the matter of employment in the State Government.

Sri Ramakrishna Hedge, former Chief Minister of Karnataka, realized that women were inadequately represented and made every effort to do justice to them. We women of Karnataka give full credit to him for his sincere efforts. In 1984-85 Sri. Ramakrishna Hegde, the then Chief Minister tried to set right the situation by providing reservation for women in the local bodies and also in the co-operative movement. Upto 20 percent reservation of seats were allotted to women in local and city Corporations. Another initative was taken in reserving 25 percent seats for women in Zilla Parishads and Mandal Parishads. At least one seat is reserved for women in the Boards of Management of co-operative institutions in Karnataka. The new law of 1993 reserves one-third seats for women and one-third for backward classes, besides reservation of seats for the SCs STS in proportion to their population.

Political Status of Dalit Women

Women constitute one half of the total population but are denied the equal share in active politics of the country. In the politics the organizational structure, leadership and sharing of power in government are mostly dominated by men. The money and caste are in important factors which play the main role in Indian politics Women participation in the political process is centered to their struggle against oppression. The social, economic status of women directly depends on their participation in the decision-making. Unfortunately all the political parties in India talk too much about equality of women, but have totally ignored the Dalit women, where their political status and participation is insignificant. It is very said that all the Dalit women have not been given the representation in all, the political parties, which reflects the social difference. Most of the women involved in politics and power sharing are from the upper caste women with political, high financial background of the family. It may be surprising to know that till 1932, the representation in legislature was only by upper caste Hindus and Dalits were totally ignored.

Dalit women's life is difficult due to patriarchal social norms prevailing among Dalits. To quote a Dalit scholar," a Dalit woman is a confused lot today she cannot rid herself of the old values nor can absorb new values. She cannot adjust to new values but she has to change." The very inner drive for Dalit woman to change is a ray of hope.

No special representation is given to the women of weaker sections, they will be politically suppressed by the minority of high caste women.

Recognizing the serious need of women's participation in politics, in the year 1987 the Janata Government in Karnataka announced 25 per cent reservation for women in Zilla Parishad and Mandal Panchayat, as per Zilla Parishad Act 1932, with a special provision of 5:1 ratio reservation to Dalit women in 25 percent women reservation, which is a very important and significant development. Due to this reservation a number of Dalit women had an opportunity to take part in active politics, 19 Dalit women as against 211 Upper Caste women in Zilla Parishad and 2469 Dalit women as against 14025 Upper Caste women in Mandal Panchayat were elected. The participation of these representatives in active politics varies. A few women have really shown good performance in the participation. But with their social and economic background and low level of education they need proper guidance and time to mature in their responsibilities in power sharing and decision-making.

The political parties should strictly implement the reservation specifically for Dalit women. Also it is responsibilities of voluntary organisations to put presser on the political parties for implementation of reservation and to create the political awareness and its importance among Dalit women.

METHODOLOGY

Concept of Dalit

According to Molesworth's Marathi English dictionary of 1831, the word 'Dalit' means ground or broken or reduced to pieces generally. The English Language Press were compelled to term this section of society as 'Dalit' instead of the more common Untouchable, Scheduled Caste, Depressed Class or even Gandhi's euphemism Dalit. It implied those who have been broken ground down by the upper classes systematically in a deliberate and active manner throughout the ageless caste system domination of society in India.

The most appropriate definition of Dalit in its contemporary usage comes from a letter written by Gangadhar Pantawane, a Professor of Marathi at Milind College and founder editor of Asmitdarsh, the organ of Dalit literature:

"To me Dalit is not a caste. He is a man exploited by the social and economic traditions of cousntry. He does not believe in God, rebirth, soul, holy books teaching separatism, Fate and Heaven because they have made him a slave. He does believe in humanism. Dalit is a symbol of change and revolution."

Need for the Study

Karnataka was the first state to pass a new law as Panchayati Raj in accordance with the 73rd Constitutional Amendment. The new law of 1993 reserves one-third seats for women and one-third for backward classes, besides reservation of seats for the SCs STS in proportion to their population.

How far the goals of reservation for Dalit women in Panchyat have been achieved in reality needs to be examined on the basis of emprical studies. This has been done in the present paper. The role of the Dalit women Panchayat members in the political decision making process has been examined critically on the basis of data collected by interviewing the Dalit women Panchayat members of Bijapur district in Karnataka.

OBJECTIVES

Aim of the present study is to highlight the role of Dalit Women in Village Panchayat in rural development.

i. To assess the socio-economic background of Dalit women in Village Panchayat.
ii. To highlight the level of participation of Dalit women in Village Panchayat.
iii. To clarify the motivations behind entry of Dalit women into Village Panchayat.
iv. To enquire into the different types of development works done by Dalit women in Village Panchayat.
v. To understand the functions and roles of the Dalit women members concerning health and family welfare activities.
vi. To highlight the role of mass media on Dalit women in Village Panchayat.

METHODOLOGY

With limited resources and time of an individual researcher, it was decided to take up the enquiry in only one district of North Karnataka, covering 14 Village Panchayat in Bijapur Taluk. The Dalit women elected in these bodies are all rural.

A study was conducted in Bijapur, a backward and draught-prone district in North Karnataka. Bijapur taluk is selected for the present study. Because there is large concentration of SC/ST (17.12%) in the taluk. It was based on the primary data obtained from 50 Dalit women Panchayat members. Bijapur taluk consists of 107 villages with 46 Villages Panchayats. Totally there are 806 elected members, among them 454 are men and 352 are women. Out of them 235 have been elected through reservation. Among them 82 SC's, 46ST's, 95 'A' category 12 'B' category and 117 Gm.

In the present study, Dalit is a broader concept which includes SCs, STs as well as other backward castes. As stated earlier Dalits are those who have been broken-ground down by the upper classes systematically in a deliberate manner. In Bijapur taluka 235 Dalit women were elected to Village Panchayat. Out of these 235 Dalit women 50 Panchayat women members have been selected randomly. The primary data has been collected through interview schedule.

FINDINGS AND ANALYSIS

Based on the empirical study the analyses is presented under two headings with one part dealing with the 'Socio-economic background' and the other with 'the role of Dalit women as Panchayat members'.

Socio-Economic Background of Dalit Women Panchayat Members

Age

Table 1
Distribution of Respondents by Age Group

Age group	*Frequency*	*Percent*
21-30	10	20
31-40	27	54
41-50	03	06
51+	10	20
Total	50	100

Age may be an important factor contributing to status and prestige of the member. Traditionally, the older ones used to lead the Panchayat. It has been found that about 74% of Dalit women representatives are from young (21-30 years) and lower middle age groups (31-40 years) and only 20% from the elder age group i.e., 51 years and above. This shows that relatively younger women have begun to replace the elderly ones.

MARITAL STATUS

As regards to the marital status of the Dalit women Panchayat members, the study revealed that an over whelming majority (90%) were married and a few of them (08%) were widowed members. One member is unmarried.

Table 2
Distribution of Respondents by Marital Status

Marital Status	*Frequency*	*Percent*
Unmarried	01	02
Married	45	90
Widow	04	08
Total	50	100

TYPE OF FAMILY

Interestingly, while looking into the type of family of the respondents, it was found that 60% of them were from nuclear families, and only 40% of them belong to joint families.

Generally, joint families contribute people for leadership position in view of their large membership. This is not confirmed by the present study as more than half of the members belong to the nuclear families.

Table 3
Distribution of Respondents by Type of Family

Type of Family	*Frequency*	*Percent*
Joint family	20	40
Nuclear family	30	60
Total	50	100

EDUCATION

In a developing democratic country, education plays an important role, particularly in local administration. However, the educational profile of the sample shows that more than half (52%) of the respondents have been illiterate, 32% have been educated up to primary level, 6% middle and 10% secondary and above. It highlight thus the level of education of Dalit women members was low.

Table 4
Distribution of Respondents by Education

Education	*Frequency*	*Percent*
Illiterate	26	52
Primary	16	32
Middle	03	06
Secondary and above	05	10
Total	50	100

OCCUPATION

Occupation is one of the important determinants of socio-economic status of women. Economic independence helps in freeing them from economic psychological control of families, in shaping assertive personality, in allowing group activity and greater access to decision making.

As regarding the occupation, 68% of Dalit women were working. Among them majority (40%) were engaged in lower status occupation, *i.e.* agricultural labourers. It is to be noted that one respondent (2%) was a teacher and three of them (6%) were petty business women. 32% of women members were housewives. They were not involved in any economically gainful employment.

II. THE ROLE OF DALIT WOMEN MEMBERS

In order to study the role of Dalit women members, data were collected on motivation behind contesting the Panchayat election, attendance in meetings, participation in development activities etc.

Motivation Behind Contesting in Elections

The largest single group of respondent (82%) was elected to the Village Panchayat for the first time. The rest of them have been in Village Panchayat for more than once.

Table 5
Motivation Behind Contesting In Elections

Motivation	*Frequency*	*Percent*
Social Service	20	40
Rural transformation	15	30
Pressure from people	09	18
Women welfare	02	04
Interested in leadership	04	08
Total	50	100

The most averred motivation (40%) behind the respondents contesting election has been social service, 30% of them cited reason of rural transformation. Few of them (18%) cited pressure from people, and 4% said desire for women welfare. It is interesting to note that 8% of women members were interested in leadership position in Village Panchayat. Thus majority of Dalit women members are interesting in village development. This shows that there is an increasing political awareness among Dalit women members.

ATTENDANCE IN PANCHAYAT MEETING

Regarding attendance in Panchayat meetings 82% of them are attending Panchayat meetings regularly, some members are reluctant to attend the meetings. The major reasons for irregular attendance of the Dalit women member in Panchayat meetings are shortage of time, poor transport facility, loss of a day's wage.

PARTICIPATION IN DEVELOPMENTAL ACTIVITIES

Majority of Dalit women (80%) know the functions and duties of Panchayat. 20% of them not aware of rural development Programmes.

The respondents have been executing variety of developmental works such as water supply, Sanction of houses, development of village roads, monitoring the activities of the Anganwadi workers.

Majority (84%) of respondents put forth their views, few (16%) mentioned that their suggesting is not taken into account simply for being women.

AWARENESS REGARDING HEALTH AND FAMILY WELFARE PROGRAMMES

A large proportion of the Dalit women members are aware of pulse polio (70%) and health and family welfare (50%). In addition the respondents are aware of family welfare activities (20%), health camps (20%), safe drinking water (16%), and environment and sanitation (10%). Most of the Dalit women members were not aware of Programmes related to environment and sanitation, safe drinking water and family welfare activities.

Table 6
Awareness Regarding Health and Family Welfare Programmes

Awareness	*Frequency*	*Percent*
Health and family welfare	20	50
Pulse Polio	35	70
Health camps	10	20
Environment and sanitation	05	10
Safe drinking water	08	16
Family welfare activities	10	20
Total	50	100

INVOLVEMENT OF DALIT WOMEN IN HEALTH AND FAMILY WELFARE PROGRAMMES

To what extent the different Programmes of health and family welfare improved due to the involvement of Dalit women members can be gauged from table 7. A majority of the members (70%) felt that immunization and vaccination programmes

Table 7
Improvement of Health and Family Welfare Programmes in their Area

Programmes	*Frequency*	*Percent*
Immunization and vaccination	35	70
Maternal and child health	20	40
Reproductive and child health Programmes	15	30
Total	50	100

improved in their areas because of their involvement followed by 40% in the maternal and child health activities. Another 30% reported that their participation improved the performance of reproductive and child health programmes.

MASS MEDIA EXPOSURE

In modern society mass media of communication constitute one of the most significant agents of psychosocial mobility. According to Deutsch (1963) mass media are the most important base of man's social and political awareness.

New means of communication are bringing revolutionary changes in the social thinking and ideological outlooks. They relate man to national and international events and emerging stream of life there from. They enlarge his sphere of socio-political thinking and vision. They are also the major source of propagation of National goals, politics, needs and problems and civil rights and privileges in developing societies like India.

From the data regarding the exposure of Dalit women to media a sizeable number of Dalit women (86%) are exposed to one or another mass media. Among them majority (50%) are exposed to T.V., Radio, and Newspaper (18% each). However, it is interesting to note that, 14% of them are not exposed to any media.

SUGGESTION FOR EFFECTIVE PERFORMANCE

For promotion of effective performance of roles by Dalit women in Villages Panchayat, particularly in the context of village development, the respondents have given several suggestions such as 'organization of adult education programme by Village Panchayat for illiterate women' (35%)' active promotion of women's development programmes by Village Panchayat' (16%), 'greater stress on compulsory attendance in Village Panchayat meeting', 'provision of knowledge of women's development programmes by Village Panchayat', 'greater stress on family planning by Village Panchayat and educated women'.

Table 8
Suggestion of Dalit Women Panchayat Members

Suggestion	*Frequency*	*Percent*
Organization of adult education Programme	18	36
Active promotion of women's development Programmes	08	16
Stress on compulsory attendance	10	20
Provision of knowledge of women's development Programmes	07	14
Stress on family planning	07	14
Total	50	100

CONCLUSION

In a nutshell, Dalit women in Village Panchayat generally are still educationally backward and economically weak. Most of them have been elected for the first time. They have been motivated by development programmes. They are generally attending meetings of the Village Panchayat and expressing their views and laying stress on varied kinds of matters and issues relating to village development. Most of them have been executing several kinds of development work like water supply, sanction of houses. Majority of Dalit women were not aware of programmes related to environment and sanitation and safe drinking water. Almost all them have been in favor of increasing women's empowerment in particular. They have generally suggested the measures of adult education, knowledge of women's development programmes and compulsory attendance for effective performance of their roles in Village Panchayat.

To sum up, Dalit women in village Panchayat, though motivated by sincere commitment to the cause of rural development in general and women's improvement in particular, are handicapped by their educational and economic backwardness and male dominated socio-cultural milieu.

SUGGESTIONS

1. Programme meant for women's development should be linked with Panchayat for more effective participation of women.

2. Interaction with illiterate elected women with enlightened rural women and educated urban elected women representatives should be arranged.
3. Co-operation of male Panchayat members is essential as they provide one of the immediate contexts.
4. To ensure participation of women in the meetings, attendance must be made compulsory. This is essential to promote their leadership qualities and self-confidence.
5. Most of the women Panchayat members are not involved in the process of making selection of the beneficiaries. So, women Panchayat members should take part in the selection of the beneficiaries of various rural development schemes.
6. Measures such as mobilization of women members and association of Panchayat with specific programmes on socio-economic issues, which affect women directly like drinking water, child care should be undertaken.

From the study it can be interpreted that the provision for the one-third reservation made in 73rd Constitutional Amendment and adopted by Karnataka Panchayat Raj Act, 1993, has ensured adequate representation to women in general and Dalit women in particular. It has helped the emergence of new Dalit women leadership in these institutions of rural level self-government, which is relatively younger.

REFERENCE

Amal Mandal, (2003), *Women in Panchayat Raj Institution,* Kanishka Publishers, New Delhi.

Bhola Nath Ghosh, (2002), *Rural Women Leadership,* Mohit Publications, New Delhi.

Madhusudhan Bandhii, (2004), "73rd Constitutional Amendment and Emerging Leadership Among the Other Backward Classes in PRIs:" The Case of Bidar District in Karnataka, Yojana, Vol. 52 (1)

R.M. Varma, (2004), "Panchayat Raj, Rhetoric & Reality", Kurukshetra, Vol. 2004 (10)

Surat Singh, (2004), "Empowerment of Women Representatives in Panchayat Raj", Kurukshetra, Vol. 2004 (10).

30

ROLE OF HIGHER EDUCATION IN WOMEN EMPOWERMENT

*Akash S. B.**

INTRODUCTION

Education is a key factor in overall development of human being, because it facilitates to increases the individual knowledge, help to aware of their rights, encourages to fighting for their rights helps to overcome the traditional barriers and it is a strategy for overall development of country. The developing country like India, the general economic situation of women being worst than that of men in respect of education, nutrition, freedom, health, life expectation, wage earning, family support, wage earning and political participation. In view of this government of India had launched special programmes for women empowerment viz., development of women's in five year plans, national policy on education 1986 on women education, national policy on education review committee 1990, programme of action 1992, national policy for empowerment of women 2001 and in tenth plan adopted three fold of strategies for empowerment of women. The main aims of these policies are to access to education and equality of learning, elimination of gender bias, providing vocational education, to provide proper training to women teacher, to encourages research and development of women studies and increases self confidence

* Lecturer, Department of Commerce, Karnatak University, PG Centre, Karwar, Karnataka

for undertaking entrepreneurial activities and sound education facilities for sustainable development of women.

The education is a vital instruments in not only empowering of the women but also to make the best of economic opportunities and bring about far reaching changes in stereotype gender status and relations between sexes and social attitudes. Thus the role of education in empowerment is not only learning of three i.e. reading, writing and arithmetic but includes awareness raising, critical analysis of various structures and acquiring knowledge for empowerment at all levels.

REASONS RESPONSIBLE FOR WOMEN EMPOWERMENT

The following are the important reasons which is responsible for women empowerment;

- Women continued to be discriminated and exploited in various level;
- The social status of women much worse than men;
- Earning capacity of the women much less than men;
- Political participation of women is negligible as compared to men;
- Life expectancy of the women communities is shorter than men;
- Women empowerment is needed to increases the capacity building of women;
- Increases the self confidence of women;
- It is needed to increases the literacy rate of women;
- Women empowerment is needed to increases the capacity to take independent decision regarding economic activities;
- It is needed for equal work time disposition;
- It is needed to improve the standard of living of women.

POLICIES, PROGRAMMES AND WOMEN EMPOWERMENT

The Indian Constitution enshrined the principle of gender equality in its Preamble, Fundamental Rights, Fundamental Duties and Directive Principles. Moreover the Constitution of

India grants equality to women, but also empowers the State to adopt measures of positive discrimination in favour of women. Within the framework of a democratic polity, our laws, development policies, Plans and programmes have aimed at women's advancement in different spheres.

FIVE YEARS PLANS AND STATUS OF WOMEN

Since first five year plans (1951-1956) have been receiving great attention to develop the status of women. But in this five-year plan development of women treated, as a subject of welfare. The second to fifth five-year plan (1956-79) continued to reflect the same welfare approach besides giving priority to women education. In sixth five year plans (1980-85), the approach is shift from welfare to development of women and in this plan adopted a multi-disciplinary approach with a special thrust on three area like health, education and employment. Under seventh plan (1985-90) the development programmes continued with major objective of increases their overall status of women. In eighth plans (1992-97) also continued to provide proper education and vocational training with view to overall development of women. In ninth plan (1997-2002) the primary objective of ninth plan is to empowerment of women and also convergence of existing services available in both women specific and women related sector. In tenth plan adopted entirely different approach of women empowerment as compared to earlier approach. It provides stronger platform for action with definite goals, targets and time frame and it adopted three fold strategies for increases the overall status of women such as social empowerment, economic empowerment and gender justice.

NATIONAL POLICY ON WOMEN EDUCATION 1986

In the year 1986, national policy on women education was enacted with view to increases the status of women. It assumed that education is a key factor in changing the status of women. In order to neutralize the accumulated desertions of the past, there will be a positive, interventionist role in empowerment of women. Through this policy women studies have been promoted as a part of different course and educational institutions encourages to take active programmes to further increases the women status. In view of this government of India have been initiated many programmes to develop the women status such as adult education for women development in age group of 15-35, increases the women access to vocational, technical, professional education and to existing emergent technologies, substantial contribution towards women equality towards crating of appropriate cell.

NATIONAL POLICY ON EDUCATION REVIEW COMMITTEE 1990

This policy has different objectives such as to provide access to education and equality of education to women, access to vocational education, ensuring adequate training and other educational facilities to women, encourages research and development of women studies, focuses on employment of women, encourages adult education, providing hostel facilities in all levels and ensure representative of women in the educational hierarchy.

THE PROGRAMME OF ACTION 1992

The export committee reported and felt that women empowerment possible through increases self-confidence and self-esteem, facilitates adequate information, knowledge and skill for economic independence, providing opportunity to women to make informed choice in the area like education, employment and health, special opportunity to ensure women to recruit and augment teacher training facilities to women.

NATIONAL POLICY OF WOMEN EMPOWERMENT 2001

The national policy on empowerment of women initiated in the year 2001.The main objectives of the policy is to bring about the advancement, development, and increases the overall status through process of changes in societal attitudes towards women, elimination of all forms of discrimination against women and encourages to active participation in social and economic activities.

ADEQUATE HOSTEL FACILITIES

Women and Child Development department implemented this scheme. The main objectives of this scheme are to provide adequate hostel facilities to workingwomen. This scheme facilitates to women to lead their life without fear, because, it provide dairy care. And it is encourages to women to under take active part in economic activities in different fields.

SERVA SHIKSH ABHIYAN

The programme was launched in the year 2000 in collaboration with the State with view to achieve the objectives of widening the scope of elementary education throughout the country. It is facilitates to bridge the gender inequality by giving due emphasis to promote education of girl child in the society and on a larger scale to afford them social justice, security and equality at par with the boy child. The programme has big ambitions like to provide quality education in the age between 6-14, providing mid day meal and it also ensure additional support to women to increases the women literacy.

THE SWA-SHAKTI PROJECT

The main aim of this project is to increases the economic status of women. The project involved organizing the women and encouraging them to under taking earning activities through SHG. The self-help groups facilitate to develop saving habits among the poor women communities, access to various promotional assistance and access large quantum of resources. In view of this over a period of time women status is increases.

SUPPORT SERVICES FOR WOMEN

In the year 1997 Balika Samridhi Yojana was launched. The main aim of this project is to changes the community attitude towards the girl child. Through this programme given grants of Rs 500 to deposit in interest bearing account in the name of girl child born after August 15, 1997 in a family below poverty line.

ADULT EDUCATION PROGRAMMES

Through this programme the National Literacy Mission came into existence with different plans and strategies. The main aim of this programme is to achieve education for all 2000 AD. This programme has specific objective viz., achieving self reliance in literacy, facilitates to acquiring the skills necessary for improving the economic status and well-being of women, facilitates to aware of the causes of deprivation and moving towards the amelioration of those oppressive conditions through organized participation in the process of overall development.

SUPPORT TO TRAINING AND EMPLOYMENT PROGRAMME TO WOMEN

The programmes come out in 1987 to achieve ambitious objective like to provide new and latest knowledge and up date skills of poor and asset less women in the traditional sector viz., agriculture, dairying, fisheries, animal husbandry, handloom, handicrafts, khadi and village industries and social forestry.

WOMEN STUDIES

The women studies now working in several universities and colleges and these institution encourages to women communities to under taking research, curriculum development, provide adequate information about availability of economic opportunities, extension services etc. The women study centre also encourages women to under take minor and major research projects and encourages women to conduct research on women issues such as literacy position of women in rural area and urban area, status of women in political field and other area.

Table 1 reveals the female literacy rate in India. During 1951 the female literacy rate were 8.86 and at the end of 2001 the female literacy rate amounting 54.16%. Thus it is clear that the female literacy rates has grown nearly seven times between 1951-2001. This is reflected also in the increase in the proportion of girls among children going to school.

Table1
Female Literacy Rate in India

Census	*Literacy rate %*
1951	8.86
1961	15.35
1971	21.97
1981	29.76
1991	39.29
2001	54.16

Sources: India Development Report, 2002

Table 2
Women Enrolment in Higher Education

Year	*Total Women Enrolment (Lakhs)*	*Enrolment per hundred men*
1950-1951	40	14
1993-1994	1664	50
2001-2002	3514	66
2002-2003	3696	67

Sources: U G C annual report 2002-03

Table 2 reveals the women enrolment in higher education per hundred men. Over a period of time has been phenomenal growth in the number of women enrolment in higher education since 1950-51. During 1950-51, 40 lakes women were registered for higher education and enrolment per hundred men amounting 14 women. However, it is clear that the number of enrolment per hundred men registered a five fold increases between 1950-51-2002-2003.

Table 3 gives information about state wise women enrolment in 2002-03. The highest percentage of women enrolment has taken place in Kerala in 2002-03 i.e.150682 constituting 60%, followed by Goa and Punjab. However over a period of time the enrolment of girls has increased in all levels of education – primary, middle and secondary. The percentage increase in female enrollment is much higher in middle and secondary levels and dropout rates among male and female children are almost the same in all three levels of education.

Table 3
State wise Women Enrolment in 2002-03

State	*Women enrolment*	*% To total Enrolment*
AP	295330	39.30
Arunachal Pradesh	1577	28.30
Assam	81458	40.50
Bihar	117628	23.81
Chattissgarh	56082	36.70
Delhi	79220	46.00
Goa	11371	58.50
Gujarath	229483	44.21
HP	38383	42.69
J& K	28071	47.10
Jharkhand	59994	30.4
Karnataka	227846	40.86
Kerala	150682	60.00
MP	176630	37.20
Mharastra	515868	41.00
Manipur	16115	44.30
Megalaya	13970	47.90
Mizoram	5249	46.70
Nagaland	4788	38.80
Orissa	123171	35.69
Punjab	128411	52.68
Sikkim	1654	40.31
TN	321583	45.10
Tripura	8219	40.80
UP	452279	38.40
Uttaranchal	46127	40
West Bengal	255382	39.40
A& N Island	1164	57.77
Chandigarh	18838	55.50
Daman & Diu	275	46.85
Pandicharry	9562	52.60
Total	3695964	40.05

Sources: UGC Annual Report

The table 4 reveals the women enrolment by different discipline in the year 2002-03. Under arts discipline 18,89,799 women enrolment taken place constituting 51.13%of total women enrolment, under science discipline women registered their name for higher education amounting 7,36,890 (19.94%

of total women enrolment), followed by commerce and management (16.48%), Medicine, engineering, education, law, veterinary science, agriculture and others. Thus it is clear that among different discipline the highest enrolment taken place in arts discipline.

Table 4
Women Enrolment by Different Discipline

Discipline	*Total Enrolment*
Arts	1889749
Commerce	736890
Science	154041
Engineering	154041
Medicine	134364
Agriculture	9332
Veterinary science	2982
Law	61947
Others	30564
Total	3695964

Source: UGC Annual report 2002-03

Table 5
Women Colleges in India

Year	*No. Of women colleges*	*Increases percentage*
1993-94	1033	-
1994-95	1107	7.16
1995-96	1146	3.52
1996-97	1195	4.2
1997-98	1260	5.4
1998-99	1359	7.8
1999-2000	1503	10.5
2000-2001	1578	4.9
2001-2002	1625	2.9
2002-2003	1650	1.5

Source: UGC Annual report

Table 5 revels the information relating to women colleges in India as on 2002-03. During 1993-93, 1033 women colleges were working it increases 7.16% over previous. During the year 1995-96, 1146 colleges were working, it is increases over previous year amounting 3.52%. Thus it is clear that the over a period of time the number of women colleges were increased in India and they have taken active and important part in providing education to women.

Table 6
UGC Refresher Courses to Women Studies

Year	*NO. Of refresher course organized*
1997-98	5
1998-99	3
1999-2000	3
2000-01	3
2001-02	-
2002-03	7
2003-04	8

Source: UGC Annual report

Table 6 provides information regarding UGC refresher course to women studies. Refresher course helps to the teaching faculty to acquire more knowledge about new area of particular discipline and it helps to refresh the teaching communities by way of providing up to date knowledge to the participants. During the year 1997-98, 5 refresher courses were conducted. In the year1998-99, 3 courses conducted by women studies and during 2000-03, 7 courses were conducted and 2003-04, 8 refresher courses conducted. Thus it is clear that women studies conducted 29 refresher courses for refreshing the women communities teaching between 1997-98 and 2003-04.

CONCLUSIONS

Education is a key factor in sustainable development because education is a vital instrument in empowering the women and it facilitates to economic opportunities to women, it turn to bring about far reaching changes in stereotype gender status and relations between sexes and social attitudes. Thus the role of education in empowerment is not only learning 'but includes awareness raising, critical analysis of various structures and acquiring knowledge for empowerment at all levels. However from the forgoing discussion it is clear that the empowerment of women has taken place due to sincere government effort and government policies and international commitment as well as pressure from NGOs. And in addition to these several important policies the government have been announced, many policies and some legislations are waiting, and Government of India has signed several international instrument of commitment towards women empowerment in view of this status of women changing very fast year by year.

REFERENCES

University News, Vol, 43, 42, October, 17-23, 2005, p. 2.

Government of India, Census of India, 2001.

WWW.Education.nic.in/htm/web/adledu.htm.

UGC Report (2002-03), Women study Centre and Cell.

UGC Guidelines (1986) Development of women studies in Indiana Universities and colleges, New Delhi.

WWW.ugc.ac.com